Business Analytics

Thank you for choosing a SAGE product!
If you have any comment, observation or feedback,
I would like to personally hear from you.

Please write to me at **contactceo@sagepub.in**

Vivek Mehra, Managing Director and CEO, SAGE India.

Bulk Sales

SAGE India offers special discounts
for bulk institutional purchases.

*For queries/orders/inspection copy requests,
write to* **textbooksales@sagepub.in**

Publishing

Would you like to publish a textbook with SAGE?
Please send your proposal to **publishtextbook@sagepub.in**

Subscribe to our mailing list

Write to marketing@sagepub.in

This book is also available as an e-book.

Business Analytics

Text and Cases

Tanushri Banerjee

Associate Professor of Information Systems, Business School,
Pandit Deendayal Petroleum University, Gandhinagar

Arindam Banerjee

Professor of Marketing, IIM Ahmedabad

⑤SAGE | TEXTS

Los Angeles | London | New Delhi
Singapore | Washington DC | Melbourne

First published in 2019 by

SAGE Publications India Pvt Ltd
B1/I-1 Mohan Cooperative Industrial Area
Mathura Road, New Delhi 110 044, India
www.sagepub.in

SAGE Publications Inc
2455 Teller Road
Thousand Oaks, California 91320, USA

SAGE Publications Ltd
1 Oliver's Yard, 55 City Road
London EC1Y 1SP, United Kingdom

SAGE Publications Asia-Pacific Pte Ltd
18 Cross Street #10-10/11/12
China Square Central
Singapore 048423

Published by Vivek Mehra for SAGE Publications India Pvt Ltd. Typeset in 10/12 pt ITC Century by AG Infographics, Delhi.

Library of Congress Cataloging-in-Publication Data Available

ISBN: 978-93-532-8710-8 (PB)

SAGE Team: Indrani Dutta, Vandana Gupta, Sonam Rana and Kanika Mathur

Contents

Detailed Contents

List of Figures

List of Tables

List of Abbreviations

ACN	AC Nielsen Corporation
AR	Augmented reality
BA	Business analytics
BI	Business intelligence
BP	Business problem
BPM	Business Performance Management
CART	Classification and regression trees
CAT	Common Admission Test
CHAID	Chi-square automatic interaction detector
CPG	Consumer packaged goods
CRAN	Comprehensive R Archive Network
CRM	Customer relationship management
DW	Data warehouse
E&P	Exploration and production
ERP	Enterprise resource planning
FMCG	Fast-moving consumer goods
GUI	Graphical user interface
HR	Human resources
IaaS	Infrastructure as a service
IoT	Internet of things
IQR	Interquartile range
IT	Information technology
KM	Knowledge management
L&D	Learning and development
MIS	Management information system
MNL	Multinomial logit
OLAP	Online analytical processing
OLS	Ordinary least squares
OLTP	Online transaction processing
PAN	Presence across nation
PCA	Principal components analysis
PoS	Point of sales
PPC	Pay per click
ROI	Return on investment

SBU	Strategic business unit
SCM	Supply chain management
SEO	Search engine optimization
SPSS	Statistical Package for the Social Sciences
T&D	Training and development
TDS	Total dollar spent

Foreword

Business Analytics as a critical requirement has crept into the corporate mindspace far and wide. It monopolizes conversation in boardrooms across the world, although in the developed markets, the usage has been reasonably wide and accepted for over a few decades now.

The resurgence of the interest in this practice domain has been fuelled by the availability of data from multiple sources, with the improvement in data collection architecture (digitalization to an extent) and the development of high-end computing facilities, which have facilitated efficient processing of the data. The notion of 'Big Data' has its evolution from these trends that have been observed in the industry.

Sure enough, it has prompted a varied set of experts to display their prowess in this domain, be it the computer scientists, the statisticians, the data management specialists or the business managers. The industry has seen immense development and application of new knowledge and expertise in mining large volumes of data. A reflection of such varied and significant creation of new ideas and knowledge is in the fact that Analytics is now known in various contours, depending on the expertise that is used. Data-driven analysts who use sophisticated technical infrastructure to manage and process the data refer to it as data science. Yet, others who work on simply managing the data and collating it intelligently in reporting formats refer to it as business intelligence. There are also traditionalists (like me), who would be more comfortable referring to it as 'data/insight driven-business problem-solving' initiative.

Be that as it may, the point to be made here is that industry has multiple views about what Analytics is supposed to be and what it can do for an organization, and more importantly, without a strong consensus on what it is across the different constituencies in the industry.

A complication due to this state of affairs is that very few industry leaders have a firm view (if at all) on how to develop infrastructure and capability within organizations for effective usage of data for business problem-solving. This is a severe problem in developing markets, although its implications are being felt in more matured markets as well.

Evidently, the world of Analytics is an evolving science and requires firm directions, especially for the next generation of business leaders to wisely invest in these new age capabilities. In this regard, a significant attempt is made by the authors in their current book by providing an end-to-end view of the necessary skills that will be useful to organizations as they build up internal capabilities in this domain.

I have rarely come across any other book (let alone a textbook) in Analytics that provides a comprehensive view of the mixture of capabilities that ideally determines the practice of Analytics. Throw in a dash of sequencing of such capabilities to leverage effective outcomes and you have a deadly tome of knowledge. I am sure the reader will sense many of these positive characteristics in this book.

I am pleased to introduce this book to all the students of Analytics. You will find this book very useful as you hone your skills in various academic training programmes across business schools. The optimal combination of management principles, data processing theory and example programming assignments will be a useful complement to classroom teaching of the practical nuances of this field. It would be worthy enough for all those who aspire to specialize in this field to study and refer this book for a long time.

Suresh Divakar
Partner, Kantar Analytics, Greater New York City Area
Formerly Heading Analytics Operations at Bristol Myers Squibb,
Avon Cosmetics and Pepsi North America

Preface

INTRODUCTION

This book can be used as a teaching material for courses taught at the graduate and post-graduate levels in the management schools. It can also be used as a teaching resource in executive programmes for corporate and faculty development programmes conducted at the business schools. It consists of a step-by-step explanation of Business Analytics in organizations in a textual form supported by a comprehensive set of cases which run across varied industry sectors. This book can be used as a textbook for a core course named Business Analytics or elective courses in Analytics in marketing, human resource, operations and finance areas. The cases provide a variety of topics to the faculty to choose from, according to the most relevant topics of discussion. It provides students the capabilities of evaluating a business case scenario; building the business problem; designing a questionnaire; identifying the data sources and data availability; logically thinking through problem-solving; using techniques such as linear regression, logistic regression, discriminant analysis, supervised and unsupervised learning algorithms, text and web analytics, sentiment analysis, market basket analysis and such others; and using application software to solve the problem and be able to interpret the results. The degree of decision-making for the cases will vary, with easy, medium and high complexity levels to allow students and faculty members to take one step at a time and build concepts systematically. Software packages such as Microsoft Excel, Statistical Package for the Social Sciences, R, Tableau and RapidMiner have to be used to solve the business problems and arrive at a decision. This course shall be offered to students who have gone through a basic course in statistics, research methodology and information systems.

Data has become an important part of managerial decision-making as correct capture, analysis and interpretation of data can result in business productivity. Data captured in structured and unstructured forms by organizations have led Business Analytics to become a strategic need for sustainability and growth in a competitive world. Descriptive, predictive and prescriptive models along with data mining techniques are being used to interpret large quantities of data for useful business insights.

FLOW OF CONTENT

There are 11 chapters in this book. The first two chapters describe the significance of Analytics in organizations. The students passing out from a business school usually take up roles of decision-makers, be it at an individual or team level. Understanding and hence building an approach of what information is important and eventually be able to filter it out to aid the decision-making process requires the knack of an analyst. This germinates from thinking analytically right from the business school level. Courses on Business Analytics have been introduced in many business schools, but there is a lack of a comprehensive course textbook that explains it end to end. We have tried to address that gap through this book. Chapters 3 and 4 emphasize the need for planning and conceptualizing the road map for the use of data to aid processes in organizations. Chapter 5 describes some of the information technology tools that have emerged as the support structure to aid correct analytical processing and outcome. Chapters 6–8 describe the various models used for churning the information set to get the desired outcome. Models and approaches vary depending on the problem statement described in the planning stage, be it historical data, descriptive data or forecasting. Chapters 9–11 emphasize the need for developing the skill for reading the outcome from the statistical results and presenting it in a form easily understood by the end user. Maintaining appropriate documentation is necessary at every stage for validation. Sometimes there is more than necessary hype about Analytics, and hence the authors have tried to emphasize that rationality in imbibing Analytics is required.

USE OF SOFTWARE

Data for each of the cases that requires working with data has been provided in Microsoft Excel spreadsheets separately in the student download section.[1] Solutions to all the case studies, including software solutions, have been provided using software tools such as Microsoft Excel, SPSS, RapidMiner, R and Tableau as appropriate. Appendices at the end of the book consist of step-by-step solved comprehensive case studies that discuss the concepts of all the chapters. The solution includes the application of all the five aforementioned software tools. This gives a good practice to students in grasping and then applying the concepts of Business Analytics with hands-on software tools. The authors recommend that the instructor of the course should provide reference to the case study at relevant intervals as he/she teaches the concepts of this coursework. Tips on installation and use of software are provided in the appendices.

Disclaimer: The authors have used several examples and caselets in the book to demonstrate particular topics in the chapters. These are only for illustration purposes and easy understanding of concepts by the reader. This bears no resemblance to any person, character or business situation in real life.

---

[1] Student download section is provided on the companion website (https://study.sagepub.in/banerjee_BA) of the book.

Acknowledgements

Both of us would like to acknowledge the immense contribution made by our respective employers (Pandit Deendayal Petroleum University and IIM Ahmedabad) in providing a very productive academic environment for us to (a) interact with enthusiastic students and business professionals, (b) research on topical issues faced in the Analytics domain and (c) facilitate documenting our ideas and thoughts on developing new approaches to the practice. It would not have been possible to get this book ready without the support of this healthy collegial environment.

We would also like to thank our academic colleagues for their constant support and feedback in numerous internal forums which have sharpened our thinking around the content of this book. To the participants of various executive programmes on Analytics that we have conducted, a special thank you for the diverse ideas that sprang up from them during the course of some very spirited discussions.

Finally, we appreciate the encouragement provided by our parents and siblings. Without their support and motivation over time, this project could not have been accomplished. The enthusiasm and affection of our children, Antara and Dhruv, led us to stay focused and devote time to conceive this book.

This book initiative has been partially funded by a grant from the Research and Publications Office of IIM Ahmedabad.

About the Authors

Tanushri Banerjee is an Associate Professor of Information Systems at the Business School at Pandit Deendayal Petroleum University (PDPU), Gandhinagar. She has 22 years of work experience divided between academia and industry. Her career is a mix of national and international job profiles, which has led her to blend industrial technological advancements into evolving academic curriculum. Prior to her current position, she was Associate Director at Duke Corporate Education (India), a joint venture between Duke University and IIM Ahmedabad. Her responsibilities included steering the operations and systems infrastructure management initiatives for India along with global executive programme design and delivery. Additionally, she has also held positions in the systems function at Abbott Laboratories Inc., Chicago, and Torrent Labs at Ahmedabad. Dr Banerjee is MS in Information Sciences from the University of Illinois, Chicago, and PhD in Management from The Maharaja Sayajirao University of Baroda. Her current interests lie in the area of business intelligence and data-driven decision-making. She has initiated the creation of Business Analytics Teaching Lab at Management School PDPU in 2018 for providing practical industry exposure to students in data-driven decision-making.

Arindam Banerjee is a Professor of Marketing at IIM Ahmedabad. He has been associated with the institute for the past 20 years as a faculty. Prior to joining the institute, he worked as an Analytics specialist in a management consulting firm based in Chicago, Illinois. He has market research experience in the United States having worked at AC Nielsen Corporation, servicing the Analytics requirement for Philip Morris Inc. As a faculty member at IIM Ahmedabad, he teaches, consults and researches in Marketing Analytics and Strategy. He has been involved in setting up the offshore Analytics operations for a global bank in India and has been an Analytics mentor for several other organizations. He is a PhD in Marketing Science from the State University of New York at Buffalo and a PGDM from IIM Lucknow.

Earlier the authors have cowritten a book on Analytics for practitioners titled *Weaving Analytics for Effective Decision-making* published by SAGE Publications.

1

Introduction to Business Analytics

Learning Objectives

After completing this chapter, students should be able to understand about the following:

- Need for business analytics
- Relation between business analytics and business intelligence (BI)
- Relation between business analytics and business performance management (BPM)
- Linking strategy to execution
- End-to-end value chain
- Decision-making with analytical outcomes for technical and non-technical end users

---

Opening Example

Rajesh Kohli has a mid-size business in the outskirts of Bangalore city in India. He manufactures and supplies packaging containers to a big pharmaceutical company. His dealings with raw material providers from neighbouring cities require him to travel every Tuesday and Friday to meet the suppliers. As business has flourished, his list of suppliers has grown over time. He believes that meeting them personally after regular intervals of time helps build stronger ties with them. After he returns from the meetings, he systematically documents the notes of the meeting. His discussions with the suppliers revolve around many factors such as the raw-material items they supply, punctuality in supply time, price they charge, discounts they offer, quality of the material, transportation charges and payment flexibilities. The transaction data associated with the suppliers over the years resides in his company database. However, considering the size and complexity of the data, his information technology (IT) team captures and retains the data as additional unused asset. For decision-making purposes, he has never used this data. He only relies on his business acumen, quick-meeting notes and long experience of doing this business. One of his key decisions has been to identify trusted and reliable suppliers in business. He has identified two key suppliers whom he can trust the most.

How has he identified these two suppliers? He has done so by relying on his confidence in business dealings and experience over time—his gut feeling. He has ignored the data captured on varied factors stated above that determine his dealings with his suppliers. Can he make a decision with certainty that these two identified suppliers are indeed the ones to be trusted the most and will continue to provide similar service in the future? The answer is: yes, he can. But not just by gut feeling. For this, he also needs to look into the transaction data on each of the factors mentioned above and their interrelated outcomes for business growth, and then derive a conclusion. His decision, thus backed with appropriate data, will state with certainty that indeed his assumption of the two key suppliers is correct. The art of filtering the necessary information from data sources using appropriate methodologies, tools and techniques that address a business decision is the genesis of business analytics.

What does the above situation describe? Every individual is making decisions daily. In our personal lives we make decisions about what to eat for breakfast, what time to leave for college/school, what to wear, anticipate traffic congestion and so on. Similarly, in the business environment, employees have been making small and large decisions in their domain of work. Decisions are based on various interlinked environmental factors. One makes the judgement based on the significance of one or more influencing factors for attaining the desired goal. Consciously or unconsciously, the weight of each of the influencing factors is taken into account before moving forward. Do we all not do so in every activity we perform on a day-to-day basis? A retail store, for instance, will decide on ordering inventory based on sale of the products or a jewellery store will provide a complimentary gift depending on the amount of the purchase or an employee is given perks based on the clients he brings for a consulting firm. Each of these decisions is based on multiple influencing factors which we shall see in the following chapters. For Rajesh, 'timely delivery of raw materials' along with 'price' could possibly be the most important factor in deciding the trusted suppliers. This **hypothesis needs to be validated** from business analytics outcomes.

Any transaction that has monetary implications creates the foundation for many business environments. As useful transactions increase over time, a formal structure emerges in the form of an organization that requires management. Several theories and management experts have discussed it in much detail. As organizations grow, with them grows the infrastructure constituting of processes and people who manage it. Business transactions encapsulate information that continue to remain useful for indefinite period of time. The environment in which the organizations operate is becoming more complex with time. You can easily find companies dealing across multiple product categories, which involves several suppliers and retailers across countries. Methods of doing business have become complex, for instance, an organization which is a leading garment brand has retail outlets and also sells online, or an electronic goods company provides after-sales service along with the sale of the product or a bank connects with its customers through its branches, online or even via the cell phone across diverse product offerings. Organizations have consciously set up methods for collecting customer feedback as a way to improve their relationship with their customers. Number of internal processes have, thus, increased to manage smooth operation across organization teams in many cases globally. All of this has generated **large amount of involuntarily captured transactional data** that may not seem to have a direct utility in the ongoing business processes of an organization. Nevertheless, companies recognize it as an asset that may be of value in the future. This has led to two issues: first, storing the information for extraction and utilization at a later time and second, understanding the value of intermixing information across various sections of the organization for business profitability. The first transformed the IT function and the second led to what we today call Business Analytics.

As students of Business Management, you will often come across several terms associated with Business Analytics such as Big Data, Data Science, Business Performance Management (BPM), Data Mining, Business Intelligence (BI), Artificial Intelligence, Machine Learning, Natural Language Processing, Data Warehousing, Internet of Things (IoT), Data Visualization and Descriptive, Predictive and Prescriptive Analytics. Throughout the text in the following chapters, the authors shall be referring to the terms as and when they apply to the topic of discussion. However, here, let us begin by briefly discussing the terms and understanding the relationship between them.

Laxmi Menon has been hired as an Analyst in the Business Analytics team of a large nationalized bank. She has undergone training during the first month of her joining the organization, where she is expected to learn and get acquainted to the responsibilities of her role as an Analyst. Her training included getting familiar with the company's enterprise system (enterprise resource planning [ERP]), how to enter and fetch relevant data, run appropriate queries and prepare the reports using online transaction processing (OLTP) for her management team. It also included learning some software tools that aid data analysis such as Microsoft Excel, SPSS and R. She was quite satisfied with this experience of learning and was eager to apply it within her work domain. However, there were a lot of apprehensions about her role in the Business Analytics team. She wondered, during her internship assignment, she had undergone a similar exposure for 2 months. At that time too, her guide (mentor) from the organization had told her that her experience in the area of Business Analytics would train her to become a Data Science professional in the future. Her several questions seemed unanswered: how is her training different from an IT specialist training, do BI and Business Analytics mean the same thing, why does she need to undergo software programming training, what is a model and so on. She also wondered how all of this together adds value to business. While the discussions seemed very exciting and promising to her, she wondered where she is expected to begin.

This is a common apprehension of any new employee in a new and evolving role in the Data Science or Business Analytics team of an organization. Referring to Figure 1.1, the reader can get an understanding of the basic terms that are used during a Business Analytics discussion. Experts in this domain have discussed them in many contexts. The authors here have tried to explain it in the most generic form.

BI can be described as a pipeline that spans across the entire realm of managing complex data in organizations for generating intelligent outcomes that aid business decision-making. It includes business objectives, methodologies, tools, techniques, models, architecture, processing and communicating desired outcomes.

Data captured by organizations have become complex with time and is now called Big Data. It is much larger in volume being captured from multiple sources. The variety of the data being captured has also increased from just textual data to images, voice and other forms. The frequency of data capture has moved from batch to continuous live data from many sources and devices. All of this data needs to be systematically preserved in the organization by the IT team in appropriate Data Warehouse or the Cloud, thus creating an information asset for the organization. Analysts and data processing experts use sophisticated query processing tools and online analytical processing (OLAP) methods for accessing the required set of information from the huge data repositories. Since the available source of information is huge, Data Mining techniques are used to establish patterns and trends by sifting through available data sets.

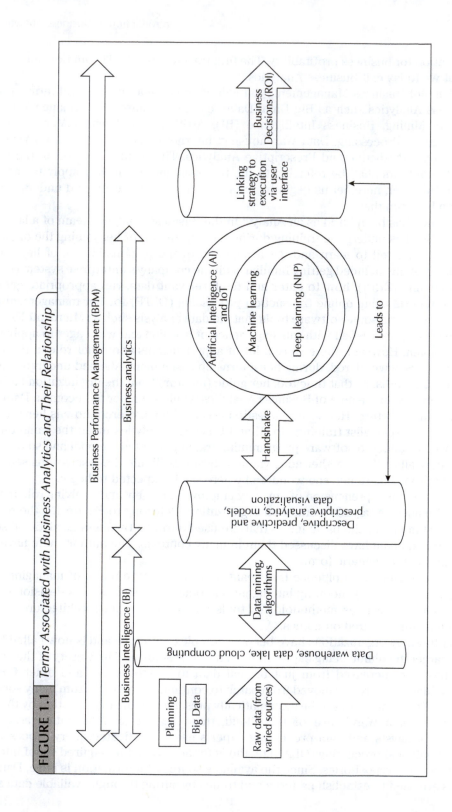

FIGURE 1.1 *Terms Associated with Business Analytics and Their Relationship*

WHAT IS BUSINESS ANALYTICS?

Business Analytics is the act of working with factual information in organizations, using appropriate lenses (tools) to identify nuggets of wisdom (insights) from them that can have direct use in influencing good decision-making. Different organizations adopt different processes to manage Analytics. Instruments, processes, data formats and processing methods may differ; however, the end objective of finding insights useful to drive decision-making remains same across all organizations.

In recent times, with the advent of high-end computing, the methodologies have undergone a transformation towards high-speed automation, at times using Artificial Intelligence, and advanced infrastructure has been invested in. Hence, analytics has taken a twist towards scaled optimization using variety and volume of data in sync with infrastructure that can churn out insights in little time. Obviously, this has led to a technical specialization in this field. Significance of Machine Learning in which machines are trained to self-learn using corrective mechanisms until they are perfect to be used as models, and further Deep Learning using Natural Language Processing which is a specialized method of machine learning where neural network is used to represent human brain behaviour is being explored.

BUSINESS ANALYTICS AND BI

Often used interchangeably, BI usually precedes Business Analytics in the evolutionary cycle. BI is about gleaning information from **past data** sources including **historical data**, hoping that some of the information would be interesting and useful to decision-makers. Business analytics, on the other hand, is led more by an objective to find specific insights or test and validate some hunches that the organization and its managers may have using appropriate tools and techniques and plan for **future business trends**. Many a time, BI is also referred to as business performance tracking using various relevant performance metrics.

BUSINESS ANALYTICS AND BPM

Business analytics and BPM are intricately linked concepts. Business analytics is a healthy support or input into organizational interventions which influence the BPM. Hence, the productivity of an organization can be highly influenced by the nature of insight generation processes in the organization and the appropriateness (criticality) of the insight to taking the right decisions for the organization. This would mean transitioning from methods and infrastructure management to having an output orientation and measuring impact of analytics infrastructure investments. The authors emphasize the need for BPM and involvement of business professionals in the entire process right from data capture to business decision-making for ensuring that the technical staff, analysts and decision scientists work towards converting business objectives into relevant outcomes. Lack of proper guidance can lead to gaps in processes such as a weak planning process, inappropriate data warehouse design, incomplete data sources and irrelevant analytics models, thus amounting to wastage of time and money and unhappy end users.

LINKING STRATEGY TO EXECUTION

Strategy is the essence of managing organizations. It is like a road map that you use to chalk out your path when you want to move from Point A to Point B.

However, everyone would appreciate that between a road map and plan and actual motion there can be instances when the plan does not work to the hilt. Hence, context-specific calls need to be taken based on requirements/challenges during execution. Business metrics are useful both in providing tactical level guidance for handling operational issues and in shaping up overall strategy. In fact, the closer the link is with facts, the better the chance that the planning and execution are precise.

THE END-TO-END VALUE CHAIN

The process of Business Analytics starts with identifying data in the organization. Data can be in any form—digital, paper or even verbal. All are useful and one needs to adopt a suitable process to harness information from the data. Traditionally, most organizations were focused on digital data (that too in organized form) to activate their analytics process. Of late, there is a realization that data can be in any form—numeric/non-numeric, digital/analogue/paper; and by using a suitable processing mechanism, information can be gleaned out of any form to be used as an input to operational process. Hence, there is a renewed interest in developing appropriate hardware and logic to glean information from all forms of data. Concurrently, the need to connect all the disparate pieces of insights into a cogent business story (inference) is important for gaining productivity. Hence, both infrastructure and algorithm development and acumen to connect the dots to build a comprehensive logic are required to build an end-to-end solution in Analytics.

Usually, the visible pieces of the process are the infrastructure and the algorithms, and hence they tend to get primacy in the planning process, though erroneously. In fact, to complete the end-to-end value chain, **the beginning and the end stages of the value creation process have to be firmly entrenched in the business issues** that require resolution. Until such connect is maintained, most analytics investments tend to be less useful.

DECISION-MAKING WITH ANALYTICAL OUTCOMES FOR TECHNICAL AND NON-TECHNICAL END USERS

This is a tricky issue. While traditional Analytics is considered to be a technical function, the outcomes from the process have to be necessarily in sync with business requirements that are used by end users who are not technology-savvy. Hence, often times in reality, there is a problem of decryption of the output for usefulness of business. Organizations have built Analytics expertise within business teams that can bridge the gap between the technical team and the business decision-makers. Various organizational models have emerged depending on the utility and dependability of business on Analytics outcomes. Organizations that rely heavily on Analytics create teams with domain experts who specialize in supporting the utility. Presenting the outcomes using appropriate visualization methods supported by storytelling methods has aided closing the gap.

REVIEW QUESTIONS

1. What has led to generation of large amounts of unconsciously captured transactional data in organizations?
2. What is Business Analytics? How has it become important with growth in business?
3. What is the need for the beginning and the end stages of the Business Analytics value creation process to be firmly entrenched in the business issues?
4. Explain the relationship between Business Analytics and BPM.
5. Explain the gap in decision-making with analytical outcomes for technical and non-technical end users.

CASE 1.1
A New Venture for an Untapped Market (Case Complexity: Easy)

Chinmay Patil hailed from a suburban city in Maharashtra. He had completed a fashion designing course in Mumbai and was picked up during a campus interview by a reputed designer garment company. He was posted in Pune. He preferred to keep his one-bedroom apartment in Mumbai. The flat in Mumbai was on the seventh floor of an 18-floor high-rise building. Six such buildings constituted the apartment complex in which he lived. Apartments were either one- or two-bedroom flats occupied by working individuals, working couples or small families. Every week on Monday morning, he used to travel to Pune and return to Mumbai on Friday evening. He had enjoyed spending the weekends in Mumbai in his familiar neighbourhood among close friends.

His commute from Mumbai to Pune and back every week was at least two hours long. It gave him enough time to think about many aspects that surrounded his life. He wondered often that although he loves his high-profile job and the travel through beautiful hilly Maharashtra landscape for work, was this something he wanted to do all his life. During his team meetings, he had often been part of conversations that discussed the customer segment in India that purchases and uses designer garments on a regular basis. The clients of his organization were mostly from the developed countries, the number from India and other emerging economies was gradually increasing. Was there an opportunity in India that remains an untapped market? This required a larger discussion about the preference, use, utility, purchase power and value for money of the Indian customer. While designer garments are for the elite few, most people in India purchase garments and continue their use till they wear out. Often stitching breaks result in small openings in the garments which cannot be worn without repair. In big cities like Mumbai, there is no tailor readily available to do these small jobs. Additionally, women of the household have a sense of fulfilment when they get their or any other member of the household's garment tailor-made. The personal touch associated with the decisions to participate in the design of the garments is an asset for the lady of the household. In big cities like Mumbai, especially the flats in which he lived, or the adjoining society where families live in big bungalows, there is very little time on hand to mend and repair their garments at home or even take the time to travel to the tailor's store, design, collect and then wear custom-made garments made by tailors. Lack of time and shortage of availability of tailors have led to discarding garment with the slightest thread tear or buy and wear whatever is available in the retail stores.

Chinmay thought, if he has to live and work in Mumbai, why not do something that gives him an avenue to tap this opportunity. He approached five women who had stitching skills. Provided them initial training. Then went door to door to drop a pamphlet that contained information about the service his small team can offer. Collect garments requiring repair work from households, repair them and return them at their convenient time. Additionally, provide tailored service for all types of garment stitching. He began with his apartment complex and the neighbouring society. For the first few weeks, he put up a small collection station at each of the two locations to build visibility and trust. Initially, the turnout was low. But as word of mouth spread through influencers about this convenient service, he started getting more clients. He would accept all kinds of work, big or small for different price ranges. Within a couple of months, he was able to create two broad categories: 'repair jobs' and 'new garments'. Within the new garments category, he created a designer wear for the elite few clients. As business grew he needed more employees. This came naturally with more men and women showing interest in joining his firm. He started receiving orders from distant locations in Mumbai. Where client base was significant, he placed a collection and delivery booth every Sunday to provide the additional service benefit. Weekend delivery trucks would ply between these locations. He also created a website to stay connected to his clients.

Exercise

1. What are the various aspects of Chinmay's business?
2. How can he attract more customers to his firm?
3. Is there a role of an influencer (someone who has been a customer) on a new client? How?
4. As Chinmay's firm grows, how can Business Analytics aid his business?

CASE 1.2
Kirana Store Introduces a Reward Programme
(Case Complexity: Medium)

This case is in two parts. Case 1.2 is about a reward programme that Jaishankar Tripathi had introduced for his clients. Case 1.3, the following case, is about Jaishankar Tripathi planning to better manage his inventory of products.

Jaishankar Tripathi owns a *kirana* store in the Bangalore city suburb. His father Hariprasad Tripathi had invested his savings in starting a business that would stock and sell daily-use commodities. The locality where Jaishankar resides has a large number of residential colonies housing middle-class families. In most houses, there would be only the male member on a salaried job who travels to Bangalore daily for work. The woman of the household does small odd jobs and manages the household. Kids go to school/college and have aspiration of higher studies.

Jaishankar's business has grown much bigger from where his father began 30 years ago. He has a store space of 15 by 15 feet divided in three broad units. His store carries all necessary grocery items starting from pulses, grains, spices, branded masalas, tea, sugar and so on. He also stocks other daily necessary items such as soaps, detergents, scrubs, tumblers and incense sticks. Jams, ketchup, sauces, beauty products occupy the shelves too. One of the units has a freezer section that keeps items such as cheese, butter, milk, breads and some other non-perishable exotic items. A third unit is kept for fresh food items such as fruits and vegetables. His attempt has been to be able to provide every item that a customer may come to buy. Seeing a customer being disappointed for lack of finding an item is a huge demotivation for him. Hence, over the years, he has carefully tried to build his stock as per the growing need of his customers. Every time he has had to decline a customer requirement, he made a note of it and tried to make it available in his store.

As business grew, he realized that keeping a count of all the different transactions was becoming difficult. What to procure, how much to procure, amount in sales, finances involved was getting complex. He also realized that most of his customers were repeat customers and there was not much he was doing to thank them for their trust in him and his services.

He decided to introduce a reward programme for his customers. This programme would be effective on a monthly basis. Customers whose monthly purchase per household amounts to ₹3,000 or more would be given a coupon of ₹150 that they can redeem on their next purchase. The total amount of purchase for the following month would not account for the ₹150 discount, while adding the purchase for that month, but instead record the total amount of the purchase. This would be a dual benefit for the customer.

Jaishankar is aware that there is competition that has come up from the big retail chain stores. Yet, he believes that his long association with his customers along with the reward programme will keep him profitable.

Data Available

A customer purchase table showing the customer name, date of purchase, bill amount in rupees for each purchase, total amount of purchase in purchase till date for the month is provided further. Data would be documented and reported per month. Although data has been provided for this case, you are not required to use any software for answering the questions below. Instead, analyse the data below and think of the best possible answers you can provide to help Jaishankar grow his business and retain his customers.

Monthly Purchase Data of Customers			
Customer Name	**Date of Purchase**	**Bill Amount (₹)**	**Total Amount of Purchase till Date (₹)**
Asha Pillai	5 June 2017	300	300
Ramesh Agarwal	5 June 2017	790	790
Jeevan Joshi	6 June 2017	220	220
Kavita Suri	7 June 2017	70	70
Manjeet Singh	7 June 2017	450	450
Ramesh Agarwal	7 June 2017	100	890
Preeti Rajan	7 June 2017	334	334
Akshay Sinha	8 June 2017	20	20

Exercise

1. How would the reward programme be a dual benefit for the customer?
2. What kind of data is important for Jaishankar to track and monitor?
3. How can he organize the data available to him for analysing it? How can he track and update a customer's consecutive household purchase over the month (note that any member of the household can come to make the purchase)?
4. What kind of analysis would be useful for him?
5. Will the reward programme be useful for Jaishankar? How?
6. What kind of analysis will he have to do to make the rewards programme successful?

Hint: In whose name is the customer registered? Hence, an ID to track customer purchase is vital.

CASE 1.3
Inventory Tracking Analysis by Jaishankar Tripathi
(Case Complexity: Hard)

Refer to Case 1.2. Jaishankar has the following data on his inventory. As business grew, he realized that keeping a count of all the different transactions was becoming difficult. What to procure, how much to procure, amount in sales and finances involved was getting complex. He would like to use business analytics for improving his inventory management across the three units of products. Every time a customer asks for a product which he is not able to provide due to zero inventory is a lost sale and opportunity for him. He knows that to survive and excel in a competitive space, he needs to keep an optimum stock of his inventory which does not add to the cost of carrying excess inventory yet leave no customer dissatisfied due to a product being out of stock. Unit 1 does not contain perishable items, Unit 2 requires a frozen unit to maintain the excess stock and Unit 3 is perishable. Hence, it needs to be procured such that there is no wastage.

Data Available

		Data of Jaishankar's Store Inventory				
Product Number	Unit Number	Product Name	Cost per Unit (₹)	Sale Price per Unit (₹)	Average Pieces on Hand	Average Pieces Sold per Year
G10200	1	Basmati rice (1 kg pack)	55	95	25	175
G10201	1	Everyday rice (1 kg pack)	20	30	100	1,000
G10202	1	Sugar (1 kg pack)	30	39	100	2,000
G10203	1	Wheat flour (5 kg pack)	250	275	50	600
G10204	1	Yellow lentil (1 kg pack)	70	84	50	750
G10205	1	Curry powder (200 gm pack)	45	59	25	200
G10206	1	Tea (500 gm pack)	150	170	50	400
G10207	1	Salt (1 kg pack)	25	30	150	2,000
G10208	1	Body lotion (large)	110	125	30	100
G10209	1	Sweet biscuits per pack	15	25	50	1,000

G10210	1	Toothpaste	60	75	30	200
G10211	2	Butter (100 gm pack)	40	45	10	75
G10212	2	Cheese (per cube)	15	20	25	50
G10213	2	Jam (1 kg pack)	130	140	10	25
G10214	2	Ketchup (1 kg pack)	75	90	30	200
G10215	2	Pasta sauce (200 gm pack)	90	150	10	25
G10216	2	Sandwich spread (200 gm pack)	80	150	10	40
G10217	2	Tamarind dip (200 gm pack)	60	150	10	50
G10218	2	Bread (medium)	12	25	5	450
G10219	2	Pizza base (2-piece pack)	25	40	5	50
G10220	2	Burger buns (2-piece pack)	15	25	5	25
G10221	3	Apples (1 kg pack)	100	140	5	150
G10222	3	Oranges (1 kg pack)	55	70	5	250
G10223	3	Bananas (1 dozen pack)	30	40	5	600
G10224	3	Potatoes (1 kg pack)	22	28	10	1,750
G10225	3	Onions (1 kg pack)	10	15	10	2,000
G10226	3	Tomatoes (1 kg pack)	8	14	10	1,800
G10227	3	Okra (500 gm pack)	30	35	10	1,500
G10228	3	Cauliflower per piece	9	14	20	1,500
G10229	3	Cabbage per piece	6	10	20	2,000

Exercise

Jaishankar wants to better manage his inventory. He feels that by doing so he can find out the cost of carrying the average inventory on hand and the total annual sales. Business Analytics would be able to help him with this requirement. Use Microsoft Excel to analyse the above data and help him answer the following questions. Add additional columns where needed. Then verify your outcomes using SPSS and R software.

1. Identify the most profitable items having a 75 per cent or more markup. And the ones that have less than 15 per cent markup. *Note:* Markup percentage = Gross profit / Unit cost.
2. Identify the items that have the most and the lowest annual sales.
3. Prepare a bar chart that compares inventory carrying cost and annual sales for top 10 selling items.
4. Is there a difference between markup and (gross) margin? Yes, they are calculated separately within a pricing model and hence have different impacts on the bottom line.

   Gross profit = Unit sale price – Unit cost
   Gross percentage margin = Gross profit / Unit sale price × 100
   Markup percentage = Gross profit / Unit cost × 100
   Which one is better for calculating profitability? Why?

5. Identify the top five items that have significant higher gross percentage margin compared to markup percentage.

Data Analytics for Business

Learning Objectives

After completing this chapter, students should be able to understand about the following:

- Why is it important to plan for an analytics culture in organizations?
- What is the approach for planning for analytics in organizations?
- Challenges of setting analytics culture in organizations
- Organization design for impactful analytics
- Data analytics in operations, human resources (HR), finance and marketing

---

Opening Example

A pharmaceutical company has retail medicine stores in various cities across India. As part of extended service, it has a small clinic in each of the stores where patients, for a nominal cost, can visit for outpatient needs. Physicians in the clinics are available for consultation from 8 am to 8 pm. Patients who come to the clinic usually purchase medicines from the store. The outpatient cases at the clinics consist primarily of regular monitoring of blood pressure, sugar and other body parameters, seasonal allergies, viral fever, stomach infections, pain management, injuries and such others. The clinics systematically capture and retain information about their patients in their database. The company is interested in cultivating personalized relation with regular patients so that it can provide better service and also be able to anticipate their requirements, eventually improving patient care by identifying potential risks associated with their health. It has made a decision to invest in a predictive model Analytics platform to address this need.

The example states a business opportunity that can be addressed by the use of Data Analytics. Business opportunity is patient (customer) delight and retention with enhanced services. In the long run it would create a positive impact on their top line. The opportunity aims to forecast patient needs in the future and based on the possibilities provide better patient care and services. After several months of discussion with experts, the solution was seen in supervised prediction analytics models. Predictive Analytics is one among the three types of Business Analytics. The three types of Business Analytics are descriptive, predictive and prescriptive, which shall be discussed in the later chapters.

PLANNING FOR ANALYTICS IN ORGANIZATIONS

Organizations are constantly making decisions that add value to business. Business decisions are made on current business performance parameters and future growth prospects. A significant part of the decision-making is predicting the future, and hence deciding next course of actions. Predictions on what the customers are most likely to buy, which employees are likely to quit, which machinery is likely to break down, which market is likely to perform better are part of everyday business decisions. Business environment has also changed adding more dimensions to processes, teams, people, new markets, technology, infrastructure and mobile employees that work together for an organization's profitability and for staying ahead in competition. BI and report generation has aided decision-making in organizations for several years. In recent times, investment into predictive analytics is being seen as a strategic move for better returns. We have discussed in Chapter 1 that today there is a lot more data available for the decision-maker, who at times is the end user to make informed decisions. Fifteen to twenty years ago, analysis of data included number crunching and use of models and algorithms that required specialized skills to build relevant statistical business models. Hence, the end-user community would be restricted to the outcomes shared by these highly technically skilled data analysts. Over time, with the advancement of technology, this gap has reduced with analysis becoming much more accessible and user-friendly. The predictive analytics capability is integrated along with business processes which can thus be used by trained end users or business analysts. If these predictions can be made more pinpointed based on factual evidence, then they are likely to add better value for an informed business decision. Organizations have realized the significance of fact-based decision-making using predictive forecasting models in the realm of Business Analytics. The objective of Predictive Analytics is to study the historical and time series data and then build models that are capable of predicting future business trends. Predictive Analytics as stated in Chapter 1 is just one type of Business Analytics. It is important that whatever form of Business Analytics an organization may incorporate, the process of Business Analytics must be planned and executed systematically to get the desired outcome. The common challenges that exist with data management and analysis in organizations can be primarily of three types:

1. Managing the huge amount of information from varied sources
2. Processing the information using appropriate tools and techniques
3. Interpreting the analysed outcomes and their application in business

In Figure 2.1, we see that the above challenges can be addressed by a structured process of Business Analytics which we shall be discussing in the following chapter of this textbook. Different organizations have either one or two of the above capabilities which get defined under the umbrella of Business Analytics. This has largely been driven by the 'business need' for which the organization began thinking about investing in Business Analytics. Over a period of time, infrastructure and skilled employees have created policies and procedures for better

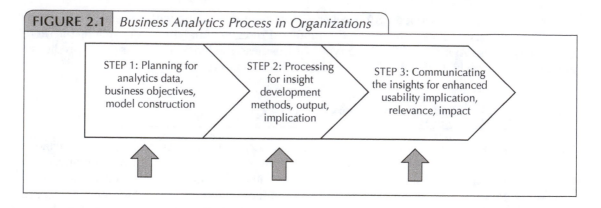

FIGURE 2.1 | *Business Analytics Process in Organizations*

management of the resources. Digital companies that manage huge amount of data may be interested in understanding which products are in demand in which region of India. Accordingly, they need to define their promotional budget for the following year. Efficient data collection and processing using statistical forecasting models and web mining methods prove to be useful. On the other hand, manufacturing companies such as cement or beverage companies monitor the processes using management information system (MIS) reports. Refinement and fine-tuning the processes with introduction of appropriate automation lead to efficiency over time. There would be companies that monitor continuous data and check for anomalies. A health care company has a temperature monitoring device that maintains certain levels of temperature in the cold storage for medicines. Any drastic change is recorded and informed by the system. All of the above examples are defined as Business Analytics. Thus, Business Analytics contributes and grows within the teams where the analytical outcomes provide the incremental value for the associated business decisions being made. Organizations that understand the significance of this additional contribution made by Analytics, plan to invest and build an Analytics culture within the organization.

CHALLENGES OF SETTING ANALYTICS CULTURE IN ORGANIZATIONS

Creating a culture involving Analytics and its acceptance in the stakeholder teams is a time-consuming process. Having the appropriate data management practices, skilled workforce, right mindset and perseverance to ensure acceptance of Analytics initiatives over time are some virtues of an analytics-rich organization. In such organizations, the top management instils belief among fellow employees in introducing and hence practising analytics as part of organizational change management.

Any organizational change comes with some resistance. But for Analytics, there are some unique complications that have to be dealt with as it evolves into a full-fledged practice. Historically, the three disciplines (a) information management, (b) processing large-scale information and (c) summarizing the processed results of analysis and hence using domain knowledge to connect it to the business problem for decision-making have remained independent of each other with shared responsibility among the members to provide contextual information as and when needed. Hence, a synergetic approach towards working under the

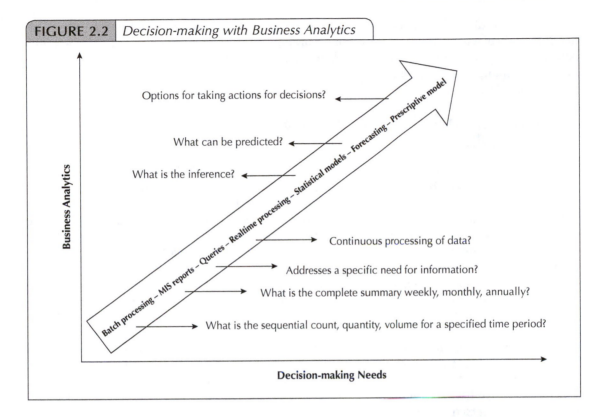

FIGURE 2.2 *Decision-making with Business Analytics*

same umbrella of business problem-solving was never felt. Research- and analytics-based decision-making has forced these three distinct skills to integrate (refer to Figure 2.1).

This could be a possible reason for Business Analytics having different meanings in different types of organizations (refer to Figure 2.2). In organizations that process information for large-scale reporting of transactions on routine basis, Business Analytics assumes the role of basic OLTP and BI (refer to Figure 1.1). Many process industries fall under this category such as cement industries, oil refineries and pharma companies that have large-scale operations. Streaming data generated on process parameters of day-to-day functioning are collated in the form of reports for monitoring company operations.

Alternatively, digital marketing companies that have gathered and managed huge reserves of data that are also processed and fed into business models define Analytics as statistical modelling or data mining. Customer segmentation, profiling, market basket analysis for determining appropriate promotional strategies and customer purchase patterns would be conducted within Business Analytics domain.

Certain organizations that have distributed and independent sets of relatively small data-bases pertaining to silos of the business operations have a hard time establishing an organized Analytics capability since their processes are not streamlined identically to process large sets of data. For instance, survey data can be used to track customer's perception about a brand and fed into a large database. A household panel is used separately to track consumer purchase data. Simultaneously, the organization may be tracking fleet data on outbound goods in their Enterprise system. Accounting systems provide information about revenue and profitability of different business units. Until and unless all these disparate sources of data are interlinked within the company data warehouse, the full capabilities of sophisticated Analytics investment are not achieved. A mechanism to provide an overall view of the business performance does not exist.

Outsourcing Analytics: Another Challenge to Creating Productive Analytic Culture

In the past 15 years outsourcing of processes (particularly Analytics) to distant geographic locales which have realized both cost advantage and specialized data processing capabilities has led to the evolution of the current stream of Analytics dominated by statistical and computational prowess. While its virtues are being debated, this separation of a few Analytic capabilities from others mentioned earlier has spurred more imbalances in the capability in many organizations and taken them away from the blended resources that have been talked about in an earlier section.

The prime mover for outsourcing Analytics processes to low-cost regions has been cost management. However, imbalances have been caused because business acumen is critical to boost up value addition in the Analytics Process. Low-cost regions which provide offshore services are associated with market conditions which are not compatible with the developed markets for whom the analytical services are rendered. The ability for resources in the offshore regions to appreciate the nuances of domain knowledge of the user (developed) markets is limited, leading to the possibility of suboptimal output. In general, technology in the form of processing capability (surfeit in its availability in low cost environ) acts as a poor substitute for business acumen to drive value addition.

Inevitably, the ideal solution to these challenges lies in the cross-pollination of skills both within and across environs to improve the competency set. Migration of experts from the domain, development of offshore environs and better work/information flows across work sites/personnel with differential skill sets can help alleviate the challenges over time.[1]

This trend towards specialization has inevitably led to the development of Analytics as a process rather than a philosophy of organizations to take rigorously deliberated decisions.

Also observed is the proliferation of specialist firms providing data processing help (stats modelling) without commensurate knowledge of business context to provide quality business advisory services.

Usually, these specialist firms have evolved into the Analytics domain using their traditional strengths in the knowledge industry. For instance, the traditional information management firms (e.g., Wipro, Infosys) have veered towards automation and reporting processes (Descriptive Analytics), whereas the algorithm-building firms (e.g., SAS, IBM) would be better positioned as modelling and optimization specialists (Predictive and Diagnostic Analytics). Traditional business advisory firms (e.g., McKinsey, BCG, Monitor Deloitte) tend to rely on their domain skills to provide prescriptions for business problems while depending on more

---

[1] Arindam Banerjee and Scott A. Williams, 'International Service Outsourcing: Using Offshore Analytics to Identify Determinants of Value-Added Outsourcing', *Strategic Outsourcing: An International Journal* 2, no. 1 (2009): 68–79.

specialized data processing partners to provide them with the analysis. The jury is still out regarding the usefulness of such specialized and piecemeal measures.

Such proliferation of specialized skill consultants and outsourced process operations has naturally had a significant influence in the way 'help-seeker' organizations view the growth of their internal capabilities in Analytics. Many decision-makers have felt that building a specialized analytics operation within the firm with statistical and computation specialist capability will be ideal for the Analytics journey. Our view is that, for most companies with fragmented information sources (which form the majority of organizations), such specialization in an evolving environment will not yield satisfactory results in the short run.

ORGANIZATIONAL DESIGN FOR IMPACTFUL ANALYTICS

Based on a research study conducted by the authors on use of Business Analytics in organizations, certain characteristics can be stated as follows:

1. **Distinct sectors of analytics usage in India:** There are three significant areas in which analytics has developed in India. They are as follows:
   a. Offshore operations, which are largely driven by expertise, and data that are imported and function on the requirements of overseas businesses that support such operations.
   b. Private sector financial institutions (primarily banks) that have started working with operational and transactional data to tailor-make their operational decision-making.
   c. Digital and web space that generates large-scale data and can be easily manipulated to provide online feed on decision changes required. But this is a fractional percentage of the total business transaction happening in India.[2] Our study does not capture this sector.

   Apart from these three domains, the rest (diverse in nature) are also there trying to catch up with limited and many times unorganized sources of data that have the potential to yield at best modest results. We have made significant efforts here to check the potential of this sector.

2. **Overall assessment of analytics process development in Indian organizations based on survey:**
   a. *Non-availability of comprehensive business data:* A prerequisite for effective data science application is the availability of data. It may be structured or semi-structured (or unstructured), but nevertheless it is important that the coverage of the available data source should be close to complete and the variety of information available is broad enough to provide a wholesome view of the business phenomenon that is studied. None of these conditions is satisfied in many organizations. A secondary concern is the unorganized state of data in many organizations which makes it difficult to develop a systematic information plan to connect to decision-making processes.

   External information regarding markets and environment is the most difficult to acquire simply because there are few private or government agencies involved in the

---

[2] 'Evolution of E-commerce in India'. Accessed 6 March 2014, http://www.pwc.in/assets/pdfs/publications/2014/evolution-of-e-commerce-in-india.pdf

collection processes. Besides, the high cost of collection of data from relatively inaccessible parts of the country (rural markets, for instance) discourages investments in such initiatives.

A consequent problem due to this non-availability of data is that the impact of data and its subsequent processing and insight into decision-making remains largely muted and incomplete.

b. *Internal data in multiple and incompatible formats:* A second dimension of the complication for some organizations that have quality business data and that get generated as a part of the business operations, such as transaction data in banks and retail stores, is their availability in different formats, which causes significant problems of consolidation. Take for instance the banking and financial services institutions in India. In the past decade and a half, there has been rapid development in computerization and automation of operations in most large public sector institutions. A consequence of this trend has been that recent data is available in standardized electronic formats but its integration (or lack of it) with data available in legacy physical systems (read: paper formats) makes it difficult to apply any data science procedures reliably to glean insights for decision-making.

c. *Dependency on heuristics for making decisions:* Given the above constraints, many business organizations remain steadfast on their dependency on heuristic business rules developed over long periods of experience and a firm connect 'with the ground'. People-driven decisions override attempts at standardization and the common refrain heard is that information is not available or incomplete to substitute the 'gut feel' with the rigours of scientific models-based decision support systems. A notable example of such a focus is the role of branch operations in managing business operations in the field. It is very apparent in rural markets, where the role of the local branch is important for taking both operational and at times strategic decisions. Here, the lack of information is substituted by the 'look and feel' of the environment, which is only possible through a decentralized branch-based operations (our respondents from the banking and financial services sectors corroborate with this view). A centralized process of decision-making using data is therefore dispensed with and substituted by a people-led decentralized organization structure.

d. *Market growth and low competition hide the virtues of analytics-driven precision in decisions:* The 'futility' of the analytics practice is also fuelled by the notion of the 'growing market syndrome'. Data scientists are supposed to extract business insights that act as a welcome succour in a highly mature and penetrated market. They are supposed to provide directions, refine decisions to hone in on the 'close to the perfect' set of decisions for an environment. However, when the markets are in the expanding phase, such extraction of precise insights from past transactions is not quite relevant. In such a situation, the importance of factual evidences based on past occurrences can easily be discounted since the growth in the market overrides the leakages of a sub-optimal decision. Precision in decision-making or the lack of it has little consequence on the year-end performance of the organization since the overall market growth many times covers up for all such inefficiencies.

e. *Technology alone has limited potential to create impact:* Offshore operations seem to have relatively less problem due to non-availability of appropriate data infrastructure, but due to their operational bases being geographically distant from policymaking units, suffer from lack of 'contextual relevance'. It was felt that embedded organizations with policymaking and analytics support working in tandem and in close coordination are necessary to ensure fructification of the true value of this domain. The domestic market imperatives being very different from the offshore challenges do not help in ensuring a sufficient flow of trained human resources (HR) that can provide adequate domain expert knowledge in offshore operations.

f. *Globalization and cross-pollination of ideas from multiple markets:* They have led to more awareness about the benefits of the data-driven processes and the role of analytics. This is not a concern area, but an optimistic note for the future. More trained resources are available in the Indian market, which has led to some traction. Higher awareness has initiated some discussion and debate regarding the appropriateness of analytics to their specific context. Openness to ideas and technology that may help in data collection and management is noted as well. Such atmosphere was non-existent five years ago. The proliferation of offshore units that use sophisticated technology has also spurred interest in indigenous companies to initiate a review of their analytic potential.

While there are enough conversations happening in the domain of Analytics, challenges in India-based operations are diverse and their origins are varied. Hence, there may not be one resolution approach that is suitable for all organizations. However, it is easy to perceive that most India-based organizations may have similar issues of data organization that may be impeding their progression in the field of Analytics.

Based on the above summary of findings and some other significant insights from our survey, we propose a framework for adoption of Analytics in Indian firms. We have specifically not considered the issues identified in the ITES industry vertical since, given its legacy, this industry is technically an 'implant' (service delivery extension) of overseas businesses and does not really merit being considered an out-and-out Indian industry.

The authors believe that the overarching drivers of analytics adoption in organizations in India are as follows:

- **The availability and constraints of/perceived need for suitable data infrastructure:** This dimension has emerged as a primary driver/constraint of Analytics deployment across multiple industry verticals. Without availability and systematic management of information databases, significant deployment of analytics is not possible. 'Ease of Access to Data/Market Data', 'Availability of Methods to capture data' and 'availability of significant proportion of relevant data and in compatible formats' are some of the parameters identified by respondents that define this construct.
- **Competitive intensity of the business environment:** This dimension, according to the authors, is an important influencer of analytics adoption as well. The critical need for competitive markets is measured strategic and tactical response to market challenges. This need is perhaps not felt in the Indian market environment as much. Industry benchmarks are not seen to have been set on minimum required Analytics capabilities for business performance. Rival organizations are not perceived to have made significant investments in analytics and hence its importance is not perceived. 'Regulated environment', 'high market growth rates' and 'low priority due to exigent needs elsewhere' are some of the parameters spelt out by respondents that define this construct.

The Adoption of Analytics in Indian Organizations: A Proposed Model

Based on these two major identified constructs, the authors offer a model that explains the adoption of analytics in India. In this pursuit, the authors are significantly influenced by a similar model proposed by Germann, Lilien and Rangaswamy.[3] While their paper looked at the drivers of 'analytics deployment' and subsequent 'firm performance', the authors have restricted themselves in their study to examining the influencers of 'analytics adoption/deployment' in firms. The authors' hunch is that evolving markets like India may require some more time to mature for them to realize the true impact of 'analytics deployment' on 'firm productivity'.

The primary driver for adopting and productively using analytics capabilities is the 'availability and access to data infrastructure' (positively related). This is supported by the views of respondents in the survey. Taking support of the model proposed by Germann (2013), the authors propose that 'competitive intensity of the business environment' has a moderating role to this relationship (negative impact of low competition). While the authors' claim is largely based on this previous research, they did obtain some evidence based on their discussion with some PSU bank executives who claimed that in their environment, 'higher order analysis was not needed, even if possible' because the banking regulator ensured a tight control over business options that could be considered.

'Availability and access to data infrastructure' investments in organizations are partly governed by:

1. Level of support from the top management ('top management advocacy'). This construct is supported by parameters identified in the research such as 'felt need for analytics', 'easy availability of turnkey solutions' and 'exposure to global standards' in analytics.
2. 'Awareness in the organization' about best practices across business environments also helps in facilitating faster adoption. Dimensions such as 'global movement of analytics talent' and also 'availability of analytics vendors' who may provide comprehensive solutions to business analytics problems and 'low/high analytics skill penetration' determine the level of awareness regarding the benefits of Analytics. There are some inputs about how awareness about best global practices has had a direct impact on the adoption of analytics in Indian organizations.

The detailed model is presented in Figure 2.3.

Deploying Business Analytics in Organizations

There are several issues faced by decision-makers, while deploying Business Analytics in their organization. There are several beliefs among the decision-makers that influence their decision in deploying Analytics as a **complementary** or **supplementary** function within their organization. There are usually two approaches to managing Analytics in an organization: the first being manage the process of Analytics and second the outcome/inference generated from Analytics. The first consists of specialists who are technology-savvy and are able to understand

---

[3] Frank Germann, Gary L. Lilien, and Arvind Rangaswamy, 'Performance Implications of Deploying Marketing Analytics', *International Journal of Research in Marketing* 30, no. 2 (2013): 114–128.

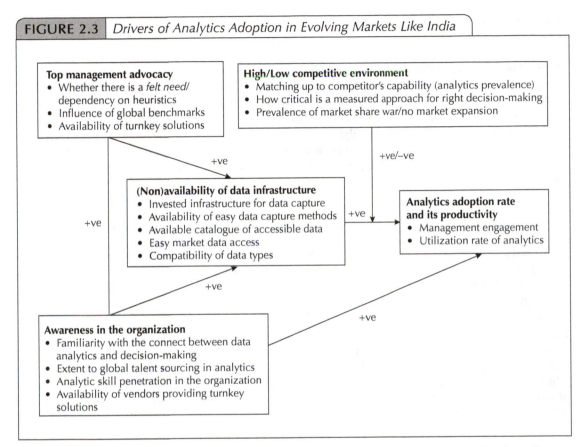

FIGURE 2.3 | *Drivers of Analytics Adoption in Evolving Markets Like India*

Source: The authors. Adapted from Arindam Banerjee and Tanushri Banerjee, 'Determinants of Analytics Process Adoption in Emerging Economies: Perspectives from the Marketing Domain in India', *Vikalpa* 42, no. 2 (2017): 95–110, doi:10.1177/0256090917704560.

business process efficiency that can be brought about by better use of Analytics. The second comprises the ones who are statisticians with business acumen to understand the business needs and be able to connect the outcomes from an Analytics model to the needs for improved organization decision-making.

Belief 1: Technology Enhancements Lead to Better Analytics

IT does have to play a role while Analytics roll out by automating and assimilating processes, and hence is an integral component during the decision-making process of building Analytics capability in organizations. However, its role is at best that of a facilitator. Need for Business Analytics is tied to organizational business needs. What are the current business opportunity areas, how is the organization performing in the present environment, what are the plans for future growth, what parameters will ascertain better business outcome. Although broadly stated, these and several such questions are the foundation for determining the need for building Analytics capability within organizations. Technology investments and their roles are part of the overall process.

Belief 2: Business Analytics Should Be a Specialized Team of Individuals within the Company

There is no one particular answer for this belief as it depends on the type of the organization. There are companies like technology solution providers or consultants where every employee is trained to do better analysis and undergoes analytics training, whereas business consulting companies will have dedicated research groups where data scientists with highly specialized skills are hired to drive Business Analytics. A third type of organizational structure requires the business team to continuously interface with the Analytics team in an embedded structure. Large data sets, and hence creation of large databases are leading organizations to think creatively to build better organizational models for Business Analytics.

Belief 3: Business Acumen Can Be Substituted by Business Analytics

While both cannot be substituted for one another, they do share a strong association. When appropriate data is available, Business Analytics can be used to challenge questions and verify hunches and subjective claims by providing relevant evidence from the Analytics outcomes. A predictive model can use appropriate data to support a future forecast by providing variety of logical possibilities to a particular decision under study. It will, however, not be able to tell you with certainty which of these possibilities should be chosen. This is where the business leader uses her Business Acumen. As an example, let us think of a doctor who listens to various symptoms of a patient, and hence tries to identify the illness. He/she has an Analytics tool in which he/she feeds the symptoms and as an output the model provides him/her with three types of causes for three different diseases. Now it would be for the doctor to use his acumen by referring to the history of past symptoms of the patient, her current condition and many such other factors to conclude on the exact illness to be treated.

Seven Steps for Creating Analytics Culture in Organizations

Leaders in organizations working towards developing a Business Analytics culture within their organization/teams should focus on the following aspects:

1. Be able to identify how Business Analytics would be adding incremental value to the already existing business.
2. Be able to sense the appropriate growth prospect of this capability within their organization. Context will vary, and hence the pace and utility will vary. However, as long as the data and the Analytical outcomes are linked to the business objectives, it will pave way towards developing an Analytics culture within the organization.
3. Be able to visualize, and hence develop the framework that connect data resources in the organizations to their utility in improving business decision-making.
4. Be able to establish measurement parameters in form of KPIs that suggest the advantage of the outcome from the Analytical processes on business performance.
5. Be able to train and build capability among the Analytics professionals to be able to effectively communicate the Analytical outcomes in the form that the end user/decision-maker is able to comprehend.

6. Be able to understand and suggest the architecture that would be necessary to accomplish the tasks 1–4.
7. Many a time, it has been seen that the investments in architecture have been made at the beginning of an Analytics capability building discussion. This may have resulted due to the purchase of canned solutions available in the market or unplanned utilization of budget allocated for infrastructure growth. This can often result in erroneous judgement unless the expected return on investment (ROI) is calculated by following Steps 1–5.

DATA ANALYTICS IN HR, MARKETING, OPERATIONS AND FINANCE

Data Analytics in HR

The HR function in an organization is about people management. An organizations' HR, its employees, is an important component for its overall growth and prosperity. Be it recruiting the appropriate resource for the specific job profiles, training them to be able contributors, identifying high performers and methods to keep them motivated, identifying low performers and the associated reasons—these basic functions are part of any HR team in an organization. With time as the organizations have grown and so its employees, managing people has become a critical part of an organizational strategy. HR management has undergone a massive transformation. Workforce management drives its decisions from data about its employees. Data can be used for any of the three purposes as may apply to the context within which the decisions are made: data to represent the details of its employees and associated performance metrics in the form of reports or dashboards, data that helps answer queries like how many employees have taken a leave of five working days on an average per month and the third where data is used for predictions like the attrition rate next year. Use of Business Analytics helps remove subjectivity from the above kind of decisions by analysing data to provide factual evidence. A five-year organizational growth plan will identify state of current organizational resources and additional resources based on monetary forecast. These changes have to be supported by appropriate talent resources. Business Analytics in HR has played a significant role in being able to assess and manage the current health of employee performance and be able to effectively plan for future.

The HR team of an organization uses a Business Analytics model (regression model) to manage diversity across teams in the organization. For example, its current requirement is to identify a resource for a leadership role who has (a) about 20 years of work experience in the business domain, (b) is a female, (c) has good interpersonal skills, (d) good communicator, (e) takes quick decisions, (f) has led large teams and (g) is a good listener. The business analytics model requires the data on all the parameters mentioned to be able to receive a set of choices from which the most appropriate resource is identified. The data for parameters 1, 2 and 6 will be directly available from databases. However, the other 4 will have to be identified from unstructured data residing in the organization in the form of minutes of team meetings, annual reports, 360-degree peer reviews and employee performance reports. The data on all parameters have to be in the same format for the model to process and provide the set of outcomes. It is then the HR team that picks the most appropriate one among the choices provided.

Data Analytics in Marketing

Business Analytics has been a big facilitator to the marketing domain in an organization that makes decision using varied sets of data in multiple categories. A decision about product categories; sales and marketing strategies: identifying leads, promotions, pricing, profits; transportation; new markets; customer data: acquisition, attrition, rewards, complain management and such others. All of these decisions are ultimately tied to the ROI that the organization makes for profitability. Analytics models for sales forecasting, market basket analysis, competitive strategies, customer satisfaction, attrition rates, choice models, enhancing customer loyalty, sensitivity analysis, campaign management are used by the marketing and sales teams in organizations.

An organization wanted to use its point of sales (PoS) data for identifying products that could be included in the upcoming buy one get one free (BOGO) summer promotion. Products that can be included would be either of the two types: (a) the ones that customers prefer to buy in summer such as soft drinks, fruit drinks, ice creams, shampoos, bath soaps and powders and (b) the ones that sit on the shelf for long durations such as jams, ready-made food mix, toothpastes of certain brands, kitchen utensils, incense sticks, biscuits and dry fruit mix. The marketing mix Analytics model uses the PoS data to identify the customer purchase behaviour for making decision on the summer promotion strategies.

Data Analytics in Operations

Company operations revolve around the supply chain management of the interlinked processes from raw material to processed goods. With the advent of Enterprise systems that connect the organization end to end and the sophistication in automation, there has been a significant role played by Business Analytics in transforming inventory management, material management, process improvement, forecasting, warehouse management, transportation/fleet management and risk analysis. Optimization models are used for estimation and forecasting varied parameters for decision-making.

A power utility company has its head office in Jaipur with power plants in 10 locations spread across the state. The power generation in the power plants operates independently that needs to adhere to company's operational norms. The company's enterprise system (ERP) is used to feed (input) and capture operational data from the power plants that is processed and stored in the company database. Business Analytics tools are used along with the ERP to analyse and share data with teams across the organization for monitoring, knowledge-building and decision-making. The managing director of the company sits in the head office in Jaipur. The Business Analytics Visualization tool is used to provide him/her a dashboard displaying relevant details through which he/she can see and monitor the 10 power plant operations. Paperwork has significantly reduced. Additionally, the speed and accuracy of decision-making have improved significantly.

Data Analytics in Finance

Financial institutions capture and retain huge amount of data that are in both structured and unstructured forms. Be it a financial organization like a bank or a finance department within a company, the business objectives are associated with measuring, documenting, analysing and providing suggestions to stakeholders in monetary transactions, thus resulting in increased revenue and reduced operating costs for the company. Automation has played a significant role in reducing routine manual interventions, providing the time to the financial managers for strategic decision-making. Business Analytics has been used for feasibility analysis, forecasting trends, break-even analysis and risk management. It has also been used for customer relationship management in banks and insurance sectors. For example, a large national bank has its operations out of Guwahati, India. A significant number of customers who had credit cards offered by the bank did not pay their bills on time. The bank had observed an increase in this trend in the past six months; however, its risk management department was unable to get a proper estimate of the number of customers faltering and the associated reasons for the same. Several in-house meetings were held to identify the possible reasons and suggestive measures, but these were not backed with structured factual data. The managers spoke from their experience of managing the credit card department. Hence, accurate decisions could not be made. The organization then decided to use a Business Analytics model for doing a feasibility analysis based on certain costs they would incur and the possible benefits it would lead to in reducing the number of faltering credit card customers. Costs would be the investment they make to fill the caveats in customer relationship management. Based on the cost and benefit analysis, the Analytics model was expected to calculate the time for breakeven in number of years. This would help the managers decide on prioritizing the costs for the expected benefits in reducing the number of customers faltering to pay their credit card bill on time.

REVIEW QUESTIONS

1. Describe the challenges of setting an Analytics culture in organizations.
2. Discuss the model of adoption of Analytics in organizations in India.
3. Discuss the issues faced by decision-makers while deploying Business Analytics in their organization in India.
4. What are the seven steps of creating an Analytics culture in organizations?
5. State how data analytics can be useful in HR, marketing, finance and operations management in organizations.

CASE 2.1
Measuring Customer Satisfaction of Service Experience
(Case Complexity: Easy)

Bakool Enterprise has established its presence in the home appliance market in India. Its four decades of existence has made it a household name for every homemaker in India. It occupies a market share of 62 per cent among strong competitors and has maintained its position for the past seven years. It mainly manufactures and sells home appliances such as refrigerators, washing machines, microwaves, ovens, kitchen chimneys and flour mills. Headquartered in the city of Udaipur, it has manufacturing units and sales offices across different parts of India. The senior management team of Bakool enterprise believes in lean manufacturing processes and building loyalty and trust among customers. This is taught and practised at every level in the organization. The CEO in his message on the company website has stated that the company strives to see the smile on the face of their customers when they operate and use an appliance manufactured by Bakool enterprise. Hence, the sale of their products is important but it is equally important to maintain the relationship of trust with their customers by providing efficient after-sales service. For instance, a customer Rajiv had recently purchased a washing machine from Bakool enterprise. After the initial monetary transactions were completed, the product reached the house of the customer on the mentioned date and time. Punctuality about time is among the core values of the organization.

During product delivery, free installation was done and all associated details for service-related calls were shared with the customer. Rajiv accordingly received the warranty card for one year which would offer him free service for any problems he might encounter within that period. During the first month of use, Rajiv had encountered a problem with the working of the equipment. He needed help, hence he called the service number and requested a visit. Within two hours, the manager of the local sales office gave him a call mentioning that an engineer would reach his residence at 10 AM the next morning to attend to the problem. He also received an SMS from Bakool enterprise mentioning that if Rajiv was satisfied with the engineer's work, he must share a three-digit number with the engineer. True to the manager's word, the engineer was at Rajiv's residence at 10 AM next morning, fixed the problem and explained to him certain checks to be done in case the problem reappears. Once Rajiv was satisfied, the engineer requested the three-digit number that he had received on his SMS to confirm his satisfaction with the service provided.

The same evening, Rajiv received a call from the customer service call centre requesting him to rate his satisfaction on a scale of 1–5. Rajiv was busy in his company meeting, but since he was pleased with the prompt service by Bakool Enterprise, he took a minute to rate it on the best scale. What did Bakool enterprise do with customer Rajiv? First, they had a happy customer who had purchased a new equipment from the company. Second, they had a satisfied customer in him with their prompt after-sales service. Third, they had the customer satisfaction captured via two direct methods: the three-digit SMS shared with the engineer by Rajiv and the feedback call from the customer service call centre. This is one such instance of the culture that prevails within Bakool Enterprise and is practised across varied products for several years. What do they do with the data? Across categories of products across cities for a large number of customers, so much of data is residing at the call centre database which is so far an asset that is lying idle.

Bakool Enterprise decided to create a Business Analytics culture within their organization wherein they would improve and automate processes for lean and agile manufacturing as well as better serve their customers. They would also be interested in extending their product line into entertainment category offering television screens, home theatres, music systems and the associated accessories. This would mean competing with an already established market with big brands.

The case does not require you to use data for analysis. You need to use your understanding of concepts from 'seven steps for creating analytics culture in organizations' and answer the following questions.

Exercise

1. Do you think Business Analytics can help Bakool Enterprise improve manufacturing processes, build stronger relationship with customers, extend their product offering and increase sales? How? Justify your answer.
2. How can the data from the call centre database assist in building a Business Analytics culture within Bakool Enterprise?

CASE 2.2
Business Analytics in an Oil Refinery
(Case Complexity: Medium)

A large oil refinery uses BI to manage its refinery operations. The major processes in any oil or petroleum refinery include processing and refining crude oil to obtain many useful products. The different stages of refining provide petroleum naphtha, gasoline (motor fuel), diesel as fuel, lubricating oil, heating oil, kerosene and liquefied petroleum gas, residuals such as asphalt and tar. The unprocessed oil, crude oil, comes from the ground. It is impure and contains a mixture of many types of hydrocarbons, hence is treated and separated by the process of oil refining. All of the by-products mentioned above have different boiling points. The process used to break the crude oil into its components is called fractional distillation. This is done by heating the crude oil, letting it vaporize and then condensing the vapour. The refineries treat the distilled products to remove impurities. These are then stored in warehouse and transported to desired locations such as petrol pumps, chemical plants and other industries.

Figure 2.4 shows the refining process of an oil refining company that uses BI and Business Analytics to make 'agile' decisions. Planning for the amount of crude oil to be processed is decided based on the availability of crude oil, the demand for crude oil and its by-products ('A_1'), the planned storage quantity ('A_2') and the market conditions. Based on the actual crude available each time and the plant and machinery resource capacity, there could be a deviation (first possibility of deviation) between the planned and the actual crude oil ('A' and 'B' in Figure 2.4) that is available on a daily basis for intake. The crude oil is then processed through fractional distillation. Due to the variation in chemical properties of crude oil and operation parameters, there could be a deviation (second possibility of deviation) between the planned and actual distillation output mix ('B' and 'C' in Figure 2.4). The dashboard provides real-time comparison between the deviation of planned and actual values for experts to make necessary agile decisions for improved performance. Data on all key parameters are stored in the company database. The processed crude oil and its by-products are then dispatched to petrol stations and other industries using lorries/trucks or pipelines. Some of it is also kept in storage for future use. Another possibility of deviation (third possibility of deviation) occurs at this point due to changing dispatched quantity 'D' due to demand variation, pipeline capacity (planned versus actual), changing storage requirement ('C'–'D'), lorry availability, wastage and such others.

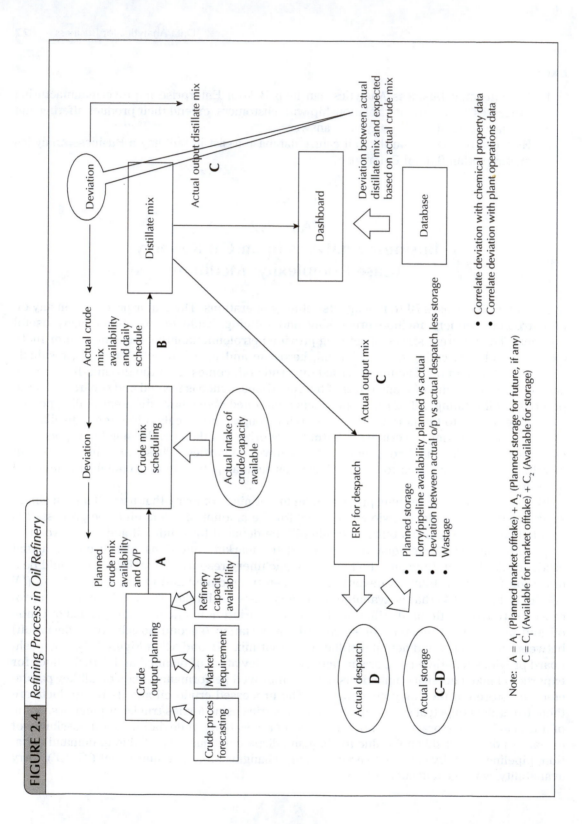

FIGURE 2.4 *Refining Process in Oil Refinery*

Exercise

1. What do you understand by 'agile decision-making' in organizations?
2. State the major processes where experts are required to make agile decisions in a crude oil refining company.
3. What is the role of Business Analytics in helping experts make agile decisions?

CASE 2.3
Bedding and Accessories Firm Embraces Business Analytics Culture (Case Complexity: Hard)

This is the case study of Lumasodia Company, a bedding and accessories firm. Before we discuss the company specifics, let us talk about certain basic employee management activities that remain common across all organizations. In organizations, employees toil to achieve short- and long-terms goals in building their career graph and thus contribute towards the organizational growth. Most employees have their work day consumed in achieving the immediate targets that involves activities and interactions with associated colleagues and departments. The management of the organization, in consultation with HR team, evaluates the performance of the employees. This is done across several parameters that rate the performance of each employee as good, average and poor which ultimately accounts into building their career growth trajectory. Organizations provide training to their employees to help them be more agile at their job. The training could be either skill-based or managerial in nature depending on what would be useful to the employee to add value to their current domain of work. An engineer designing an aircraft spare part would benefit from a skill-based training that educates him in new designing techniques that are being used by similar organizations. Alternatively, a manager of a team may be very good in subject matter but requires training in interpersonal skills. This training in return is expected to improve the performance of the employees. Training and development (T&D) of employees is usually managed by the HR department of organizations. However, in large companies, T&D may be a separate department taking care of the T&D needs of organizations.

After the training needs have been identified, how does the T&D department go about providing the training? Organizations have followed different models depending on the number of employees to be trained, the type of training to be provided, the frequency of the training needed and the level of the employees in the organization to be trained (top management, mid-level management, operational teams and individual contributors). These are as follows:

Model 1: The training is conducted in-house, that is, within the organization premises by their employees who are considered to be experts in certain fields.

Model 2: The training is conducted in-house by experts who are invited from outside the organization. The engagement with the experts is via consultancy assignments.

Model 3: The employees are sent to an educational institution for a short-term training course where faculty members from the institution/university conduct the classes. These are termed as management development programmes (MDPs).

Model 4: The organization ties up with an executive education and consulting firm for long-duration training programmes for educating their employees.

Lumasodia Company has 4,000 employees working for them across India. Headquartered in Chandigarh, they specialize in bedding and accessories. Started as a small backyard business, the three generations of Lumasodia family have built the business with care and innovation such that it has grown beyond expectations with dignity. The beginning was with selling hand-woven blankets at very reasonable prices. Women of the household participated in sewing the blankets, whereas men would source the raw material from nearby villages. In the sheer cold weather of north India, the blankets were in great demand. Rajshekhar, the eldest in the Lumasodia family, accumulated funds to buy a space in the industrial estate of the city from where the business could be carried out with ease. Soon the product range increased, where they started manufacturing and selling bedsheets, bedcovers, pillows, pillow covers, comforters, quilts, baby beddings and curtains. Their customers were of three kinds: purchasers from their retail stores, online shoppers which included billing and shipping to overseas customers and wholesale buyers such as hotels and hospitals. Managing the business required skilled employees. The top management that made strategic decisions had significant presence from the Lumasodia family. However, the organization's hierarchical chart was flat with team leaders managing their respective domains and simultaneously interacting with other teams to ensure overall productivity. At the end of each day and for every significant outcome, the employees were required to fill and update details on an ERP system for shared knowledge. This information was used to plan and monitor optimum inventory, manpower allocation for processes in the manufacturing unit, packaging and warehouse management, customer call centre management, salesforce and marketing efficiency. The top management wanted to create a Business Analytics culture within the organization where each employee understood the value of the information he/she uploaded on to the enterprise system and was able to use it for better decision-making. The operation of the company was huge and wherever possible automation had already been done to build process efficiency. But is there still a scope for improvement? The management along with T&D team decided to provide training to all employees in the organization in an effort to build an Analytics culture in the organization (refer Figure 2.5).

The employees in transaction processing roles like field sales executives, and customers interfacing employees such as order takers and complaint handling, billing desk, fleet and ware-house operators would be provided training using Model 1 where more experienced employees within the organization would be training them in batches. This training would primarily consist of efficient methods of logging information into the enterprise system—framing and constructing the information that is easily understood by all. This might also include training in English language proficiency, where needed. The next in the pyramid would be their managers, the line managers, who would be provided training using Model 2. This would include use of basic querying tools, report generations, accessing and processing information from various sources and some software knowledge for using spreadsheets. External experts would come in and train them on analytics skills and team management. The mid-level managers would be provided training by immersion programmes as described in Model 3. Utility of planning and building hypothesis and then validating it using analytics models, optimization techniques, visualization methods, forecasting future trends and communicating results in an easily understandable form would be key focus areas of the training. Top management would be trained by a global executive education firm as in Model 4—how an analytics culture brings value to an organization's end-to-end value chain, competitors who have used it

---

FIGURE 2.5 | *Business Analytics Culture at Lumasodia Company*

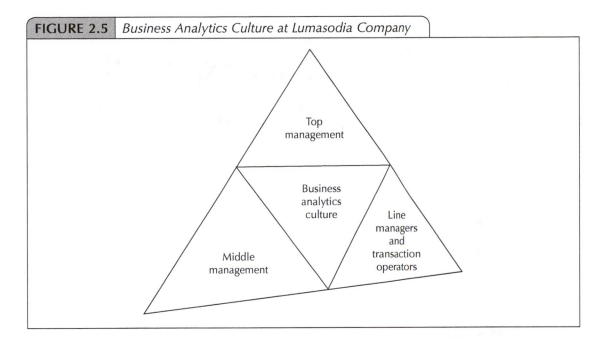

---

for better results, global trends, investment options and measuring the ROI. Based on the costs and expected benefits, the economic feasibility worksheet suggests that the company would breakeven in two-and-a-half years.

Exercise

You are required to list the benefits that the organization would gain from providing the training to all its employees. Think of the advantages that a Business Analytics culture provides to operations, finance, HR and marketing; connect it to the bedding and accessories organization and the four models used for the training.

3

Data Exploration in Business Analytics

Learning Objectives

After completing this chapter, students should be able to understand about the following:

- Different sources of data
- Different types of data
- Relevant data points to address business objectives
- What is available versus what is good to have
- Untapped data sources

Opening Example

Sanjana Pillai had just completed her MBA and had received a job offer of customer relationship manager in a multinational organization through campus placement. Life seemed to be going just the way she had dreamt it to be. Now that she was 23 years of age, her parents had spoken to her about getting married and settling down. She wanted to get some work experience before getting married, but she was also excited about formally announcing to everyone about her relationship with her classmate and boyfriend Rudra Dixit. She sat down with her parents and expressed her desire to settle down with Rudra. Things went well, parents of both sides met and the day for their wedding was announced. She and Rudra met several times to plan their wedding and honeymoon destination. Month and date for the wedding depended on many things such as (a) when both Sanjana and Rudra could get time off from work, (b) vacation time for parents, siblings, relatives and cousins for participating in their wedding, (c) most suitable weather conditions, (d) availability of hotels, (e) price variations of resources during the year and (f) venue for wedding. They also had to plan on the menu items, dress and jewellery, shopping list, beautician, car bookings, flight bookings, destination for honeymoon, *sangeet* (music) during the wedding.

The opening example narrates a social story of every household where the son or the daughter of the house completes education, gets to an age when parents along with the prospective bride/groom decide the marriage and the wedding takes place.

Let us look at the same example from the point of view of a business analyst. For a very different objective, **you wear the lens of a business analyst** and look at the pieces of data (attributes/variables) that exist in this whole wedding planning process of Sanjana and Rudra, it will draw an interesting list. **Variables** are characteristics of items of interest that vary. We measure, control, manipulate and test variables for inferences. A **construct** is a broad topic that is being studied. Variables are used to describe the construct in a measurable form. Two types of marriage options have been discussed, love marriage versus arranged marriage (prospective bride and groom meet with parents' consent and decide on life together. There are many variations of arranged marriage in India.). These can be described as two constructs. Here, Sanjana and Rudra have decided on love marriage. In this example, ideal marriage planning would be the specific construct under study. Variables include months when both Sanjana and Rudra would get time off from work, this coinciding with vacation months of family members. Months would be either of the months of January, May, June or December. Weather conditions are ideal from the months of November to February in most parts of India. Hotels and venue are available at different price ranges. Menu items for breakfast, lunch and dinner for at least four days required planning. Car booking, flight booking, destination for honeymoon all have several options to choose from. These variables would all be considered together, with interrelated effects, to define an ideal marriage planning and execution by parents on both sides.

The business analyst can pick these and similar other data points from marriages being executed in several households to generate a huge data set over time. This data set can further be analysed to work out optimal solutions for wedding planning/execution customized services for many others like Sanjana and Rudra. The basic starting point is the capture of data which are of two types: categorical and numerical.

Asking a student who has gone through a statistics or research methodology class, what is central tendency or difference between a dependent and independent variable, chances are that concepts would have already become hazy. Possible reason could be gaps in relating the business problem-solving methodology to the underlying mathematics, algorithms and modelling techniques covered in both the courses. Often, in the midst of a rigorous course curriculum, the courses are taught back to back. In such a situation, the student learns what is delivered by the faculty in class from the point of performing well in examination. Once done, the information goes back to the shelves along with the books, thus inhibiting the retention of knowledge to be taken forward to other specialized courses. The elective courses in the second year of an MBA programme are built upon courses taught in the first year of the programme. The basic concepts of both the courses mentioned above form the backbone of the Business Analytics course. Frameworks built with clear knowledge of the basic concepts are closer to perfection in analysing and interpreting real-world business problems and opportunities. Chapters 3 and 6 will revisit some of the concepts covered in previous courses. We shall be sequentially discussing the relevant topics with examples that will form the foundation of some of the later chapters. Applied research has been used in business decision-making in areas of marketing, sales, production, operations, finance to either solve an existing problem or get a better understanding of an existing opportunity. The examples have been created using SPSS software. Instructions for using the software are provided in the appendices at the end of the book.

UNDERSTAND DIFFERENT SOURCES OF DATA

There are mainly two sources of data: secondary and primary. **Secondary sources** include prior research done, trade journals, magazines, electronic content, organization data, reports, census, store panel data and such others. **Primary data** is collected using **qualitative methods** like focus group interviews and/or depth interviews or **quantitative data** collection methods like observation methods or survey questionnaire administered in person, by email, by Internet and/or by telephone. The collected secondary data supports significant part of the exploratory research. **Exploratory research** is conducted to identify the specific components of a business discussion that can be taken forward for research in the form of problem-solving or opportunity. It provides clarity based on what is derived from existing body of knowledge provided by other sources. Descriptive and causal research can be supported by both secondary and primary data. **Descriptive research** provides a systematic description of the facts that exist for a situation under study. **Causal research** looks for relationships that exist within the variables under study to form a cause-and-effect relationship. The authors have discussed in Chapter 5 how Big Data has led to the creation of data warehouses in organizations to capture, retain and analyse relevant data for competitive advantage.

UNDERSTAND DIFFERENT TYPES OF DATA

There are several ways in which data can be segregated. We shall follow the two major types of data: **categorical** and **numerical** (Figure 3.1). The primary question is when we encounter a variable, how can we slot it as categorical or numerical. You have probably already answered in your mind that the variable on which a mathematical operation is done is meaningful is numerical otherwise it is categorical. Let us make it still simpler with a quick litmus test. If you can perform an average of the data set which is meaningful, then it is numerical data else it is categorical. Simple, isn't it? Let us check it out with some examples:

1. Length of arm
2. Mode of transportation to office

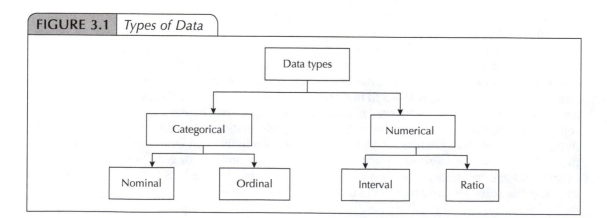

FIGURE 3.1   *Types of Data*

3. Time of travel to office
4. Money spent at restaurants last year
5. City of residence/hometown
6. Postal code
7. Hours slept at night
8. Duration of a movie
9. Favourite sport
10. Date of birth

Out of the 10 data variables mentioned, mode of transportation (2), city of residence (5), postal code (6), favourite sport (9) and date of birth (10) are categorical. Rest of the variables are numerical. How many could you get correct? On all five slotted as categorical, taking an average of the data set has no meaning for the business analyst. The postal code and date of birth are special cases where the data set appears as numbers many a times mis-leading the analyst to slot it as numerical.

In the opening example, the variables can be classified as categorical and numerical. For instance, the venue for the wedding, the desination for honeymoon, month for wedding and menu items are categorical, whereas price range for booking hotels, cars and flights would be numerical. The business analyst may be further interested in finding out what type of wedding is in trend among young adults like Sanjana and Rudra—love or arranged marriage. When informed about a love affair as Sanjana did, in how many cases had the parents agreed, cooperated and made the love marriage happen as desired? What would be the average spending for such weddings? What would be some suggestions on planning weddings similar to that done by family members of Sanjana and Rudra? These and similar analyses can begin with a hypothesis which we shall discuss in Chapter 6. For now, let us go back to our discussion on data types.

The categorical data is partitioned into **nominal** and **ordinal** data types. A categorical data is ordinal if the instance of that variable can be arranged in a particular order. For example, grades of students of a class are A, B, C and D, where A is the highest in order and D is the lowest. Where the instances do not have any particular order, data is called nominal.

A **frequency table** can be an informative representation built from the categorical variable showing the actual count and percentage frequency. Let us take an example to understand better. In a manufacturing firm, there are 10 types of equipment that are operated on a regular basis. At times, when the equipment gets broken, repair is scheduled for running it again. The equipment description table (Table 3.1) describes 10 equipment along with their location. The variable 'Equipment No.' represents the equipment number (51–60). They are located in three rooms—1, 2 and 3. The adjoining column 'Location' represents the room where it is located. There are two other variables: 'Price (in INR)' is the price of purchase of the equipment and 'Time of Use (Months)' is the number of months that the equipment has been in use since the date of purchase at the manufacturing unit.

Of these 10 equipment, an annual record is maintained of the equipment that have broken down and repair work is done to run them again. Table 3.2 lists 15 repair records of the 10 equipment in the manufacturing unit for the year 2018. The variable 'Equipment No.' shows the equipment that was repaired and the adjoining column 'Location' shows where it is located.

TABLE 3.1	*Equipment Description*			
S. No.	Equipment No.	Location	Price (in ₹)	Time of Use (Months)
1	51	Room 1	25,000	28
2	52	Room 1	20,000	24
3	53	Room 1	16,000	36
4	54	Room 2	60,000	24
5	55	Room 2	56,000	28
6	56	Room 2	58,000	26
7	57	Room 3	90,000	18
8	58	Room 3	98,000	22
9	59	Room 3	105,000	35
10	60	Room 3	120,000	29

TABLE 3.2	*Equipment Repair Record*	
S. No.	Equipment No.	Location
1	55	Room 2
2	52	Room 1
3	54	Room 2
4	57	Room 3
5	54	Room 2
6	57	Room 3
7	55	Room 2
8	54	Room 2
9	52	Room 1
10	58	Room 3
11	51	Room 1
12	55	Room 2
13	58	Room 3
14	56	Room 2
15	52	Room 1

Table 3.3 shows a count of the number of times an equipment was repaired in 2018 along with cumulative frequency and proportion.

Figure 3.2 shows the same information in graphical form. The column chart represents the frequency (count) of repair of the equipment on the x-axis, whereas y-axis shows the number of times it was repaired. It is evident that equipment 52, 54 and 55 were repaired maximum number of times.

TABLE 3.3	*Frequency of Equipment Repair*		
Equipment No.	**Frequency**	**Cumulative Frequency**	**Proportion**
51	1	1	0.06666667
52	3	4	0.2
54	3	7	0.2
55	3	10	0.2
56	1	11	0.06666667
57	2	13	0.13333333
58	2	15	0.13333333

The pie chart (Figure 3.3) shows the location of the equipment in the three rooms. As can be seen, out of the total number of equipment repaired, Room 1 has approximately 26 per cent of the equipment, Room 2 has 46 per cent and Room 3 has 26 per cent.

The numerical data type is partitioned into **interval** and **ratio**. These variables denote the distance between the categories which are identical. For instance, a variable recording the time of an equipment was allowed to operate from 10 minutes to 15 minutes. Associated time for each instance of Time recorded is either 10, 11, 12, 13, 14 or 15. Distance between each of the six categories is one minute. How can you differentiate between an interval and ratio data type? The difference between interval and ratio data type is that the latter begins from a zero point, for example, height, weight, length, years of experience.

Data type can also be seen as **discrete** and **continuous**. For example, a five-point Likert scale/item in a survey questionnaire for product satisfaction variable which provides an option from very satisfactory to least satisfactory is discrete and ordinal. It has finite number of values. There is a

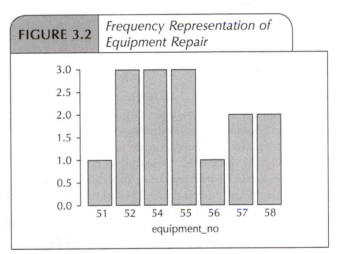

FIGURE 3.2 *Frequency Representation of Equipment Repair*

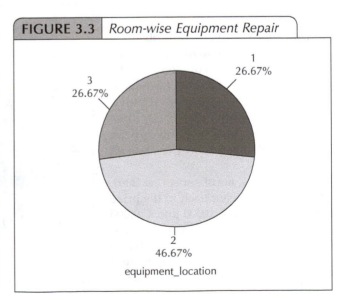

FIGURE 3.3 *Room-wise Equipment Repair*

TABLE 3.4	Descriptive Statistics						
	Mean	**Median**	**Min**	**Max**	**Kurtosis**	**Skewness**	**Range**
Price	55,350	57,000	10,500	120,000	−1.501	0.304	109,500
Time of use	27	27	18	36	−1.083	0.201	18

lot of debate among experts about whether parametric tests should be used on Likert scales. Likert scales in many situations are treated as continuous.

How satisfied are you with the product?

- ○ Least satisfied
- ○ Somewhat dissatisfied
- ○ Neutral
- ○ Somewhat satisfied
- ○ Very satisfied

Now suppose you are measuring the volume of sales of the product, marks obtained out of 50 by students in a class, age of employees in an organization; they have several values. These would be considered as continuous variables.

For the manufacturing firm, as has been mentioned in Table 3.1, both price and time of use are numerical variables. Descriptive statistics is the basic form of representing numerical variables. It can be inferred from Table 3.4 that the average price of the 10 equipment is ₹55,350, with minimum price being ₹10,500 and maximum being ₹120,000. The average use of equipment has been 27 months since the date of purchase with the minimum being 18 months and the maximum being 36 months.

Figures 3.4 and 3.5 represent **histograms** showing the probability distribution of the two numerical data variables: price of equipment and the time in months that the equipment has been in use, respectively. It shows the frequency of the variable by class interval. The class intervals are on x-axis and the frequency per class on y-axis.

In Figure 3.4, we observe that there are three equipment each in the price range from ₹0 to ₹20,000 and ₹40,000 to ₹60,000. There are two equipment in the price range from ₹80,000 to ₹100,000. There is one equipment each in the price range from ₹20,000

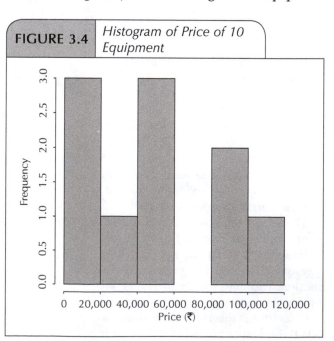

FIGURE 3.4   Histogram of Price of 10 Equipment

to ₹40,000 and ₹100,000 to ₹120,000. There are no equipment in the price range from ₹60,000 to ₹80,000.

In Figure 3.5, we observe that there are four equipment in use for 25–30 months from the time of purchase. There are three equipment in use for 20–25 months from the time of purchase. There is one equipment in use for 15–20 months, 30–35 months and 35–40 months, respectively.

Now suppose the manufacturing unit keeps a record of equipment repairs done for the past seven years. An outcome and a graph that compare the frequency of repairs done on an equipment for each of the seven years shall make a **time series** analysis. Another way of looking at the data could be as follows: the manufacturing unit has its offices in three different cities with exactly the same equipment and office layout in terms of equipment per room. A comparative analysis for repairs done on equipment at each of the three offices for the past year is **cross-section** data analysis.

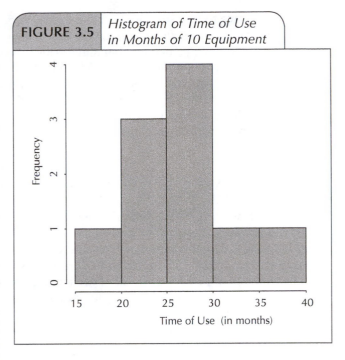

FIGURE 3.5 *Histogram of Time of Use in Months of 10 Equipment*

This concept will be further elaborated and explained in chart section in Chapter 9 in the section on data visualization.

IDENTIFY RELEVANT DATA POINTS TO ADDRESS BUSINESS OBJECTIVES

A data set obtained as a consequence of transactional information processing is an asset for the organization, used primarily to publish MIS reports. Examples in the marketing domain could be report of sales data of products category and region wise; in HR domain, report on hours worked by employees department wise; in finance domain, report on net profit of an organization region and year wise; in the operations management domain, report on inventory replenished by store city wise and so on. The reports are based on information capture. IT set-ups and software aid the capture of transactional data and hence processing it into information. The question would be, is all the data captured relevant for processing into information? Who decides this? This is where the role of a business analyst comes in, in being able to identify the relevant data points based on domain knowledge expertise and what is beneficial for the client to aid in decision-making process. Suvarna Kumar was in-charge of a large retail store in Central Mumbai. The transactional data of sales was processed every day in the form of daily sales report. As a keen business manager, he observed that most of his customers paid using a credit card during checkout. He suggested to his management that if the customers could be given an incentive to use a particular bank credit card, it would lead to better streamlining of information for the organization along with enhancing customer loyalty and delight. Eventually, the store partnered with a national bank in the locality for offering the incentive of a 5 per cent cashback to the customer who purchased using the bank's credit card. It was an easy change to implement, as most customers living in the vicinity already possessed a credit card of that bank. It required regular use by the customer of that card during checking out after their purchase. Mr Suvarna was thus able to identify a key relevant data point to build customer loyalty and benefit with the organizational sustainability and growth.

WHAT IS AVAILABLE VERSUS WHAT IS GOOD TO HAVE

One of the drawbacks of Big Data that has been discussed in many forums is the capture of **quality data** with multiple variables derived from the humongous data dumps. It gets overwhelming for the business analysts and decision-makers to make meaning of everything that is disguised in the data unless done through a systematic process in place. There can be many arguments to justify the stand of organizations on this challenge. First argument is that the business leaders in organizations understand their requirements and based on that they store, retrieve and process data variables that make meaning to their business decisions. In this case, the organizations are perplexed about the additional data that resides in their database with no use for the organization. Should organizations continue to bear this additional cost of keeping this data? A contrary argument states that there could be additional insights from the otherwise unfamiliar data. This would also result in cost of hiring specialists to make meaning out of this data that could possibly lead to competitive advantage or business growth. There is no single answer to this, leading to organizations experimenting to find answers. Consulting firms and software organizations have partnered with organizations to pave the way for identifying solutions. It is a constantly evolving process in the world of digital information capture.

UNTAPPED DATA SOURCES

Transactional data that we discussed in the previous sections are the main sources of data for organizations. Digital data capture and Big Data have increased the complexity of data in terms of size of data capture, frequency of data capture batch versus streaming data and the varied forms of data such as video, audio, graphs, images, photographs, textual data and web statistics. Data that is available in structured form is processed into information. Certain other raw data are unstructured/semi-structured in nature such as images, customer reviews, online behaviour of customers and sentiments of stakeholders. Within the unstructured/semi-structured data capture, there are two possibilities. There is a conscious capture, for example, of graphs generated from daily logs that have a well-defined process in place in the organization for processing and interpreting the data. However, there is also a significant other set of unstructured/semi-structured data that comes naturally as a part of organization data capture, which the company executives may not have clue of taking forward. These are the **untapped** data sources.

Organizations have put in a lot of mind and money to streamline untapped data sources. There is enough information on the internet about what your customers have to say about you, how they make a purchase on the Net, what they like and to what extent, what are some stumbling blocks for improvement and the competitive analysis. Sensor technology, IoT and data warehousing concepts with enterprise systems, text/web mining and sentiment analysis are some of the ways organizations have tried to beat this challenge. Those who have been able to build it systematically along with data scientists have claimed their name to fame.

The experts have augmented the existing resources with optimal methods of quality data capture from untapped sources and further systematically interpreted it to make meaningful insights for enhanced business decisions for organizations.

REVIEW QUESTIONS

1. What are the different sources of data? How are they useful?
2. What are the different types of data? How can you differentiate between a categorical and a numerical variable?
3. What are some basic ways of processing categorical and numerical data?
4. What is the process of identifying relevant data points to address business objectives?
5. What are untapped data sources? Explain with the help of an example from your university some possible sources of untapped data that may otherwise be useful to capture.

CASE 3.1
Where Is the Data in the Cars? (Case Complexity: Easy)

Arvind Rastogi owns a dealership in cars. He has a big retail store on the city highway close to the airport. He maintains a small database of the cars. The data set for cars is available in the student download section.[1] The variables in the data set are about cars: their technical features, their price, safety features and overall acceptability of the car. It has 1,728 instances (rows) in the data set.

All are categorical variables. The variables 'buying' and 'maintenance' refer to the price and the required maintenance of the car, respectively. Both have four values: very high, high, medium and low. The variable 'doors' signifies the number of doors the car has. The variable 'persons' refers to whether it can accommodate two, four or more people in the car. The variable 'luggage_boot' refers to its size as small, medium or big. The variable 'safety' refers to the safety features of the car either low, medium or high. The variable 'overall' refers to the overall acceptability of the car by the customers. Snapshot of data is provided further for reference. Cars that have not been sold for the past two years have been termed as 'unacceptable' by customers (see the table on the next page).

[1] ftp://ftp.ics.uci.edu/pub/machine-learning-databases/car/

Buying	Maintenance	Doors	Persons	Lug_boot	Safety	Overall
vhigh	vhigh	2	2	small	low	unacc
vhigh	vhigh	2	2	small	med	unacc
vhigh	vhigh	2	2	small	high	unacc
vhigh	vhigh	2	2	med	low	unacc
vhigh	vhigh	2	2	med	med	unacc
vhigh	vhigh	2	2	med	high	unacc
vhigh	vhigh	2	2	big	low	unacc
vhigh	vhigh	2	2	big	med	unacc
vhigh	vhigh	2	2	big	high	unacc
vhigh	vhigh	2	4	small	low	unacc
vhigh	vhigh	2	4	small	med	unacc
vhigh	vhigh	2	4	small	high	unacc
vhigh	vhigh	2	4	med	low	unacc
vhigh	vhigh	2	4	med	med	unacc
vhigh	vhigh	2	4	med	high	unacc
vhigh	vhigh	2	4	big	low	unacc
vhigh	vhigh	2	4	big	med	unacc
vhigh	vhigh	2	4	big	high	unacc
vhigh	vhigh	2	More	small	low	unacc
vhigh	vhigh	2	More	small	med	unacc
vhigh	vhigh	2	More	small	high	unacc
vhigh	vhigh	2	More	med	low	unacc
vhigh	vhigh	2	More	med	med	unacc
vhigh	vhigh	2	More	med	high	unacc
vhigh	vhigh	2	More	big	low	unacc
vhigh	vhigh	2	More	big	med	unacc
vhigh	vhigh	2	More	big	high	unacc
vhigh	vhigh	3	2	small	low	unacc

Exercise

1. Go to the student download section and download the data table. Use SPSS to create a frequency table of all the variables. Draw relevant bar and pie charts, and hence interpret your findings.
2. Help Arvind identify broadly which features and their combination are most popular in terms of acceptance by customers.

CASE 3.2
Salary Packages of Graduating Students
(Case Complexity: Medium)

The table 'Graduation' has been provided in the student download section. The data has randomly selected 60 records of students from a management institute that have graduated from an MBA programme in the past 3 years. The data variables include the following: gender (0 female, 1 male), year of graduation (2018—3, 2017—2 and 2016—1). The area of specialization of the student (marketing—1, finance—2, Operations—3 and HR—4) along with the starting salary package amount in INR has been mentioned. A snapshot of the data is provided for reference below.

S. No.	Batch	Gender	Specialization	Salary (₹)
1	1	1	1	700,000
2	1	0	1	650,000
3	1	1	3	400,000
4	1	0	4	420,000
5	1	1	2	500,000
6	1	1	3	350,000
7	1	0	2	470,000
8	1	0	2	350,000
9	1	1	3	400,000
10	1	1	1	600,000
11	1	1	1	600,000
12	1	1	1	700,000
13	1	0	2	680,000
14	1	0	3	500,000
15	1	0	4	450,000
16	1	0	2	550,000
17	1	0	3	550,000
18	1	0	4	400,000
19	1	1	1	700,000
20	1	1	2	900,000
21	2	1	3	400,000
22	2	1	4	600,000
23	2	1	1	750,000

Exercise

Go to the student download section and download the 'Graduation' data table. Identify the categorical and numerical data types. Perform frequency count of batch, gender and specialization. Also do the descriptive analysis of salary. State your findings.

CASE 3.3
What Went Wrong at Rozana Terminal? (Case Complexity: Hard)

Rozana Terminal has positioned itself as the common man's retail store for fresh produce and other household needs. It has its presence in several locations across major cities in India. Their supply chain system has grown over time, enabling them to provide farm fresh fruits and vegetables to customers from 8 AM to 10 PM all days of the week.

The management is enthusiastic about continuous improvement (Kaizen) and strives hard to provide a good customer experience to all its customers. Each store has a store manager under whom a group of trained staff operate in two shifts. The stores sell goods 5 per cent lower than the market price, hence attract large number of buyers. Customers who get all that they want at one-stop shopping location have got locked in over time and are profiled as 'loyal' customers. Loyalty is primarily driven by quality products, in-store shopping experience, everyday low prices and promotions and offers of free products on purchase made for certain amounts. For instance, purchase worth ₹1,000 in one bill would fetch a packet of biscuits, ₹2,000 would fetch a packet of detergent and so on. This certainly brought customer delight.

Recently, the stores have been revamped to improve the overall ambience. The primary objective was to free up space by reorganizing the shelves that contain the goods. This would allow customers to move around with their shopping carts with ease, be able to find their products easily and a quick checkout. Several other improvements were added. The older billing and checkout procedure required the customers to first complete their purchase, and then have each item go through the barcode scanner at the checkout counter. The store employees were specially trained to operate the scanner device and payment system with ease. For fresh produce, the items were weighed at the checkout counter and priced accordingly. At times, during rush hours or weekends, there would be long queues at checkout.

The employees in a team meeting discussed with the store manager to find an innovative way to faster checkout. The store managers across stores agreed upon this being a perennial problem and brainstormed it to find a solution. As part of the new design of the stores, weighing machines were stationed near the fresh produce aisles. The customers were now required to complete their purchase of fresh fruits and vegetables and hence go to the weighing counters. Two store employees would weigh each produce in the shopping cart to provide a label containing the weight and the associated price. The checkout counter would then only be required to scan the label. This was done in anticipation of reducing the billing time, and hence the queue at the checkout counters.

All went as planned. The store employees were provided the adequate training to operate the new equipment. Billing at checkout was faster, thus reducing the queues. Additional staff was hired at each store to seamlessly manage the change. A staff was posted at the entrance of each store to greet the customers with a smile, provide the shopping cart and briefly guide on the recent store upgrade.

Within two months after the stores were redone, customer footfalls started reducing. The store managers observed this sudden decline in customers, thus affecting their top line. They checked their database and were surprised to see that certain loyal customers had not visited them since the past few weeks.

What could have gone wrong? Was it to do with the recent changes in the store or something else? To come to an informed conclusion, they decided to conduct a survey with their existing customers to understand their views on customer shopping experience in the stores. A prominent research agency helped them with the survey.

After detailed focus group interviews with the store managers, the questionnaire was prepared based on significant attributes that impacted the overall customer experience. Variables to be tested included availability of products, ease of finding a product in the store, price of an item, freshness of produce, store timings, helpful staff, store ambience (lighting, temperature, cleanliness, space between isles, arrangement of items in the aisles and size of shopping cart), billing time, security and parking space. The questionnaire was provided to customers who visited the store for the following two weeks. Each customer was supposed to fill the survey only once. The responses were grouped in two types of customers: loyal (who have been visiting the store weekly or frequently for at least the past one year) and those who have recently started coming to the store. The outcome of the survey did not reveal any spurious variable that could be identified as the cause for the problem. Then what went wrong...?

Exercise

1. Identify the categorical and numerical variables.
2. Think of possible untapped data sources which can identify significant variables and can help them identify the cause of the problems. Explain your reasoning.

4

Mapping Chart for Analytics Outcome

Learning Objectives

After completing this chapter, students should be able to understand about the following:

- Planning the Analytics road map
- Problem formulation: identification and simplification into manageable parts
- Designing the research matrix
- Building a model: connecting the business problem to an analysis platform

---

Opening Example

A Volvo bus service provider runs buses from New Delhi to various nearby destinations which are places of interest for the tourists. New Delhi, being the capital of India and geographically located close to the heart of the country, gets a large number of tourists throughout the year. The passengers include tourists travelling to New Delhi and nearby places from across India, transit passengers who change routes for travelling from one city to another, foreign tourists who like to do road journeys as part of their travel itinerary and business professionals who come

IMAGE 4.1[1]

[1] Image taken from https://www.pngfly.com/png-22rmmd/

to New Delhi or nearby cities for office work. Ravi Chabra, the owner of the Volvo bus service, makes a decent profit to keep his business viable.

He has tie-ups with many travel agents across the world and also maintains a website for allowing online bookings. His major routes are to the cities in northern India. He is contemplating expansion of his services to other parts of India. This is based on the feedback received on his services directly from passengers and also from his channel partners. Owing to lack of a firm understanding of what that would involve and how/where to begin, he approached a frequent traveller and friend Sanjeev Duggal to provide him guidance. During previous trips, he had heard Sanjeev narrate stories of how he and his consultancy firm had helped organizations plan and grow their business. Sanjeev found this an interesting assignment and as part of giving back to society, he decided to help Ravi Chabra with his business expansion plan. He started with the various pieces of data and various aspects of the Volvo service that Ravi had collected over time in his computer. Then he sat down to work on the problem formulation and research matrix. Using BA, he wanted to work out a BA model for Ravi to understand the tangible options for further investment and growth. Sanjeev was convinced that this action plan backed with Ravi's Volvo operations' historical data and the research matrix created by him would help Ravi in taking decisions for business growth.

PLANNING THE ANALYTICS ROAD MAP

Analytics has multiple definitions in today's world. Some associate the term with applied statistics using business data, others with computer algorithms which happen to miraculously predict outcomes with near perfection and still others believe it is all about 'smart' dashboards which depict various intelligent business metrics periodically. What is implicitly assumed (perhaps!), but not articulated openly is that Analytics has a lot to do with using business data of various forms to assist in resolving business problems. As someone quite succinctly said, 'As an Analytics professional, my job is to tell useful business stories—except my stories are always backed by data'. The advantage that Analytics provides is that, through the intelligent use of data processing tools, it develops insights that help in ensuring a level of objectivity in decision-making. That does not preclude the role of emotions in influencing decisions (we would leave that to decision-makers to decide). But it does provide an alternative and often times rational basis to seek resolution to problems. At times, it acts as a neutral input to a vexing political debate in organizations by providing a purely objective view to the problem. This is true only if there is available data to ignite such objective analysis. Analysis, as you will appreciate, is also objective as long as the neutrality of the data is maintained.

How then should a business organization plan its Analytics initiatives? A simple response to that would be to weave it tightly with the decision-making process of the organization at various levels. Computer algorithms and statistical applications are helpful; however in the end, the objective would be to provide insights through appropriate processing that is easy to understand, reliable and relevant to the point that it will support decision-making. Hence, processing tools are like surgical tools—just like the surgeon needs to know which tool to use (or the sequence in which a set of tools to use), a good Analytics professional needs a road map to select appropriate tools and data to create the right insight for the purpose of resolving a business problem.

Building a Productive Analytics Initiative in the Organization

What is a good way to start the initiative? Many business professionals relate Analytics to programming, algorithm development and predictive accuracy—something, as we have already stated, like 'holding a pair of scissors and looking for something to use it on'. But then, every business problem is not like a 'shearing task'. Therefore, before using a tool, it is important to understand the necessary processing that is required on the available format of data to be able to generate appropriate wisdom.

There are steps involved in developing a good Analytics initiative. Like all managerial processes, they are—planning, execution (processing) and delivery (communicating). In Chapter 2, we introduced a process flow chart that depicts the Analytics project execution process (Figure 2.1). Here we shall describe each of the stages in some detail below before embarking upon the key elements in the planning process. The rest of the book will provide insights into the other stages of the Analytics initiative:

1. **Planning:** A good point to start any support initiative is to ask 'what needs support'. Organizations have problems aplenty and many times have little to bank upon except the experience stock of its employees. A place to begin is to understand the way problems are resolved currently and the history behind the evolution of the same. This is more like absorbing as much of the context as possible to form your own perspective about the problem and the resolution path. Sometimes it is also termed as context immersion. Most significant organizational problems are complex and are not suitable to be tackled by one 'uber' analysis. Hence, these problems need to be simplified into smaller bits that lend themselves to a suite of individual analyses. It is possibly the most difficult step since many times organizations do not have (a) one problem and (b) any consensus among its constituents about 'what is the problem'. More on this stage will be dealt with in the next section.

2. **Processing:** A well-defined problem with high contextual familiarity is the desired platform to develop an execution plan for the Analytics project. Problems which are complex have been broken into simpler issues (which add up to resolving the complex problem). Each of these issues requires an analysis plan, which includes the data to be used, the format in which the data will be obtained and the processing sequence to be followed to get to the result (sequence of tools to be used for a certain set of data). This requires a fairly good understanding of the analysis tools, a visualization of what might be the output from the processing done using the tool and its implication on the resolution of the problem. Planning the execution also requires assessment of what processing tools to deploy given the nature of available data resources and the anticipated outcome and its value. An example of the same is described in a later section of this chapter.

3. **Communicating:** Delivery is about repackaging the insights from various analyses to provide leads on the resolution to the problem. In short, it is about communicating a business story that describes the solution but is significantly backed by insights from the analyses. Strong data scientists find this task tad difficult since it is an 'art' (not a science) to be able to creatively use analyses' output to string together a compelling prescription to the decision-maker. Many a time, analysts have to be prepared with 'push backs' from decision-makers to provide evidence to claim back. Be prepared to provide evidence as required. Part of the preparation for delivery is to proactively ascertain what evidence

may be needed to claim back. More importantly, it needs to be ascertained as to what assumptions are being made (when evidences are lacking) and whether the assumptions are reasonable to an extent. A later chapter in this book will provide more inputs on how the communication strategy should be devised to make effective business presentations using Analytics output.

Next, we focus on the details of the planning stage of an Analytics initiative. If any stage in the Analytics project is to be deemed critical, it is the problem formulation (definition) stage. If the problem is well defined, the chances of the project ending successfully are high. If not, the effort put in may go in vain. The value of a correct answer for a wrong question is insignificant (if not zero).

PROBLEM FORMULATION: IDENTIFICATION AND SIMPLIFICATION INTO MANAGEABLE PARTS

Problem definition can be termed as the process of determining the key questions that decision-makers in organizations really need answers to, so that the business performance can be managed better. While this seems simple, it is rarely very easy to get a clear buy-in from everybody in the organization as to what is the true problem.

For instance, a reasonably successful packaging material manufacturer may look at a new opportunity in a new domain and may want to evaluate its prospects in the new market— 'should it enter the new market?' A different and pertinent question could be—'can it make significantly more profits by entering the new market?'

Every important stakeholder in the organization may have their unique perspective about what may be a problem in the organization. For instance, an important stakeholder (part of the ownership structure of the organization) may not be keen on entering the new market. In which case, the analysis and assessment of the new opportunity is a matter of little consequence to the organization (or to the stakeholder).

Further, consider the problem 'Can the organization make additional profits by entering the new market?' This is a broad question, normally what decision-makers grapple with. This question can only be answered by dividing it into smaller set of questions that are more amenable to analysis. This may be pertaining to, 'How much more packaging material can be sold, at what price can we sell them, are there new methods or processes required to make packaging material for this new market, and is there a cost implication?' These are smaller and more specific questions that lend themselves to analysis, and hence are easier to handle. Another aspect of problem definition is therefore the ability to deconstruct larger questions into smaller ones that lend themselves to better research and analysis. A further point that needs to be reiterated—deconstructing is alright for analysis, however, at the end of the research (Analytics) project, the answers have to be 'reconstructed' to provide the right response to the decision-maker's broad question.

The process of identifying the right problem is not an easy one. Most executives in organizations have a vague definition of the problem that they grapple with on a daily basis. Executives are often impatient, if pushed too much about defining the problem at a high level of specificity and may also, at times, perceive the researcher or the Analytics provider to be unnecessarily 'meticulous' beyond reason—unless the researcher is a close personal contact of the executive.

Also, it is important to remember that at times the problem definition may be also couched in some personal objectives (personal agenda) of various executives or decision-makers in the firm. It is important to be able to sift through these personal interests (notwithstanding the difficulty) to be able to get clarity on what may be the true objectives of the firm.

Good problem definition, like in any business problem-solving context, is of utmost importance in managing an effective Analytics process. Perhaps, it is something that is not paid too much attention in the hurly burly of today's Analytics practice! Like any effective business problem-solver, Analytics professionals need to deep dive into the context to be able to discern the true issues that require resolution through Analytics or otherwise. This may require multiple conversations across executives in the context to be able to mull over their 'vague' assessments of the problems and setting aside personal agendas of several executives to finally bring together a consensus in the firm about the true problem that demands a resolution.

DESIGNING THE RESEARCH MATRIX

A good way to scope out an identified problem to initiate the process of resolution is to build a research matrix. Figure 4.1 provides a depiction of a research matrix. It is a hierarchical framework that originates from the business problem identified (at the top) and progressively breaks the problem into small but nested components that are more amenable to research and analysis.

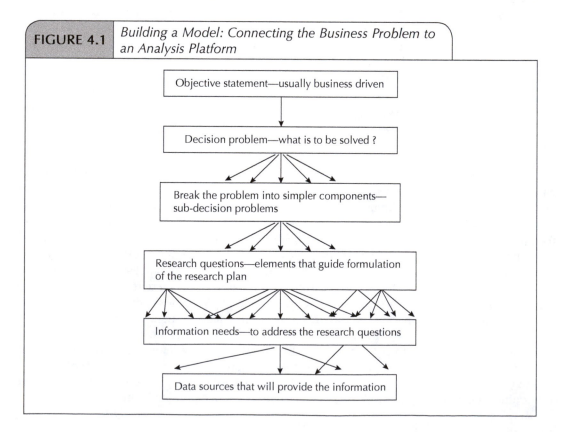

FIGURE 4.1   *Building a Model: Connecting the Business Problem to an Analysis Platform*

Objective statement—usually business driven

Decision problem—what is to be solved ?

Break the problem into simpler components—sub-decision problems

Research questions—elements that guide formulation of the research plan

Information needs—to address the research questions

Data sources that will provide the information

Evidently, it is a difficult process for most beginners in analytical problem-solving since it involves the discipline of building a 'hierarchical tree' of issues that are connected systematically to the business problem. This process is also called fragmenting the problem into components that are mutually independent of each other, but collectively define the higher order issue (problem).

Most problems are associated with an objective that is determined by the firm and has to be met. The decision problem is closely associated with the objective identified. Usually, there is a dilemma in the firm about how to meet the stated objectives, and hence it is phrased as the decision problem. The rest of the research matrix is developed in the lines of what has already been described earlier. Disintegrate larger problems into smaller ones and develop research questions that are easy to answer. Notice that as we go down the matrix, the issues are more elemental and easier to visualize. Naturally, analysts prefer to deal with research questions, however executives and decision-makers are more interested in the larger business issues (top of the hierarchy). Here lies the challenge for the analysts to bridge the divide between what inputs help organizations take decisions, and how they may be sourced through answers to more elementary research questions.

Effective Analytics solution systems are supposed to provide that connection between the operational aspects of analysis (that uses sophisticated data processing methodology) and the development of answers to business solutions based on a creative amalgamation of those relatively elementary analytic insights. The research matrix is a good reference to ensure that such connections are maintained.

An example of such a research matrix for a generic problem of a firm evaluating the prospect of entering a new business opportunity is depicted in Figure 4.2. This matrix is oriented differently from Figure 4.1 since the hierarchical 'blow up' is horizontal (left to right). It is important to note that the 'objective' is progressively 'blown up' to analysis questions (research questions) which can further be linked individually to the sources of information and specific data that may be needed to conduct the analysis to get the answers to the pertinent questions identified. In short, this provides a complete picture from the executive's problem statement to elementary pieces of information that may be required to provide a complete resolution of the problem. As stated earlier, the discipline of linking the research questions (and information sources) back to the business problem ensures an effective way of linking up downstream analyses (using Analytics processes) to a communication channel back to the decision-maker. Effective communication is a good way to ensure that decision-makers value the role of analysts in the organization. This may just be the catalyst required to prime the importance of the Analytics function.

While the practice of building a research matrix before conducting specific analyses is a good approach, it may be adapted to the specific requirements of the context. An example of the same is given in Figure 4.3 that depicts an adaption of the concept of research matrix used to create a plan for developing an organization-wide information system for a tobacco marketing company. All the critical line functions of this tobacco marketing company are identified and the necessary decision-making elements of each of the functions are listed. A comprehensive list of information/analyses that could support the ongoing decision-making process has also been identified (on the right side of the figure). Next, the possible information requirements for each of the analyses were identified for the organization to conduct an audit as to whether the necessary information was available internally. Figure 4.3 only lists the potential analyses that can be conducted to support decision-making.

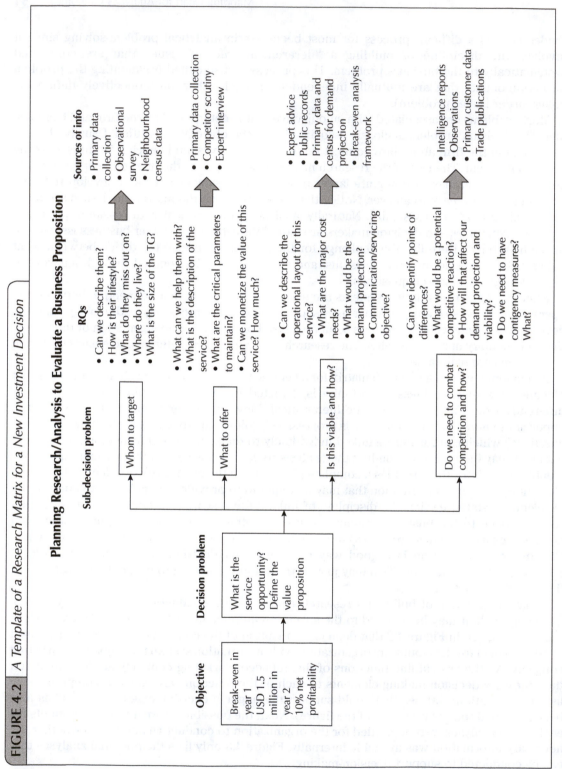

Planning Research/Analysis to Evaluate a Business Proposition

Objective

Break-even in year 1
USD 1.5 million in year 2
10% net profitability

Decision problem

What is the service opportunity? Define the value proposition

Sub-decision problem

Whom to target

What to offer

Is this viable and how?

Do we need to combat competition and how?

RQs

- Can we describe them?
- How is their lifestyle?
- What do they miss out on?
- Where do they live?
- What is the size of the TG?

- What can we help them with?
- What is the description of the service?
- What are the critical parameters to maintain?
- Can we monetize the value of this service? How much?

- Can we describe the operational layout for this service?
- What are the major cost needs?
- What would be the demand projection?
- Communication/servicing objective?

- Can we identify points of differences?
- What would be a potential competitive reaction?
- How will that affect our demand projection and viability?
- Do we need to have contigency measures? What?

Sources of info

- Primary data collection
- Observational survey
- Neighbourhood census data

- Primary data collection
- Competitor scrutiny
- Expert interview

- Expert advice
- Public records
- Primary data and census for demand projection
- Break-even analysis framework

- Intelligence reports
- Observations
- Primary customer data
- Trade publications

Notes: RQs, research questions; TG, target group.

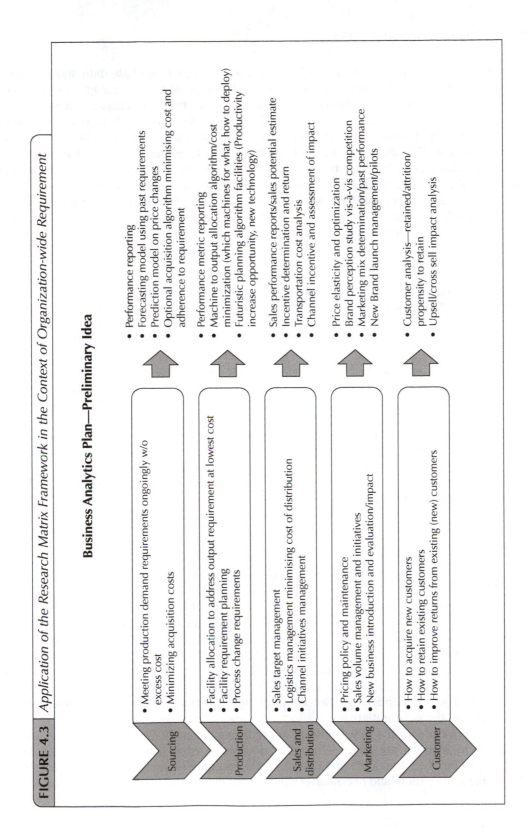

Business Analytics Plan—Preliminary Idea

Sourcing
- Meeting production demand requirements ongoingly w/o excess cost
- Minimizing acquisition costs

→
- Performance reporting
- Forecasting model using past requirements
- Prediction model on price changes
- Optional acquisition algorithm minimising cost and adherence to requirement

Production
- Facility allocation to address output requirement at lowest cost
- Facility requirement planning
- Process change requirements

→
- Performance metric reporting
- Machine to output allocation algorithm/cost minimization (which machines for what, how to deploy)
- Futuristic planning algorithm facilities (Productivity increase opportunity, new technology)

Sales and distribution
- Sales target management
- Logistics management minimising cost of distribution
- Channel initiatives management

→
- Sales performance reports/sales potential estimate
- Incentive determination and return
- Transportation cost analysis
- Channel incentive and assessment of impact

Marketing
- Pricing policy and maintenance
- Sales volume management and initiatives
- New business introduction and evaluation/impact

→
- Price elasticity and optimization
- Brand perception study vis-à-vis competition
- Marketing mix determination/past performance
- New Brand launch management/pilots

Customer
- How to acquire new customers
- How to retain existing customers
- How to improve returns from existing (new) customers

→
- Customer analysis—retained/attrition/ propensity to retain
- Upsell/cross sell impact analysis

The chart in the figure can be easily extended on the right to include data and information requirements for executives in the organization to identify, collate and manage key information resources that are needed to support the organizations functions on a regular basis.

The point here is to emphasize the need for a structured approach to organize complex business problems into smaller parts (together they make up the whole) which are relatively easier to analyse. The discipline of a hierarchical structure ensures that all elements once analysed can be pieced together to form the contour of the resolution plan for the complex business problem. Also, it has been found to appeal to many decision-makers, since they can relate to how their perceptibly complex problems can be systematically exploded to more simple dimensions. Readers may note that this is a disciplined approach and usually the experience of doing this multiple times leads to being closer to perfection.

How does the research matrix help?

Apart from being a convenient representation of complex problems into simpler components, the research matrix is also able to identify critical analyses components that are important for problem-solving. It is able to identify data requirements and critically the gaps in the data which may impede analyses. Most business settings have such lacuna in the data warehouse. However, what is necessary is a critical assessment of what information pieces are important and available and what are not. Typically, the unavailable ones require some deliberation—should the organization invest in gathering them (additional costs) or can they make reasonable assumptions on the same in the analyses.

The assumptions play a significant role in analyses since it is important to ascertain the sensitivity of our analyses to the type of assumptions made. If the sensitivity is high (dependence of the output on the assumptions made is high), it depicts the 'weakness' of our analysis, since it is highly dependent on the assumption made. In such cases, organizations need to reassess the assumptions and check the reasonableness of the same. In case of doubt, clearly, the decision to invest in getting facts to replace assumptions may be reviewed.

BUILDING A MODEL: CONNECTING THE RESEARCH QUESTION TO A RESOLUTION APPROACH

The planning component of Analytics goes well beyond connecting business problems to data requirements (through a research matrix). For individual analysis (say customer attrition analysis), an element of planning is required to visualize the expected outcome from the analysis and how it can be used by the business for its objectives. Many analysts concentrate on building a model and showing the analytical results. However, a precursor to building a model would be the need to assess the necessary conditions in which a model will be deemed useful for a business application. Some forethought on this matter is often times useful to deploy effort in the right initiative.

Models can be descriptive (explanatory) or predictive in nature. Descriptive models are generally useful to identify the antecedents (or associates) of a significant business outcome. Therefore, to build such models that associate the outcome to some surrogate metrics or control variables, analysts would necessarily have to evaluate the plausible relevance (importance) of the association in the context of the decision that may be influenced. Does the association provide an insight that is useful to calibrate decisions? Sometimes, it may so happen that the important associations between antecedent (explanatory) variables and the outcome remain hidden because other variables have an overpowering impact on the association due to a problem called 'multi-collinearity' among variables (see Chapter 6). It is important during the planning stage to identify and select variables (in terms of priority) that need to be studied together to describe (or explain) the outcome which may be a useful input to the decision-making process.

Let us take an example to illustrate this point. Mr Amin owns a chain of retail stores in a large Indian city. Recently, Amin has been promoting a new store in his chain in an upscale neighbourhood of the city by providing a price discount over the selling price of most products. He has been doing this promotion for the past three months. Simultaneously, he has also spent money on local radio advertisement in the city to announce the opening of his new store. Business has grown well over the past three months, and now Amin would like to check if he can reduce his radio spots and/or reduce his discounts in a phased manner and still retain his sales. However, since he invested in both of them simultaneously, he is not sure if it is prudent to reduce one or the other, or both. The dilemma is—'What was more important to make the sales happen in the new store?' Hard to identify through a model since both discount and local advertising were seemingly responsible jointly to make sales happen and, hence, they both may be equally important. No model can tell for sure in such situations. Anticipating a situation of this kind is of utmost importance to Analytics executives before embarking upon any data processing. In this particular instance, when no specific managerial ploy can be uniquely attributed to the success of the new store, it may be worthwhile to assume that both the measures are simultaneously important. In certain instances, it is possible to tease out the individual impacts of the different measures (discount and advertisement) using appropriate methods in spite of them being employed together for a fair amount of time. However, care must be taken to report such independent attribution since the events occurred with both the ploys happening together for most of the times.

Variables (dimensions) to be included in explanatory or descriptive models have to be carefully selected to ensure their relevance to the decision-making context, their probable impact on the outcome and their association with other dimensions that may not be highlighted in the model. The latter issue is about describing the context in which the explanation or association is provided. For example, in Mr Amin's case, if he had opened his new store during the festival season, the impact of the managerial ploys should be caveated with this fact. Perhaps, the impact of his ploys may have been of a different order if the store had been opened during some other month of the year.

Alternative explanatory models (or descriptive models) of the same context can be looked upon as different but (usually) partial views of the same phenomenon. Different descriptive models provide different views of the same phenomenon that may be at variance with each other since they provide a partial and differently oriented perspective of the same phenomenon. Planning activities in building descriptive models include creatively visualizing what (and which) views of the problem may be most insightful before actually launching to the processing (or analysis) of the data. In other words, a prior sensing (premise) of what may be a sensible way to portray or build a model may be helpful in getting a better output. This step is very different from the theoretical view of data mining which seemingly assumes that data processing would yield insights without the need for a prior postulation.

Planning Predictive Models

Predictive models, on the other hand, are meant to provide a reliable estimate of future outcomes, irrespective of whether they can explain the phenomenon (unlike explanatory model). Given the radical difference in objectives, predictive models have the mandate of providing an accurate forecast of the future. For instance, forecast of sales or prediction of a certain trait in individuals or correctly classifying individuals into predetermined categories (segments). For each of these objectives mentioned, predictive models are expected to perform with minimum inaccuracy—close to zero variability in the forecast of sales to the actual sales, or minimum erroneous classification of individuals or prediction of traits. The reality is, however, different from these utopian aspirations. No matter how sophisticated they are, most models tend to have in-built inaccuracies. How then can analysts plan to build useful models when they are all seemingly 'wrong'?

The answer to the above question lies in the definition of the usefulness of a model. Most models can still perform with positive results, so long as the benefit of prediction is higher than the cost of the inaccuracy in the prediction. We shall take two different examples to illustrate this point.

Let us assume that the sales volume for a future year is to be forecasted using a prediction (forecasting model). If the forecast obtained is inaccurate by a certain margin (say 20% on both higher and lower sides), will it be useful to rely on the forecast? It will necessarily depend on whether the firm can 'tolerate' this level of inaccuracy, that is, either bear the loss of overestimating or underestimating the forecast, or has the capability of readjusting its capacity (production) on seeing the actual deviation from forecast within the band of 20 per cent. Then the model is useful to the firm. However, if the forecast inaccuracy is higher (say, ±40%) which adds to the cost of inaccurate prediction so much that the output has no positive value, in this case the forecasting models will be useless to the firm.

Similarly, when classifying individuals into groups, a wrong classification may be attributed to a cost since a misclassification can lead to a missed opportunity. If the opportunity cost of such misclassification can be quantified during the planning stage, it can be compared with the useful outcome of the classification model and an assessment can be made about the overall benefit of such classification models.

Figure 4.4 illustrates one such example. This is an example of targeting a segment of customers (say, in marketing activities). We would like to proactively provide an extra incentive to the 'As' in the hope that they respond favourably and cause a positive impact on our business performance. At the same time, we would like to make sure that the 'B's' do not get the same incentive, since it would be a waste of our resources. The challenge is to predict who is 'A' and not 'B' beforehand so that the incentive can be directed to them well in time for them to respond favourably. Hence the need for a classification model that predicts their cluster representation (basis some surrogate profile variables) accurately well before they actually reveal their actual identity (A or B). Examples of such business segments include (a) profitable customers versus non-profitable customers, (b) high potential versus low potential employee and (c) high-risk versus low-risk debtors.

Most classification models have a leakage as depicted in the figure. If 'A' is the target cluster that the firm is interested in to deploy the marketing intervention (and interventions come at a cost, as stated earlier), the firm would be naturally worried about misclassifying 'B's' as 'A', since the intervention is not meant for them.

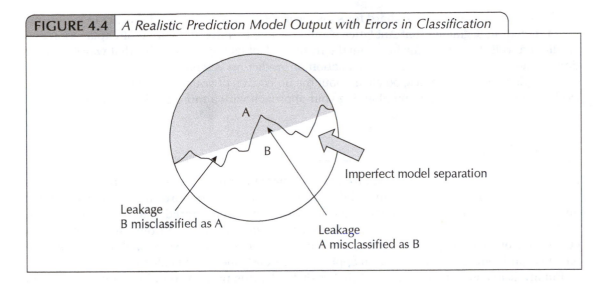

FIGURE 4.4 | *A Realistic Prediction Model Output with Errors in Classification*

The cost associated with the intervention is therefore wasted in proportion to the amount of 'B's' that are targeted along with the 'A's'. Similarly, there is an opportunity cost of missing out on the 'A's' that have been erroneously classified (as 'B's'). All said and done, if the benefit of identifying a large proportion of the 'A' through this prediction model overrides the wasted effort of directing some of the intervention to the misclassified 'B's' (and also the cost of losing out on some of the misclassified 'A's'), then the usefulness of the model is confirmed. As the famous British mathematician, George E. P. Box, had once said, 'All models are wrong, but some models are useful'. Endorsing a similar view, we have now established a rationale to determine the usefulness of essentially 'imperfect' models.

The implication of this discourse is simple. Prior to embarking upon analyses (data processing/model building), developing a hunch on what may be useful to the end user is a good game plan. This may involve understanding what may help explain a phenomenon better (or impactfully), in case the outcome is explanation or what may be the maximum inaccuracy that can be tolerated, in case the outcome is to predict.

A final note of caution to new analysts: the utopian desire of all of us is to build information systems (and models) that fully explain the phenomenon and concurrently predict the future accurately. Hard to say if such systems exist or perhaps will exist in the foreseeable future. This is largely due to (a) the lack of comprehensive data in most organizations and (b) our lack of understanding of a social phenomenon in its perfect detail.

Explanation will most probably remain imperfect (as stated earlier) and prediction too will be largely inaccurate. More importantly, most explanation models may not be a good instrument to predict and vice versa. This is because in our imperfect domain, the focus of building models is different given the differences in the objectives. Relevant but partial views of a phenomenon may be a good way to provide a useful business diagnostic (within a reasonable cost), but the 'partial' view may just be the reason why the model may not achieve the objectives of predicting future outcomes accurately. In other words, a good business story may provide very useful insights for planning future initiatives, but may fall short of achieving the target of 'exactly' predicting future outcomes.

This last point is many times hard for some users of Analytics to accept. For there is a strong belief in certain segments that Analytics should be able to solve the puzzle of explanation and prediction well. Nothing is further from the truth. And let us hope it remains that way for a long time—since the hope of bettering explanation or prediction is what lends value to this profession. As planners of Analytics, be clear about the objectives of your stated work—prediction or explanation—and embark upon planning your approach with a more realistic objective.

CONCLUSION

It may be prudent for organizations to invest in planning Analytics activities properly before making significant investments in building infrastructure to support such initiatives. While investments in technology, processes and infrastructure are material gain for organizations, such initiatives may not be productive without doing due diligence on their focus on solving business problems. A good way to ensure such connection is to work backwards from the business problems to their resolution approaches as described in this chapter.

Finally, it needs to be emphasized that realistically it is perceived to be easier to invest in the analytic infrastructure (easier since it is tangible/visible investment) than developing the approach towards prudent investment. The latter, many times, is assumed to evolve with the passage of time and experience of using the infrastructure. While there is some truth in this statement, it should also be noted that a significant turnkey investment in analytic infrastructure may be overwhelming for organizations with nascent capabilities. And hence the experience of grappling with a process that is hard to intelligently manipulate because of a lack of requisite capabilities may lead to a spiral of negative productivity. It is therefore useful to consider investments in a phased manner wherein the experience of the previous stage provides a better planned approach for future enhancements in infrastructure and capabilities.

REVIEW QUESTIONS

1. Explain the role of planning in an Analytics initiative.
2. Highlight some of the key challenges in developing a research matrix.
3. Should the objectives of an explanatory model be different from a predictive model? Why or why not?
4. Analytic infrastructure is easy to build, but productivity of the infrastructure is harder to improve. Can you explain some of the reasons for this problem?

CASE 4.1
Managing Change during a Technology Upgrade in a Garment Manufacturing Company (Case Complexity: Easy)

Dotra Garments is a manufacturer of women fashion wear in India. It has its manufacturing unit near Amritsar and employs 450 men and women for different job roles. It sources the fabric but does the designing and manufacturing in-house. Rustam Cama and his wife own the company and have done fair business for the past 15 years. The company has a tie-up with suppliers who provide the fabric and other design components and accessories such as buttons, laces and threads. Raw material is maintained in the inventory. Employees in the manufacturing unit are trained to operate the machines for stitching garments as per latest trends and fashion. Both Rustam and his wife have relied on agile manufacturing processes to run their business. Based on the constantly changing needs of customers, which is prevalent in the garment industry, the organizations need to make physical, administrative and technological changes.

Agile manufacturing system comprises the methods of total quality management (TQM), just in time (JIT) and lean manufacturing practices. The difference is that agile manufacturing focuses on personalized products and less on lot size compared to lean manufacturing.[2]

Employees in the manufacturing plant are not very keen on embracing continuous change that comes with agile manufacturing systems. They have shown reluctance in the past in moving from current method of work routine. The changes in the manufacturing processes have brought about automation in the company leading to fear of losing their jobs. Rustam has always treated all his employees as one big family. He understands their fear, and hence to keep them calm and motivated, he conducts an annual get together to show appreciation for their contribution.

It was again that part of the year where a new technological change in the manufacturing unit had to be brought about, impacting 100 or more workers. The combination of software and hardware would build an Analytics model that would allow him to predict the sales in his current product categories, thus a significant step towards agile manufacturing upgrade. He was not sure if this transition would provide additional value to his business.

Exercise

Rustam has to involve his employees in the needs analysis conversation to identify if Analytics transition is necessary. Help him plan his conversation with his employees such that he is able to instil confidence in them as co-decision-makers. Thus, encouraging them to participate in providing candid inputs.

CASE 4.2
Students Gear Up for Planning the Annual Management Symposium (Case Complexity: Medium)

It is that time of the year when MBA students of Supreme Institute are called by faculty members for discussing the Management Symposium to be hosted in three months' time. Being a progressive business institute, it has always believed that every event organized by them would be led by their students with appropriate guidance provided by the faculty members. This is part of an applied learning methodology for inculcating learning by doing. The Management Symposium is conducted once every year. Several stalwarts from big organizations visit the institute and interact with the students. Being a business school, the focus remains on

---

[2] http://www.textotex.com/application/static/data/file/eng/Mehmet%20KUCUK.pdf

learning provided across all domains—marketing, sales, HR, finance, strategy and now the sought-after domain of BA.

Out of the 120 students on campus across two-year MBA programme, the second-year students lead the event and the first-year students join as followers. A core team of students is formed, that forms its subsequent subcommittee. An event of this nature requires proper planning and execution by the committee members. The objectives of the symposium are as follows:

1. To create learning environment by interaction between industry professionals and students.
2. To understand the new business trends in organizations.
3. To create possibilities of summer internships and placements.

The students are required to plan a schedule for a two-day symposium. The designed schedule must accommodate talks, panel discussions and workshops by business professionals across all domains of business from different industry sectors. Other aspects of planning and management include creating a budget in consultation with faculty incharge and getting approval of director, logistical planning such as room for the event, food, beverage, transport, guest pickup, drop and their boarding and lodging. Guests have to be contacted for seeking possibility of their travelling to the institute for the event and follow it up with an invitation. One student would have a list of 10 guests whom she/he would call to convert into a speaker.

Exercise

Based on Figure 4.2, create a research matrix to plan and execute this event.

CASE 4.3
Introducing Reverse Mentoring at Saujanya Bank
(Case Complexity: Hard)

The senior management team at Saujanya Bank has an efficient learning and development (L&D) team based at their head office in Pune, Maharashtra. Ms Chanchal Mitra has been leading the L&D team for the past five years. She is a very sharp professional with an eye for identifying talent in employees. Her structured method of working has brought laurels to the team. Employees within the organization have been trained both in skill development and leadership at various levels. Her infectious smile has improved interpersonal relationship among the employees of the organization.

Every year she travels to business schools to pick up students during campus placements. Her team has designed a well-researched orientation programme for new hires that requires them to go through a rigorous training for the first three months in different departments of the bank. They are then placed in their location of work. Her amicable nature has led her to have informal friendly conversations during lunch time with the new energetic employees.

She has observed that these newly hired students who are in their twenties have a great attraction for technology-assisted tools and gadgets. The apps and gadgets have stormed the marketplace with multiple options and functionalities. This being a recent development, the older generation in the organization is not able to cope nor is interested in learning. She has been wondering for quite some time if this can be in some way made beneficial for the organization.

Chanchal has heard and read a lot about reverse mentoring—how the younger generation in organizations impart knowledge to the older-in-age employees of an organization. It is an interesting concept, however a very sensitive issue. She thought that with the current changes in technology happening so fast that impacts the financial business, a new and emerging term 'fintech' is being adopted by financial institutions. She wondered, can reverse mentoring be introduced as a knowledge-sharing learning exercise within the organization. The design can be prepared by her team for what to exchange in a semi-formal setting. In order to manage ego not getting hurt, it has to begin with a conversation with business teams.

Exercise

Help Chanchal plan and design a research matrix on how to launch and make the reverse mentoring learning exercise successful.

5   Technology Infrastructure for Business Analytics

Learning Objectives

After completing this chapter, students should be able to understand about the following:

- Relation between Information Technology and Business Analytics (BA)
- Checks for an organization's technology readiness for BA
- Role of data warehousing in BA
- Data lakes versus data marts
- Cloud computing and BA
- Internet of things (IoT) complements BA
- The Analytics-powered organization

Opening Example

Yash Menon has been appointed as the Data Science lead in a global fast food chain organization. His assigned role is to identify and hence roll out BA within the organization to support the manufacturing, sales and services in various geographies. Fast food chains have to cater to the local taste to remain competitive. Hence, they rely on a robust IT infrastructure that seamlessly manages information management across multiple processes. Yash wonders that his job will be to marry the virtues of BA to this robust technology infrastructure to generate the necessary impact. He will have to propose the changes without any major disruption to the existing operations. He will have to work with the sales and marketing teams, as well as regional leaders, to understand the key metrics they track and how they utilize them for business decisions and thorough assessment of their returns and criticality. Then he will be able to create a road map for additional value that BA might provide. This compelling story has to be supported by the adequate technology infrastructure which will have to be sourced and coupled with the existing infrastructure. He has to educate employees who do regular analysis for seeking information to aid decision-making to move towards inculcating Analytics within their teams for better decision-making.

In this chapter the authors have discussed the role that IT has played in supporting the sustainability and growth of BA culture in organizations. Each technological concept mentioned in this chapter is a huge field of study in itself, the virtues of which have been discussed in great detail in books related to the area of IT. Some are also taught as areas of specialization in the engineering schools. This chapter does not intend to get into detail of their technological know-how. However, as business professionals of the future, students need to understand the merits of each of the technological infrastructure pieces that add up in supporting growth of BA in organizations or in some cases being the genesis of pushing business leaders to think of embracing BA culture in organizations.

Let us draw a simple analogy from everyday life to understand this relationship. A creeper plant[1] requires support to bloom and grow as shown in the above figure. When nurtured and provided the appropriate backbone support, it provides the necessary grace to the beauty of the house. The house can be compared to an organization, and the creeper is similar to the business decisions made by the executives of the organization. These decisions have to be precise and are closely interlaced to organizational processes. The backbone support provided to the creeper corresponds to the IT infrastructure, and the correct mix of nurture, care and nutrition provided to the creeper to grow can be compared to BA. All of these together provide the healthy growth of the creeper—fact-based decision-making.

RELATING IT TO BA

When organizations work with data in search of outcomes that aid the overall business environment, we come across both the terms 'analysis' and 'Analytics'. Analysis is the act of breaking up something into parts and examining them for a meaningful outcome. Analytics is the analysis of data that is done logically aided by sciences (statistics, computers, models, algorithms and so on). Is there actually a point when organizations transit from analysis to Analytics or is it a part of the organizations' nomenclature? Earlier, analysis resulted as an outcome of number crunching using a pen and a paper. As organizations grew and so did the technological means of supporting them such as digitization, automation, multiple touch points with customers, batch to continuous processing, working in global teams across the globe and need for sharing information as part of change management, there was a gradual transition from simple analysis to Analytics. BI methods for business are part of boardroom strategy discussions.

[1] https://openclipart.org/detail/185364/grape-vine

Our students who graduate from the masters programme (MBA) often get placed in BA teams in organizations. Two of our students were picked by IT majors. We were curious to know their job responsibilities. One of the students said that her team is involved in assimilating data from various data sources of the organization for relationship and pattern analysis. Most of the data is structured and categorical in nature; hence, statistical software for categorical data analysis is used. The second student said that his team was involved in rollout of a technology solution for a client in a developed nation. The data is mostly unstructured in nature whereby feasibility tests have to be conducted against the requirements specified by the client. This involves using a statistical software package for predictive analysis. This supports the fact that analysis based on facts is termed as BA, and its application varies depending on the context in which it is used. One such example is given below.

Yash Menon is getting ready to participate in a discussion with senior management. He has the difficult task of answering an otherwise very simple query of a senior management executive: What do you think our organization needs to do in terms of a technology infrastructure upgrade to be able to incorporate a BA culture within our organization? Yash needs to think across multiple aspects before being able to answer the question supported by appropriate facts. He needs to understand the current IT infrastructure. For this, he needs to find out the answers to the following and many other similar questions: How have employees used it to process data? What kind of data analysis is done by teams within the organization? What kind of advanced data analysis would be beneficial to the end users? What IT infrastructure would be needed to support the enhanced forms of analysis? Would it be possible to expand and build on the current IT set-up or would it be a completely new purchase and installation? He wonders that the employees of the organization do use BA when working with data. The difference is that it is referred to as higher forms of data analysis that uses modelling techniques and algorithms. Creating an Analytics culture, as the senior management proposes, by upgrading the current BA set-up requires significant amount of work.

CHECKS FOR AN ORGANIZATION'S TECHNOLOGY READINESS FOR BA

He picked up his notebook and pen to conduct the necessary research and then summarized his findings across the following four aspects (Figure 5.1).

1. Identify need for BA

In order to bring about a change in an organization, it is vital to understand and document the reason for the proposed change. Additionally, clearly state and convince all stakeholders about the additional value that the proposed change would bring to the business, including the impact of the change for the respective teams. For Yash to be able to carry out this exercise, he will have to meet all the stakeholders and conduct focus groups, as well as in-depth interviews with them. During the course of the conversations, he will have to try to understand the current working environment of the teams and the business decisions they take on a regular basis. As a next step, he needs to try to link it to the analysis that each of these teams conducts to aid their decision-making process. Would additional interpretations in more sophisticated form or

FIGURE 5.1 *Steps to Identify Need for Creating BA Culture in Organizations*

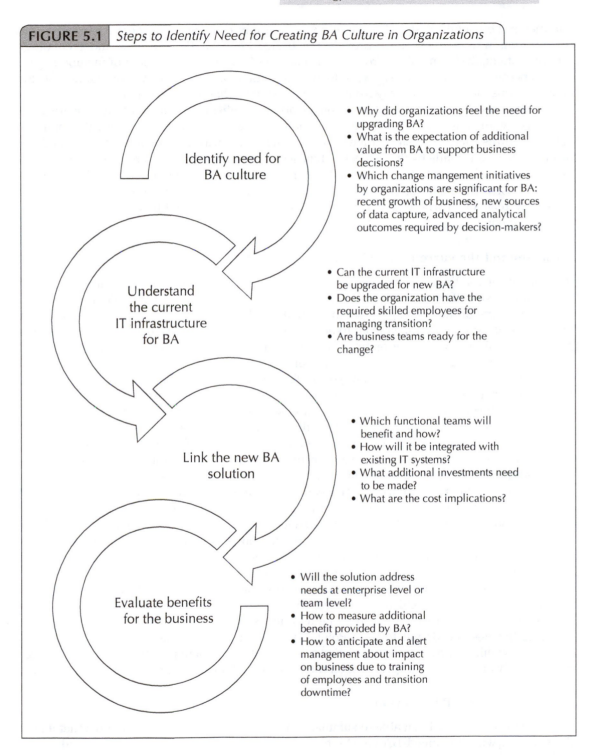

Identify need for BA culture

- Why did organizations feel the need for upgrading BA?
- What is the expectation of additional value from BA to support business decisions?
- Which change mangement initiatives by organizations are significant for BA: recent growth of business, new sources of data capture, advanced analytical outcomes required by decision-makers?

Understand the current IT infrastructure for BA

- Can the current IT infrastructure be upgraded for new BA?
- Does the organization have the required skilled employees for managing transition?
- Are business teams ready for the change?

Link the new BA solution

- Which functional teams will benefit and how?
- How will it be integrated with existing IT systems?
- What additional investments need to be made?
- What are the cost implications?

Evaluate benefits for the business

- Will the solution address needs at enterprise level or team level?
- How to measure additional benefit provided by BA?
- How to anticipate and alert management about impact on business due to training of employees and transition downtime?

parameters be useful? Yash will have in his team a mix of business leaders from within the organization who will primarily provide the bridge between the business and technology groups, data analysts, members from the IT team, statisticians and a couple of members from the respective business teams who focus on data analysis. During the course of his conversations, he shall stay away from any conversations that involve technology.

It is often observed that during a BA conversation, the client gets carried away narrating the challenges with IT infrastructure—hardware and software—and its integration with company data and infrastructure. Yash will have to steer the conversation to understand the kinds of business decisions made by the respective business teams and to what degree the analytics tool facilitates data interpretation, manipulation and inferences by the end users. He needs to further possess the Business Acumen to be able to understand how data is interpreted by the respective teams and where are the gaps which can be closed to aid better interpretation for decision-making.

2. Understand the current IT infrastructure for BA

It is important for Yash and his team to evaluate the existing BA solution from its technical standpoint. Yash will try to compare the inputs received from business heads (Point 1) and map it to BA features of the existing BA solution. Analytics has very different meaning for different business leaders: it could range from frequency analysis of categorical data to a 3-D graphical predictive analysis tool. Many organizations use the optimization model for monitoring and calibration purposes. New technology solutions for BA by big technology companies have flooded the market in the past few years. They have provided solutions for descriptive, predictive and prescriptive analytics. The solutions have also emphasized the significance of integrating information from varied information sources for rich and faster decision-making, the need for considering the pace at which data is captured, in some cases it is real time in nature, and compartmentalized the consolidated data effectively for separate decision-making teams. These solutions have been developed to complement the existing enterprise solutions that prevail in most big companies. The existing enterprise solutions in organizations are either designed as modular solutions for respective functional teams that tie into the overall organization information system or they exist as pieces of solutions like CRM systems, SCM systems or knowledge management (KM) systems. The KM systems have subsequently been able to create an organizational-level centralized knowledge base that allows sharing of knowledge and best practices across global locations. These platforms have also facilitated basic-level analysis of information as required by managers for decision-making. The software packages and solutions in the market are very tempting as they promise advanced analytics and premium outcomes. The end user is lured without complete clarity of the end result. The challenge for Yash and his team would be as follows: to evaluate whether, for fulfilling the changing business needs put forth in Point 1, there is a need for the purchase of a new BA solution or would an upgrade to the existing solution suffice. Cost implications, ROI, technology compatibility and data security all rest on the shoulders of Yash and his team.

3. Linking the new BA solution

Yash and his team have been able to summarize from the findings in Points 1 and 2 that a new BA solution with advanced BA capability will address the requirements of the end users.

Yash's next task would be to evaluate the new BI solution in terms of its compatibility with the existing technology infrastructure within the organization. There are different types of organizational structures: it could be a large organization with centralized resources at one location (family business firms), or an organization in India with offices in several locations (a bank or a manufacturing company), or a brick and mortar company that has online presence too, or a completely online company. Yash, based on his understanding of business of his company, will evaluate integration of the new BI solution with the old in terms of technology upgrade, data capture (ETL—extraction, transformation, loading) methods, new sources and types of data, storage and information security concerns, sharing of information across teams and the costs involved.

4. Evaluate benefits for the business

If Yash and his team are able to present a convincing case in the senior management meeting that gets a positive response, he will need to plan for its implementation. In large organizations, the practice is to perform a pilot test with a group of prospective users. Any immediate implementation and user interface issues can be taken care of at this point. After successfully conducting the pilot test, it is implemented to the larger user group. The implementation is usually done in a phased manner, meaning piece by piece. After users become comfortable with the first phase rollout, the next phase is considered. This creates minimal downtime in business, manages the training of employees and smooth transition. However, Yash pauses for a minute and wonders is it all that easy? No, any technology upgrade comes with teething problems. The magic lies in how well it is planned to be able to do a smooth transition. So the question goes back to whether technology first or data analytics first? Here we are considering data analytics as the need for managers to make faster decisions aided by judicious data interpretation based on facts. Yash is a firm believer that the following viewpoint, although theoretically may seem easy, practically can never be possible: *firms invest in a technology solution first and then think of what additional benefits it may provide for better decision-making*. He picks up a piece of paper and a pencil and jots down the questions that he needs to be prepared to answer to the management: Is the investment necessary? What is it that we are not doing now gets solved by the technology solution? What business analytics decisions are we thinking about doing differently? How much of customization is involved and does the vendor promise the customization from the canned solution? Who champions it internally within the organization, is the team of champions experienced enough to understand the business needs and convert the requirements during the rollout? Has the required feasibility analysis for break-even on costs incurred in purchasing the technology solution and meeting up to the competitors been done? What do the numbers say? Who provides the training for the new technology? Does it actually aid better decision-making?

The cyclic process adopted by technology companies has been in place for a long time. It includes coming up with new ways of capturing data, processing it into information-based technological solutions, followed by organizations adopting these technology solutions and thus consciously or unconsciously building a huge repository of data. With so many different choices talking of benefits to business in different forms, the organizations are treading carefully. More so because it is not just about the technology solution, but also about meeting the challenges of all pieces of adoption of technology needs to fall in line together for the desired outcome. Some decisions to purchase new technology solutions come from end users

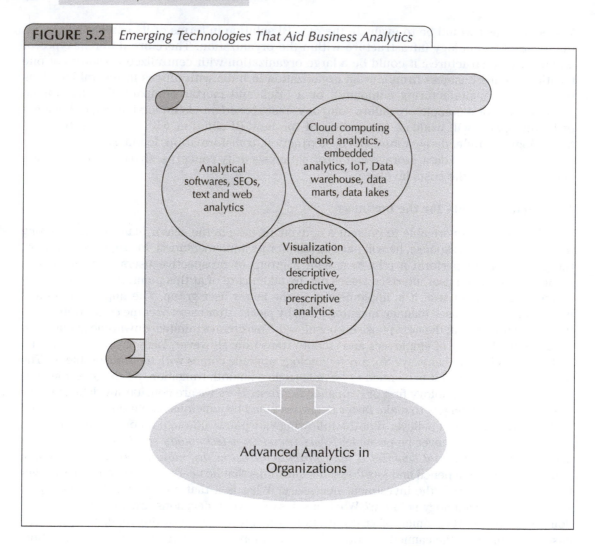

FIGURE 5.2   *Emerging Technologies That Aid Business Analytics*

who are practitioners and know that a particular analytical tool will facilitate better decision-making. In such cases, a particular group of users is provided with technology upgrade/purchase for the specific needs ensuring that it ties in the overall firm architecture. In other cases, technology solutions (software or hardware) are purchased at the enterprise level which affects a large group of users. Figure 5.2 lists some of the technologies that have led to our discussion on BA.

There are three bubbles in Figure 5.2 representing three handles of IT infrastructure support required for BA in organizations. The first bubble consists the DW, cloud computing, IoT, data mart and data lakes, which are primarily software and hardware tools and techniques that will be discussed further in this chapter. The second bubble consists of search engine optimization (SEO), web and text analytics which will be discussed in Chapter 8. The third bubble consists of visualization methods and the types of analytics which will also be discussed in Chapter 9.

A natural gas processing and distribution company in India uses BA while planning for laying pipeline in India. It has built a network of trunk pipelines covering length across India. It plays a key role as a gas market developer in India for decades catering to major industrial sectors such as power, fertilizers and city gas distribution. While laying new pipes, it is done such that it is close to demand centres (customer locations). This has direct cost implication on a day-to-day service, resulting in huge cost savings. Route mapping (path to follow) for new pipelines and capacity considerations work with multivariate scenarios using statistical software to determine minimum length between points. Laying is normally straight unless there are impediments like a forest area, which have to be avoided due to environmental concerns. Laying pipeline is expensive, and hence proper diagnosis and planning need to be done by the rollout teams so that there are no surprises after a work has been initiated. It is based on the analysis of higher order carried out at the functional team level using enterprise data—quoted to be BA.

ROLE OF DATA WAREHOUSING IN BA

You must have studied in your information systems course about data warehousing concepts. DW is a repository of historical and current data that is of significance to decision-making teams in organizations. These humongous data stores of time series data are used for BA. Data that is stored in the DW is mostly in a structured form that can be readily available for analysis by business teams. At an enterprise level, it provides precise, dependable and, in some cases, real-time information to managers on company operations and processes, thereby enabling them to make decisions based on facts. Many decision support operations such as querying, data mining, reporting and online analytical processing can be performed using the DW. Its high cost has restrained its use in large companies. However, with the need for establishing a BA culture in organizations, data warehousing has been adopted by major companies. The enterprise-wide DW integrates data from many different sources with scalable architecture. Data can be in many formats such as text, audio, video and images, and in many instances, they can be captured in real time. This huge volume of data of varied nature is cleansed and processed so that they can be brought in a standard format for use by BI and BA professionals.

A bakery chain has established outlets in all the metropolitan cities in India and has been successfully running the business for the past 10 years. It carries a range of products from different kinds of sweet and salty biscuits (cookies), cakes, pastries and chocolates. Customers of all ages visit their store, thus making it a popular brand in households, offices and party food items. During the company meeting, a section of the employees mentioned an interesting idea to the CEO. They said that there were customers in their city who had repeatedly requested to introduce 'paan' (betel leaf)-flavoured chocolates. People in India have always enjoyed a paan after major meals—lunch or dinner. Paan-flavoured chocolates could be a substitute for the same which could be eaten by children, young adults and elderly people. The CEO found this idea interesting, decided to bounce it by the cross-section of employees who had come for the company meeting. He mentioned it during his address speech to his employees. Initially, there was a silence, then laughter with most employees voting in favour of experimenting the idea. For the decision to go ahead, they would require company-wide data on customers and their preference, purchase pattern, time series data on last five years' sales, manufacturing needs for the new product, forecast the market for such product and whether it would be profitable, marketing the new product and such other. This could only be possible by studying and analysing huge volumes of enterprise data. The company used DW with BA to make a decision on the idea.

DATA LAKES VERSUS DATA MARTS

DWs have a well-designed repository wherein data resides in a structured form. Analytical processes are carried out by business leaders using software packages. For specific functional teams, at times, data marts are created to serve specific business needs. The data marts, which are a subset of the DW, allow access rights for specific functional teams or user groups and speed up the process of query, data transfer and analysis at individual department level. Business leaders have been asking Yash and his team about data lakes in recent times. Data lakes are similar to DWs as both are used to store data. However, data lakes store data in raw form in large scale as is captured from the source unlike DW where it is stored methodically to facilitate analytical processes. In many organizations, business leaders are using a hybrid solution for their analytical needs. The raw data, whether unstructured data, text, audio, video, web data, sensor data, are all stored together in a data lake. It can compartmentalize the data depending on the source from where it is received or the requirement of the business teams. Simple analysis on this data can provide insights that may be of interest to the business teams. This analysis result can be fed to the enterprise DW where further analytical tests can be carried out.

Banking industry is striving to be agile to face stiff competition in the consumer banking space. Customers are becoming more demanding, and banks are making efforts to provide fast quality service from across the world. Customer data in retail banking resides in enterprise DW on a centralized server and is distributed across locations depending on the business team needs. It consists of gathering real-time data from various customer touch points, be it from a bank branch location, ATMs, web banking or mobile banking. Enterprise data lakes have injected agility in providing banking services at lower costs. Data is picked from all customer touch points and processed in the data lake to be fed into the enterprise DW.

CLOUD COMPUTING AND BA

The advent of cloud computing came as a refreshing relief to business across the globe. Cloud computing is the technology used to provide on-demand sharing of resources (data, storage and applications) and processing tools via Internet. It allows sharing of resources across various locations from servers hosted on the Internet. This has direct implication on saving costs as it implies maintaining less local infrastructure with the additional benefit of exchanging and sharing information across virtual teams. The three basic methodologies that are prevalent for cloud computing are (i) Infrastructure as a Service (IaaS) wherein the organization utilizes storage capacity space on a provider's infrastructure, (ii) Platform as a Service (PaaS) wherein the development tools for application development are on provider's infrastructure and (iii) Software as a Service (SaaS) wherein the provider provides web services like email over the Internet in a distributed model. It offers the flexibility of paying for computer resources on a pay per use basis or on demand basis. Cloud computing can be private (data within the organization premises controlled and distributed by a centralized server), public (hosted on a provider's server) or a mix of both called hybrid service which allows maintaining privacy of confidential company data yet outsource the mundane bulky routine data processing tasks. The logic is very simple and understood by top management of organizations for implementing the cloud strategy. Since 2009, many companies have begun going the cloud computing way for faster decision-making.

Cloud computing has provided immense cost benefits and flexibility in the different industry sectors, manufacturing and service, with the benefit of scalability. Fast-moving consumer goods (FMCG) companies have adopted this technology to manage huge volume of customer and operational data processing. IaaS has reduced the requirement of maintaining large technology infrastructure within the organization. Additionally, real-time data can be pulled in from various sources and analysed for providing better service to customers as well as internal operational decisions. Research teams across the globe can collaborate and work on projects hosted in the cloud. The customer touch points such as retail stores, online transactions and payment gateways have information on customers' purchase patterns, product choice, frequency of purchase, payment methods, loyalty cards and other specific details. Thus, the entire customer data is managed on the cloud. Operational decisions on inventory management, transportation routes, warehousing, weather and complaint handling can be done using data on the cloud. This allows internal decision-makers to focus on strategic-level issues rather than day-to-day operations.

Analytical Software Packages

Business leaders who have made decisions based on outcomes of statistical analysis have been passionate about the features of the analytical software being used, be it Google Analytics, Oracle Analytics Cloud, IBM Analytics, R software, SPSS or Advanced Microsoft Excel. They do not necessarily need to understand the coding; however, the features of the packages help them articulate their business needs into possible inputs to the analytical software. Yash and his team will always be there to facilitate but one must remember that the analytical process outcome must be such that it is useful[2] for the business leader. Many new software packages are available in the market, and IT companies are providing support for necessary rollout and after-sales support.

INTERNET OF THINGS (IOT) COMPLEMENTS BA

With the advent of time, the top management of the organization where Yash worked was told about Cloud Analytics with IoT Gateways. That surely becomes confusing. Analytics itself means an advanced form of statistics for a common man. The top management executives start

---

[2] Useful here means that it can be understood and interpreted by the user group and further insights aid decision-making.

to wonder when the company is doing well with analysis using Cloud computing, what is the need for Cloud Analytics with IoT Gateways? What ain't broke why fix it? On the other side, the technology executives have a convincing story on the benefits of this emerging technology. Collecting information from varied sensor devices is the need of the hour to be able to track and understand data being generated simultaneously from varied sources. IoT is the internetworking of physical devices, vehicles, homes, buildings and other items containing sensor electronics, software, sensors, network connectivity that enable these elements to collect and exchange data. The advantage of IoT allows objects to be sensed and/or controlled over existing network infrastructure. This results in better efficiency, accuracy and cost benefits for the organization. Usually this requires a phased upgrade to the existing technology infrastructure. IoT has many applications in the industry sectors. For instance, it is used in Wi-Fi tracking systems, predicting equipment failure, radio frequency identification chips (RFID) in inventory tracking, managing kiosks, smart transportation management, smart energy management and smart cities. From the IT side, it is important to ensure that the complexity involved provides seamless dialogue between machines, hard disks and the cloud.

A global healthcare firm had purchased a temperature and humidity monitoring system from a vendor to monitor 400 sensitive items stored in the refrigeration unit at their company headquarters. The system was customized to suit the needs of the user group within the organization. It had installed sensors at critical locations in the refrigeration unit from where it would capture information and generate log at regular intervals. In case of any irregularity, it would generate a beep with an LED (light emitting diode) light indicator for required action. It would also suggest possible corrective actions. At the end of every month, it would provide a report of abnormalities that occurred during the month and the corrective measures which were taken. This data would also be recorded in the enterprise DW. This falls in the category of basic analytics with IoT. Building smart homes and offices with IoT technologies, monitoring patients, wearable IoT devices capturing people data and smart cities are huge applications of IoT.

There are other situations where data gets captured as a result of a technology tool that is being used in the organization. The business leaders are aware that such volumes of data exist; however, they do not know what to do with it—keep it or junk it. There is always the inner voice that echoes—there may be gold residing within this data, it just needs to be unfolded. Many organizations have made efforts to understand and analyse the data for useful business insights. Analytics as it may seem popular and trending in recent times is an age-old practice in organizations. It is the culture within an organization that would allow it to change nomenclature with the changing environment; else it would remain with the same nomenclature and keep improving on processes as the need of the business changes.

THE ANALYTICS-POWERED ORGANIZATION

Here the authors make a reference to Figure 2.1, the structured process of BA. The Analytics-powered organization supports this value chain with the IT infrastructure for the business domain expert to make appropriate decisions. The amount of data available to the business teams in organizations has brought a sure change in the way teams operate and make decisions. Spontaneous judgemental remarks by a senior member in the team based on gut feeling and claiming it on years of work experience can be challenged by a new joinee based on factual evidence. Business leaders ensure that judgemental remarks need to be supported by information. This information may be a result of quick analysis using spreadsheet software or complex statistical analysis, the significance lies in understanding the outcome of the analysis and interpreting it to address the objectives of the problem statement. This has cultivated an environment of fact-based decision-making within organizations. Additionally, there are huge reserves of data on company servers. Enthusiastic business leaders make attempts to look at data sitting idle on the servers—data that has been captured as a result of running certain routine business processes. Their attempt is to identify usefulness of the data by finding the gold that can be reaped from its appropriate analysis and interpretation.

We as academicians meet industry leaders during short-term training programmes organized for them at our institute. They are in decision-making roles from various industry segments. In the classroom discussions on analytics, there is excitement among them to share their role as BA drivers within their respective organizations. The nature of their work includes analysis of categorical data, tracking and monitoring using optimization models, descriptive and trend analysis, predictive analytics and text/web analytics. It can be concluded that there is a gradual move from analysis to analytics, yet technology surfaces in the discussion very quickly. As business leaders, one must continue to focus on business needs and develop the skills to interpret outcomes from analytical processing results. Furthermore, based on interpretation, they must be able to create useful insights that aid agile decision-making. Technology tools will continue to remain a platform (see Figure 5.3), appropriate use, ably calibrated by domain knowledge, will provide desired results.

| FIGURE 5.3 | *Joining the Dots of Analytics* |

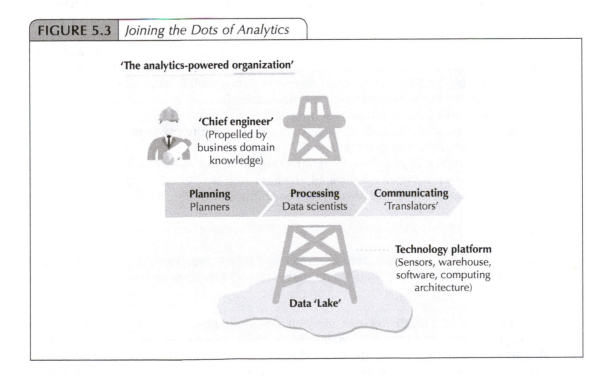

'The analytics-powered organization'

'Chief engineer'
(Propelled by business domain knowledge)

| Planning | Processing | Communicating |
| Planners | Data scientists | 'Translators' |

Technology platform
(Sensors, warehouse, software, computing architecture)

Data 'Lake'

REVIEW QUESTIONS

1. What are some checks to ascertain that an organization is ready for BA? Explain with the help of an example.
2. With the help of a figure, explain the different categories of emerging technologies that aid BA.
3. Explain the role of the following technology concepts for an organization that is planning to adopt BA:
   a. DW
   b. Data lake
   c. Data mart
   d. Cloud computing
   e. IoT
4. What is an Analytics-powered organization? Explain with the help of a figure.

CASE 5.1
Role of Data Science in Upstream Oil and Gas Companies in India (Case Complexity: Easy)

A petroleum company in India, mainly focusing on exploration and production (E&P), has been in existence for three decades. This is part of the upstream activities of the company with the other two being midstream and downstream. As part of E&P, it looks for possibilities of crude oil and natural gas underground and beneath water, which also includes unconventional gases like coal bed methane; drilling of the oil wells and bringing the crude oil or natural gas to the surface by efficiently operating the wells. It has strived to establish its position in the global market in efficient methods of E&P. Current challenges for the organization include high maintenance costs, old infrastructure requiring upgrade, unplanned downtime, constantly changing regulatory policies, shortage of skilled workforce, security concerns, identifying ways to cut losses and disaster recovery mechanism.

A new drilling project begins first by conducting an aerial survey followed by ground survey. If proper leads have been established, the next step is to create drilling test beds for conducting preliminary drilling and identifying possibilities of finding wells. Data captured is in raw form.

Mainly two types of data are captured during the E&P activity:

1. Raw Seismic data (aerial and ground [surface and sub-surface]) gets collected and stored
2. Data from the Wells (production, drilling, lab data and logs) captured at defined levels of depth

Raw data samples of Seismic log data and Well data are analysed further in the technology centre DW. The entire organization is connected via the enterprise system (ERP) that facilitates sharing and using data among the teams. The Seismic data are unstructured and require advanced methods to pre-process, cleanse and then store for further analysis. The Well data on the other hand are structured transactional data. Due to complex processes that exist in the entire value chain, there is minimal possibility of experimentation. Decision-making is primarily based on certain automated processes and models. Client and project teams require information for planning and forecasting while making decision on carrying out seismic activities in new fields. Additionally, when actual well-drilling activity is carried out, historical data provides useful information. BI tools and data analytics are used for creating standard reports, running queries and generating maps in gradient colours for highlighting relevant data points for depth and clarity. Visualization of the data in the desired form is key to appropriate decision-making. With changing technology there have been concerns about data security. Digital oil fields, cloud and IoT and intelligent wells are some new advancements in BA that are being contemplated by the management team for an organization's upstream activities. The following figure lists the data types that are captured during upstream activities for decision-making.

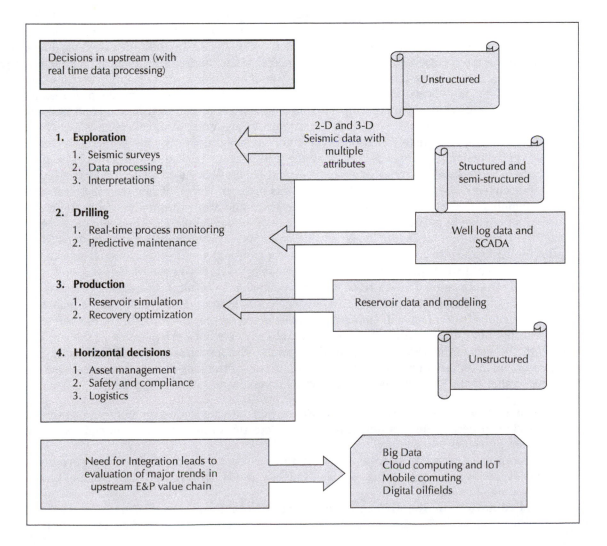

Exercise

Research the Internet to find why the data variables have been mentioned as structured and unstructured. Further, state what advice you would provide as a Data Science expert to the management team that is contemplating investing in digital oil fields, cloud and IoT, and intelligent wells.

CASE 5.2
Identify IT Upgrade Need in a Pharmaceutical Company
(Case Complexity: Medium)

Preventive Diagnostics Limited is a pharmaceutical company headquartered in Noida, India. The four business units of the company manufacture a wide range of pharmaceutical products in the generic group, diagnostic devices, equipment for medical use and nutritional products. These products are regularly supplied to hospitals, diagnostic laboratories, clinics, blood banks and emergency care centres. It has its oldest factory on the outskirts of Noida city where a work-force of 4,000 employees work in three different shifts for manufacturing products across all business units. It also has manufacturing units on the outskirts of Pune, Hyderabad and Kolkata. The total number of employees across all the manufacturing units, head office, satellite offices and sales staff is approximately 10,000. As the company has grown over the years, it has faced difficulty in maintaining a proper record of all the transactions that happen in the organization. Earlier there were lesser number of employees and clients who used their products. Hence, manufacturing could be planned such that there was optimum usage of raw materials and staff time to maintain desired inventory levels, process them and store finished goods in the ware-house, thus efficiently managing the supply chain with its stakeholders. The technology team within the organization has so far made several attempts to bring an enterprise system (ERP) vendor for deployment of automation in some of the operational modules. The limited investment made in this regard and lack of buy-in from senior management have been the key reason for its failure. The efforts made by the IT team have not been able to result in transition of employees from their regular method of operating to a new enterprise system. Additionally, the IT team had made suggestions to conduct staff training for transitioning employees smoothly to the new plat-form. This has not caught much interest due to the already existing work pressure of the employ-ees. With the success of the business over the years, all operational parameters have grown without bound in different directions with no definite way of tracking the basic processes across the entire value chain. The caveats exist across the company in the following areas:

1. **The orders received:** When, from whom, first time or repeat customer, quantity of product ordered, bill amount, time to complete the order, product shipped, payment received, reorder possibility
2. **Manufacturing of products:** Sourcing raw materials, maintaining desired inventory levels, mixing and processing, packing finished goods, storage and warehousing levels, shipping of goods
3. **Coordination among different units:** Sharing of information, sharing best practices, hiring new staff, monitoring staff performance, training staff, reduce duplication of

information, managing remote sales team on the fields, senior management being able to monitor performance parameters

4. **Financial management:** Track financial parameters, identify wastage and losses, identify profitable segments, forecast a five-year plan to increase revenue

All of the above indicate that there are silos within the organization with each manufacturing segment performing independently and no particular method to make decisions at an enterprise level. So far, organization leaders have depended on these blocks of information to make decisions as needed. However, now the need has emerged for proactive decision-making. Rita Shastri took the lead from the Business Research and Technology team of the company to solve this problem. She recommended an enterprise system (ERP) with BA as the future course of action. She was given the task of identifying what IT upgrade would be necessary to meet the needs.

Exercise

On the basis of Figure 5.1, you shall help Rita Shastri design a set of structured and unstructured questions to collect information from end users and top management about their day-to-day activities and what they feel is good to have. She intends to analyse the information collected through the questionnaire, hence link it with the proposed technology upgrade she has in mind.

CASE 5.3
Business Analytics Questionnaire for Fast Food Chain
(Case Complexity: Hard)

In the past five years, there has been a significant number of fast food restaurants that have come up in India. Some are local catering to the local taste of their customers, whereas others are PAN (presence across nation) India, even serving Indian versions of some global snack items. Sussado is one such fast food chain operating PAN India. It provides the complete list of menu items containing Indian and contemporary snack items from 7 AM to 11 PM. Customers can pre-order for take away via mobile app, website or just a phone call. The outlets offer seating arrangements for dining. They have experimented with certain menu items under the category 'Sussado specials' which are popular among their customers. A dashboard in each store outlet provides the staff and store managers with real-time information on sales. This trend of quick bite meals all through the day has grown due to the changing life style of people in India, who have shown affinity for small-size affordable meals on the go. The restaurants in turn have to be agile in terms of quick service, catering to long queues, efficient billing, quality and taste of food, sizable menu list, and hence keep customers happy to remain profitable. It is equally important to simplify store operation and provide the staff and management real-time information for driving revenue targets.

A few blocks away from Sussado outlet in Gurgaon, there is exactly another similar fast food restaurant. Sussado is immensely popular, whereas the other is not. Sussado's store manager, Raghav Sharma, believes that it has been possible due to the magic of capturing the behaviour of the customers and converting them into actionable insights for creating customer delight.

This coupled with lean operations management has helped them simplify processes of production and services leading to reduced wastage. Understanding the customer behaviour has become all the more necessary in a fast-paced business of fast food restaurants.

In a food chain industry, broadly BA can be adopted for customer management, improving operations, supply chain management, managing the HR, expansion into new territories and monitoring financial performance. Sussado has a dynamic real-time information enterprise architecture (ERP) driven by the BA framework supported by IT infrastructure.

Following are some possible ways through which a fast food chain like Sussado can use BA for better decision-making for enhancing its business.

1. Superior end-to-end service experience for the customer:
   a. Quick billing
   b. Coupon number display for every order
   c. Reduced wait time
   d. Courteous behaviour of staff at counter
   e. Quality and packaging/spread of food served
   f. Additional services like preference to sit outside/indoor, preference of drinks
   g. Improve the service for drive-through or take away menus
2. Automate handling of customer complaints and feedback:
   a. Rather than writing in notebooks, store it in company database for quick analysis and resolution
   b. Address gaps in customer requirements to improve margins
3. On-time home delivery:
   a. Take data from road, traffic, weather, and hence predict time taken to deliver
   b. Where they live, what they prefer to order, what they are willing to spend for home delivery
4. Optimal workforce utilization:
   a. Train staff
   b. Free staff from mundane administrative work
   c. Empower teams to take ownership
   d. Train and motivate employees based on which shifts they manage
   e. Share best practices across different locations
5. Automate reporting by region, city, area:
   a. Centralized review and maintenance of company reports to reduce information silos and multiple copies of same information in different places across the organization
   b. Share relevant sales data faster to offer promotions
   c. Perform market basket analysis to improve sales (which items are popular, most frequently purchased, purchased together, purchased by singles/family/kids/elderly/take away/home delivery)
6. Build a scalable model that focuses on key metrics.
7. Capture real-time information using sensors and widgets:
   a. Monitor and track customer touch point experience from mobile apps, internet, store outlets, social media comments
   b. Sentiment analysis to monitor customer experience over social media
8. A cloud-based dashboard in every store outlet for information sharing and monitoring among Sussado staff and company executives.

9. Optimize inventory planning and replenishments.
10. Drive innovation by sharing new ideas real time.
11. Forecast new regions of expansion.

The major concern with Sussado top management is whether they should invest further in IT architecture such as DW, Cloud computing and IoT for the above-mentioned BA outcomes. Currently, they have an enterprise system (ERP) that operates out of a company database.

You are a data scientist who needs to create a 'requirements set' for understanding the need for IT-enabled BA at Sussado. This 'requirements set' will help identify if further investment in IT infrastructure is needed.

The employees of the organization will be respondents to a questionnaire that will be used to answer the questions for the top management. The 11 points mentioned above list the different ways BA can be useful in enhancing business at Sussado.

Exercise

Based on your understanding of designing a questionnaire in your research methodology course and discussion in Chapters 4 and 5 of this book, you are required to design a questionnaire for the store employees for gathering inputs on where BA could improve operations and customer delight. Remember, 'none of the questions should pose a technology' question to the respondent but your job will be to design it such that the 'responses lead to a "requirements set"' that will help to decide on further course of action for IT investment for the top management team.

Analytical Methods for Parametric and Non-parametric Data

Opening Example

Every year, about two lakh students in India appear for the Common Admission Test (CAT) for securing admission across business schools of repute in the postgraduate programmes. This is a computer-based examination that tests the students' verbal ability (VA), quantitative ability (QA), data interpretation (DI), logical reasoning (LR) and reading comprehension (RC). Every year, one of the Indian Institutes of Management (IIMs) is responsible for conducting the examination.

Students receive their score as a percentile which ranks them vis-à-vis the performance of all those who appeared for the examination. A lot of effort goes into preparation for this competitive examination and the ones who get very high scores feel they have achieved a significant milestone in their education period of life. This, they feel, guarantees them a seat in a reputed business school in India. But does a high score in CAT guarantee a seat in big business schools? The answer is No, it is only a qualifier for being considered for further admission process. While it is desirable to have a high CAT score to get an interview call for admission to the business institutes, the students have to go through a two-step selection process. The second part, which is the rigorous interview process, filters out the selected students based on how they performed during the group discussion (GD), personal interview (PI) and written ability test (WAT). This may vary from institute to institute. Hence, there is always the uncertainty and risk involved in not getting selected during the admission interview process even after securing a very high CAT score. Several variables and metrics are considered together by the business schools' admission teams for finalizing the list of admitted students. This is a structured and prolonged process carried out every year, where analysis of data variables and their relationships play an important role.

IMAGE 6.1[1]

Similar to Chapter 3, in this chapter we shall revisit some of the topics that you have studied in your business research methods and statistics class.

SIGNIFICANCE OF SAMPLING IN BUSINESS RESEARCH

Discussion on population and sample is a key element of any research data. Data being the fuel for BA, a sound understanding of data and related concepts becomes important for an analyst. As you might recollect, **population** is the entire collection of items under study. For instance, suppose a research team is interested in understanding the behaviour of teenagers from the age group of 14–17 by gender and by geographic location, it will provide several different and interesting outcomes. All teenagers who fall under this definition in the entire universe will be the population under study.

The characteristics of the individuals (variables/attributes) who form the population help define the **target group**. For our example, it would be boys and girls who are within the age group of 14–17, belong to any nationality in the world and are securing school education. Once the research team decides the objectives of the research, a clear and detailed definition of the target group is necessary to avoid any ambiguity in the future.

The question that follows is, will it be possible to reach out to every single teenager on the globe who falls under the definition of the target group for conducting a perfect and complete research. There may be several challenges in conducting this global study, such as the time required, the budget required, resources available, and mode of identifying and reaching the individuals. Rather, a smaller group that has characteristics of the population under study would be able to provide an outcome that the researcher intends to investigate. This small

[1] https://bschool.careers360.com/articles/cat

FIGURE 6.1   *Types of Sampling Techniques*

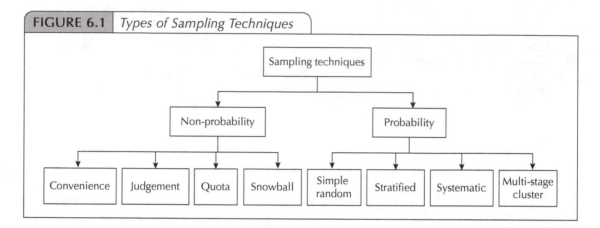

group that is a representation of the population under study and has all the characteristics of the population is called a **sample**.

Sampling techniques are used for both basic and applied research. As you might recollect, there are primarily two types of sampling techniques: probability and non-probability sampling (Figure 6.1). In probability sampling, every item in the sample has an equal chance of getting selected, whereas in non-probability technique, interventions such as likelihood of reach, human intelligence and grouping methods are used.

There are four types of non-probability sampling techniques. Suppose a researcher is interested in finding out how satisfied customers are with the smart electricity meters installed in their house. They will prefer to go to a locality where there has been recent installation of smart meters, pick houses based on convenience of reach and conduct the survey. This is **convenience** sampling.

Let us now consider another situation. Suppose the researcher lives in that locality and is aware of households that would provide him sufficient time to complete the survey with candid responses. He will use **judgement** sampling in selecting those households.

Further, let us consider a third situation. Suppose the researcher needs 30 respondents: 10 from a family of 4 individuals (parents and two young children), 10 from couples with no children and 10 from single occupants. He would make his selection of sample accordingly, where each of the three quota needs equal representation. Here the researcher will plan a quota to achieve. It is called **quota** sampling.

A Snowball gathers snow as it rolls. Let us assume that the researcher is not sure about residents who work in a multinational firm. He needs to approach and collect responses from them. However, this being a sensitive issue, he cannot directly ask a respondent during the survey. So he goes about asking for reference from individuals whom he knows fulfil his requirement and have completed the survey. This is called **snowball** sampling.

The probability sampling techniques can also be bifurcated into four types. **Simple random** sampling emphasizes on the fact that the possibility of choosing a respondent from any household remains the same as any other household.

Alternatively, the researcher might decide that since all the 60 houses have smart meter installed, he/she will make a random start and then choose every third house. This is **systematic random** sampling.

Let us go back to our discussion on quota sampling. Within each specified quota, if the researcher uses simple random sampling, it is called stratified sampling technique. Let us consider the three quotas—one that has four family members, second being couples with no children and third being single occupant. The respondents need to have a certain specified monthly family income of say X amount. Within each quota, if such respondents are chosen using simple random sampling, it would result into **stratified** sampling. The characteristics within a strata are similar and are predefined.

In **multi-stage cluster** sampling, two or more steps of the probability sampling are used. In cluster sampling, the individual respondent is not important but group of elements are clubbed together. This technique is used for widely dispersed population. Let us assume that a researcher is investigating hygiene in fast food restaurants across 150 cities in India. Planning to survey all the fast food restaurants in 150 cities by using simple random sampling would yield a very dispersed sample. It would lead to investment of immense time and travel for the researcher and results could be erroneous. Hence, two types of probability sampling techniques can be used by the researcher. First, the sample of cities can be selected using random sampling and then fast food restaurants can be selected within each of the 10 cities using random sampling. He/she would randomly sample and select 10 cities from among all the cities. Each city would be a cluster of all fast food restaurants existing in that city. Further, a sample of 20 fast food restaurants can be selected from each of the 10 cities (clusters) using simple random sampling. Results thus obtained using a two-step process would yield more accurate results.

As authors have mentioned, the discussion on sampling data is necessary for an analyst to plan the analytics road map. Certain other concepts on confidence interval, hypothesis testing, cross- tabulation and correlation will be discussed in this chapter which also provide the base for BA planning and execution.

CONFIDENCE INTERVAL AND HYPOTHESIS TESTING

A university that is located on the outskirts of the city limits has undergraduate, postgraduate and PhD programmes in various disciplines. Every year about 1,000 students who are admitted are provided residential accommodation in hostels on the university campus. However, there is no housing facility for about 250 faculty and staff members on the campus. They commute every day from the city. The range of travel each way for the employees is between 10 and 30 km every day (to and fro). Using probability sampling technique, if we take a sample of 16 employees from the population of employees, the mean distance travelled every day comes to 12.5 km. The standard deviation for the population is 20 (estimated from the sample). The question is, how we can be sure that 12.5 mean is a true representation of the population mean. If we take several samples and find the mean, each time it will be different. The difference of the means from the population sample when plotted will generate a bell-shaped curve as shown in Figure 6.2.

The shape confirms that half of the sample means are lower than the population mean and the other half are higher than the population mean. The curve tails off at the ends, indicating that fewer sample means fall in those regions. The sampling error/standard error of the mean/ standard deviation of a sampling distribution is the degree of the variation of the sample mean

FIGURE 6.2	*Bell-shaped Curve Distribution of Sample Means*

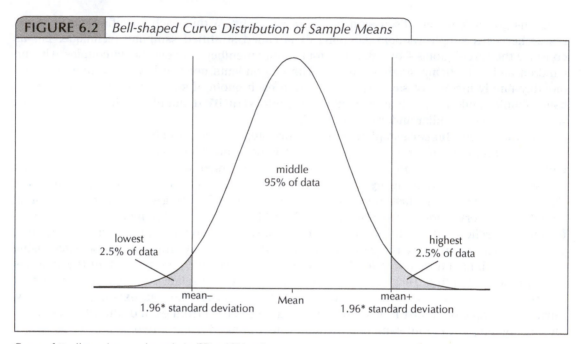

Source: http://www.icse.xyz/msor/ssim/SDandCI.html

in comparison to the population mean. Figure 6.2 shows the representation. We know from sampling theory that 68 per cent of all sample means fall between plus or minus 1.00 standard deviation from the population mean and 95 per cent of all sample means fall between plus or minus 1.96 standard deviation from the population mean. The latter statement is used by researchers to test their research findings. It implies that the researcher can be 95 per cent confident that the population mean lies within plus or minus 1.96 standard deviations from the sample mean. The shaded portion represents the 5 per cent divided into 2.5 per cent on each side considered as the region of rejection. For our example, the standard error of the mean is

$$20\sqrt{16} = 5$$

If the sample has been selected using probability sampling technique, the researcher can be 95 per cent sure that the population mean will lie between the sample mean plus or minus 1.96 multiplied by the standard error of the mean. This interval is termed as confidence interval. For our example,

The lower limit is $12.5 - (1.96 \times 5) = 2.7$

The upper limit is $12.5 + (1.96 \times 5) = 22.3$

Hence, the population mean lies between the confidence interval 2.7 and 22.3.

Analysts test several hypotheses based on objectives of a research problem or opportunity. In most cases, the investment of time, money and resources is done because the analyst intends to test the possibility of accepting an alternate hypothesis. As you have studied in Statistics and BRM courses, the confidence interval is used to accept or reject the null hypothesis based on statistical tests conducted on the sample data. For a 95 per cent confidence interval, the null hypothesis gets rejected if the 'p' value in the outcome is less than 0.05, indicating that the value lies in the 5 per cent rejection region.

CROSS-TABULATION

Cross-tabulation or contingency tables are ways of grouping variables to analyse the relationships between them. They are used for categorical data—groups of data in categories that are mutually exclusive.

We just discussed the example of 250 employees of a university who commute daily to work. Both male and female employees commute using various modes of travel. Primarily, there are three modes: four-wheeler (personal), two-wheeler (personal) and public transport. If you observe carefully, the two variables—gender and mode of travel—are categorical in nature. As we have seen in Chapter 3, the analyst can do a frequency count by variable and generate charts for visual representation and understanding. The researcher may be further interested in understanding the relationship between the two variables. He/she may seek answer to the following question: What is the distribution of travel mode personal versus public by the gender? Tables 6.1 and 6.2 represent the outcome. Pivot tables in Microsoft Excel and cross-tabulation in SPSS will generate the cross-tabulation table.

It can be inferred from the cross-tabulation (Table 6.1) that use of personal vehicles is higher for commuting to work. Of the 95 women, 73.68 per cent use personal vehicles and 26.31 per cent use public transport. For men, 64.52 per cent use personal vehicles and 35.48 per cent use public transport. This represents the distribution by gender.

Another way of interpreting the outcome can be by the mode of transportation. Out of the 170 employees using personal vehicles, 41.18 per cent are women and 58.82 per cent are men. Similarly, for public transport, 31.25 per cent women compared to 68.75 per cent men use public transportation. It can be inferred that women have higher preference for using personal vehicles as compared to public transport than men.

TABLE 6.1 | *Cross-tabulation 1*

	Personal	Public	
Female	70 (73.68%)	25 (26.31%)	95
Male	100 (64.52%)	55 (35.48%)	155
			250

TABLE 6.2 | *Cross-tabulation 2*

	Personal	Public	
Female	70 (41.18%)	25 (31.25%)	
Male	100 (58.82%)	55 (68.75%)	
	170	80	250

CORRELATION

The authors have mentioned in the previous section that cross-tabulation is used for grouping and comparing categorical data. When the variables are numerical, the degree of strength of the relationship between them is expressed by correlation. The variables need to be numerical and continuous in nature, for example, age, height, weight, sales volume, number of units sold per day. The correlation is expressed by 'r' which has a value from +1 to –1. Positive values indicate positive correlation (as one variable increases so does the other and vice versa). For instance, the relationship between salary and motivation. Negative values indicate negative correlation (as one increases the other decreases and vice versa). For instance, the relationship between use of pesticides and diseases in plants.

Table 6.3 lists the latitude and temperature measured in the month of January for 12 cities. Figure 6.3 shows the correlation between the two numerical continuous variables 'latitude' and 'January temperature'. As we observe from the figure, there is negative correlation between the two variables. As latitude (height) increases it becomes cooler.

FACTOR ANALYSIS

At this stage, we move from single-variable (univariate) and two-variable (bivariate) analysis, such as correlation, to multiple-variable (multivariate) analysis.

A correlation is a useful input into conducting various types of Factor Analysis. A commonly used variant of Factor Analysis is the Principal Components Analysis (PCA), also referred as Exploratory Factor Analysis.

In PCA, all associations among variables of interest are identified (in numeric terms through a correlational analysis). Conceptually, higher correlation (absolute value) implies redundancy in the information since the association among the variables is predictable, and hence any one

TABLE 6.3	*Latitude and Temperature in January*	
City	**Latitude**	**January Temperature**
A	61	13
B	30	49.1
C	47	6.7
D	38	32.9
E	43	22
F	21	72.6
G	34	56
H	43	15.6
I	45	11.2
J	47	37.2
K	38	48.5
L	28	59.8

FIGURE 6.3 | *Correlation between the Variables*

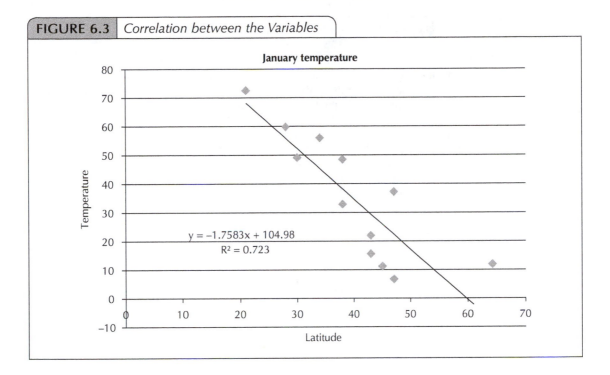

variable of a bunch of correlated variables can represent others reliably. In this process, we are able to reduce the number of unique (uncorrelated) variables that may be used for further analyses. This process is also called the dimension reduction methodology.

The PCA is a good way of bunching variables which are highly correlated with each other. However, often times in real data sets the correlation among the variables is not strong enough to visually discern groups of variables that are associated highly with each other, and hence the PCA methodology is used to assist in identifying the groups.

Exploration is a process that falls midway between an application of science and the artistic dexterity of the analyst. Careful observation of the data, forming impressions of the information based on newer discoveries of associations and applying right judgement are required traits of the data analyst for making superior inferencing from the data.

We must emphasize over here that many times exploratory analysis will not follow a standard set of rules and norms. Instead, the process of identifying groups of correlated variables using PCA is quasi-scientific and has a large judgemental component. It develops as newer insights are revealed from the data. Domain knowledge is critical for applying the appropriate judgement calls. Hence, for more insightful exploratory analysis, the data analyst and the user groups need to actively work in a collaborative manner.

Box 6.1 provides an example output of Exploratory Factor Analysis that is conducted to group variables (dimensions) on which products/brands/goods are rated into broader categories based on the similarity in the way respondents (customers) view these variables. This similarity is measured as correlation among the variables. The factor analysis routine (PCA) attempts to categorize variables based on their association with other variables into groups of variables that are highly correlated with each other. Such correlations are obtained from the nature in which customers (respondents) report their assessment of these variables.

BOX 6.1 | *Example of Exploratory Factor Analysis*

Automobile Research Foundation (ARF) conducted research on customer preferences for automobiles on multiple relevant evaluation criteria (nine variables) for automobiles. In order to ascertain if all these dimensions were independently useful, they decided to ask customers for the importance rating of each of these variables. Using the importance rating scores of a customer sample, they conducted Factor Analysis to see if the variables were associated with each other.

The Analysis results showed that there are three broad categories of variables: (a) Pick Up and Power, (b) Size, Luggage Space and Roominess and (c) Gas Mileage and Maintenance Cost. The categories (Factors 1, 2, 3) are identified below and their association with the original variables are given in terms of Factor Loadings. Price, Seating Capacity and Operating Costs seem to have more 'diffused' association with multiple categories (based on their Factor Loadings—usually between ±1).

Percentage of Total Variance explained

	1	2	3
	33.976	13.141	9.527

Rotated Loading Matrix (VARIMAX, Gamma = 1.0000)

Factors → Variables ↓	1	2	3
Pick Up	0.139	0.105	0.641
Power	0.100	0.109	0.772
Size	0.780	0.165	0.094
Luggage Space	0.720	−0.123	0.274
Seating Capacity	0.431	0.025	0.570
Roominess	0.702	0.281	0.166
Operating Cost	0.031	0.583	0.462
Price	0.301	0.295	0.455
Gas Mileage	−0.009	0.807	0.178
Maintenance Costs	0.255	0.745	−0.023

Note: Factor loading closer to 1 or −1 infer higher association. The highlights in the above data demonstrate association with multiple categories.

For instance, based on similarity in customer ratings of vehicles, (a) Luggage Space, (B) Size and (c) Roominess are regarded similarly, and hence categorized together as part of the same 'Factor' (group of correlated variables). Similarly, (a) Pick Up and (b) Power are categorized as a different 'Factor' given that they are similar to each other based on correlations (Factor loadings give an indication of the similarity of the variable with a Factor, closer to 1 or −1 means higher association). Some variables, however, do not have a firm association with any category, for instance, Price, Operating Cost and Seating capacity.

As stated earlier, Factor Analysis (PCA) provides a platform to reduce data without a commensurate reduction in the information content of the data. Using correlation as the basis of commonality across variables, it groups variables with similar 'information' and bunches them together (each one of the variables represents others). In applications, this is a useful way to summarize the information into tighter dimensions, helpful for understanding and interpreting the information.

Marketing user groups in business organizations may be curious to know more about their customers' preferences for their products. For instance, they may like to group the dimensions on which they see customers base their purchases and try to categorize those dimensions into broader and lesser number groups (based on how similar they are perceived by customers). This would enable them to understand purchase drivers better. Such objectives can be met by running Factor Analysis described above.

More information on the utility of the Factor Analysis and other forms of Exploratory Analysis are better presented in standard textbooks on 'Research Methodology for Business Applications'.

REGRESSION (OLS) MODELS

Ordinary Least Squares (OLS) regression models, another type of multivariate analyses, are very prolifically used as prediction models. The basic requirement for developing these models is an outcome variable that is measured on a continuous scale (interval or ratio) and juxtaposed on the outcome variable should be some relevant predictor (explanatory) variable, also measured usually on a continuous scale. This modelling technique is actually another form of correlation analyses across multiple variables. The theme of these models is the association of one target variable (outcome) to other explanatory (predictor) variables, which may also be termed as 'antecedent'[2] variables. Equation 1 depicts a typical linear regression model where the explanatory (antecedent) variables (X_1, X_2, X_3) are supposed to be associated with an outcome variable (Y). The measure of the associations is given by the corresponding coefficient (β).

The model-building process attempts to fit a linear additive function (we assume this mathematical form) of the explanatory variables to the outcome variable (see Figure 6.4). In the process, the weights (coefficients, β) of the predictor variables are determined in such a way that the summation of the variables (adjusted by their weights) has a value closest to the value of the outcome variable (the best fit equation). As a consequence, the unexplainable 'error' component (ϵ) is minimized.

$$Y = \alpha + \beta_1 X_1 + \beta_2 X_2 + \beta_3 X_3 + \epsilon \tag{1}$$

The closer the fit is to the actual data (higher R^2),[3] the better is the chance that the equation will be able to predict outcomes based on values of the input (explanatory) variables. However, there is no guarantee that the models will continue to predict well across other data samples, unless the nature of the data remains largely the same.

The standardized coefficient (the magnitude) signifies the importance of the variable in determining the value of the outcome. The sign (+ve or –ve) determines the nature of the relationship between the outcome and the variable. For instance, the weight associated with the price variable in determining sales will normally have a negative value, signifying an opposite relationship between price and sales (see Figure 6.5).

---

[2] Antecedence is only proven by the domain in which the model is being built and not by the correlation among the variables.

[3] See a chapter on regression analysis in a statistics book for details.

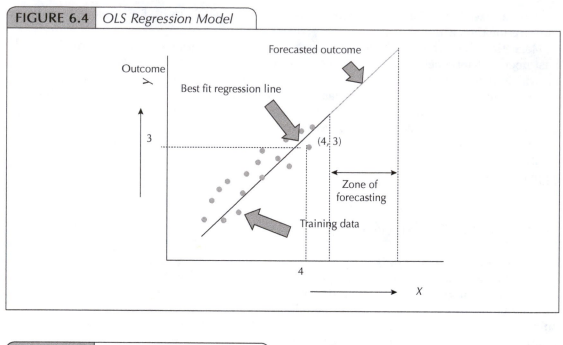

FIGURE 6.4 *OLS Regression Model*

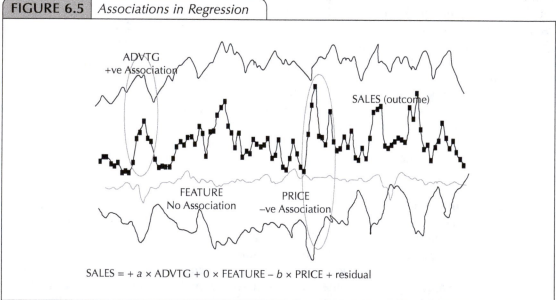

FIGURE 6.5 *Associations in Regression*

SALES = + a × ADVTG + 0 × FEATURE − b × PRICE + residual

The model which is developed on a training sample is tested across multiple validation samples to check on the reliability of its prediction power before it is approved for use.

Figure 6.6 is a typical output obtained when a regression is run over data. The (un)standardized coefficients indicate the relationship between each of the explanatory variables and the outcome variable (referred as dependent variable in Figure 6.6). The 'std. error' is a measure of

FIGURE 6.6	*Output from a Regression Model*

Coefficients[a]

Model		Unstandardized Coefficients		Standardized Coefficients	t	Sig.
		B	Std. Error	Beta		
1	(Constant)	1551.790	91.168	–	17.021	.000
	HS	113.159	36.427	.159	2.945	.003
	HI	33.393	12.572	.105	2.656	.008
	FHRD1	−321.095	125.457	−.135	−2.559	.011
	FHRD2	−518.188	152.779	−.143	−3.392	.001
	FHRD3	−596.491	197.591	−.105	−3.019	.003
	FHRD4	−590.167	372.881	−.048	−1.583	.114
	ORD1	−119.476	76.923	−.047	−1.553	.121
	DOGS	39.621	33.646	.036	1.178	.239
	CATS	39.884	34.600	.034	1.153	.249
	FHA	8.308	21.441	.013	.387	.698
	PCD1	−214.965	125.057	−.065	−1.719	.086
	PCD2	−42.625	142.162	−.010	−.300	.764
	PCD3	297.743	131.655	.077	2.262	.024
	PCD4	−301.714	162.732	−.073	−1.854	.064
	PCD5	389.813	264.250	.047	1.475	.140
	PCD6	286.715	177.111	.057	1.619	.106
	PCD7	66.546	332.025	.007	.200	.841

a. Dependent variable: TDS

Predictor variables	Association	Fuzziness of association (smaller is lower)	Strength of the relationship with outcome
⬆	⬆	⬆	⬆

the 'fuzziness' of the relationship (higher the number, larger the fuzziness about the existence of the relationship). The unstandardized coefficient and the 'std. error' together determine the strength of the relationship and is indicated by the 't'. Higher the absolute 't' value, stronger the relationship between the specific predictor variable and the outcome variable.

Predictive power can sometimes be increased in the training sample by using more complex mathematical functions instead of a simple additive linear regression model. Non-linear functions, sector-wise functional forms of different order and incorporating discontinuity in the functions are various ways to customize the prediction model given the nature of distribution of the outcome variable in the training sample. However, like other models such as separation models (logistic models, dealt in the next chapter), too much customization may not provide reliability of prediction, since many such models are not able to perform up to mark in independent validation exercises. Hence, the seasoned practitioners have to match the level of customization of the model to the sample data against the need for reliable prediction across other sample data. This exercise is usually context-driven and depends on the nature of data that is used to build and valid models.

Predictive models are relatively easier to specify compared to diagnostic models that identify associations between profile variables and the outcome. In the latter, the identification of a logical association is relatively more important. Reliable prediction is not the main aim of developing these models as much as being able to identify the 'causation' of a certain behaviour outcome.

Developing diagnostic regression models requires a curious mix of technical acumen and contextual familiarity to pick the right profile variables; ensure that the impact of each variable is exactly measured without the confounding due to multicollinearity in the profile variables. This is as much an art as it is a science and it is left to the experienced analyst to take the right calls.

Linear regression models are widely discussed and literature is openly available. We would encourage the readers to seek appropriate references for a more detailed exposition of these models.

MULTICOLLINEARITY

The coefficients of the explanatory variables in a regression model are supposed to provide a measure of the association between the explanatory (predictor) variable and the outcome variable. In the previous section, we have already described how the strength of the association is determined together by the magnitude of the coefficient and the level of 'fuzziness' in the coefficient (std. error). Usually, when two explanatory variables are correlated, the regression model is unable to tease out the independent associations of each of the explanatory variables with the outcome variable, since the former have an association among them as well. This is clearly depicted in the example given in Figure 6.7.

| **FIGURE 6.7** | *Problem of Multicollinearity* |

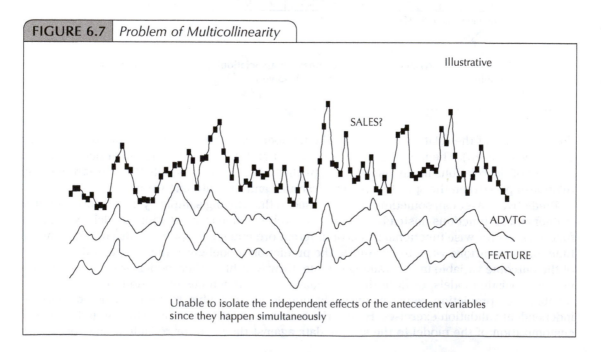

If you carefully look at the data stream of ADVTG and FEATURE (both explanatory variables) with SALES, they look exactly the same, that is, a very high positive correlation. It is a situation where the two marketing variables have been consistently manipulated together. In this context, it would be impossible to find the independent association of ADVTG or FEATURE on SALES separately. Since the marketing mix variables are always manipulated together in the same way, the effect on SALES will be due to their combined effect.

This is a hypothetical example of multicollinearity just to explain the point. In reality, even when correlations are moderate, effect of multicollinearity is noticed in terms of higher 'fuzziness' in coefficients, weakening the association with the outcome variables.

Multicollinearity is a usual problem in a diagnostic regression model which is meant to identify the strength of the relationships of predictor variables with outcome variable. If the true strength of the relationship is 'hidden' due to the correlation of an explanatory variable with another, the objective of identifying relationships among variables (predictor and outcome variables) becomes difficult.

There are no technical solutions to avoid multicollinearity. It is an artefact of the data and represents the way the variables are aligned in the real world.

A partial solution to this problem is to run Factor Analysis (PCA) on the group of explanatory variables to categorize them based on their correlation. Thereafter, one variable from each group of correlated variables may be used as an explanatory variable in the regression model. However, in this example, separate association of each of the variables in a group (FACTOR) with the outcome variable cannot be determined. Other partial methods to solve the problem like step-wise regression do not always provide useful answers to support a diagnosis. Hence, manoeuvring around a multicollinearity problem that makes diagnosis complicated requires some creativity and prior experience of handling such problems and does not usually have a standard solution.

FORECASTING AND TIME SERIES ANALYSIS

So far we have been discussing about regression models in the context of unravelling associations between explanatory variables and the outcome variable. However, there are many applications where the primary role of the model is to find a relationship between explanatory variable and the outcome, in order to predict/forecast outcomes in the future. Such models are termed as forecasting models. Sometimes predictive models are also used to visualize potential future outcomes in anticipation to changes in explanatory variables. Such models are called scenario planning models (or scenario visualization models). Both forecasting and scenario visualization models require high degree of predictive accuracy to be useful. Hence, R^2 of these models are usually expected to be very high (although this is just one of the many necessary conditions).

The explanatory variables in the estimated regression model are manipulated with new values (as per the anticipation of the future) and the estimated outcome is computed (refer Equation 1). The 'std. error' of the estimated outcome (is associated with the R^2) can also be computed from the model. This provides a 'band of uncertainty' of the true value of the outcome around the estimated outcome (see Figure 6.8).

Smaller the band of uncertainty, higher is the confidence in the estimated outcome (or forecast). The actual outcome is a function of many other dimensions (such as future changes

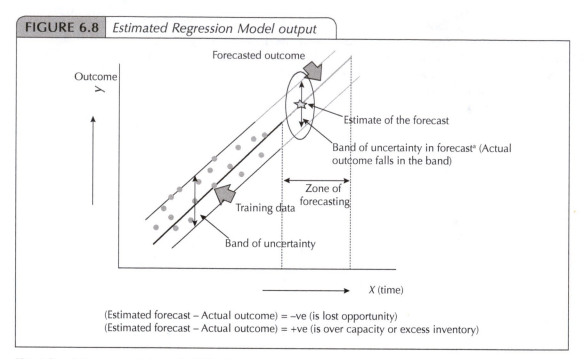

FIGURE 6.8 | *Estimated Regression Model output*

(Estimated forecast – Actual outcome) = –ve (is lost opportunity)
(Estimated forecast – Actual outcome) = +ve (is over capacity or excess inventory)

Note: [a] Simplistic representation to build intuition.

in the environment and their plausible impact on the outcome) that cannot be incorporated in the model estimated on back (historic) data. Hence, the confidence on the expected outcome depends on the analysts' assessment of whether the futuristic environment is similar in characteristic to the past (from where data has been sourced to build the model). If the future is significantly different from the present or the past, no scenario planner or forecasting model built using past (back) data will be reliable enough to provide a satisfactory forecast.

Time series analysis is a form of forecasting models that is estimated using historically (time-based) collected data of outcomes that are used to project the expected outcome for the future (see Figure 6.9).

A typical structure of the time series (Autoregressive) model is given below:

$$Y_{t+1} = \beta_t Y_t + \beta_{t-1} Y_{t-1} + \beta_{t-2} Y_{t-2} + \beta_{t-3} Y_{t-3} + \beta_{t-4} Y_{t-4} + Y_{t+1} X_{t+1} + \mathcal{E}_{t+1} \tag{2}$$

The forecasted value of the future ($t+1$ time period, Y_{t+1}) is a function of past outcomes (Y_t, Y_{t-1}, Y_{t-2}, Y_{t-3}, Y_{t-4}) and some explanatory variables in the future (X_{t+1}) and an unexplained component ($\mathcal{E}_{t+1}$). The technical condition to be met to enable estimating a regression model (OLS) to compute the coefficients of the past outcomes and the explanatory variables is that the errors ($\mathcal{E}_{t+1}$) are perfectly random and uncorrelated.

The time series model above represents a situation where the forecasted value of the future is assumed to be significantly driven by the past outcomes (although there may be a part that is determined by the explanatory variable). The point that we would like to emphasize is that in forecasting models using time series data, the objective is not so much as to explain the reasons for a certain expected outcome, it is more about predicting the future accurately. If the

FIGURE 6.9   *Time Series Analysis*

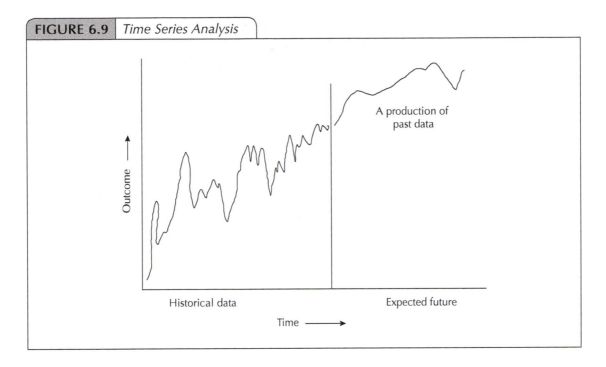

past outcomes have a significant role to explain the future (as in the above Autoregressive model), the model will have met its expectation—in spite of a significant lack in its explanation of the reasons for such an outcome.

The point being made above is that some models forecast well, others explain better but do not forecast well. Ideally, models should be such that they explain and predict well—that would need us to know every bit of the relationship between the outcome and the explanatory variables very well. Such models are rarely possible in reality (utopian) due to many reasons: (a) lack of adequate data, (b) lack of adequate understanding of the associations that cause an outcome and (c) the complexity of the associations that make the perfect model meaningless from an application perspective. Hence, as stated earlier (in Chapter 4), most models are wrong, but then they may be useful in their specific context, so long as we are clear about the objectives of building them.

HETEROSCEDASTICITY IN TIME SERIES MODELS

While on the subject of time series analysis, it is prudent talk about the properties of the unexplained part (ϵ_{t+1}) of the model. This is normally assumed to be random (normally distributed) and uncorrelated across successive observations, although in most practitioner settings, analysts rarely check on the actual distribution of the errors to validate if the model is correct (not that we would like to ratify such practice).

While this assumption does not hold in many cases and we choose to ignore such violations, in time series models it may be worth some consideration. See Figure 6.10 that provides a

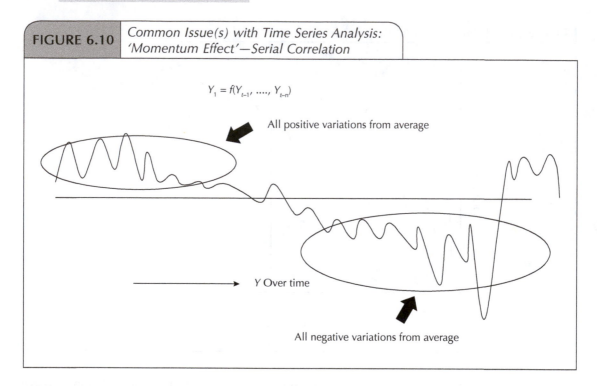

FIGURE 6.10 Common Issue(s) with Time Series Analysis: 'Momentum Effect'—Serial Correlation

$$Y_1 = f(Y_{t-1}, ..., Y_{t-n})$$

All positive variations from average

Y Over time

All negative variations from average

description of a non-random error distribution that is obtained from the baseline time series model. The figure provides a series of estimated errors obtained after running the model that predicts Y_t from past data of (Y). The nature of the error plot shows serial correlation across the sequence of errors and does not satisfy the conditions of uncorrelated random normal distribution of errors. Such correlated errors (if the error is positive from the mean, chances of the next error being positive is high and vice versa) are termed as heteroscedastic errors, and are a violation of the assumptions of the regression model. Technically, this distortion needs to be addressed to build a 'better'[4] model.

Several methods can be employed to get rid of this problem in the model, such as the inclusion of more lagged output variables and a 'differencing' variable. The Durbin–Watson test is employed to ascertain whether the serial correlation in the errors has been resolved.[5]

There is another way to interpret the limitation of the model due to the presence of correlation among the errors. A serially correlated error series (or any other correlation) implies that there is a pattern in the outcomes in the past that has not been captured in the model, and therefore continues to remain as part of the error (measured as the correlation among errors). This should be a concern to analysts because if any remnant pattern that is left in the error is not exploited by appropriately factoring it in the forecasting model, the performance of the model is evidently compromised. Hence, from an application point of view

---

[4] A technically sound model. The statistical properties of the estimate of coefficients in an OLS model are invalid when the errors are correlated. Generalized least squares (GLS) is the appropriate model instead of the OLS.

[5] Refer to the chapter on Time Series Analysis in a standard econometrics book.

as well (and not just for technical correctness), it is necessary to augment the model to tease out any consistent patterns in the error that hitherto may not have been exploited to improve the forecasting performance of the model.

CONCLUSION

Our chapter on multivariate analyses (parametric and non-parametric methods) concludes over here. A significant part of the chapter covered ordinary regression analysis that uses interval-scaled data and has widespread applications in diagnostic, planning and forecasting outcomes in industry. They can be either causal or correlational/associative models, depending upon the specification of the context in which they are built. In the next chapter, we will describe regression models when the outcome variable is nominal/ordinal scaled.

REVIEW QUESTIONS

1. Explain the different types of sampling techniques with examples.
2. What is the relationship between sampling, confidence interval, hypothesis testing and BA?
3. What is the difference between cross-tabulation and correlation? Can cross-tabulation be done on numerical data? Explain your reasoning.
4. Explain the concept of Exploratory Factor Analysis. What is the method adopted to reduce dimensions using Factor Analysis?
5. Ordinary regression is a causal model or a correlation model. Explain.
6. Explain the difference between a diagnostic regression model and a forecasting model. How does the problem of multicollinearity affect a diagnostic model?
7. Explain the problem of heteroscedasticity. Why is it important to omit the problem in a forecasting model?

CASE 6.1
Should Vishwa Take the Loan? (Case Complexity: Easy)

Vishwa Sinha has a small store beside a gas station (petrol pump) on a state highway. He believes his location attracts travellers to his store, who stop by the gas station. Among the items he carries, he has created six categories of products. They are snack items (chips, biscuits, munchies, rolls, crackers); chocolates of all types including mints, candies and mouth fresheners; beverages (mineral water, fruit juices, soft drinks, milk shakes and yogurt shakes); sweets (bakery items and Indian sweets); ice creams and accessories for men and women. As a special service, he allows use of a toilet which is free of cost. Those who use the toilet have to go past his store. He believes that people who visit the toilet have an inclination to peek into his store resulting in increased footfall converting to purchase of goods. He has five employees who are paid a daily wage of ₹30 each.

Considering the growth of his business in the past few years, he plans to extend his offerings to customers by adding a small food outlet to the store. With the food outlet, he feels his revenue will grow.

For making this happen, he has consulted well-wishers who have helped him with a rough calculation. His total estimated expenditure for adding the food outlet to the store will be ₹250,000. He currently has some saving in the bank which he plans to use for this purpose. Additionally, he will require to take a loan of ₹100,000.

The pro forma income statement template has been provided in the student download section. A snapshot of the template is provided as follows (Table 6.4). The base period sales for the year 2018 is ₹180,000.

TABLE 6.4 | *Pro Forma Income Statement Template*

Vishwa's Store				
Pro Forma Income Statement				
Prepared on: 15 January 2019				
	2018	2019	2020	2021
Sales				
Snacks				
Chocolates				
Beverages				
Sweets				
Ice-creams				
Accessories				
Total sales				
Cost of goods sold				
Snacks				
Chocolates				
Beverages				
Sweets				
Ice-creams				
Accessories				
Total cost of goods sold				
Gross profit				
Operating expenses				
General and administrative				
Wages				
Total operating expenses				

Income before taxes					
Income taxes					
Net income					
Assumptions					
Base period sales	**₹180,000.00**				
Store items	**% of Sales**	**CGS**		**Rates**	
Snacks	17.00	10.00%		2019 Growth	7.25
Chocolates	18.00	10.00%		2020 Growth	7.75
Beverages	21.50	15.00%		2021 Growth	8.25
Sweets	10.00	5.00%		Tax	35.00
Ice-creams	21.00	5.00%			
Accessories	12.50	15.00%			
	100.00			Salaries	
Operating expenses					
General and administrative	8.75				
Daily wage	₹30.00				
				No. of Employees	5

Source: Lisa Miller (2007). *MIS Cases: Decision Making with Application Software* (pp. 13–18). Pearson. ISBN 978-81-317-2104-9

Exercise

The percentage sale by category, cost of goods sold by category, other operating expenditures, tax and expected growth rate for the next three years are provided in the template. Using Microsoft Excel, based on calculated net income, you have to suggest if Vishwa should take the loan of ₹100,000 or not?

He will also be required to conduct a survey with customers visiting his store to understand their views on a possible food outlet in his store. What kind of sampling technique will he use?

CASE 6.2
Who Is the Star Sales Representative Performer for the Month at Laced Education? (Case Complexity: Medium)

Lace Education Services is a distributor of office items and stationary goods. It has its distribution presence in central, eastern and western parts of India. It primarily deals in five items: pens, pencils, pen sets, binders and small desks for writing. It has employed 11 sales representatives for selling the items to the end target customer in their designated regions. Every month the revenue for each item sold by the representatives is documented in a spreadsheet. This is for the month

TABLE 6.5 *Region-wise Sales by Representatives*

S. No.	Region	Rep. First Name	Rep. Last Name	Item	Units Sold	Unit Price	Total Revenue
1	Central	Varsha	Shah	Binder	94	19.99	
2	East	Ajay	Agarwal	Binder	81	19.99	
3	Central	Rahul	Sharma	Binder	87	15	
4	East	Ajay	Agarwal	Pen Set	74	15.99	
5	West	Piyali	Mitra	Binder	57	19.99	
6	Central	Rajiv	Rana	Pen Set	42	23.95	
7	Central	Rajiv	Rana	Binder	50	19.99	
8	West	Javed	Patel	Desk	3	275	
9	Central	Sukanya	Rao	Binder	80	8.99	
10	Central	Laxman	Rajan	Pen Set	55	12.49	
11	Central	Rajiv	Rana	Desk	5	125	
12	East	Sharda	Agnihotri	Pen	64	8.99	
.	.	.	.	.	.	.	
.	.	.	.	.	.	.	
.	.	.	.	.	.	.	
.	.	.	.	.	.	.	

of September. Each representative is given a target of 100 items to sell every month. A snapshot of the data provided in the student download section is as follows (Table 6.5).

Forty-three records have been documented in the data on region-wise sale of items by the 11 representatives for September. As you can see from the data, it has documented the item sold, representative's first and last name, the region, units sold and unit price. Use Microsoft Excel to derive the following results:

Exercise

1. You are required to calculate the total revenue and the items remaining from a target of 100 units.
2. Prepare a cross-tabulation table using pivot tables to represent the following. Analyse the result for each table.
   a. Total revenue by item per region
   b. Total revenue by representative per region
   c. Total revenue by representative by region for each representative
3. Prepare a graph for the results obtained in Question 2.
4. The star sales representative performer at Laced Education is determined by the person who made the largest revenue and/or who had the least number of units remaining to sell across all items provided. Who is the star sales representative performer for the month of September?

CASE 6.3
What Drives Customer Satisfaction at a Gas Station?
(Case Complexity: Hard)

Deep Goyal owns a petrol pump in the heart of the city. Being close to the marketplace and office headquarters, it is a busy street all year long. There are many daily commuters who stop by his petrol pump to keep their vehicles running.

Deep knows that his customers have many choices within a few kilometres distance. There are about five petrol pumps in the vicinity. Still there are a few familiar faces who are regular to his gas station.

His upbringing in a business family had taught him good business values which he follows in doing everyday business. He has always wanted his customers to be satisfied with his services. From the time the customer enters the petrol pump, there should be minimum waiting time until the process of filling petrol/diesel is completed and the billing for the transaction is done. He has also trained his staff to behave professionally with the customers in lean time or during busy times. The cleanliness maintained at the gas station is important for him. He has worked very hard to provide a hassle-free clean service. He has also ensured that the quality of the diesel/petrol is never compromised.

One day, he decided to carry out a survey with his customers. He wanted to find out how satisfied his customers were with his petrol pump services. Additionally, the respondents were requested to rate the following experiences: the wait time for filling petrol/diesel, the billing time for the transaction, quality of petrol/diesel he provides, the cleanliness maintained at the petrol pump and the behaviour of the staff members. Data on all six variables were collected using a five-point Likert scale where 5 indicated the highest agreement and 1 indicated the lowest agreement. A snapshot of the data collected is provided in Table 6.6. Thirty responses were collected. The data is available in the student download section.

TABLE 6.6 *Survey Data at Petrol Pump*

S. No.	Form No.	First Name	Last Name	Satisfaction	Time to Fill	Time to Bill	Quality	Cleanliness	Staff
1	3312	Girish	Kumar	5	12	5	4	1	2
2	3456	Anand	Dutta	1	23	7	2	2	1
3	3457	Raj	Sinha	1	30	6	2	2	1
4	4566	Vijay	Tondon	2	22	6	2	2	2
5	3458	Priyanka	Awasthi	1	23	6	5	1	1
6	6612	Parul	Bhatt	5	12	4	5	3	5
7	2345	Ravi	Rao	5	12	5	5	3	4
8	5678	Ravindra	Vora	5	11	3	4	3	4
9	3478	Ujjwal	Rathod	5	10	5	4	4	4
10	3333	Rita	Sheth	4	10	5	4	5	4
.	.	.	.	.	.	.	.	.	.
.	.	.	.	.	.	.	.	.	.

Exercise

You are required to download the data from the student download section. Then use Microsoft Excel Data Analysis pack to do the following analysis:

1. Establish a correlation between the six variables. Interpret your findings.
2. Using satisfaction as the dependent variable, run a linear regression on the data. Which of the variables significantly drive customer satisfaction?
3. Is the regression model a good model? Support your answer with appropriate output obtained from the model.

Analytical Methods for Complex Data

Learning Objectives

After completing this chapter, students should be able to understand about the following:

- Analytical methods for discrete data: logistic regression models
- Estimating logit models
- Evaluating the performance of the logit model
- Other 'separation' models: multiple discriminant analysis
- Probit models
- Choice-based conjoint methodology

Opening Example

Petrol and diesel cars are rapidly getting replaced by electric cars globally. Decreasing cost, longer battery life and more number of charging points have been attributed to the rapid growth of electric car market share. In an article in a newspaper publication,[1] there has been a discussion around the concern of waste that will get accumulated over the years by discarding lithium ion batteries from electric cars. This would create a big waste management

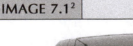

IMAGE 7.1[2]

---

[1] https://www.theguardian.com/sustainable-business/2017/aug/10/electric-cars-big-battery-waste-problem-lithium-recycling

[2] https://www.stuff.co.nz/motoring/111367821/what-happens-to-all-those-ev-batteries

problem and environmental hazard. According to the International Energy Agency estimate, there will be 140 million electric cars globally by the year 2030 generating 11 million tonnes of worn-out lithium ion batteries.

These discarded batteries will have to be recycled. Organizations globally have suggested several options for managing this impending and fast approaching environmental problem. One thought being considered is of recycling the discarded batteries at affordable cost. Making the cost affordable is currently a challenge. Another alternative being considered is of reusing a battery that is no more usable for electric vehicles for other purposes. It can be broken and repackaged for use in home energy storage. There are also options being considered to make the extracted material from these worn-out batteries reusable. Commercial plants and new technologies are being considered which can handle recycling of a large number of discarded batteries. The data for working out optimum solutions is very complex. Solution possibilities are in the forecasting stage. BA and the advanced methods discussed in this chapter can aid the decision-making process.

As we see in the above example, there are two to three options being discussed by experts for processing worn-out electric car batteries. If we see from a data type perspective, 'option' is a categorical variable (not interval scaled). There are many attributes (variables) being taken into account while deciding the environmental-friendly ways of managing this waste, be it reusing the batteries for other purposes or recycling them using new technologies. It is a case of choosing an option from the ones available depending on the impact of the variables being considered. Variables such as cost of recycling, cost of storage, cost of new technology and number of batteries that can be processed at one time could be varied to see the impact on the resultant choice. Analytical models have described such situations in the realm of logistic regression or logit which shall be discussed in this chapter. This is a special case of regression analysis.

ANALYTICAL METHODS FOR DISCRETE DATA: LOGISTIC REGRESSION MODELS

Brand Choice Modelling: An Application of Multinomial Logit

We have touched upon regression analysis and OLS in Chapter 6. Just to reiterate, regression analysis is used to build a causal relationship between a dependent variable, say sales volume, and a set of independent variables, say price, discount, advertising, store display. A causal relationship is more like a one-way influencer relationship—price or advertising changes have an impact on the changes in sales volume in the retail store. However, the reverse is not proven. Significantly, the business impact is estimated as changes in a continuous variable either in monetary terms (total volume worth in rupees) or, in the actual number of units or net weight sold (total number of kg). The dependent variable is interval scaled (loosely described as continuous variable).

The problem becomes somewhat intriguing when the **dependent variable is not interval scaled.** For instance, if instead of sales volume of a particular brand of soap, we have to examine the effect of competitive measures on the consumer's proclivity towards a brand, exhibited in terms of her choice say, if the price differential (difference in price of the two brands of the same pack size) is changed from ₹50 to ₹30, what impact does it have on the consumer's inclination to buy *Dove* over a competing brand, say, *Fiama*? (To keep the problem manageable, let us assume for now that the market has only these two brands to offer.) Of course, we can certainly incorporate other significant effects of the market that influence the choice decision, but the point that we are making here is that there is a structural change in the model from the one we were describing for volume changes. Instead of sales volume, we have a **nominal variable**—choice between *Dove* and *Fiama* as a dependent variable. The independent variable is also modified from price-to-price differential. Philosophically, the problem remains what we have solved before in regression analysis, except that the structure has changed.

How Do We Build a Model to Predict Brand Choice?

Let us take a stylized version of a real-life situation. Supposing Prakash, a young college-going lad has to purchase a bar of soap from the marketplace. He has only two options to choose from and he has to exercise his option to buy one of them (and only one bar of soap). Let us say, the options are soap Brand A and soap Brand B. How will he exercise his choice?

Simplistically put, Prakash would choose the soap that he likes more—assuming that he has experienced both of them. Of course, if his choice is not so firm, he may switch across the two brands on occasions, depending upon his preference for a particular brand on a specific occasion. This preference may be driven by rational dimensions such as price variations, boredom from past purchase and an attractive deal (freebies given on certain occasions). We could attribute all these dimensions to a composite and name it as Utility. When the Utility of A is greater than the Utility of B, Prakash should choose to buy Brand A for sure.

$$\text{Choose Brand A, if } U_A > U_B$$

For a market observer this sounds too simple. In many occasions, it is impossible to be sure of what is the true Utility of A or B for Prakash because of his own idiosyncrasy or sometimes due to unforeseen changes in the market conditions. For instance, on a particular day, Prakash went to the store planning to buy Brand A (given that the Utility of A is high for him), but is informed by the store manager that Brand A is not available. This situation was never anticipated, and all of a sudden, the non-availability of A imposes a severe penalty on Prakash's perception of Brand A. Prakash may still seek out Brand A at another store, that would incur an extra cost of seeking out the brand in a different store. Therefore, for that particular occasion, beyond the known (planned) dimensions of utilities of A and B, there are some unexpected costs (benefits) that emerge, which can never be anticipated and may be varied across occasions. We could therefore operationalize the decision-making process as

$$\text{Choose Brand A on any occasion, if } U_A + \epsilon_A > U_B + \epsilon_B$$

Here, the introduction of utility (ϵ_A, ϵ_B) due to idiosyncratic and unexpected dimensions takes account of all the unknown, unanticipated elements that may affect the utility on a specific occasion. It is these unknown elements that make the observable phenomenon not totally certain (it is stochastic).

The above equation for brand choice A can be rewritten as $\epsilon_A > U_B - U_A + \epsilon_B$.

So long as ϵ_A (the uncertain component of utility of A) is greater than the difference in the known components of utility plus the uncertain component of B (ϵ_B), the observed choice should be Brand A.

In the absence of any information about the nature and intensity of the uncertain component, it can be assumed that values of ϵ_A and ϵ_B are unbounded (the unknown utilities can take any value on a range $+\infty$ and $-\infty$). There is a fixed chance (probability) that the above inequality is satisfied. It is the summation of all possible instances when the value of ϵ_A is greater than ϵ_B by the least amount which is the difference in the known utilities ($U_A - U_B$).

A bit of discrete integration of those instances gives rise to the actual percentage of times (probability) Brand A will be purchased as

$$\text{Pr } (A) = \{\exp (U_A)/(\exp [U_A] + \exp [U_B])\} \quad \text{(exp means exponential)} \tag{1}$$

'Pr (A)' is the estimated probability that Brand A will be chosen by the customer on a particular shopping occasion. The probability is dependent on the Utility (transformation of the utility—exp) of both brands. It is not very difficult to imply that the probability of choosing A is dependent not only on its own utility (U_A), but also on utility provided by the competitive brand (U_B). Hence, the final outcome is a derivative of the relative perceived strength of the brands in a particular shopping occasion.

Similarly, the probability of choosing B is

$$1 - \text{Pr } (A), \text{ that is,} \quad \text{Pr } (B) = \{\exp (U_B)/(\exp [U_A] + \exp [U_B])\} \tag{2}$$

The two probabilities have to add up to one, indicating that these are the only two options that the customer can opt for, in our stylized example. However, it is easy to incorporate the possibility of many other options, and also the possibility of 'non-purchase' in the model to make it more realistic and generalizable.

Now, let us turn our attention to the utility function. Suffice to say that the Utility for each brand can be represented as (illustrative):

$$U_A = a_A + b_1 \times (\text{Price})_A + b_2 \times (\text{Discount})_A + b_3 \times (\text{Other marketing mix elements})_A \tag{3}$$

The utility is composed of some specific Brand 'A' related dimensions, say product attributes (we refer to them as 'a') and some marketing mix variables specifically attributable to the brand. The 'bs' are similar to the regression coefficients that one measures in OLS; to us they are more like the impact (sensitivity) of the particular parameter on the utility.

To complete the argument, Brand B will have its own utility function, with parameters that pertain to the brand ('a', price, discount, and other marketing mix variables and so on). The impact coefficients 'bs' are the same as the ones in the A's utility function. Like in regression models, the objective of this calibrating model (also called the **logit model**) is to estimate the 'bs' or the impact coefficients.

It is not very difficult to perceive that choice probability (Pr) of a particular brand is not only dependent upon its own set of parameters (marketing mix or others), but also on the alternative's (competitive) values for the same parameters. Mathematically tuned readers will appreciate our attempt to transform the original equation (1) into the following:

$$\text{Pr } (A) = \{\exp (U_A - U_B)/(\exp [U_A - U_B] + 1)\} \tag{4}$$

where

$(U_A - U_B) = (a_A - a_B) + b_1 \times ([\text{Price}]_A - [\text{Price}]_B) + b_2 \times ([\text{Discount}]_A - [\text{Discount}]_B) + b_3 \times$ (difference of other pertinent measures across the brands).

Similarly,

$$Pr(B) = \{(1)/(\exp [U_A - U_B] + 1)\}$$

Hopefully, this transformation will help appreciate the fact that choice of brand is dependent on not only what a particular brand's marketing mix is, but also what the competition is up to (hence, the predictors are transformed as differences). After estimating the coefficients, one can use this mathematical formulation to simulate what the choice probabilities may be if one changes some parameter (within reasonable ranges) with respect to competition.

Recapitulating the significance of the impact coefficients ('*bs*'): the magnitude and the direction (positive or negative) of the coefficients will determine which parameter (e.g., marketing mix or brand specific), rather the difference in the parameter values of the two brands, will impact the relative share of A versus B.

A generalized form of a multinomial logit (MNL) when there are more than two direct options to choose from is given below:

$$Pr (A) = \exp (U_A)/\Sigma \{\exp (U_i) (i \in a \text{ set of options that includes } A)$$

The set has as many options that are considered to be direct competitors over which the person makes a choice. This kind of choice model is also called **conditional logit**. The options have different utility values based on the specific value for each option of each of the dimensions that constitute the utility function.

Polytomous Logit

Let us, for a change, assume that we would like to predict a customer's usage of a telephone service. Specifically, we would like to predict if, Ramya, the customer, will attrite and move to some other telephone services. Propensity to attrite may be dependent on various customer profile characteristics such as Ramya's age, her socio-economic status and the length of her current association with the telephone service provider. Specifically, the two states in which Ramya may belong are: (a) past customer or/and (b) existing customer. In this type of modelling, an entity's profile variables will be used to predict which state she may be in.

$$Pr \text{ (Leaving the telephone service)} = \exp \text{ (Profile characteristic)}/$$
$$\{1 + \exp \text{ (Profile characteristic)}\}$$

$$\text{Profile characteristic} = a + b_1 \times \text{age} + b_2 \times \text{length of association} +$$
$$b_3 \times \text{other socio-economic profile variables} + b_4 \times \cdots.$$

In this particular case, the possibility of leaving the relationship or staying pertains to the same entity. Hence, the individual state-based profile characteristic (utility) is a composite of the entities profile variables (values) and their weights that determine influence on the propensity measure. The interpretation of '*bs*' is the relative influence of the profile variable (say, age) to enhance the propensity to stay compared to the benchmark state of 'leaving' the relationship with the service provider (telephone company).

The major difference between polytomous logit and conditional logit (as described earlier) is that the variables that determine a 'utility' function (Profile characteristic) are associated with the entity in case of **polytomous logit**. Whereas in the conditional logit, the 'utility' function is derived from the variables (and their values) associated with the specific alternatives.

In our original example of brand choice during a soap purchase occasion, a polytomous logit can also be formulated at times (when option-specific variables are irrelevant in a context). Instead of option (brand)-specific predictor variables, the respondent characteristics (demographics, attitude and so on) are used to predict their choice outcome. For instance, the probability of choosing A will be

$$\Pr(A) = \{\exp(U_{\text{Respondent}})/(\exp[U_{\text{Respondent}}] + 1)\} \tag{5}$$

where $U_{\text{Respondent}} = \Sigma [\beta X (\text{respondent characteristics such as age, income, attitude and so on})]$

Similarly,

$$\Pr(B) = \{1/(\exp[U_{\text{Respondent}}] + 1)\}$$

Note that the 'β' coefficients determine the strength and the direction of influence of the respondent characteristic on the propensity to choose the alternative (A). As earlier, the probabilities of choice for the two options add up to 1. The direction of influence that the characteristics have on the propensity to choose the other brand (B) will all be opposite to their influence on A.

Polytomous logits have widespread application in banking and insurance sector to model consumer attrition, profitability and risk. Retailing and telecom are the other sectors where applications of such models have been widely reported. In practice, their applications have had far-reaching business impact compared to conditional logit models, mainly because of the ease of operationalizing such models.

A more complex but realistic hybrid model would incorporate both option-specific and respondent (customer)-specific variables to explain the choice of the brand. These models are termed as mixed logit models.

ESTIMATING LOGIT MODELS

Recalling the normal regression case, the OLS technique uses the principle of 'minimizing' the variance (squared difference of the actual volume to that obtained by the predictor function). In a brand choice example, or in the general case of logit, the dependent variable is discrete (e.g., the person chose A or B on a certain purchase occasion). This is more like assigning a probability of choice of 1 for the chosen brand and 0 for the brand not chosen. Logit estimation (maximum likelihood method) tries to estimate coefficients that will 'maximize' the probability of choosing the brand that was actually chosen on 'every' purchase occasion (note the stress on word 'every').

For a live example, if one is given a string of purchases and the corresponding marketing mix differentials for each purchase occasion:

Occasion 1   Brand chosen A
Occasion 2   Brand chosen B
Occasion 3   Brand chosen B
Occasion 4   Brand chosen A
Occasion 5   Brand chosen B
Occasion 6   Brand chosen B

In this example, the logit model will try to estimate the coefficients such that:

The likelihood function or the joint probability of all six purchases are maximized:
$$\Pr(A) \times \Pr(B) \times \Pr(B) \times \Pr(A) \times \Pr(B) \times \Pr(B).$$

It is now worth talking about applications of this model. Obviously, it does not take much thinking to anticipate that consumer choice prediction in marketing research function is done using this technique. Market research organizations such as Information Resources Inc (IRI) and AC Nielsen Corporation (ACN) collect individual household level data (panel data) from a large representative sample of households (over 40,000 each in the last decade) in the United States. ACN has a similar panel in India as well. Data such as brands bought, amount bought, price paid, any discounts obtained, coupons used and any store displays seen by the customer are recorded for every purchase occasion. This database provides a rich source of information to the consumer packaged goods (CPG) industry in the United States on consumer price elasticity, brand loyalty and product assortment issues. Logit modelling is a common statistical technique used to develop choice prediction models and build further complex choice–quantity models (what brands do consumers buy and how much do they buy based on the marketing mix variables as well as product and consumer attributes such as loyalty and value).

The example that we discussed earlier is the case of two choices. Two-choice logit models are appropriately called **binary logit or logistic regression**. Usually, in situations where one brand is a market leader and the researcher would like to study the effect of competitive pricing on the market share of the leader, binary logit is the way to go. (Note that the estimated probability which is obtained from the logit model can be construed as estimated market share too.)

The world is far more complex than what can be accommodated in a binary logit model. Most choice situations have multiple alternatives or brands. In situations like these, an extension of the binary logit is used, which is widely known as the **MNL**. A reference on the same was provided earlier in this chapter. Even more complicated models, like hierarchical (nested) logits, attempt to model both 'Direct' and 'Indirect' competitors, which are models closer to the reality. However, more realistic models are also complicated and harder to estimate and additionally do not have the intuitive 'feel' that simpler models provide. Hence, in practice, most applications of logit modelling are reduced to a two-state case (also popularly termed as logistic regression).

EVALUATING THE PERFORMANCE OF THE LOGIT MODEL

There is a significant point of difference between the evaluation of the performance of the regression models and that of the logistic regression model (logit, in general). While regression models are evaluated on 'fit'—the difference between the estimated value and the actual value of the target variable—logistic regression models have no such absolute output. Instead, they compute the probability of the target alternative. For perfect prediction, the probability of the actual alternative should be always 'one' (or very close to it). However, in reality, the probability of the actual alternative may vary depending upon the 'fit' of the model. When the explanatory power of the model is very less, the computed probability of the actual alternative may be randomly dispersed.

Most useful models will have a skew (towards one) in the computed probability for the actual alternative. But it is still a probability of an alternative and not the prediction of a value (as in case of a regression model). How then is the predicted alternative identified?

The illustrative example at the end of this chapter describes the process of predicting outcomes. Essentially, a cut-off probability (on the higher side) is pre-decided to predict the alternative. The predicted alternative is compared with the actual and if they match, it is termed as a 'Hit'. The 'Hit' percentage (proportion of 'Hit') is used as a basis to evaluate the performance of the model.

While there are more scientific bases of calculating model performance (refer to a book on statistics) from an application point of view, we have found the above measure to be intuitively appealing.

OTHER 'SEPARATION' MODELS

Multiple discriminant analysis is an alternative technique which is used when the predictive variable is a nominal/classification variable (discrete). For example, if one were to identify the type of individuals who buy mutual funds as against ones who do not consider mutual funds as an investment option based on household/demographic characteristics and other relevant behavioural traits of the respondent, multiple discriminant analysis would be a good approach to develop a classification routine that decides group identities. Note that the logit model is also used for classification purposes in such cross-sectional analysis. The only plausible advantage for discriminant analysis, with its ability to estimate multiple discriminant functions (number of functions being related to the number of categories), is its potential to do a far better job at classification than a simple utility formulation used in most MNL models.

However, it is important to note that the construction of the discriminant function is significantly different from that of the logit model and makes different assumptions regarding the nature of the dependent variable. Logits, on the other hand, are very powerful tools to develop prediction models, given the elasticity determination, whereas discriminant analysis often times yield good classification models. We will invite the reader to use other reference material to understand the operationalization of discriminant analysis. Suffice to say that in terms of business applications, logistic regression (logit models) addresses all practical problems that can be dealt with discriminant analysis and hence the latter does not provide additional advantages in business applications. Besides, logit models are a far more elegant approach to modelling a phenomenon.

PROBIT MODELS

A reference must also be made of probit models that specifically fall under the genre of logit models. In section on logit, we introduced the idiosyncratic utility term ϵ and developed the logit model around this stochastic term. Usually, a stochastic term ϵ is qualified by a frequency distribution (probability density function) which denotes the frequency of occurrences of various possible values of ϵ. In building the logit model we specifically ignore the nature of this frequency distribution. In reality, different assumptions of the ϵ yield different choice models. If the frequency distribution is assumed to be 'extreme-value' distribution, the logit model is derived using the discrete integration mentioned in the section on logit. However, a normal distribution assumption yields a probit model.

From an application perspective, logit models or probit models do not have any significant differences. It is just that the assumptions in the stochastic components are different. Normally, probit models are harder to compute (given the nature of the specification of the model), and hence most applications of discrete dependent variables (nominal scaled dependent variable) use logistic (logit) models.

For the sake of completeness, readers may note that in some specific instances, theoretically, probits are more useful than logits, though such occasions arise very rarely in business applications. In market structure analysis when competitors (options) differ in their closeness to each other (direct versus indirect competition), a probit model may be able to address the conditions better than logit. Of course, the complexity of estimating a probit model remains and hence few, if at all, examples of probit applications exist in business operations.

CHOICE-BASED 'CONJOINT' METHODOLOGY

Logit models are not only used to model secondary sourced data on consumer choice (data sourced from actual purchases made) as described earlier but also used in simulated experiments where respondents are asked to 'choose' one out of many pre-configured alternatives. The simulated environment replicates a purchase environment, except that the alternatives presented to the respondent may be manipulated (along with others that exist in the real marketplace). Alternatives are configured by manipulating the presence (or absence) of a set of pre-decided product features and offered to respondents as an option set from which one alternative is chosen.

Such experiments (also called choice-based conjoint experiments) are normally conducted to record consumer choices based on their assessment of product features available in various alternatives. Choices across respondents are associated with the features present in the options using a logit model to determine the 'valuation' of respective features. The 'b' parameters estimated (see Equation (3)) correspond to the weights (valuation) assigned to the presence of a certain feature (usually a dummy variable is used to signify the presence/absence of the feature) in an alternative. Usually, such experiments are conducted on a cross-sectional sample of respondents to identify optimal mix of features for new product development.

Choice-based conjoint experiments are widely used in business applications in new product/ service development initiatives across industries as diverse as credit cards, tractors to personal gadgets.

An Illustrative Example of Logistic Regression

Let us consider an example of profiling customers of a bank into two categories based on their riskiness (propensity to default on their loans). This is a standard application of polytomous logit models in practice where past data of customers is accumulated and they are categorized as high risk (1, grey) or low risk (0, black). Of course, this is a simplistic basis to profile customers (in reality, there could be more categories), but for the objective of illustrating the application, this stylized example can be considered to be a fair representation of reality.

Figure 7.1 shows a data stream of customers, categorized as high risk or low risk. Overlaying an explanatory variable (profile variable) on this data stream of risk classification, one can observe a plausible association between the values of the explanatory variable and the corresponding categorization of the customer. Logit models capture these associations in the form of a mathematical relationship given in Figure 7.2.

The mathematical relationship in Figure 7.2 portrays the relationship between the explanatory variable (*X*) and the possibility of the respondent being a 'high risk' (1, grey) customer. If the weight (*β*) is positive, a higher value of the explanatory variable increases the chance of the customer being 'high risk'. The complementary probability of the customer being 'low risk' is given by: 1 – Probability of being 'high risk' (1, grey).

FIGURE 7.1 | *Categorized Data Stream of Customers*

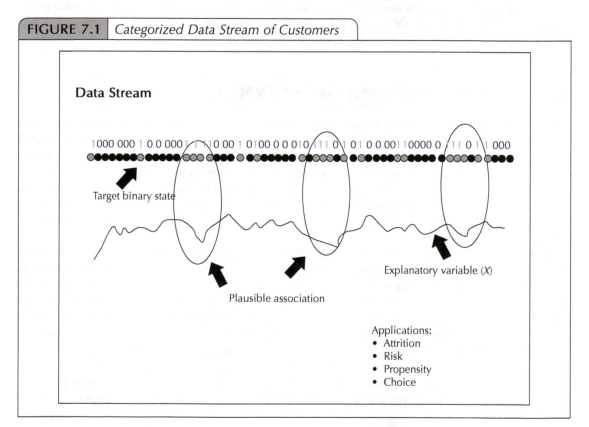

FIGURE 7.2 | *Relationship between Explanatory Variable and High Risk*

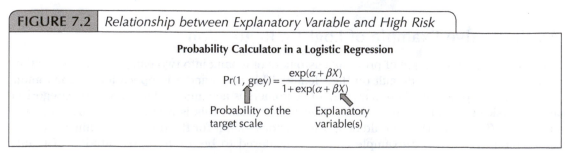

Probability Calculator in a Logistic Regression

$$\Pr(1, \text{grey}) = \frac{\exp(\alpha + \beta X)}{1 + \exp(\alpha + \beta X)}$$

Probability of the target scale   Explanatory variable(s)

You may note that while the actual phenomenon is discrete, a respondent can be categorized either as 'high risk' or as 'low risk', the logit model churns out the probability of being categorized as one or the other. Therefore, in a sense, the model provides a chance of every customer being in one category or the other—there are no discrete categorization. At best, customers may be termed as having very high probability of being in one or the other category (probability close to '1' or '0').

How to Estimate This Model?

It is appropriate to describe the data first before we discuss the estimation routine. As shown in Figure 7.1, the data is usually cross-sectional (one record for every customer) which includes his/her classification as 'high risk' (1, grey) or 'low risk' (0, black) and an array of profile variables that characterize the customers. The profile variables could be demographic variables, past behaviour records, information gathered about the customer from external sources and all other appropriate data that can be associated with the customer. An illustration of a typical data set is given in Figure 7.3. The programming codes to run the estimation of the logit model (using R codes) with this data set is given in Figure 7.4.

A truncated output obtained using this estimation technique is provided in Figure 7.5. It describes the impact of each of the profile variables used in the model on the probability of categorizing the customer as 'high risk'. As explained earlier, if the impact coefficient is positive, it implies that the higher value of the corresponding variable has a positive impact on the probability of the customer being 'high risk'.

| FIGURE 7.3 | *Sample Data Set 'Your_Data'* |

Sample Data Set: Current Customers of the Bank

Customer id	Risk Category	Past Default	Amount of Debt (₹)	Number of Dependents	Insolvency in Past Year	Income Level (₹)	Age
1001	1	Yes (1)	1,000	0	Yes (1)	19,000	21
1002	0	No (0)	2,339	1	Yes (1)	22,000	44
1003	0	No (0)	4,000	3	No (0)	31,000	22
1004	0	Yes (1)	1,500	4	No (0)	25,000	25
1005	1	No (0)	367	0	Yes (1)	33,000	56
1006	1	Yes (1)	23,000	0	No (0)	50,000	34
1007	1	No (0)	2,500	1	Yes (1)	45,000	43
1010	1	Yes (1)	4,500	2	No (0)	23,000	23
1014	0	No (0)	345	3	No (0)	67,000	26
1025	1	Yes (1)	6,790	5	No (0)	40,000	33
1026	0	No (0)	45	0	Yes (1)	12,000	23
1031	1	No (0)	0	0	No (0)	16,000	33
1044	0	Yes (1)	0	3	Yes (1)	44,000	41

FIGURE 7.4 | *R-Codes for Logistic Regression (for Data Set Named 'Your_Data')*

```
#Logistic Regression (Target Variable: RiskCategory)
#(Explanatory Variables: PastDefault, Amount of Debt, , Income Level, Age)
#Codes for "your_data" Data
filmdata=read.csv(file.choose(),header=T)#Read "your_data".csv
fullModel = glm( RiskCategory ~ PastDefault + Amount of Debt +
Income Level + Age, family=binomial (link="logit"),data=filmdata)
summary(fullModel)
```

FIGURE 7.5 | *Output from the Model*

Example output

Variable (x)	Estimate (β)	Chi-square	Inference
"Evidenced of Past Payment Default" (Yes)	0.01	9.14	Positive impact on Target Probability
"Amount of Unsecured Debt"	0.02	8.02	Positive impact on Target Probability
"Number of dependents in the Family"	0.77	6.10	Positive impact on Probability
"Insolvency Record in the past year" (Yes)	0.69	5.23	Positive impact on Target Probability
"Income Level"	−0.06	1.08	Negative impact on Target Probability (insignificant)
"Age"	−1.39	0.31	Negative impact on Target Probability (insignificant)

Effect Size   Strength of Association

How Do We Use the Estimated Model to Classify a New Case as 'High risk' or 'Low Risk'?

Using the impact coefficient, a probability of being 'high risk' for every case, new or existing cases, is calculated. Ideally, a perfect model would have probabilities as '1' ('0') depending upon whether the case is a high-risk one or otherwise. However, our analogue model will only compute a probability value close to '1'. Most models are nowhere close to perfect and yield

FIGURE 7.6 *Deciding the Prediction Rule*

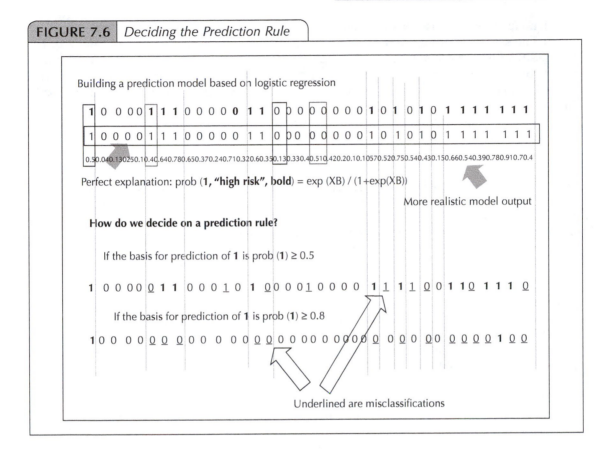

lower than '1' probability for 'high-risk' cases. The first three rows of Figure 7.6 illustrate this point. The first row is just a series of cases that are actually 'high risk' or 'low risk'. The second row is the utopian condition of the model computing perfect probability of 'high risk' category. The third row is the realistic case of computed probabilities. You would expect that the 'high risk' category (1, bold) should have high probability. Usually, a good model should exhibit such an output. But sometimes there could be misfits as depicted in Figure 7.6. A good rule to use to classify new cases would be to use a probability over 0.5 as a case of 'high risk' profile. Of course, as can be seen, sometimes you run the risk of misclassifying cases too.

What Should Be a Good Classification Rule for New Cases?

That brings us to a dilemma that many modellers face while interpreting the output of a logistic model. The output never provides a perfect answer to a classification problem, it is always probabilistic. And hence, sometimes a simplistic rule such as high probability may fail to classify the case appropriately (especially when the explanatory power of the model is weak). In such situations, the model will need to assign a certain cost of misclassification of one of the two categories and be conservative in its approach to classification. Figure 7.6 provides an illustration of the same. As seen, if the basis of classifying a 'high risk' is made more rigid (0.8 probability or more), none of the 'low risk' cases is misclassified. However, this conservatism comes at a cost. As you can see, there are more cases of 'high risk' that are now misclassified as 'low risk'. The misclassification rates would be just the opposite, had we have taken a 'liberal' cut-off for 'high risk' (probability of less than 0.5 for classifying a 'high risk'). The appropriate classification rule depends upon the context and on the misclassification which is considered to be more costly. For instance, if you definitely want to weed out 'high risk' profile at the cost of losing some good prospects ('low risk' profile), in our illustration, we would definitely keep a liberal rule for classifying 'high risk' cases.

Practical Example in Discriminant and Logistic Regression Analysis

After an in-depth understanding of different types of advanced analytics methods, let us work on some data to perform logit and discriminant model analysis.

Logit Example

A new advertisement was shown to a group of individuals to get their views on whether the advertisement is conveying information to prospective customers on the product details of the company. After the advertisement was completed, the viewers were asked to fill a survey questionnaire containing six questions. The questions measured the views of the audience on the following six variables for the advertisement:

1. Whether the advertisement did communicate the intended message or not.
2. Whether the complete range of products was appropriately communicated.
3. The emotional connect has been appropriately demonstrated.
4. The usability of the products was appropriately stressed upon.
5. The locations for availability of products.
6. The price of the products.

Each question was measured on a five-point Likert scale, where 1 indicated low agreement and 5 indicated high agreement. As shown in Table 7.1, balanced sample of 30 respondents has been taken from the large data set of which 15 have said yes and other 15 have said no for the question on advertisement communicating the intended message. The analyst wants to predict the probability of a responder saying 'yes' as a function of product range, emotion and usability.

The logit model, using the maximum likelihood estimation method, was used to arrive at the results. View is a categorical variable with two options 'yes' and 'no'. The table has recorded 'yes' as 1 and 'no' as 0. This will be the dependent variable. Here, a condition can be set such that if the predicted probability is greater than 0.5, then the predicted value of dependent variable Y can be set to 1, or otherwise it can be set to 0. The predicted value of Y can then be compared to the actual value to decide on the number of correctly predicted values. The output obtained from the above table using SPSS is shown in Table 7.2. Number of statistical values can be inferred. However, from a business analyst's point of view, there are certain outcomes that you must know to decide on the quality of the model. They have been explained below. Those who are interested in detailed statistical interpretations can look up books in advanced statistics.

TABLE 7.1	Respondents' Views on Advertisement					
S. No.	View	Product Range	Emotion	Usability	Availability	Price
1	1	5	3	4	4	4
2	1	4	4	3	4	5
3	1	4	2	3	3	4
4	1	5	3	3	4	5
5	1	5	4	4	3	5
6	1	4	5	3	2	5
7	1	5	3	4	4	4
8	1	4	2	4	5	5
9	1	3	1	4	3	4
10	1	5	2	4	2	3
11	1	4	3	5	1	4
12	1	4	4	4	2	5
13	1	5	2	3	3	4
14	1	4	3	4	4	5
15	0	5	2	5	5	4
16	0	2	1	2	4	3
17	0	1	4	1	3	3
18	0	2	1	3	2	3
19	0	3	1	2	2	3
20	0	3	2	1	5	2
21	0	2	3	2	2	3
22	0	1	2	1	5	2
23	0	1	5	2	4	3
24	0	2	5	3	2	3
25	0	1	3	2	1	3
26	0	2	2	1	2	2
27	0	2	5	1	3	1
28	0	1	2	1	4	2
29	0	2	3	2	4	3
30	0	1	5	2	3	2

It can be concluded that respondents who feel that the advertisement has appropriately displayed the complete range of products tend to agree that the advertisement has communicated the intended message. Thus, managers who wish to prepare advertisements of similar nature need to highlight the product range as that turns out to be the single most deciding factor for the success of an advertisement in communicating a message to prospective customers.

| TABLE 7.2 | *Output of Logistic Regression* |

(a) Case Processing Summary

Unweighted Cases[a]		*N*	Per Cent
Selected cases	Included in analysis	30	100.0
	Missing cases	0	0.0
	Total	30	100.0
Unselected cases		0	0.0
Total		30	100.0

Note: [a] If weight is in effect, see classification table for the total number of cases.

(b) Dependent Variable Encoding

Original Value	Internal Value
No	0
Yes	1

(c) Model Summary

Step	−2 Log Likelihood	Cox and Snell R^2	Nagelkerke R^2
1	14.232[a]	0.596	0.796

Note: [a] Estimation terminated at iteration number 6 because parameter estimates changed by less than 0.001.

(d) Classification Table[a]

		Predicted		
		View		Percentage Correct
	Observed	No	Yes	
Step 1	View No	15	1	93.8
	Yes	1	13	92.9
	Overall Percentage		93.3	

Note: [a] The cut value is 0.500.

(e) Variables in the Equation

		B	S.E.	Wald	df	Sig.	Exp(B)
Step 1[a]	PRODUCT RANGE	1.749	0.825	4.489	1	0.034	5.747
	EMOTION	0.282	0.510	0.307	1	0.579	1.326
	USABILITY	0.645	0.824	0.613	1	0.434	1.906
	Constant	−8.449	3.086	7.497	1	0.006	0.000

Notes: [a] Variable(s) entered on Step 1: PRODUCTRANGE, EMOTION, USABILITY.
- We can infer from Table 7.2 that 30 sample data have been used with no missing value.
- Nagelkerke R^2 of 79.6 per cent indicates a good fit of the model. This is similar to the coefficient of determination R^2 in linear regression model (Chapter 6).
- Wald's statistic gives a measure of the significance of each of the measured variables. It is chi-square distributed with 1 degree of freedom for numeric variables. For our example, we observe that it is significant (0.034) only for 'product range' variable.
- The classification table shows that 28 out of 30 cases have been correctly predicted, which results in 93.3 per cent.

Discriminant Example

Employees of an organization are sent for leadership training every year. The decision of their selection for the training (eligibility) depends on three factors (variables):

1. Team size they manage in numbers.
2. The degree of innovation they have demonstrated in their leadership role.
3. The efforts they have put in keeping all their team members motivated.

Eligibility is a categorical dependent variable with two options. The metric variable team size managed by each employee is based on the people who belong to his project team. The other two metric variables have been rated on a five-point Likert scale, where 1 indicates low and 5 indicates high. As shown in Table 7.3, balanced sample of 40 respondents has been taken from the large data set of which 15 are eligible (1) and other 15 are not (2). The sample is divided into two parts: 30 instances are part of the analysis sample which form the discriminant model and the other 10 form the holdout sample used to test and validate the model. The analyst wants to identify the combination of independent variable (team size, innovation, motivation) that will best discriminate the categories of the dependent variable (eligibility).

TABLE 7.3	*Analysis and Holdout Sample of Employee_Training*

(a) Analysis Sample

S. No.	Employee_ID	Eligibility	Team Size	Innovation	Motivation
1	21668	1	40	2	4
2	21730	1	45	1	5
3	21779	1	60	4	5
4	21425	1	50	3	5
5	21333	1	60	2	5
6	21542	1	45	4	4
7	21256	1	55	1	5
8	21111	1	32	5	4
9	21666	1	58	2	5
10	21350	1	66	1	4
11	21354	1	69	1	4
12	21874	1	70	3	5
13	21720	1	40	1	3
14	21970	1	50	2	5
15	21660	1	60	4	5
16	21222	2	12	5	2

(Table 7.3 Continued)

(Table 7.3 Continued)

S. No.	Employee_ID	Eligibility	Team Size	Innovation	Motivation
17	21590	2	15	5	2
18	21780	2	20	5	2
19	21530	2	15	3	2
20	21840	2	22	4	3
21	21213	2	21	3	2
22	21431	2	14	5	1
23	21546	2	24	2	1
24	21652	2	21	3	1
25	21766	2	10	4	2
26	21879	2	2	3	1
27	21865	2	14	2	3
28	21540	2	15	2	2
29	21998	2	14	2	1
30	21967	2	12	1	2

(b) Holdout Sample

S. No.	Employee_ID	Eligibility	Team Size	Innovation	Motivation
1	21131	1	50	4	4
2	21141	1	55	1	5
3	21136	1	40	4	5
4	21148	1	70	3	5
5	21170	1	45	2	5
6	21150	2	25	4	2
7	21189	2	12	4	1
8	21191	2	16	5	2
9	21152	2	11	2	1
10	21143	2	5	4	2

The discriminant model output obtained from Table 7.3 by using SPSS is shown in Table 7.4. Number of statistical values can be inferred. However, from a business analyst point of view, there are certain outcomes that you must know to decide on the quality of the model. They have been explained below. Those who are interested in detailed statistical interpretations can look up books in advanced statistics.

TABLE 7.4	SPSS Output of Two Group Discriminant Analysis

(a) Group Statistics

Eligibility		Mean	Std. Deviation	Valid N (List-wise)	
				Unweighted	Weighted
1	Team Size	53.33	11.381	15	15
	Innovation	2.40	1.352	15	15
	Motivation	4.53	0.640	15	15
2	Team Size	15.40	5.604	15	15
	Innovation	3.27	1.335	15	15
	Motivation	1.80	0.676	15	15
Total	Team Size	34.37	21.209	30	30
	Innovation	2.83	1.392	30	30
	Motivation	3.17	1.533	30	30

(b) Tests of Equality of Group Means

	Wilks' Lambda	F	df1	df2	Sig.
Team Size	0.173	134.126	1	28	0.000
Innovation	0.900	3.121	1	28	0.088
Motivation	0.178	129.308	1	28	0.000

(c) Pooled within-Groups Matrices

		Team Size	Innovation	Motivation
Correlation	Team Size	1.000	−0.141	0.294
	Innovation	−0.141	1.000	0.105
	Motivation	0.294	0.105	1.000

(d) Eigenvalues

Function	Eigenvalue	% of Variance	Cumulative %	Canonical Correlation
1	7.348[a]	100.0	100.0	0.938

Note: [a] First 1 canonical discriminant functions were used in the analysis.

(e) Wilks' Lambda

Test of Function(s)	Wilks' Lambda	Chi-Square	df	Sig.
1	0.120	56.234	3	0.000

(Table 7.4 Continued)

(Table 7.4 Continued)

(f) Standardized Canonical Discriminant Function Coefficients

	Function
	1
Team Size	0.610
Innovation	−0.103
Motivation	0.625

(g) Structure Matrix

	Function
	1
Team Size	0.807
Motivation	0.793
Innovation	−0.123

Notes: Pooled within-groups correlations between discriminating variables and standardized canonical discriminant functions.

Variables ordered by absolute size of correlation within function.

(h) Functions at Group Centroids

	Function
Eligibility	**1**
1	2.619
2	−2.619

Notes: Unstandardized canonical discriminant functions evaluated at group means

Classification Statistics

(i) Classification Processing Summary

Processed		31
Excluded	Missing or out-of-range group codes	0
	At least one missing discriminating variable	1
Used in Output		30

(j) Prior Probabilities for Groups

		Cases Used in Analysis	
Eligibility	**Prior**	**Unweighted**	**Weighted**
1	0.500	15	15.000
2	0.500	15	15.000
Total	1.000	30	30.000

(k) Classification Results[b,c]

		Eligibility	Predicted Group Membership		Total
			1	2	
Original	Count	1	15	0	15
		2	0	15	15
	%	1	100.0	0.0	100.0
		2	0.0	100.0	100.0
Cross-validated[a]	Count	1	14	1	15
		2	0	15	15
	%	1	93.3	6.7	100.0
		2	0.0	100.0	100.0

Notes: [a] Cross validation is done only for these cases in the analysis. In cross validation, each case is classified by the functions derived from all cases other than that case.
[b] 100.0% of original grouped cases correctly classified.
[c] 96.7% of cross-validated grouped cases correctly classified.

Holdout Sample

(l) Classification Results[b,c]

		Eligibility	Predicted Group Membership		Total
			1	2	
Original	Count	1	5	0	5
		2	1	4	5
	%	1	100.0	0.0	100.0
		2	20.0	80.0	100.0
Cross-validated[a]	Count	1	4	1	5
		2	1	4	5
	%	1	80.0	20.0	100.0
		2	20.0	80.0	100.0

Notes: [a] Cross-validation is done only for those cases in the analysis. In cross-validation, each case is classified by the functions derived from all cases other than that case.
[b] 90.0 % of original grouped cases correctly classified.
[c] 80.0% of cross-validated grouped cases correctly classified.

Inference

Eigenvalues: It is the ratio of the between group to within group sum of squares. Larger values are desirable.

Wilks' lambda: It is the ratio of the within group sum of squares to the total sum of squares. It has value ranging from 0 to 1. Values close to 0 indicate chances of different group means.

1. It can be inferred from the statistics group means and standard deviations that the two groups vary more in terms of team size than the other variables.
2. In 'test of equality of group means', the univariate F value is significant for only two variables, 'team size' and 'motivation'. Thus, indicating them to decide on eligibility of selection for training.
3. The pooled within-group correlation is low, hence there will not be a problem of multicollinearity between the variables.
4. The eigenvalue is 7.348 and explains for 100% variance.
5. The canonical correlation associated with this discriminant function is 0.938. The square of this correlation is 0.88. Thus, 88% of the variance in eligibility selection is explained by this model.
6. Wilks' lambda is used to test null hypothesis that the means of all discriminant functions are equal in all the groups. The decision is based on the significance level and chi-square value. For our example, Wilks' lambda is 0.120 with a chi-square value of 56.234 at 5 degrees of freedom and is significant at 0.05 level.
7. Predictors with relatively large standardized values usually contribute more towards explaining the discriminant function. For our example, we can conclude that 'motivation' 0.625 is more significant than 'team size' 0.610 in discriminating between the two groups.
8. The validation sample is used for developing the classification matrix. In a two-group discriminant function, a record will be assigned to the group with the closest centroid. As mentioned above, the hit ratio is the percentage of correctly classified records in the holdout sample. It can be determined by adding the elements in the diagonal and dividing by the total number of records. For our example, we conclude the following:
   a. In the analysis sample, 100.0% of original grouped cases correctly classified.
   b. In the analysis sample, 96.7% of cross-validated grouped cases correctly classified.
   c. In the holdout sample, 90.0% of original grouped cases correctly classified.

With two groups of similar size, a chance hit ratio can be of 50%. Here there is significant improvement over chance, normally considered good if above 25%. All three values are beyond 25% improvement. The validity of the discriminant model can be considered to be acceptable.

CONCLUSION

The authors hope that this description of logit models would help the reader appreciate the key model difference in comparison with regression models. While the objectives are similar, regression and logits differ significantly in the approach to construction of the model. Also, the requirements for using a specific modelling approach depends on the nature of the dependent variable. In logit (choice) models, the dependent variable is usually nominal scaled as against interval scaled variable used in regression. The different methods used to draw inference from data described until chapter 7 have been summarized in Table 7.5.

TABLE 7.5	*Different Methods in Brief*		
Test Type	**Independent Variable**	**Dependent Variable**	**Analysis**
1. Chi-Square	Categorical (Non-metric)	Categorical (Non-metric)	1. Frequency counts. 2. No specification of independent and dependent variable is necessary. 3. If chi-square value is higher than critical value, then a significant association between the variables exists. 4. Reject null hypothesis stating no association between the variables exists.
2. T/Z test	Numerical (Metric)	Numerical (Metric)	1. Compares means of 2 different samples or paired samples. 2. No specification of independent and dependent variable is necessary. 3. If t or z value is higher than critical value (or p value is lower than alpha), then the means of the 2 samples are different. 4. Reject null hypothesis stating means of the 2 samples is same.
3. ANOVA (one-way)	Categorical (Non-metric)—one	Numerical (Metric)—one	1. Compare means of 3 or more samples. 2. Independent variable can be split into groups for comparison. 3. If F value is higher than critical value (p value is lower than alpha), then at least one of the means is different, and hence independent variable **does have** significant effect on dependent variable. 4. Reject null hypothesis stating means of all samples is same.
4. ANOVA (N-way)	Categorical (Non-metric)—more than one	Numerical (Metric)—one	1. Compare means of 3 or more samples. 2. Independent variable can be split into groups for comparison. 3. If F value of Model is higher than critical value (p value lower than alpha), then check two way interaction values. 4. If the p value is higher than alpha value, then we conclude that there exists strong dependency among the independent variable and further independent effect analysis is not required. However, if p value is lower (significant), then we look at F and p values of the independent variables. 5. If p values are significant, then the one with higher F value is concluded to create more impact.

(Table 7.5 Continued)

(Table 7.5 Continued)

Test Type	Independent Variable	Dependent Variable	Analysis
5. MANOVA	Categorical (Non-metric)—more than one	Numerical (Metric)—more than one	1. Used when 2 or more dependent variables are correlated. Else if no correlation, then ANOVA on each variable separately should be done.
6. Regression (OLS) bivariate	Numerical (Metric)—more than one	Numerical (Metric)—one	1. Develops relationship between dependent and independent variables. 2. Usually, if R^2 and F values are higher, model is significant. 3. Look for individual t values for variable level significance.
7. Multiple regression	Numerical (Metric)—more than one	Numerical (Metric)—more than one	As above, however, look for multicollinearity by seeing the VIF factor. If higher than 5, conclude that multicollinearity exists.
8. Regression with dummy variables	Numerical (Metric) / categorical—more than one	Numerical (Metric)—more than one	
9. Discriminant analysis	Numerical (Metric)—more than one	Categorical (Non-metric)—more than one	1. Decide which category (cluster) the variable belongs to. 2. Done by dividing sample into analysis and holdout sample. 3. Difference in Mean values of variables, correlation for multicollinearity, Eigen value (like F value), Wilks lambda, significance p value of model and hit ratio are used for analysis.
10. Binary logit	Numerical (Metric)—more than one	Categorical (Non-metric)—more than one	1. Decides likelihood to belong to which group of dependent variable. 2. Nagelkerke R^2 explains model strength. 3. Classification table denotes percentage of correct predictions. 4. Wald value is like t-value for individual variable assessment.

REVIEW QUESTIONS

1. Describe differences in model construction between OLS (regression) and logistic regression. What type of data will suit a causal model based on logistic regression?
2. What is the difference between logistic regression and MNL? Can an MNL model be reduced to a simpler logistic regression?
3. What is the maximum likelihood method of estimating a logit model?
4. What is the difference between 'conditional logit' and 'polytomous logit'?

CASE 7.1
Tranquils'.com Determines Leads (sales) from Its Website
(Case Complexity: Easy)

Ayurveda is a method of medication that has its connection with olden times in India. It refers to a natural method of healing using herbs, metals, minerals and simple healing techniques. In recent era, the consciousness towards use of natural products has made Ayurveda find presence in homes in India in the form of either medicine or natural beauty products.

Tranquils'.com has been launched by a group of Ayurvedic practitioners. They have used their years of experience in this field to develop natural beauty and hair care products. Their lab is equipped with the latest technology to process natural herbs and prepare a mixture based on research formulae to create high-quality products. Their product range includes: skin care creams, massage oils and lotions; bath and body care formulations, face wash, scrubs, soaps, shower gel; and hair care shampoos, oils and conditioners.

They realized that it was becoming difficult to target this product range to a niche customer segment and equally becoming difficult to market. Hence, the team came up with a website Tranquils'.com (for case discussion purpose only). With an objective to reach a larger audience, the advantage of having a website is to have more prospective customers visiting the site. The sales team was interested in knowing the following: From among the people who visit the site, and how many can be considered as sales leads? You shall help the sales team define a customer lead.

Exercise

1. Search and visit a website that would be similar to Tranquils'.com. From the product offering, identify the characteristics of a prospective customer.
2. What kind of behaviour recorded by web mining (refer to Chapter 5) would be useful in defining a sales lead?
3. Create a template of a table listing the variables that would assist in using a binary logit model to categorize website visitors as 'lead' and 'no lead'.

CASE 7.2
Hotel Owner Decides to Measure Quality of Service
(Case Complexity: Medium)

A three-star budget hotel in the business park area of Hyderabad city remains completely booked 365 days of the year. There have been 'one-day' visitors or ones who book for short durations, mostly corporate customers who need a place to stay closer to their office. There are also regular customers, who have an arrangement of spending certain days of the week working out of the Hyderabad office location. For Janak Rao, it does not matter who comes and for what duration. He has always believed in quality service.

While checking out, he requests every customer to fill a very short survey with four attributes on a five-point scale that helps him measure quality of the service provided by his hotel. Here 5 indicates good and 1 indicates poor. The attributes are opinion on room cleanliness, food at the hotel restaurant, attitude of staff and billing procedure. Based on the responses, he divides the service quality as 'satisfactory' and 'not satisfactory'. Quality thus is a categorical variable, where '1' indicates satisfactory and '0' indicates unsatisfactory. Table 7.6 shows the data for 30 customers, 15 of them are satisfied with the quality and the other 15 are not satisfied.

TABLE 7.6   *Response of Customers*

S. No.	Quality	Cleanliness	Food	Staff	Billing
1	1	5	3	2	4
2	1	5	3	3	4
3	1	5	3	2	5
4	1	5	2	2	5
5	1	5	2	2	5
6	1	5	2	3	5
7	1	4	3	3	4
8	1	4	3	3	4
9	1	4	4	3	5
10	1	4	3	2	5
11	1	5	3	2	5
12	1	5	4	2	5
13	1	2	1	1	3
14	1	4	2	1	3
15	1	4	2	3	4
16	0	4	2	4	2
17	0	2	2	4	3
18	0	2	3	2	2
19	0	2	2	2	3
20	0	3	2	2	2
21	0	1	2	1	3
22	0	1	3	1	2
23	0	1	2	3	2
24	0	3	2	3	3
25	0	3	1	4	1
26	0	2	4	2	1
27	0	1	1	1	1
28	0	2	2	2	3
29	0	2	2	2	3
30	0	2	2	2	2

Exercise

1. Using the data sample of 30 respondents, use logistic regression in SPSS to estimate the probability of customer being satisfied or not satisfied with the quality of service. You can refer Appendix D for software guidance.
2. There are certain statistics associated with logistic regression analysis that you have studied in this chapter. Analyse them from your results:
   a. Model fit using Nagelkerke R^2. It can be established that if the value is 0.5 or greater, then the value of quality is set to 1. If the value is less than 0.5, then the value is set to 0.
   b. The classification table for correct and incorrect predictions.
   c. Wald's statistics for identifying the significance and direction of the estimated coefficients.
   d. The p value.

CASE 7.3
Budget Accommodation for College-going Students
(Case Complexity: Hard)

After finishing school education, students seek out admission in universities across various locations in India. While some of the universities have student hostel accommodation, a majority of them are unable to accommodate all the students who are admitted to their residential programmes. Students who leave home to study at a location away from the comforts of home have to simultaneously look for an accommodation.

With several universities and institutes coming up across India, the need for an assured comfortable accommodation has risen. Several property owners and home owners have begun a structured method of offering budget housing to students every year. These could be in the form of a room where the student stays as a paying guest (PG) or full house accommodating a group of students.

Sadhana Pancholi and her husband Arvind lived in a township close to the Central University. They have four grown-up married children who have moved to other cities. They own a two-bedroom flat in the township. Each of their four children also owns a flat in the same township. Arvind and Sadhana had maintained the flats for their children for the first three years. However, with time and lack of use, the deterioration was very fast. Sadhana had heard from her neighbours that parents of students who get admitted to the university often come looking for possible accommodation in the township.

They made a decision to let out the four flats of their children on rent to the students every year. They have been doing so now for the past six years. At the beginning of every new academic year, parents along with their ward visit them to discuss the possibility of budget housing. Several factors are considered such as the locality and its safety, the proximity to the university, food, furnished, laundry service, medical options, recreational activity, 24 hours electricity and water. The flats maintained by Arvind and Sadhana have all these facilities on an 'as required' basis. They have budget accommodation in two price ranges: ₹5,000 and ₹7,000 per month. Parents make a decision on going for either of the accommodation option based on their ward's need and the importance of the facility. Sadhana has collected responses from the parents on the significance they attach to each of the above-mentioned factors while picking either of the location. Two of their flats are in the interior of the township which are priced at ₹5,000, whereas the other two are closer to the university which are priced at 7,000. They have organized the other features in these flats based on the responses from parents over the years. Thirty responses from among a large number of respondents have been shown in Table 7.7. These responses contain the preference that parents attach to four attributes (proximity to university, food service, on-demand laundry and need for continuous electricity) on a scale of 1–5, where 5 is high and 1 is low.

In Tables 7.7 and 7.8, the price range '1' indicates ₹5,000 and '2' indicates ₹7,000 per month.

TABLE 7.7	*Preference of Budget Housing (Analysis Sample)*				
S. No.	**Price Range**	**Preference towards Proximity**	**Food**	**Laundry**	**Electricity**
1	1	2	2	3	4
2	1	1	3	2	4
3	1	1	3	3	4
4	1	2	4	3	4
5	1	3	2	3	4
6	1	2	2	3	4
7	1	2	2	2	4
8	1	3	2	1	4
9	1	1	3	1	4
10	1	1	3	1	4
11	1	2	1	4	4
12	1	2	1	4	5
13	1	1	1	4	5
14	1	2	2	4	5
15	1	3	4	4	5
16	2	5	5	4	5
17	2	5	5	5	5
18	2	5	3	5	5
19	2	4	2	4	5
20	2	4	4	5	5
21	2	4	4	4	4
22	2	4	5	4	5
23	2	5	3	4	5
24	2	4	3	4	5

25	2	5	5	4	4
26	2	5	5	4	3
27	2	5	5	5	3
28	2	5	3	5	5
29	2	4	2	4	5
30	2	4	4	5	5

TABLE 7.8 *Preference of Budget Housing (Holdout/Validation Sample)*

S. No.	Price Range	Preference towards Proximity	Food	Laundry	Electricity
1	1	2	2	3	4
2	1	1	3	2	4
3	1	3	2	1	4
4	1	1	3	1	4
5	1	1	3	1	4
6	2	5	5	4	5
7	2	5	5	5	5
8	2	5	3	5	5
9	2	4	4	4	5
10	2	4	4	5	5

Exercise

1. Using a two-group direct discriminant analysis, identify if the preference that exists for two price ranges is significantly different. Use SPSS to obtain and analyse your results. You can refer to Appendix D for software guidance.
2. There are certain statistics associated with discriminant analysis that you have seen in this chapter. Analyse them from your results:
   a. Classification matrix (confusion matrix): Number of correctly and wrongly classified cases.
   b. Eigenvalues: It is the ratio of the between group to within group sum of squares. Larger values are desirable.
   c. Wilks' lambda: It is the ratio of the within-group sum of squares to the total sum of squares. It has a value ranging from 0 to 1. Values close to 0 indicate chances of different group means.
   d. Others include F value, p value, correlation matrix, canonical correlation and group means.

Data Mining Methods in Business Analytics

Opening Example

Nisha is not much of an Internet buyer, she prefers to do her shopping by going to a physical store. On Monday last week, she received a call from her childhood friend that she would be visiting her over the weekend. Nisha was scheduled to be on an overseas assignment all of that week and would be back in India just in time to receive her friend at home. Her friend is from a Maharashtrian family (Maharashtra, western state of India) and is an theist (believes in God). She wanted to gift her a statue of Lord Ganesha, the God with the elephant head, who protects from all obstacles and provides wisdom and well-being. With very little time on hand after her return to India, she reluctantly decided to check it out online. To her surprise, she was able to find numerous statues in varied sizes, forms and made of different materials, many more options than she could have found in any physical store. A pleasure to her eyes, it made her job so simple to click, compare and decide based on several parameters that would define her final purchase. The websites also provided guidance in the form of other customers profiled in Nisha's segment who had purchased a statue she had viewed and simultaneously also purchased or viewed a similar item. There was a listing of items that were frequently bought together to assist her in her purchase decision. What else did she need? From the cosy sofa of her drawing room, she got a choice of multiple products and recommendations for purchase. Product description, price, delivery options, discount, flexible payment methods—all bundled together. She was tired looking around the websites that evening and hence decided to defer her purchase to the next morning. Next day she was flooded with digital advertisements of Ganesha idol across websites.

In the situation described above, the website has used data mining techniques to provide customers like Nisha with the best surfing and shopping experience online. Understanding her requirements as soon as possible and then working towards providing her and similar customers the ease of shopping to decide, select and buy the product of their choice from innumerable options is a key feature of data mining techniques. A large number of data mining techniques are being used by organizations to manage their customers by getting a better understanding about their needs and purchase behaviour for improving organizational processes for efficient operations, managing employees and other stakeholders, financial decisions and strategic needs.

Students in a business school are exposed to a course on statistics in the first year followed by Business Research Methods. These are generally compulsory courses that every student is required to study. These become foundation courses for them to step into the world of domain-specific decision-making backed with data. An important concept, 'data mining', is referred to during case study discussions. Although the term data mining may be new and significantly discussed in reference to BA, the concepts are very old and have basis in statistical and mathematical techniques. If you ask the definition of Data Mining to a student who has moved into second year of an MBA programme, there is a standard answer: 'It helps analysts relate and identify patterns within huge reserves of data.' What is pattern and how is this different from BA? Additionally, is it only about patterns? Let us explore….

WHAT IS DATA MINING?

Data mining is used to describe the method of discovering or mining knowledge from large reserves of data. It is a term used to describe the process through which previously unknown patterns in data are discovered. In literature, data mining is defined as 'the nontrivial process of identifying valid, novel, potentially useful, and ultimately understandable patterns in data stored in structured databases', where the data are organized in records structured by categorical and numerical variables (Fayyad et al., 1996, https://www.aaai.org/ojs/index.php/aimagazine/article/view/1230/1131).

Every year, in the educational institutions, a large amount of student data gets generated. This consists of the personal data collected about the students such as their name, age, gender, educational background, parents' education and where they belong. During the course of the programme in which students are enrolled, information about them such as classroom participation, grades, projects, internships, preference for elective courses, extra-curricular activities and hostel details is maintained. Let us assume that a Management institute's data centre decides to create a data mining tool that would allow predicting the *best profile* for a student graduating out of their institute. Here, 'best profile' means the profile customized to each graduating student based on all aspects that define his/her values as an individual, capabilities and skills suited for employability. Hence, empowering the institution to be able to recommend the perfect job suitable for him/her during placement. The current method followed by the institute for shortlisting students is purely based on the student performance. However, in an effort towards customization and improving effectiveness, they plan to mine historical alumni data regarding personal details, performance details and personality details, and compare it with the respective alumni's job profile. Thus, develop a forecasting model that would be able to predict and recommend jobs for existing students.

There is a huge amount of data that gets generated during organizational processes. Moving towards the culture of digitization and automation, organizations have consciously or otherwise collected enormous amounts of unstructured data. Looking for patterns within this data using algorithms could be of significant value to provide a competitive edge to an organization. Is there some merit to doing it and what should organizations do to identify that the kind of knowledge generated from this exercise would aid better decision-making. This is where data mining becomes important to organizations. Being able to tie the decision-making needs to data mining outcomes has become an area of key interest to organizations. Statistical and mathematical models and techniques have been extended under the umbrella of data mining.

DATA MINING AND BA

There has been a realization globally of the hidden virtues of untapped data that lies in the data warehouse of organizations. The cost of technology has reduced over the years along with new methods and technologies being developed for data processing and storage. Data mining does refer to extracting knowledge from large data sets which otherwise make no meaning in itself. The recent efforts by certain software vendors have extended the definition of data mining to include presenting the outcome of a data mining technique in a form easily understood by the end user. This delves into the territory of data analysis. We shall see in the examples that follow how using mainstream data mining software (like RapidMiner) can provide such aided analysis to the end user who could possibly be a Business Analyst. It is then for the Business Analyst to interpret and present it in a form that provides additional insights to the clients. Data Mining is thus an integral component feeding into BA as discussed in Chapter 1.

DATA MINING AND MACHINE LEARNING

Data Mining is applied on large data sets which are historical in nature, residing in organization data warehouse. The learning methods used to extract, train and model the data using algorithms are known as Machine Learning. There are primarily two types of Machine Learning methods: unsupervised and supervised (Figure 8.1). The data sets are extracted (training data set) and studied for patterns within them hence identifying relationships that would generate additional learning. No specific criterion is mentioned by the analyst, rather the natural partitioning provides description of the attributes. This is called the Unsupervised Learning Method. We shall see two types of Unsupervised Learning methods: Clustering and Association.

If models are built by considering certain variables of interest, training data sets used for prediction and rules pre-specified by the analyst, it is termed as Supervised Learning. A sample data set is used to build and train the model. This is then tested using a holdout sample data for

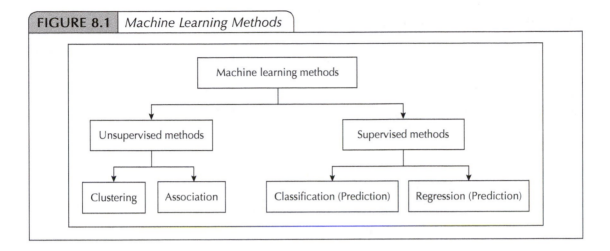

FIGURE 8.1 | *Machine Learning Methods*

consistency of the model. As a third step, it is used to test data in actual world for prediction and forecasting. We shall see two types of Supervised Learning techniques: Classification and Regression. For the examples used for demonstration of both these data mining techniques, we shall split the data set into training and holdout sample as explained in the respective sections.

DATA MINING METHOD: CLUSTER ANALYSIS

It uses as an optimizing technique to group the data in relevant buckets (classes) where objects within each bucket are similar in nature and the buckets are significantly different from each other. The algorithm that operates within the training data set has no predefined bucket, rather similarity in characteristics is used to identify the grouping of variables. The analyst who has the business domain expertise will rerun the algorithm several times to decide on the optimum number of clusters based on the BP under study.

Here, we shall see one of the clustering techniques by using an example. The *k*-means clustering technique starts with a random partition of the training data set. This is an iterative process, where the centre of each partition called centroid is calculated (Figure 8.2). Considering the Euclidean distance function as the criteria for the nearest neighbour, data objects are reassigned into relevant clusters. The new centroid is calculated taking the average of all members for each attribute.

We shall be using RapidMiner software for explaining each technique and the interpretation of its outcomes. Please see Appendix D for details on downloading, installing and use of RapidMiner software.

All the data sets used in this chapter are available in the student download section for exercise.

The Iris flower data set used for Clustering data mining exercise is present in the sample data set section in RapidMiner that you have downloaded to your device. The Iris flower data set[1] consists of samples from each of the three species of Iris flower: Iris Sentosa, Iris Virginica and

---

[1] http://archive.ics.uci.edu/ml/datasets/Iris

FIGURE 8.2 *Cluster Assignments and Centroids*

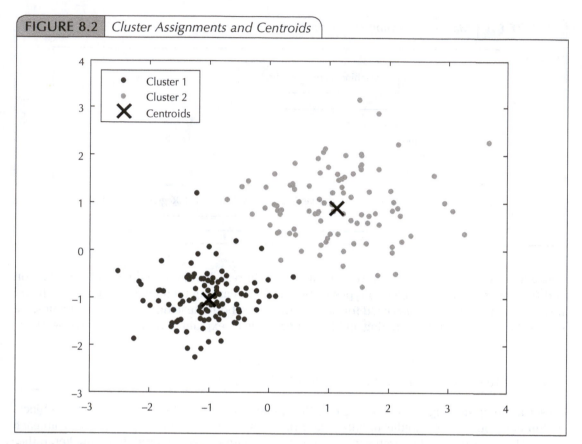

Source: https://www.mathworks.com/help/stats/kmeans.html

Iris Versicolor. Each flower has four attributes in centimetres: sepal length and width, petal length and width. In the 150 sample data set provided in RapidMiner, 'a1' is sepal length, 'a2' is sepal width, 'a3' is petal length and 'a4' is petal width. We have assumed that the class of the flower is unknown and allowed the data set to naturally group into clusters using the k-means algorithm in RapidMiner. Refer to Figure 8.3 to see the operators that have been used. Before beginning any process in RapidMiner, create your own folder to store your work as explained in Appendix D. The Iris data set can be brought to your folder in the 'data' section to further work on it. Pull the data set into the process screen. Use the normalize operator to standardize the sample values for comparison between them. The 'Clustering' and 'performance' operators will create the required number of clusters as mentioned by the user. Here we have created three clusters.

The output as in Figure 8.4 shows 3 clusters for the 150 samples. Cluster '0' has 44 records, cluster '1' has 56 records and cluster '2' has 50 records. This has evenly distributed the records across the clusters. You can try with more or less number of clusters and see the outcome and finally choose the one that most clearly defines your clusters. For this example, we have stopped at three clusters.

FIGURE 8.3 *Clustering in RapidMiner*

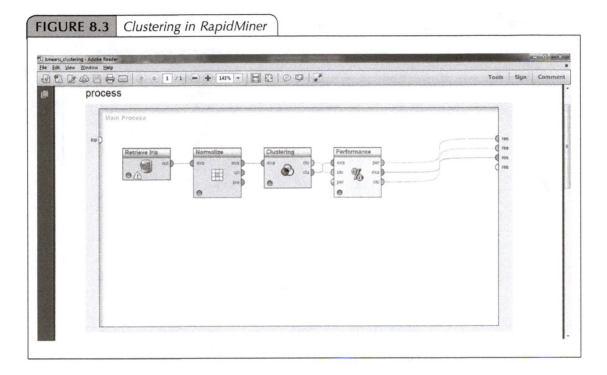

FIGURE 8.4 *Clustering Algorithm Output in RapidMiner*

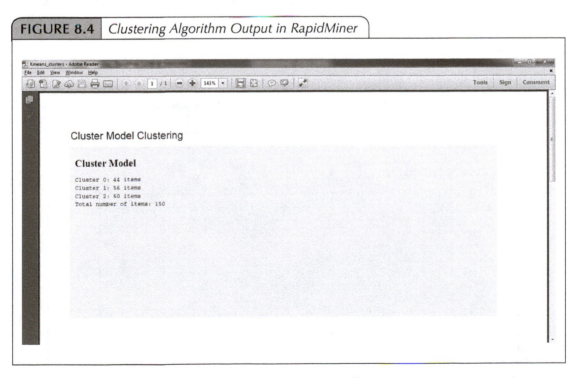

FIGURE 8.5 | *Normalized Dataset by Cluster*

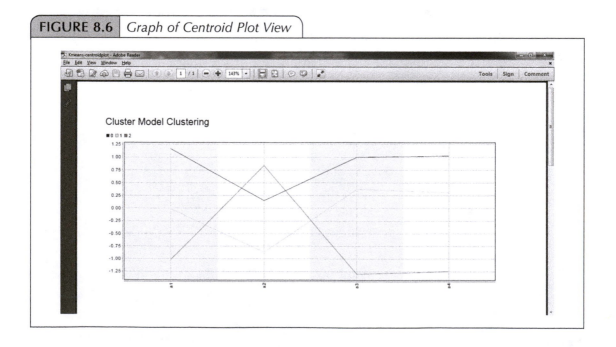

Figure 8.5 shows a snapshot of the normalized data set in each cluster.

Figure 8.6 is a graphical representation of the centroid plot view of four attributes across three clusters. It is clearly evident that 'a2' sepal width centroid stands apart from the other three centroids for each cluster. It is also evident from the example set output in Figure 8.5.

FIGURE 8.6 | *Graph of Centroid Plot View*

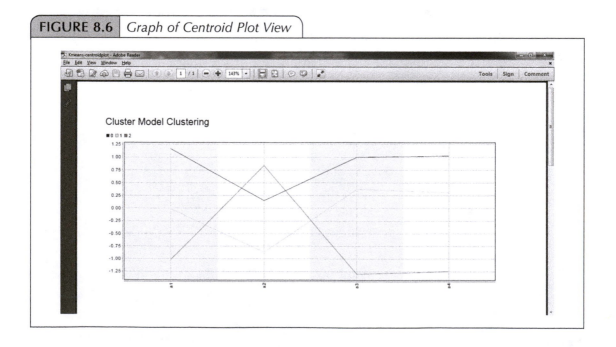

DATA MINING METHOD: ASSOCIATION TECHNIQUE

Association, a common word used in English, means a common link or relation between individuals or groups. Similarly, in data mining, Association technique refers to linkages or occurrences of objects together over a period of time. The Apriori algorithm is used in Association rule mining where frequently occurring objects are identified. This method has widespread use in medicine, pharmacy, telecommunication, retail, financial fraud handling and banking. In retail, the popular Association rule mining application is referred to as market basket analysis, where transactional data at large retail stores and supermarkets are analysed for enhancing knowledge on customer behaviour and products assortments purchased. They are used for tracking products purchased together, aisle management by placing frequently purchased items together, cross selling, promotions, bundling of products and pricing.

The following example discusses market basket analysis in RapidMiner, using the data set 'market basket' provided in student material download. It has 30 sample receipts of customers of a supermarket. Each receipt is used to identify if the customer has purchased one or more of the following products: milk, eggs, bread, ketchup, pasta, jam, butter and sugar. To avoid complexity in this illustration, we have excluded attributes such as packaging size, brand and price. The goal is to use the Association rule mining algorithm (Figure 8.7) to identify products that are frequently purchased together. The numerical to binomial operator changes all variables to binomial which can have only two values 'true' or 'false'. This helps in associating similar occurrence of each instance of the objects. By default, a zero value is mapped to false, all others are true. The FP Growth operator identifies and groups items occurring together and the frequency of their occurrence together. The Create Association operator creates the Association rule using an if–then pattern. For example: 'If the customer has purchased a shirt, he is 70 per cent sure to buy a handkerchief'. Such outcomes are very informative suggestions for the retail store owner.

| FIGURE 8.7 | *Association Rule in RapidMiner* |

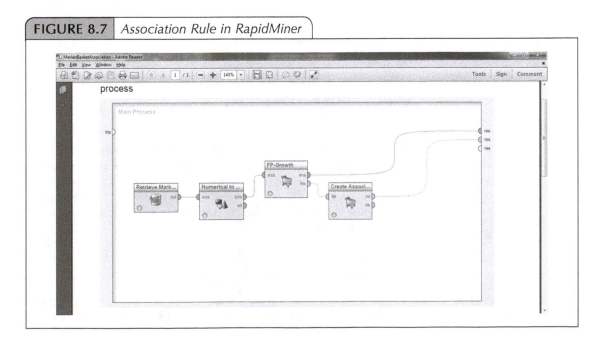

The outcomes of the Association rule are analysed using three common metrics:

1. **Support:** How frequently do the Items A and B occur together in the same transaction in an existing data set (Figure 8.8).

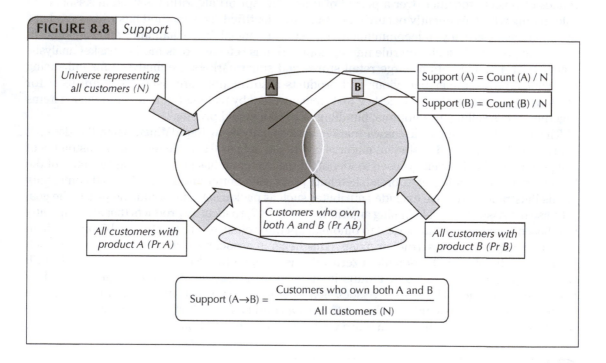

FIGURE 8.8   *Support*

Universe representing all customers (N)

A   B

Support (A) = Count (A) / N

Support (B) = Count (B) / N

Customers who own both A and B (Pr AB)

All customers with product A (Pr A)

All customers with product B (Pr B)

$$\text{Support (A→B)} = \frac{\text{Customers who own both A and B}}{\text{All customers (N)}}$$

2. **Confidence:** The probability of occurrence of B in a transaction when A is present (conditional probability) (Figure 8.9). Values range from 0 to 1, where 1 indicates 100 per cent occurrence.

$$x\% = \frac{\Pr(A,B)}{\Pr(A)} = \Pr(B \mid A)$$

3. **Lift:** The ratio of confidence of A and B occurring together to the expected confidence of them occurring together (Figure 8.10). The expected confidence is the product of the support values of A and B divided by the support value of A and support value of B. This shows how much more likely a customer is to buy the consequent, given the antecedent, as compared to the baseline rate of purchasing the consequent in the overall population. Values > 1 indicate a positive relationship.

$$\frac{\Pr(A,B)}{\Pr(A)\Pr(B)} = \frac{\Pr(B \mid A)}{\Pr(B)}$$

Let us go back to our example. The variables and the outcome of the rule are shown in Figures 8.11 and 8.12. As we see, the highest support is for milk and jam to occur together in our sample

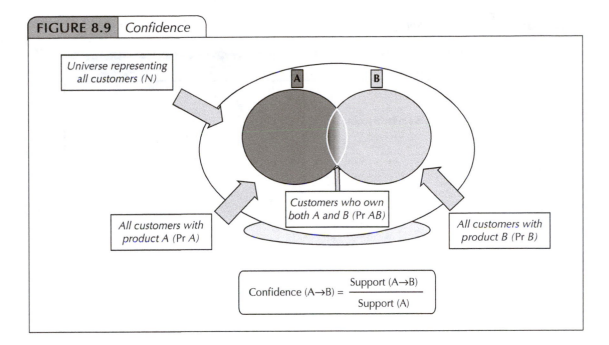

FIGURE 8.9 *Confidence*

Universe representing all customers (N)

All customers with product A (Pr A)

Customers who own both A and B (Pr AB)

All customers with product B (Pr B)

$$\text{Confidence (A} \rightarrow \text{B)} = \frac{\text{Support (A} \rightarrow \text{B)}}{\text{Support (A)}}$$

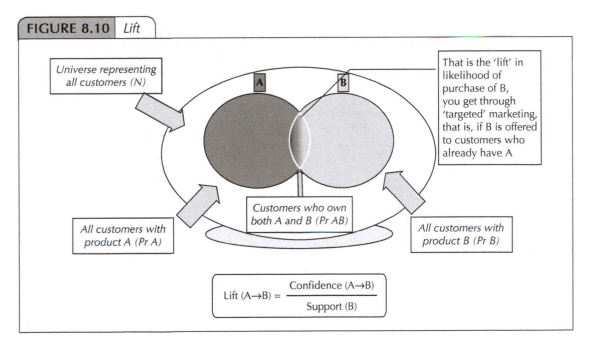

FIGURE 8.10 *Lift*

Universe representing all customers (N)

That is the 'lift' in likelihood of purchase of B, you get through 'targeted' marketing, that is, if B is offered to customers who already have A

All customers with product A (Pr A)

Customers who own both A and B (Pr AB)

All customers with product B (Pr B)

$$\text{Lift (A} \rightarrow \text{B)} = \frac{\text{Confidence (A} \rightarrow \text{B)}}{\text{Support (B)}}$$

data set which is 0.533 (53%). The confidence of occurrence of jam when milk is present is 1 (100%). The lift is 1.875. Similarly, for support for butter when bread is present is 46.7 per cent, confidence is 100 per cent and lift is 2.

FIGURE 8.11 *Example Set*

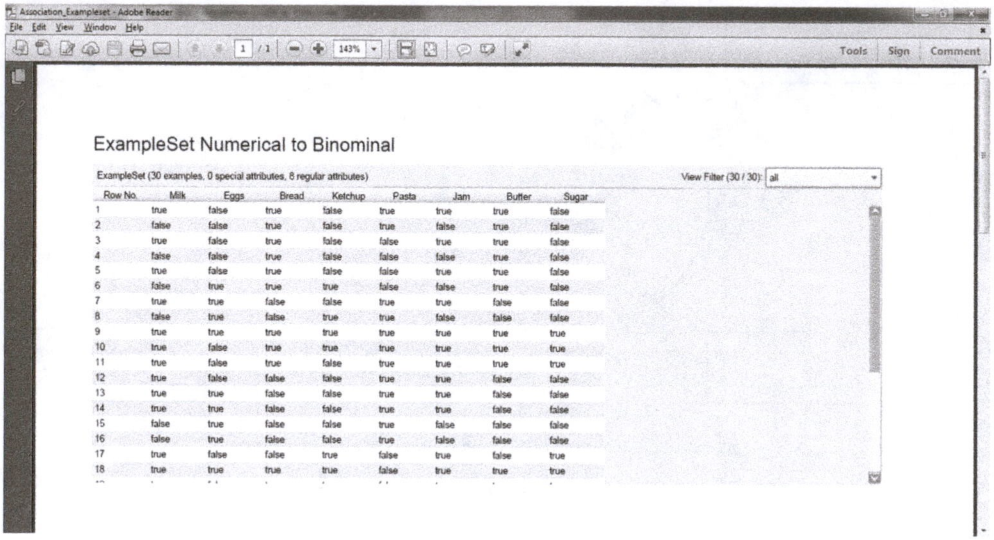

Row No.	Milk	Eggs	Bread	Ketchup	Pasta	Jam	Butter	Sugar
1	true	false	true	false	true	true	true	false
2	false	false	true	false	true	false	true	false
3	true	false	true	false	false	true	true	false
4	false	false	true	false	false	false	true	false
5	true	false	true	false	false	true	true	false
6	false	true	true	true	false	false	true	false
7	true	true	false	false	true	true	false	false
8	false	true	false	true	true	false	false	false
9	true	true	true	true	true	true	true	true
10	true	false	true	true	true	true	true	true
11	true	false	true	false	true	true	true	true
12	true	false	false	false	true	true	false	false
13	true	true	false	false	true	true	false	false
14	true	true	false	false	true	true	false	false
15	false	true	false	false	true	false	false	false
16	false	true	false	false	true	false	false	false
17	true	false	false	true	false	true	false	true
18	true	true	true	true	false	true	true	true

FIGURE 8.12 *Association Rule for Example Set*

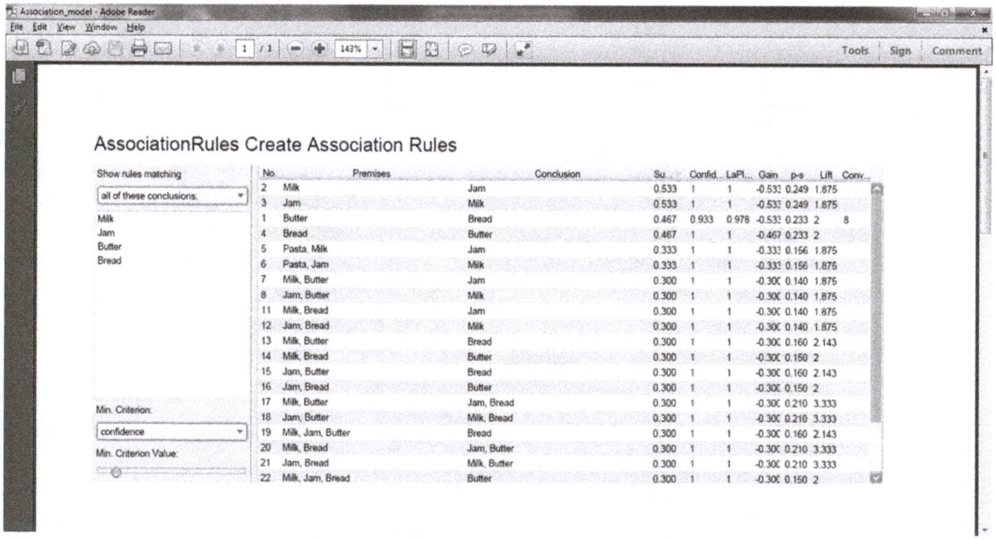

No.	Premises	Conclusion	Su...	Confid...	LaPl...	Gain	p-s	Lift	Conv...
2	Milk	Jam	0.533	1	1	-0.53	0.249	1.875	
3	Jam	Milk	0.533	1	1	-0.53	0.249	1.875	
1	Butter	Bread	0.467	0.933	0.978	-0.53	0.233	2	8
4	Bread	Butter	0.467	1	1	-0.467	0.233	2	
5	Pasta, Milk	Jam	0.333	1	1	-0.33	0.156	1.875	
6	Pasta, Jam	Milk	0.333	1	1	-0.33	0.156	1.875	
7	Milk, Butter	Jam	0.300	1	1	-0.30	0.140	1.875	
8	Jam, Butter	Milk	0.300	1	1	-0.30	0.140	1.875	
11	Milk, Bread	Jam	0.300	1	1	-0.30	0.140	1.875	
12	Jam, Bread	Milk	0.300	1	1	-0.30	0.140	1.875	
13	Milk, Butter	Bread	0.300	1	1	-0.30	0.160	2.143	
14	Milk, Bread	Butter	0.300	1	1	-0.30	0.150	2	
15	Jam, Butter	Bread	0.300	1	1	-0.30	0.160	2.143	
16	Jam, Bread	Butter	0.300	1	1	-0.30	0.150	2	
17	Milk, Butter	Jam, Bread	0.300	1	1	-0.30	0.210	3.333	
18	Jam, Butter	Milk, Bread	0.300	1	1	-0.30	0.210	3.333	
19	Milk, Jam, Butter	Bread	0.300	1	1	-0.30	0.160	2.143	
20	Milk, Bread	Jam, Butter	0.300	1	1	-0.30	0.210	3.333	
21	Jam, Bread	Milk, Butter	0.300	1	1	-0.30	0.210	3.333	
22	Milk, Jam, Bread	Butter	0.300	1	1	-0.30	0.150	2	

DATA MINING METHOD: CLASSIFICATION DECISION TREE

Classification is a Supervised Data Mining method, which is used for prediction in business decision-making. A model is created using historical data and variables of interest. The relationships between the variables are studied for interesting patterns that can identify and predict a common variable of interest. Decision Tree and Logistic Regression are two techniques used in Classification. Decision Tree algorithm is used to classify data into predefined pure classes. It begins with the root node as the starting point with the complete data. Then it splits the data using branches that dissect the data into groups of significant common attributes. The end of the branch is called a leaf node which is a group/class label. If the class can be split further to make it more refined, it continues till all elements of the class are similar.

The authors have used the Iris flower database to demonstrate this algorithm in RapidMiner. This time it is assumed that class labels are predefined in contrary to Clustering where the groups had to be identified. In Figures 8.13 and 8.14 we have used the operator Decision Tree on the Iris data set. Each flower has four attributes in centimetres: sepal length and width, petal length and width. In the 150 sample data set provided in RapidMiner, 'a1' is sepal length, 'a2' is sepal width, 'a3' is petal length and 'a4' is petal width.

| FIGURE 8.13 | *Decision Tree in RapidMiner* |

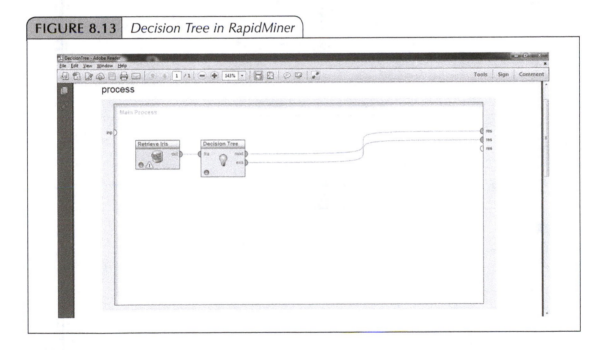

The Decision Tree in Figure 8.15 starts with 'a3' petal length as the root node. It then branches based on 'a4' petal width and 'a3' petal length to create pure classes of the three species of flowers.

DATA MINING METHOD: CLASSIFICATION LOGISTIC REGRESSION ANALYTICS

Logistic Regression (logit) has been explained in detail in the previous chapter. Here, we shall look at its application as a Supervised Classification model. The logit model will require the dependent variable to be categorical that will eventually predict the data sets in either of the classes. The 'petrol pump' data set has been used to build and test the model. It consists of 30

FIGURE 8.14 *Example Set Iris*

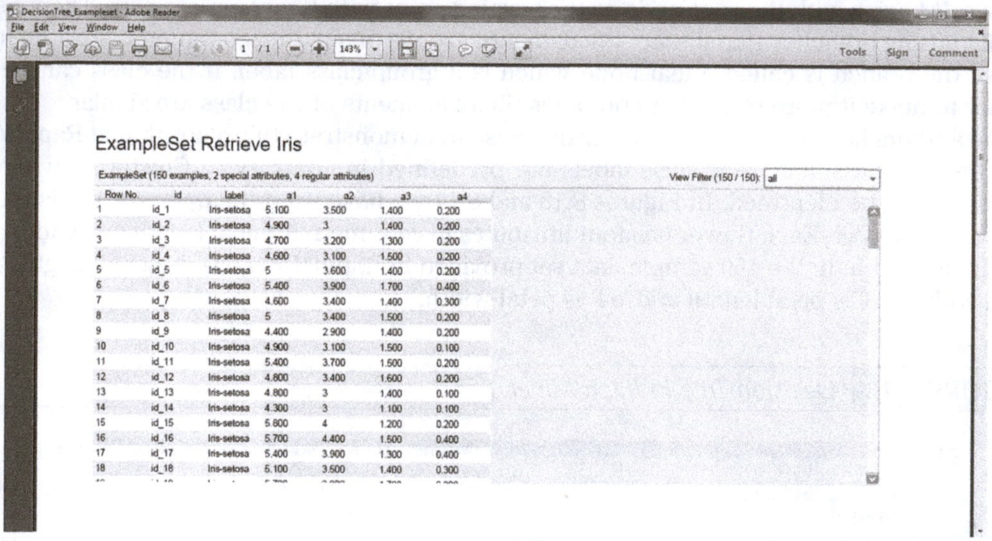

ExampleSet Retrieve Iris

ExampleSet (150 examples, 2 special attributes, 4 regular attributes)

View Filter (150 / 150): all

Row No.	id	label	a1	a2	a3	a4
1	id_1	Iris-setosa	5.100	3.500	1.400	0.200
2	id_2	Iris-setosa	4.900	3	1.400	0.200
3	id_3	Iris-setosa	4.700	3.200	1.300	0.200
4	id_4	Iris-setosa	4.600	3.100	1.500	0.200
5	id_5	Iris-setosa	5	3.600	1.400	0.200
6	id_6	Iris-setosa	5.400	3.900	1.700	0.400
7	id_7	Iris-setosa	4.600	3.400	1.400	0.300
8	id_8	Iris-setosa	5	3.400	1.500	0.200
9	id_9	Iris-setosa	4.400	2.900	1.400	0.200
10	id_10	Iris-setosa	4.900	3.100	1.500	0.100
11	id_11	Iris-setosa	5.400	3.700	1.500	0.200
12	id_12	Iris-setosa	4.800	3.400	1.600	0.200
13	id_13	Iris-setosa	4.800	3	1.400	0.100
14	id_14	Iris-setosa	4.300	3	1.100	0.100
15	id_15	Iris-setosa	5.800	4	1.200	0.200
16	id_16	Iris-setosa	5.700	4.400	1.500	0.400
17	id_17	Iris-setosa	5.400	3.900	1.300	0.400
18	id_18	Iris-setosa	5.100	3.500	1.400	0.300

FIGURE 8.15 *Decision Tree Output in RapidMiner*

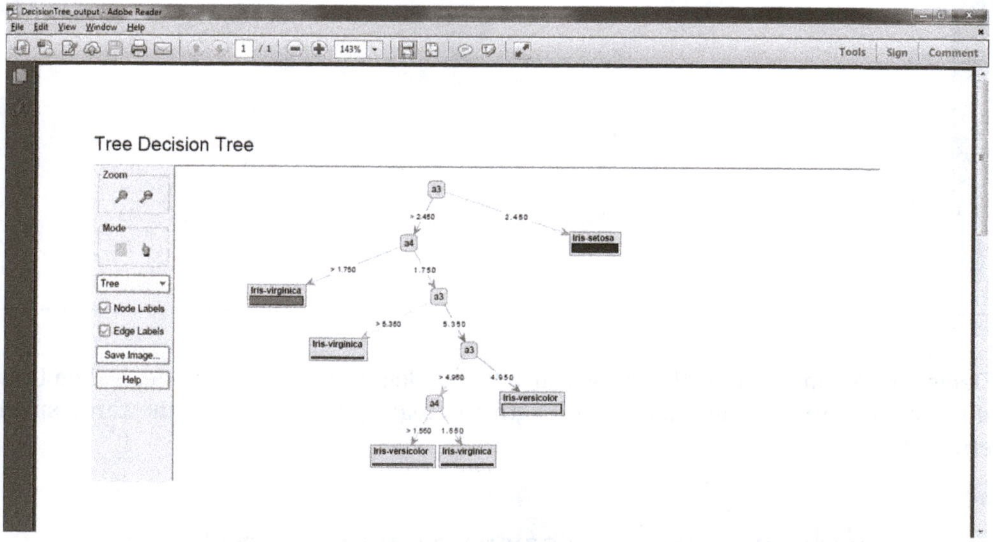

samples of customers at a petrol pump who were asked a few questions on their experience at the petrol pump. The survey also captured if the customer was a new customer or repeat (has visited previously) customer. RapidMiner operators have been used to create the model as seen in Figure 8.16.

FIGURE 8.16 *Logit in RapidMiner*

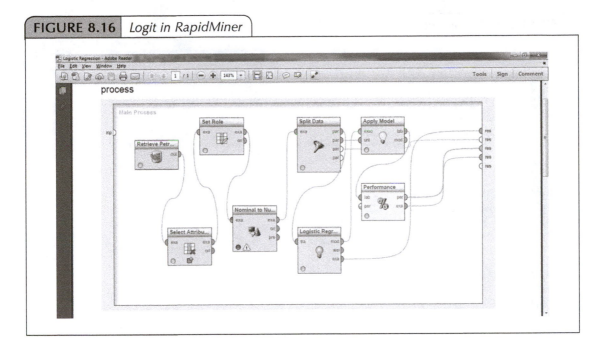

The 30 sample data has been split into 70 per cent being the training set data (21 instances) and 30 per cent being the holdout sample as shown in the Figures 8.17 and 8.18. As we can observe, the holdout sample has predicted eight out of the nine instances correctly.

FIGURE 8.17 *Training Data Set for Logit*

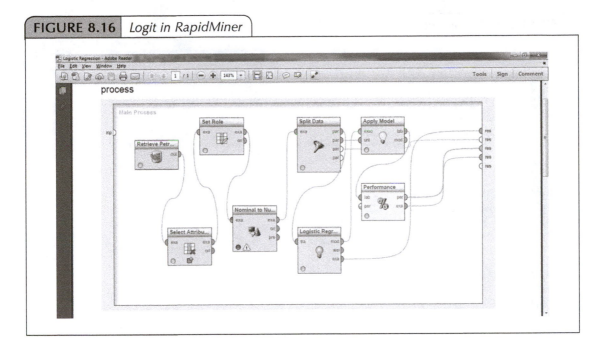

| FIGURE 8.18 | *Holdout Sample for Logit* |

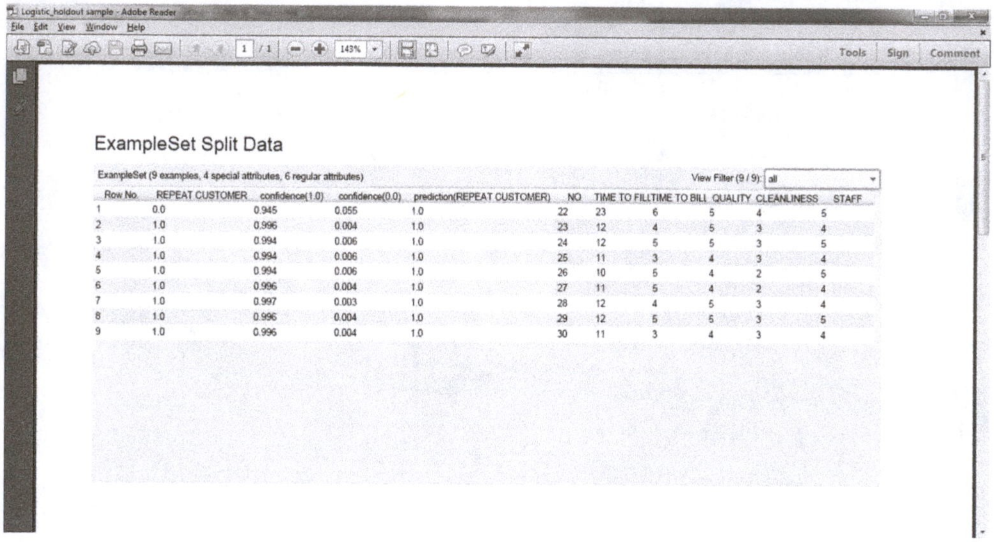

ExampleSet Split Data

ExampleSet (9 examples, 4 special attributes, 6 regular attributes)   View Filter (9 / 9): all

Row No.	REPEAT CUSTOMER	confidence(1.0)	confidence(0.0)	prediction(REPEAT CUSTOMER)	NO	TIME TO FILL	TIME TO BILL	QUALITY	CLEANLINESS	STAFF
1	0.0	0.945	0.055	1.0	22	23	6	5	4	5
2	1.0	0.996	0.004	1.0	23	12	4	5	3	4
3	1.0	0.994	0.006	1.0	24	12	5	5	3	5
4	1.0	0.994	0.006	1.0	25	11	3	4	3	4
5	1.0	0.994	0.006	1.0	26	10	5	4	2	5
6	1.0	0.996	0.004	1.0	27	11	5	4	2	4
7	1.0	0.997	0.003	1.0	28	12	4	5	3	4
8	1.0	0.996	0.004	1.0	29	12	5	5	3	5
9	1.0	0.996	0.004	1.0	30	11	3	4	3	4

The classification matrix in Figure 8.19 indicates 88.89 per cent accuracy of the model, where eight instances are predicted correctly, whereas one instance is wrongly predicted. The example has two classes: a repeat customer is indicated as 1 and a new customer as 0. The diagonal from upper left to lower right indicates correct predictions. A repeat customer has been predicted by the model as 1 in 88.89 per cent of cases.

| FIGURE 8.19 | *Classification Matrix for Example Set* |

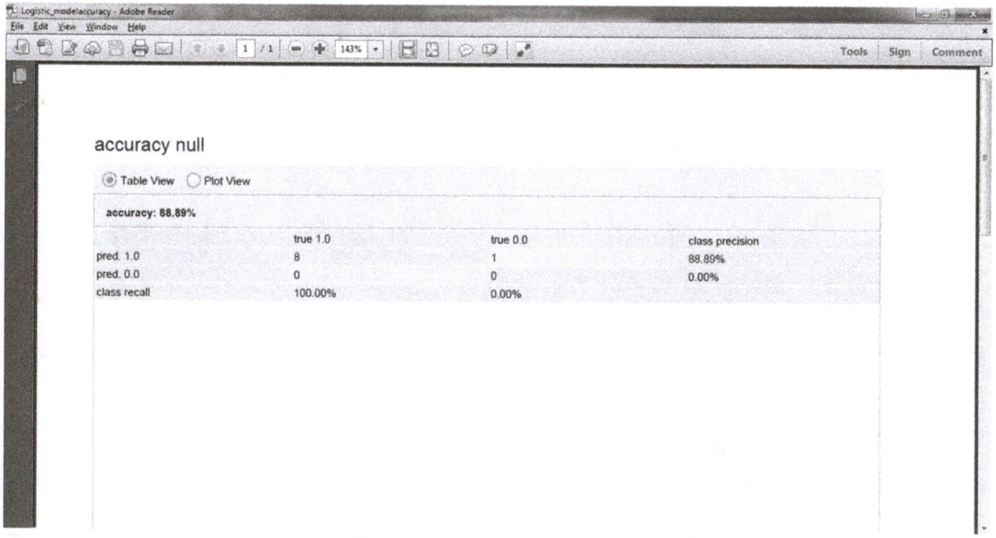

accuracy null

○ Table View   ○ Plot View

accuracy: 88.89%

	true 1.0	true 0.0	class precision
pred. 1.0	8	1	88.89%
pred. 0.0	0	0	0.00%
class recall	100.00%	0.00%	

Accuracy% = correctly predicted instances (both positive and negative) / total instances in holdout sample × 100 = 8/9 × 100 = 88.89%.

The Accuracy percentage is an indication of the strength of the trained classifier model in predicting real-life data. Hence this value should be high.

DATA MINING METHOD: PREDICTION—LINEAR REGRESSION

Linear Regression has been discussed in detail in Chapter 6. Here we shall work to create a trained Linear Regression model using RapidMiner that can be used to predict future outcomes. The Employee data set has 11 variables and 474 instances. The variables are the Employee ID, Gender, Birthdate, Education in years, Job category, Salary when research was conducted, Salary when they joined the company, Number of months they are with the current organization, Previous work experience and if they are in the minority category. A column has been added that calculates the difference in the salary from the time they joined the organization called 'Difference'. The model will use this numerical variable as the dependent variable. The other variables will be fed into the model to identify what drove higher raise in salary.

The operators used in the model are shown in Figure 8.20. The Set Role operator is used to define Difference as the dependent variable. There are several categorical variables among the independent variables. The operator Nominal to Numerical is used to dummy code the categorical variables.

The Split Data operator has been used to split the data into 70% (332 instances) training data set and 30% (142 instances) as holdout sample for testing the model. Figure 8.21 indicates the predicted value of the dependent variable in the holdout sample data.

| FIGURE 8.20 | *Linear Regression in RapidMiner* |

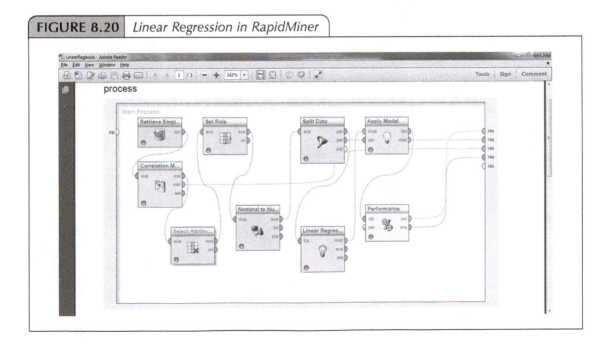

FIGURE 8.21 *Training Data Set for Linear Regression*

ExampleSet Split Data

ExampleSet (142 examples, 2 special attributes, 10 regular attributes)   View Filter (142 / 142): all

Row No.	Difference	prediction(Differe...	Gender_m	Gender_f	Job Catego...	Job Catego...	Job Catego...	ID	Education i...	Job time (m...	Previous ex...	Minority
1	19050	14002.500	0	1	0	1	0	333	15	75	5	0
2	13500	7961.138	0	1	0	1	0	334	12	75	32	1
3	16200	9582.667	1	0	0	0	1	335	8	74	408	0
4	26010	29940.819	1	0	1	0	0	336	16	74	45	0
5	14550	10397.910	0	1	0	1	0	337	12	74	2	0
6	5700	5952.354	0	1	0	1	0	338	8	74	43	0
7	13050	1100.568	0	1	0	1	0	339	8	74	281	0
8	9300	398.952	0	1	0	1	0	340	8	74	318	0
9	25650	19103.979	1	0	1	0	0	341	12	74	272	1
10	10200	5634.963	0	1	0	1	0	342	12	74	117	1
11	43500	27039.336	1	0	1	0	0	343	16	73	150	0
12	19200	11412.121	1	0	0	1	0	344	12	73	72	0
13	5700	9623.534	0	1	0	1	0	345	12	73	7	0
14	9000	12122.178	0	1	0	1	0	346	15	73	22	0
15	11100	5185.103	0	1	0	1	0	347	12	73	228	0
16	26750	26946.464	0	1	1	0	0	348	16	73	15	0
17	16350	6851.283	0	1	0	1	0	349	17	73	375	0

The output from the correlation matrix shows the strength of the relation between respective variables (Figure 8.22). The meaningful positive correlation is between the Salary Raise and Education where we see a 58.8% correlation.

FIGURE 8.22 *Correlation Matrix*

Correlation Matrix Correlation Matrix

Attributes	ID	Gender	Birth date	Education i...	Job Category	Salary in ye...	Beginning s...	Difference	Job time (m...	Previous ex...	Minority
ID	1	0.079	0.054	-0.057	0.006	-0.096	0.008	-0.157	-0.998	-0.003	-0.032
Gender	0.079	1	-0.051	-0.356	0.144	-0.450	-0.457	-0.378	-0.066	-0.165	-0.076
Birth date	0.054	-0.051	1	0.281	-0.223	0.144	0.009	0.220	-0.053	-0.802	-0.111
Education in years	-0.057	-0.356	0.281	1	-0.633	0.661	0.633	0.582	0.047	-0.252	-0.133
Job Category	0.006	0.144	-0.223	-0.633	1	-0.680	-0.667	-0.588	0.004	0.301	0.234
Salary in year 1995	-0.096	-0.450	0.144	0.661	-0.680	1	0.880	0.938	0.084	-0.097	-0.177
Beginning salary	0.008	-0.457	0.009	0.633	-0.667	0.880	1	0.662	-0.020	0.045	-0.158
Difference	-0.157	-0.378	0.220	0.582	-0.588	0.938	0.662	1	0.147	-0.187	-0.165
Job time (months)	-0.998	-0.066	-0.053	0.047	0.004	0.084	-0.020	0.147	1	0.003	0.050
Previous experience (months)	-0.003	-0.165	-0.802	-0.252	0.301	-0.097	0.045	-0.187	0.003	1	0.145
Minority	-0.032	-0.076	-0.111	-0.133	0.234	-0.177	-0.158	-0.165	0.050	0.145	1

| FIGURE 8.23 | *Regression Output in RapidMiner* |

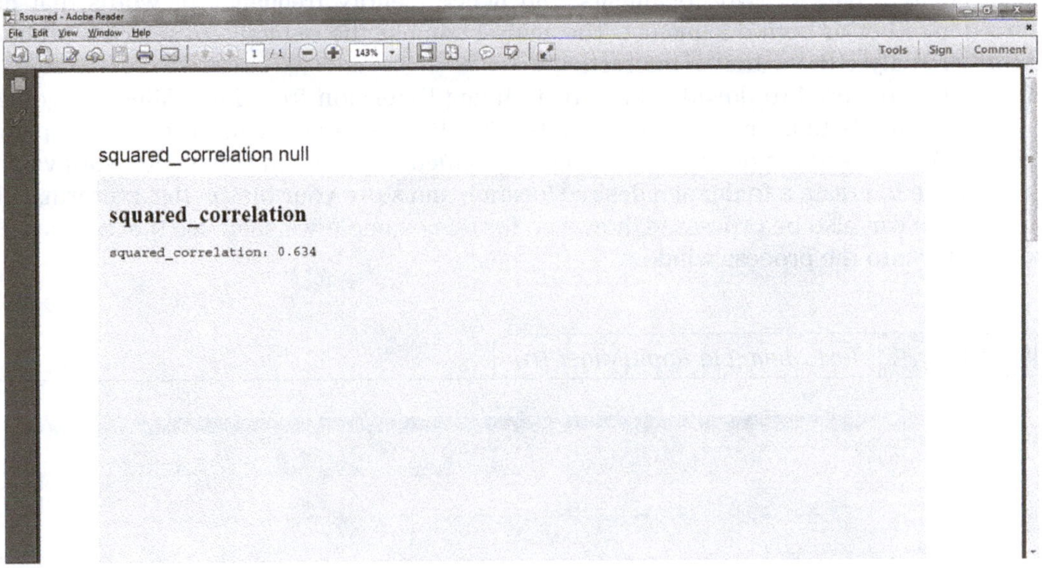

The output of the Linear Regression model is shown in Figure 8.23.

The significant variables of interest with very low p values are the Education in years and Previous experience which have a positive impact on Salary Raise. The R^2 value of the model is 63.4 per cent indicating that 63.4 per cent of the change in Salary Raise can be explained by the independent variables.

DATA MINING METHOD: TEXT ANALYTICS

The data mining methods described so far have all dealt with structured data. However, there is almost 80% company data that exists in unstructured form. Big data and sophisticated data capture systems have collected and retained huge volumes of data in varied forms in organizations, for example, reports, customer reviews, employee feedbacks, machinery description, project reports and reviews, complaints handling, error image logs and such others. Text mining is the process of extracting useful patterns from such unstructured data resources. Natural Language Processing is used for creating the Text Mining model. An interesting aspect of Text Mining is to study sentiments within the outcome by classifying it as positive and negative sentiments. This has been used widely in research and business decision-making. For instance, owners of a car model can be asked to write a paragraph on their experience about using the car. These can be documented in the form of text files. These files can then be analysed using text mining to identify favourable and unfavourable responses. The model is the medium to identify the sentiments, however it is up to the analyst to make the outcome more pure to align with the BP on hand.

The following example demonstrates a Text Mining example using RapidMiner. The documents describe the causes of poverty[2] in India. RapidMiner operators have been used to read the textual data in two documents, and hence identify frequency of words that have occurred in either or both documents. The analyst can use the outcome to selectively choose and further analyse the words of interest.

You will be required to download the Text Mining Extension from RapidMiner by going to the Help menu. Details are in Appendix D. The Process document from Files operator (Figure 8.24) will read the documents from the specified file location and create word vectors. It is advisable to create a folder at a desired location and store your files in the .txt form. Other forms of files can also be processed, however, for this example we shall use the .txt files. Pull this operator into the process window.

FIGURE 8.24 | *Text Mining in RapidMiner (A)*

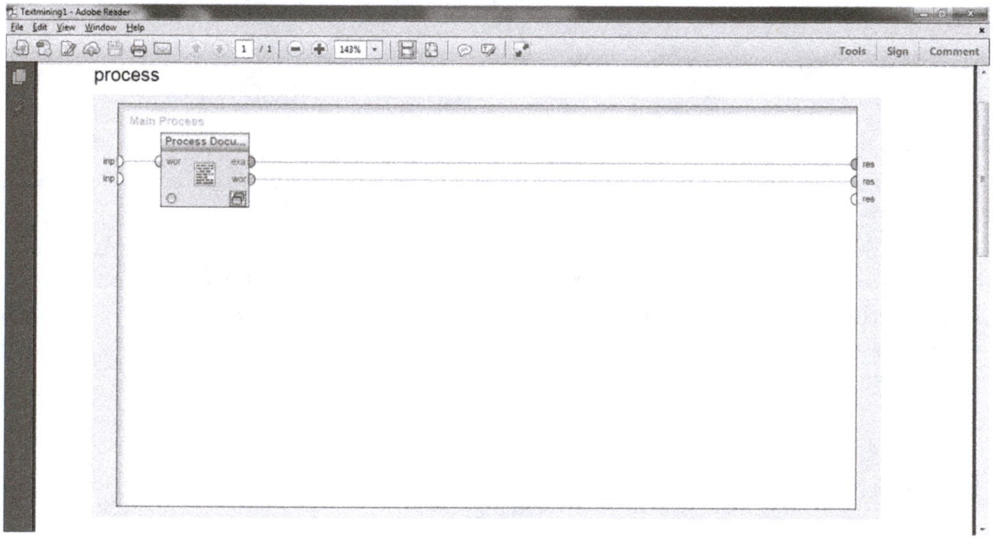

On double clicking the operator, another process window opens (Figure 8.25) where you are required to add the text mining operators. The tokenize operator splits the document text into a sequence of tokens. The Transform Cases operator transforms all the letters of the documents into either lower or upper case as specified. The Filter Stop Words operator removes all commonly occurring words in English such as 'the', 'a' and 'an'. The Generate n-Grams operator creates bundle of frequently occurring tokens. The Filter tokens operator retains token of pre-specified minimum and maximum lengths only. These thus create a clean repository of frequently occurring words in the document.

---

[2] https://learn.culturalindia.net/essay-poverty-india-causes-effects-solutions.html

FIGURE 8.25	*Text Mining in RapidMiner (B)*

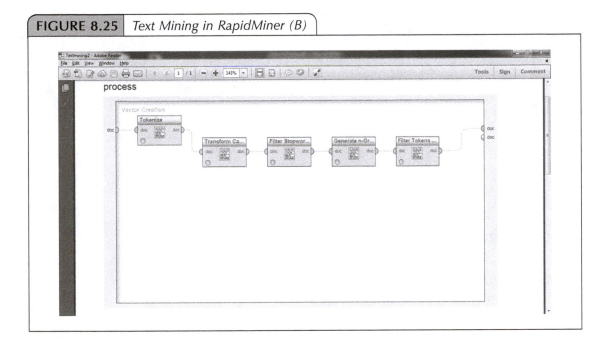

Break points can be out on operators to see interim results. For instance, if you wish to see the tokenized document, insert a breakpoint after the operator executes. Figure 8.26 shows the tokenized outcome in upper pane and the actual document in the lower pane.

FIGURE 8.26	*Tokenized Document*

| FIGURE 8.27 | Text Mining Output in RapidMiner |

WordList Process Documents from Files

Word	Attribute Name	Total Occurences	Document Occurences	PovertyIndia
poverty	poverty	76	2	76
country	country	31	1	31
lack	lack	28	1	28
poor	poor	28	1	28
income	income	27	1	27
india	india	24	2	24
people	people	20	1	20
economy	economy	19	1	19
education	education	19	1	19
population	population	18	1	18
health	health	17	1	17
economic	economic	16	1	16
society	society	16	1	16
children	children	14	1	14
family	family	14	1	14
families	families	12	1	12
government	government	12	1	12
labour	labour	12	1	12
social	social	12	1	12
effects	effects	10	1	10

We can infer from the outcome (Figure 8.27) that the word poverty has occurred 76 times in two documents, whereas country has occurred 31 times in 1 document. Related to poverty, frequently occurring words of interest for the decision-maker could be people, income, education, health and so on.

Search Engine Optimization

SEO has become a topic of discussion in the industry corridors since the time companies started operating online retail stores along with brick and mortar presence followed by companies that offered buying completely online. SEO captures what customers search for based on keywords of the site, the time spent on each page and so on number of visits. It also includes optimizing the site to show up at the top during display of search results by the search engines like Google. Appearing in more searches means the possibility of a visit resulting into a sale of product on the website. Higher level of analytics are performed based on metrics captured for consumer search behaviour. Several online sites such as stattools.com, statvoo. com, informer.com and similarityweb.com have used website usage metrics information and have analysed it using SEO tools and statistical methods.

Text and Web Analytics

A huge amount of data exists in an unstructured form on the Internet. Websites have been created with a large amount of textual content. There are opinion and discussion sites containing text in threads of continuous conversations. Blogs and personal homepages generate unstructured data. Retail sites contain unstructured information such as the textual data of the website content, customer buying habits, queries and complaints, social media posts and research reports. Analysts have developed ways of mining this rich source of data for developing insights that can be useful for business growth and profitability. Sentiments that are expressed by stakeholders are a rich source of information, if analysed can generate interesting business insights. Statistical methods like web and text analytics for evaluating web and textual content on the websites have become important in analysing unstructured data. Sentiment analysis also known as opinion mining forms an important component of industry requirement where opinion expressed by individual in textual content is analysed using natural language processing for subjective responses. Opinions are identified and categorized for positive or negative sentiments expressed by the respondents.

Text mining/analytics, also known as text data mining or knowledge discovery in textual databases, is the semi-automated process of extracting patterns (useful information and knowledge) from large amount of unstructured data sources. Text mining is the same as data mining in that it has the same purpose and uses the same processes, but with text mining, the input to the process is a collection of unstructured (or less structured) data files such as Word documents, PDF files, text excerpts and XML files. In essence, text mining can be thought of as a process (with two main steps) that starts with imposing structure to the text-based data sources followed by extracting relevant information and knowledge from this structured text-based data using data mining techniques and tools.

The World Wide Web is perhaps the world's largest data and text repository, and the amount of information on the web is growing rapidly every day. A lot of interesting information can be found online: whose homepage is linked to which other pages, how many people have links to a specific web page and how a particular site is organized. In addition, each visitor to a website, each search on a search engine, each click on a link and each transaction on an e-commerce site creates additional data. Although unstructured textual data in the form of web pages coded in HTML or XML are the dominant content of the web, the web infrastructure also contains hyperlink information (connections to other web pages) and usage information (logs of visitors' interactions with websites), all of which provide rich data for knowledge discovery. Analysis of this information can help us make better use of websites and also aid us in enhancing relationships and providing value to the visitors of our own websites. Web mining (or web data mining) is the process of discovering intrinsic relationships (i.e., interesting and useful information) from web data, which are expressed in the form of textual, linkage or usage information.[3]

REAL ANALYTICS: TEXT AND WEB ANALYTICS IN ONLINE GROCERY

With a growing number of e-tailers providing an online platform for grocery shopping, competition has entered the online grocery shopping market in India. Research and academic discussion forums debate competitive strategies for their growth and survival. Some of the common attributes of measuring online presence in a competitive market include the bouquet of product categories offered, the ability to service PAN India, competitive pricing, on-time delivery of products and services, discounts offered through deals and coupons, maintaining quality, managing suppliers and handling consumer complaints effectively. While the content displayed on the website is important along with the look and feel, easy loading of pages, quick navigation

---

[3] E. Turban, R. Sharda, D. Delen, and D. King, *Business Intelligence: A Managerial Approach*, 2nd ed. (Pearson, 2011).

between web page links, appearing in searches, referrals from other websites and a desirable revenue model, equally important is to maintain the optimum products in the inventory, on time-delivery, cashback options, deals and discounts, payment options and handling customer queries and complaints. All of these activities generate a huge amount of data that are structured as well as unstructured in nature. Some of the data is consciously captured by the organizations which are used by their Analytics teams to do descriptive and predictive analysis and devise competitive strategies and metrics for measurement of their success online. A case on Online Grocery stores written by the authors is provided in Appendix B.

REVIEW QUESTIONS

1. What is the relationship between Data Mining and Machine Learning?
2. State the two major types of Machine Learning methods.
3. What is Association technique? Where can it be useful in business?
4. What is Clustering technique? How is it different from the Classification technique?
5. What is text mining? How is it relevant in business?

CASE 8.1
Switching Cell Phones: A Gender- and Age-related Analysis at Panacea (Case Complexity: Easy)

A large retail store chain in India, Panacea, caters to electronic items and household electrical goods. Necessity being the mother of invention, it has in its 10 years of existence found ways and means to innovate providing joy to customers. One of the fast-moving goods is the cell phone category. Cell phones have touched the hearts of many creating an everlasting emotional bond with the owner. Rajesh Prasad and Tina Bansal were recent recruits at one of the Panacea stores in Noida. They had both studied together during their BBA undergraduate programme and were very good friends. What brought them closer was their fascination for cell phones. Tina admired the look and feel, the features and the brand ambassadors associated with the phones, and hence curiously observe the kind of user group that would own the mobile. Rajesh was analytical by nature and his passion drove him to compare price versus technical features of a phone and the affordability for consumer purchase. Both have spent, as part of their hobby, numerable hours comparing cell phones of varied brands from different cell phone manufacturers.

This passion and love for cell phones led to Rajesh and Tina getting hired at Panacea. They were part of the team that managed the store outlet display of cell phones. Their team manager Gaurang Maiti had explained the new recruits about their job profiles, and hence how it fits into the overall performance of their team. Gaurang heads a team of six members who have primarily managed the section of the store where cell phones are kept on display for prospective buyers to inspect and hence make a decision to purchase. Training is provided from time to time to the members on features of the cell phones and communication skills to be able to professionally explain the features as well as answer queries of prospective customers. Rajesh and Tina performed very well in the first six months thus winning the confidence of Gaurang. They further suggested to Gaurang that cell phones have become easily substitutable items, thus fall under the category of FMCG.

Switching cell phones has become a common trend among young adults. Rajesh observed that the urge to switch a cell phone device differed by age group. The age group beyond 50 years had less inclination of proactively switching a device and preferred to continue until it broke. With senior citizens, the requirement was limited to providing them the ease of reaching a person or service when necessary. Tina observed on job that men and women of same age group have very different uses of a cell phone device. During her conversations with prospective customers, she had learnt a lot about the preference criteria considerations of men and women during purchase of a cell phone. Customers had declined a purchase due to criteria such as colour, weight, perceived complicated features and even the emotional bond they share with their current mobile phone. While at times a purchase was made without much discussion, just by holding a new device for the first time. Price of a device has been a secondary criterion during those times. Tina sighed… such are the varying emotions during purchase of this device. Data on all of these parameters is regularly captured by the team working under Gaurang but nothing much has been done with it. Tina along with Rajesh decided to conduct a research study to understand the purchase pattern by age and gender that would assist their team in better understanding their prospective customers leading to additional sales. What kind of data mining techniques can they use to derive at some conclusions?

Exercise

Prepare a research matrix that will help Tina and Rajesh to carry out this research project using data mining methods. Further, refer to the data provided to you. Perform *k*-means Clustering using RapidMiner.

CASE 8.2
Infant Mortality Rate versus Income[4] (Case Complexity: Medium)

Research Sadhana team took up the study of understanding the change in infant mortality rate across the world in different countries. As declared by UNICEF, infant mortality rate is the probability that a child born in a specific year will die before reaching the age of one, if subject to current age-specific mortality rates. It is expressed as a rate per 1,000 live births. From available sources, they studied data of about 250 countries. Death in children is caused due to several reasons: malnutrition, weak health of mother, unhealthy conditions after birth, birth defects, post-birth infections and so on. A lot has been done to protect the child and the mother during and after birth so that both lead a healthy life. This has led to reducing the infant mortality rate across the globe.

One of the huge contributors towards this change is the increase in income level per person. Research Sadhana team also acquired global income level per person data with projection from relevant data sources. This includes gross domestic product per capita by purchasing power parities (in international dollars, fixed 2005 prices). The indicative numbers have taken into account the inflation and differences in the cost of living between countries. Cross-country data for 2005 is mainly based on the 2005 round of the International

---

[4] Taken from Source of data Gapminder.com

Comparison Program. Estimates based on other sources were used for the other countries. Real growth rates were linked to the 2005 levels.

Exercise

Use supervised technique Linear Regression RapidMiner to mine data and analyse data from the 2 datasets. Hence, state the effect of income on infant mortality rate. Perform classification using Logistic regression and Decision tree. Explain your outcome.

CASE 8.3
What Drives Popularity among School-going Kids?
(Case Complexity: High)

A research study was conducted to find out how school-going kids interact with their peers while they are at school. The study included various aspects such as demographic information—gender, race, age—school they belonged to, financial status and the district they belonged to—urban, suburban or rural. It also asked questions to understand what defined 'being popular' in school out of the four attributes: getting good grades, being handsome or pretty, good in sports, being rich. The sample consisted of 478 students from Grade 4 to 6. Data was collected using a structured questionnaire. The demographic data collected was categorical in nature. The section on gauging popularity was numerical data measured on a scale of 1–4, where 1 is most important and 4 is least important. (Note: during inference keep the direction of the scale in mind).[5]

The attributes' definitions are as follows:

1. Gender: Boy, girl
2. Grade: 4, 5, 6
3. Age: 7, 9, 10, 11, 12, 13
4. Race: Other, white
5. Urban/rural: Urban, suburban, rural
6. School: 9 options
7. Popularity (scale of 1–4)
   a. Grades: 1, 2, 3, 4
   b. Good in sports: 1, 2, 3, 4
   c. Handsome/pretty: 1, 2, 3, 4
   d. Being rich: 1, 2, 3, 4

Exercise

Download the data from the student download section. Perform Decision Tree and Linear Regression using RapidMiner. State your analysis.

---

[5] Taken from data source: this data set of 478 instances was obtained from http://lib.stat.cmu.edu/DASL/Datafiles/PopularKids.html

Interpreting the Statistical Outcomes

Learning Objectives

After completing this chapter, students should be able to understand about the following:

- Need for developing skill to understand the statistical outcome
- Data visualization methods
- Capability mix for BA

Opening Example

Jewellery Company Uses Augmented Reality in Retail Stores[1]

At PC Jewellers, a reputed jewellery brand in India, customers can try out jewellery using the iPad with the StyleDotMe's MirrAR platform. This is an Augmented Reality (AR) application in the jewellery market, where the entire catalogue of earrings can be the 'AR experience' of the customer contemplating the purchase of an earring. Artificial Intelligence uses the images produced by a computer and superimposes it on real-world objects. The MirrAR platform identifies customer's face from the camera and then matches earrings such that it appears that the customer is wearing them. Thus, the customer is able to try and test the earring in real time without the actual presence of the jewellery. In order to browse through a catalogue of thousands of designs, the customer needs to look at the iPad which acts as 'Smart Mirror'. It works with a variable that does face mapping and maps skin tone of customers, approximate age, time spent on each item and her mood to gauge reaction to a particular design. Based on these variables, it recommends the designs that may cater to her taste, and hence may be inclined towards purchasing. The customer can try the jewellery virtually by clicking on the ornament. This reduces the amount of inventory required to be managed at the stores and also leads to customers making faster decision on purchases. This also helps them generate a lot of structured and unstructured data to use BA for determining variations in customer preferences by region and predict new trends in fashion.

---

[1] https://www.financialexpress.com/industry/technology/tech-in-the-showroom-augmented-reality-adds-sparkle-at-jewellery-stores/1281820/

NEED FOR DEVELOPING SKILL TO UNDERSTAND THE STATISTICAL OUTCOME

As students of a business school and management professionals of the future, it is important to understand why statistical investigations are conducted in research, and hence be able to judiciously make meaning of the underlying outcomes from data-enriched processes. What creates value is to be able to link the business objectives to a particular outcome such that it makes meaning for your client or customer. We see in the opening example of PC Jewellers that the variables make all the difference in managing lower inventory and increasing sales. Algorithms and statistical methods shall link the variables to provide outcomes to the analyst. Gauging the value of the outcomes for use in business is a skill that the analysts and decision science professionals develop over time. To be able to put it in the language that the end user/client would be able to appreciate and value for use in business raises instant gratitude and appreciation. For this, as business school students, you need to be adept at reading a statistical outcome and be able to create a story to describe how it would meet an objective for the client. Future roles of business executives for many of you may not require you to operate any statistical tool, technique or develop an algorithm in your professional career. However, one who understands the basics of these to apply in the business domain is a sought-after resource in the industry. Be able to clearly understand and reason with a statistical outcome. Sieve out what is important from the several possibilities spun out from the Analytics model.

Ruby, Minal and Sanjana are three friends studying at a business school (Figure 9.1). They had decided to gift themselves a cell phone during the Deepavali festival. What variable categories will decide their purchase of a cell phone? You have probably already started counting them on your finger. Budget, need, usage, demographics, life style and status would be the major categories. Under each category there would be multiple variables. Suppose a research study is conducted to study the purchase intent of a cell phone of girls similar to Ruby, Minal and Sanjana. The outcome indicates that the significant variables are cash money available on hand (under budget), communicating with friends and family (under need), hours of daily study (under life style) and hours of sleep (under life style). The robust Analytics model has done a good analysis of using the sample data to provide the significant variables that impact the intent of purchasing cell phone by customers like Ruby, Minal and Sanjana. Of the four variables in the outcome, the analyst now has to decide what to keep and what to discard based on what is relevant to address the business objective. It is evident that the first two—cash money available on

FIGURE 9.1 | *Three Friends*

Source: Image taken from MS Word clipart.

hand (under budget) and communicating with friends and family (under need)—can be considered as impacting variables. The question is about the other two: hours of daily study (under life style) and hours of sleep (under life style), where a direct conclusion cannot be made. Role of the analyst is significant in being able to make this decision. At this point, the analyst may feel that the latter two variables are non-essential. However, he/she cannot completely discard the finding. The analyst will create a storyboard to communicate the outcome. Data visualization plays an important role in communicating to the end user the relevant and probably irrelevant impact of outcomes on the business objective. Through the use of graphical methods, outcomes can be represented in many forms for quick decision-making by the clients.

DATA VISUALIZATION METHODS

Visualization has been an important component of data analytics. Irrespective of the size of data, if sophisticated analysis can be done quickly and results presented in ways that showcase patterns and allow querying and exploration, theory has said people across all levels in your organization can make faster and more effective decisions. Two friends Tarun and Varun work for the same organization. They have worked with the same boss for many years. Varun walks into Tarun's office and tells him that the boss is again grumpy this morning. Tarun rolls his eyes and knows exactly what Varun is saying.... Grumpy defined by attributes such as short communication, no eye contact, stiff chin and no smile on the face.

Let us look at some everyday examples before we get into specifics. Let us think of a situation. Two girls are good friends in college. One tells the other, hey there is a beautiful girl who has joined our college. The first has seen the girl, the second has not. The second girl would tend to imagine the beauty of the girl (Figure 9.2). Depending on what she believes as the attributes of beauty, she might visualize her looks accordingly. Each person has a definition of beauty that is based on a set of attributes linked together. As the proverb goes 'beauty is in the eyes of the beholder' meaning what one individual may find beautiful may not appeal to someone else. It will vary from person to person based on what defines beautiful for them.

The other day my friend said that the food at the multi-cuisine restaurant in the neighbourhood is awesome. What is the definition of 'awesome'? In my mind, I would visualize the platter the way I enjoy it most in any multi-cuisine restaurant. It could be any of the four possibilities shown in Figure 9.3 or a

FIGURE 9.2 | *Varying Imagination*

Source: creamstime.com

FIGURE 9.3 *Food Platter*

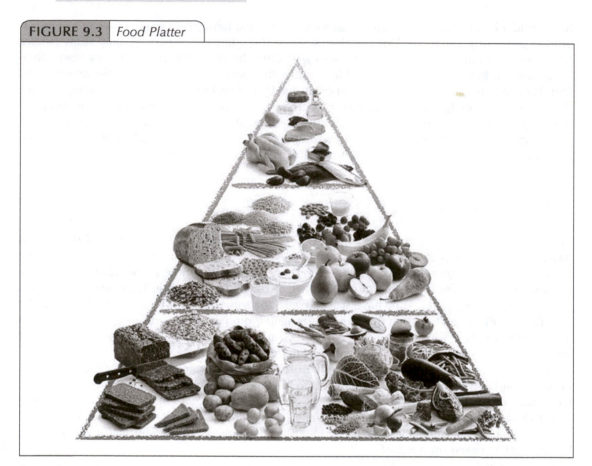

Source: Image taken from MS Word clipart.

combination of them or maybe something entirely different. I can agree with my friend only when I actually try it out and validate it.

Ramesh Thakar is planning a family vacation in summer which would be an 'ideal' beach vacation. He will probably do all his bookings via a travel agent for getting a comprehensive package. He will also do his independent research by collecting information from his friends, relatives, associates, colleagues and also perform research on the internet. Customer reviews that are publicly available on several websites will be particularly helpful. He will also surf through the net for pictures of locations and hotel accommodation. Putting all of the information together, he will plan his vacation.

In all the above three cases we are dealing with multiple variables, building a hypothesis and then validating it by establishing relationships between these variables. It is a part of everyday decision-making. Many of the words in Data Analytics and Research have come from everyday life. Words like 'attributes/variables' that form the basis of data analytics and the word 'hypothesis', that is, the gut feel that gets validated by systematically measuring the attributes are part of normal English conversation. Mining clean data from among the complex data repositories and using visualization methods have aided better decision-making.

The point that the authors are trying to make is that there are three stages of using visualization for decision-making with data.

Exploratory: Looking at introducing other methods of payment as the competitor did so.
Descriptive diagnostic mode: Sales data, product faults
Predictive: What will be the consequences if I offer a promotion or install air conditioners in my residence?

The pictorial representation is particularly useful in such cases, especially when you are trying to find relationships from hundreds and thousands of variables to determine their relative importance.

Additionally, in all the above three examples, we see that individual's personal experience, advise from an expert, secondary research to gather relevant information as per the need of research work to be carried out and data analytics using current and historical data assist in the visualization process (Figure 9.4). The efforts thus lead to reducing ambiguity, and hence effective business decision-making.

If an analyst is working with massive amounts of data, a common challenge is the representation of the results of data exploration and analysis in a way that is not overwhelming. The analyst may need a new way of looking at data—one that collapses and condenses the results in an easily understood form with the help of graphs and charts that decision-makers are adept at using for graphical forms of representation.

Where is it relevant in data analytics?

1. **To complement the business objectives:** Plan and organize what needs to be visualized
   a. Simplify and communicate information in graphical form
   b. Relevance to the domain and context
   c. Balance between aesthetic form and function
   d. Ability of end user to comprehend the outcome
2. **Manage complexity of the data:** Evaluate size, type, frequency of capture, processing parameters, infrastructure support, expertise, cost
   a. Nominal, ordinal, numerical, text (data types)
   b. Similarity, difference, order, proportion, grouping, trend (need for visualization)
   c. Points, lines, trees, networks, maps, grids, areas, dashboards (visualization methods)

The authors shall refer to these with the help of some simple examples for clarity in understanding.

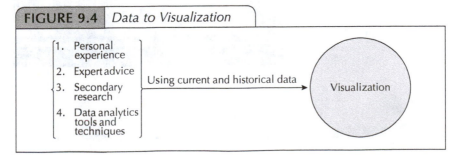

FIGURE 9.4 *Data to Visualization*

Case of One-Sample Analysis and Interpretation

A survey agency conducted a research to ascertain the time spent on social media by working executives per day either using laptop, desktop or mobile devices. The company assumed that the average time spent was 100 minutes. A sample size of 50 customers was randomly taken to check the same.

What is the best way to understand the spread of the sample data? A histogram would be a good representation of the data. It is a graphical way of representing the frequency distribution of the data categories. A normal distribution line can be superimposed if the data is numerical such that it represents the skewness of the distribution. Figure 9.5 representing Excel output represents the histogram with a positive right hand skew.

Do we need a t test? What would it represent? It would allow the test for rejecting or accepting the null hypothesis. In this example, the null hypothesis would be as follows: the average time spent on social media by working executives per day is 100 minutes.

The t test result from SPSS in Figure 9.6 shows that the p value is higher than 0.05, so at 95 per cent confidence interval the null hypothesis cannot be rejected. What else would the analyst be interested in finding? Are there outliers? What is the sample mean?

A box plot would be a good representation of the sample data to identify outliers.

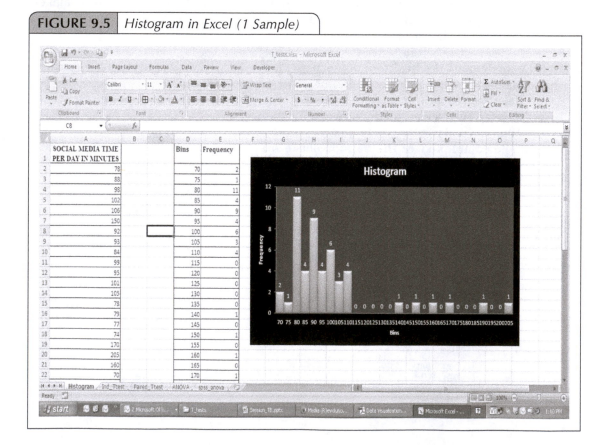

FIGURE 9.5   *Histogram in Excel (1 Sample)*

| FIGURE 9.6 | *Result Obtained from t-Test in Excel (1 Sample)* |

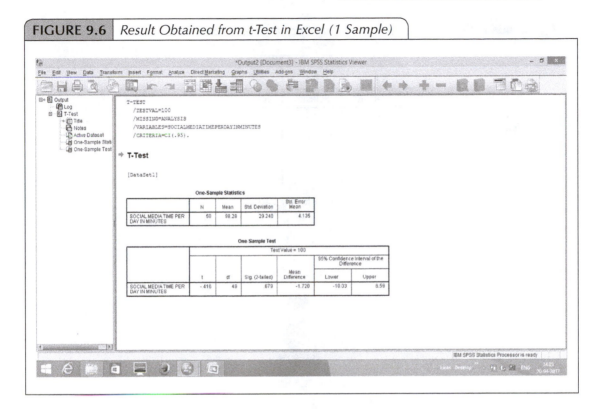

Figure 9.7 represents the box plot and the descriptive statistics of the sample from SPSS. It is evident from the output that 50 percentile of the values lie within 79 and 101 which is the Inter Quartile Range (IQR). Median is at 89, which is closer to the lower value 79, thus indicating a right skew. Values within 1.5 IQR (which calculates to 101 plus 33 upper value) form the whiskers, 109 being the last value from the sample. Anything beyond that is a 'moderate outlier' in SPSS. So 139 is an outlier. Anything beyond three times IQR is an 'extreme outlier'. It is always suggestive for the analyst to look back at the data and evaluate the moderate outliers. Extreme outliers need to be decided to be omitted, as presence of outlier will affect the mean, not the median.

The Inference for this example would be as follows:

1. Null hypothesis cannot be rejected. Browsing time is on an average 100 minutes per day.
2. The distribution is skewed on the lower side (positive and right), as seen from histogram.
3. The same can be concluded as mean is higher than the median.
4. Moderate and extreme outliers have been detected which can be reviewed for further analysis.

Let us consider another example for you to practise upon. Data has been provided in the student download section. An ice cream manufacturing company is interested in finding the number of single scoop ice creams consumed by an individual per month. A survey was conducted where the particular question was asked to the responder and response was

| FIGURE 9.7 | Box Plot and Descriptive Statistics in SPSS (1 Sample) |

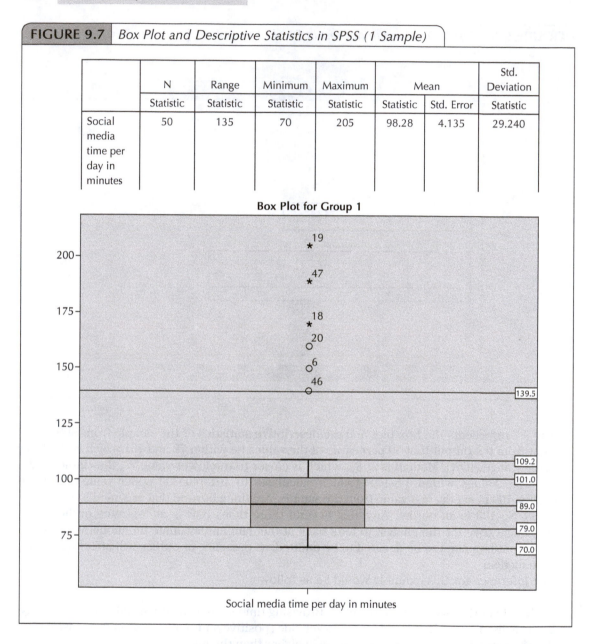

	N	Range	Minimum	Maximum	Mean		Std. Deviation
	Statistic	Statistic	Statistic	Statistic	Statistic	Std. Error	Statistic
Social media time per day in minutes	50	135	70	205	98.28	4.135	29.240

Box Plot for Group 1

Social media time per day in minutes

collected. Nineteen responses were picked up randomly to get a broad idea of the result. Draw a histogram and box plot to visualize the result. The results appear as per Figures 9.8–9.10.

The Inference for this example would be as follows:

1. The distribution is slightly skewed on the upper side (negative and left), as seen from histogram.
2. The same can be concluded as median (23) is higher than the mean (22.74).
3. No outliers detected.

FIGURE 9.8 | *Histogram in Excel (Icecream Scoop)*

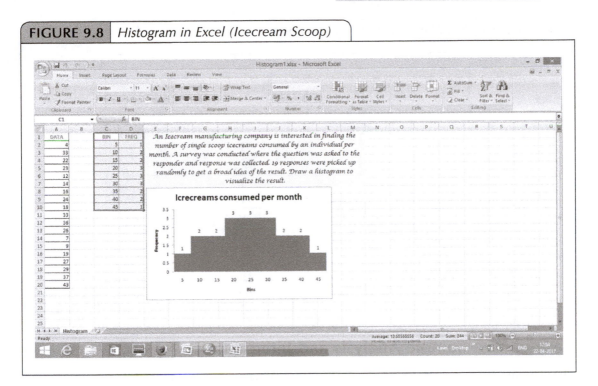

FIGURE 9.9 | *Histogram in SPSS (Icecream Scoop)*

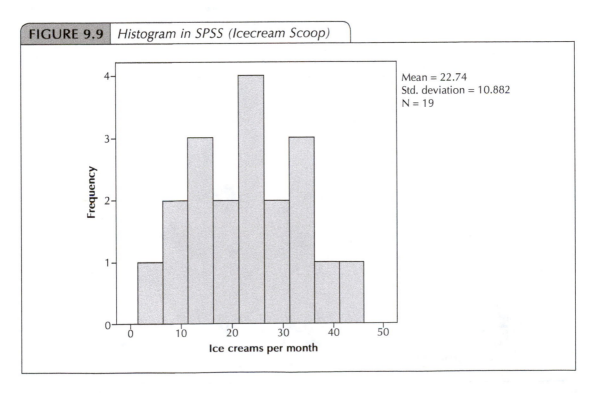

FIGURE 9.10   *Box Plot in SPSS (Icecream Scoop)*

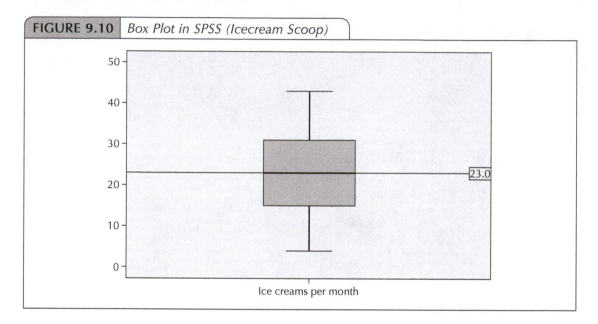

Ice creams per month

Case of Two-Sample Analysis and Interpretation

The sample data discussed in the above example has been taken from two different cities. Each sample size is of 50 working executives. A snapshot of the data set is shown in Figure 9.11 and is also available for download in the student download section.

FIGURE 9.11   *Data Snapshot (2 Samples)*

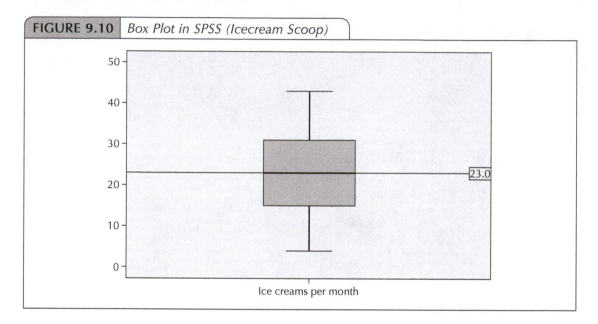

The null hypothesis states that there is no difference between the mean browsing times of the two samples. An independent sample *t* test has been conducted using both Microsoft Excel and SPSS. Results are shown in Figures 9.12 and 9.13.

FIGURE 9.12 | *Result Obtained from t-Test in Excel (2 Samples)*

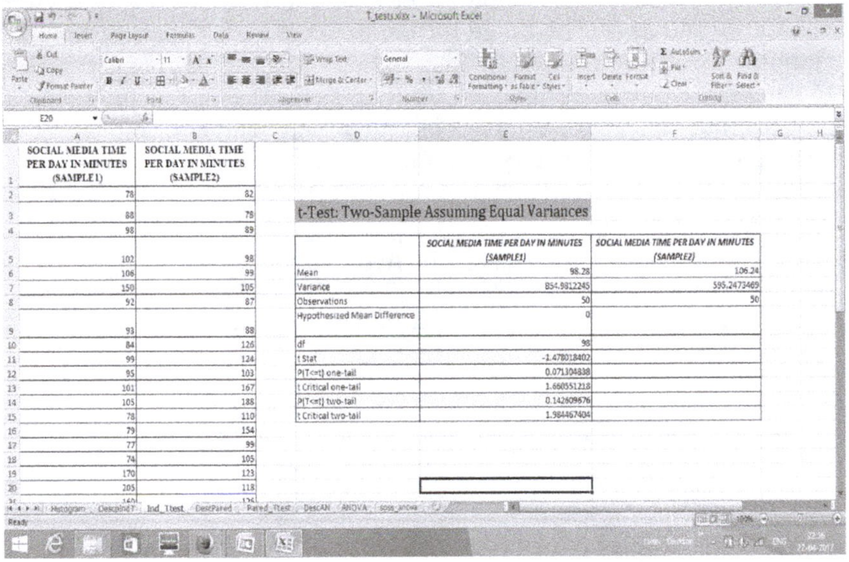

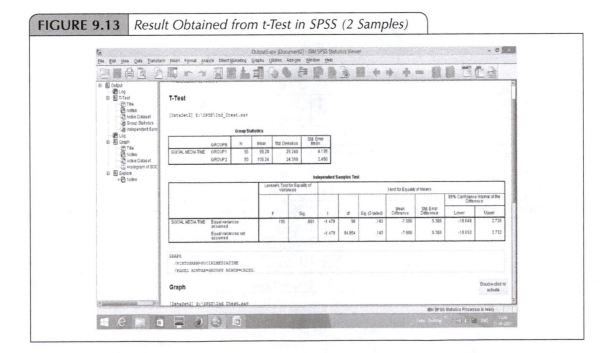

FIGURE 9.13 | *Result Obtained from t-Test in SPSS (2 Samples)*

It is evident from both the results that the p value is '0.143' which is higher than 0.05. Hence, null hypothesis cannot be rejected at 95 per cent confidence interval. It can be concluded from the results of independent sample t test that there is no difference between the means of the two samples.

The histograms for the two sample data sets are represented in Figure 9.14 along with descriptive statistical information. The individual means can be compared to the grand mean for understanding the nature of the sample spread. Both are right skewed as mean is greater than the median in both cases. The range for Sample 1 is larger than Sample 2 with higher standard deviation.

Figure 9.15 shows the box plots obtained from SPSS for the two sample data sets. A quick observation reveals that median for Sample 2 is higher than Sample 1. Additionally, the number of outliers in Sample 2 is less compared to Sample 1.

FIGURE 9.14 | *Social Media Time per Day for Two Groups*

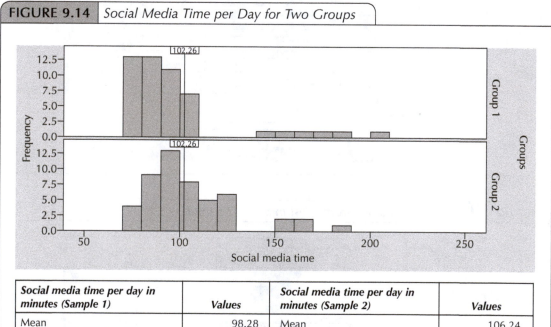

Social media time per day in minutes (Sample 1)	Values	Social media time per day in minutes (Sample 2)	Values
Mean	98.28	Mean	106.24
Standard error	4.135169221	Standard error	3.450354611
Median	89	Median	99
Mode	78	Mode	99
Standard deviation	29.24006198	Standard deviation	24.39769143
Range	135	Range	112
Minimum	70	Minimum	76
Maximum	205	Maximum	188
Count	50	Count	50

FIGURE 9.15   *Box Plot for Two Groups*

Social media time per day in minutes (Sample 1)	Values	Social media time per day in minutes (Sample 2)	Values
Mean	98.28	Mean	106.24
Standard error	4.135169	Standard error	3.450354611
Median	89	Median	99
Mode	78	Mode	99
Std. deviation	29.24006	Std. deviation	24.39769143

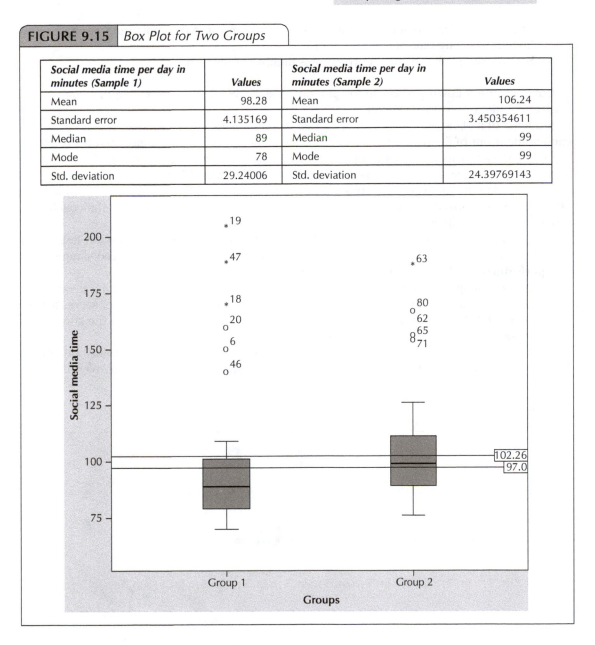

The inference for these example sets would be as follows:

1. Based on *t* test, there is no significant difference between the browsing time of two samples, and hence cannot be rejected.
2. The distribution is skewed on the lower side (positive) for both samples, as seen from the histogram.

3. The median for the second sample is higher than the first, indicating comparatively higher browsing time across the sample.
4. Second sample has a comparatively less number of outliers.

Consider the following example for practice. Use SPSS after downloading the sample data set from student download section.

Students of a class were administered a test in mathematics. Performance was recorded for each student out of 50 marks. Following this, a coaching session was conducted for the same group of students to help them cope with concepts in class which they might have been individually struggling with vis-à-vis other students in the class. Then, another maths test was administered to the same group of students and performance was recorded for each student out of 50 marks. A snapshot of the score obtained by the students before and after the coaching is represented in the Figure 9.16.

The mathematics teacher was interested in finding out if the coaching session helped the students perform better in the second test as compared to the first test. A paired sample t test was performed using SPSS on the two score data sets (Figure 9.17).

The paired sample t test is significant at 95 per cent confidence interval with a p value less than 0.05, indicating that the means of both the samples are different. We also observe that the mean value of Test 2 is higher, indicating a positive impact of the coaching on the students. It can be concluded thus that there was a positive impact of coaching.

Histogram gives a confused picture with not much clarity on who actually benefitted (Figure 9.18). The mean of second test is higher, indicating a positive higher overall performance in Test 2.

FIGURE 9.16 | Data Snapshot (Mathematics Test)

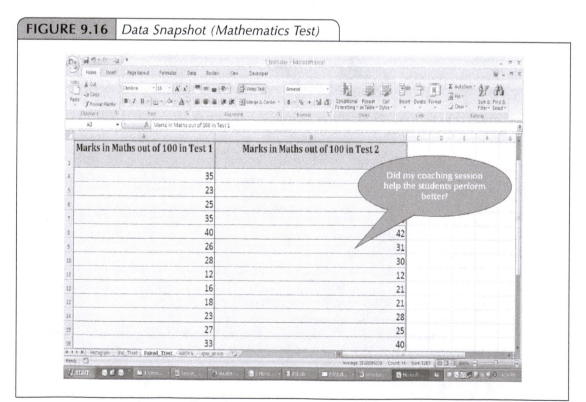

| FIGURE 9.17 | *Result Obtained from t Test in Excel (Mathematics Test)* |

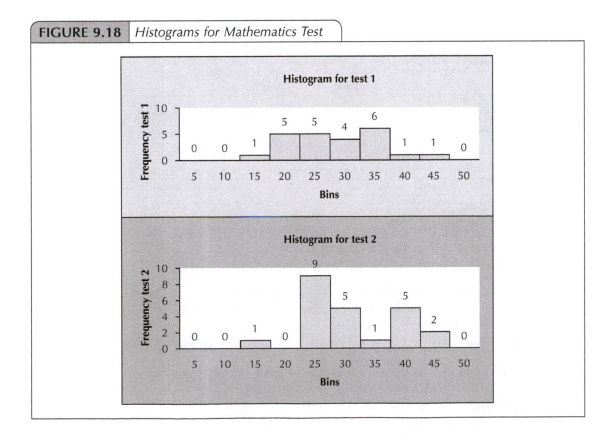

| FIGURE 9.18 | *Histograms for Mathematics Test* |

FIGURE 9.19 | *Students' Performance Before and After Maths Test*

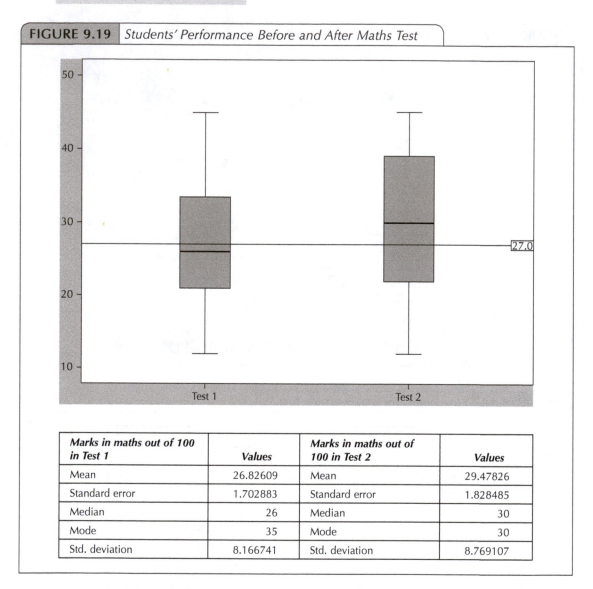

Marks in maths out of 100 in Test 1	Values	Marks in maths out of 100 in Test 2	Values
Mean	26.82609	Mean	29.47826
Standard error	1.702883	Standard error	1.828485
Median	26	Median	30
Mode	35	Mode	30
Std. deviation	8.166741	Std. deviation	8.769107

The box plot in Figure 9.19 reveals that the variance is higher in Test 2. The median of Test 2 is also higher compared to Test 1 but the mode is lower.

The Inference for this example would be as follows:

1. Paired sample *t* test indicates that the coaching session was impactful.
2. Histogram suggests that although median for Test 2 is higher, the performance spread is not very encouraging.
3. Box plot indicates that the sample values for Test 2 have a much larger spread compared to Test 1.
4. Median is higher but mode is lower. It may be good to look at the students who performed better with the coaching session and focus on them.

Case of Three or More Sample Analysis and Interpretation

Let us now extend the example of social media browsing time to three cities. Figure 9.20 is a snapshot of time spent on social media per day by business executives in three cities. A sample of 50 has been collected from each of the three cities. The analyst is interested in finding if there is a difference in browsing time among the business executives of the three cities.

The one-way ANOVA test would be an ideal test to compare the means of the three sample data sets. The null hypothesis would state that there is no difference between the means of the browsing time on social media of business executives across the three cities. The null hypothesis will be rejected if at least one of the means is different. Here browsing time would be the independent numerical variable. The three cities would be the categorical dependent variables. The outcome of the ANOVA test using Microsoft Excel is shown in the Figure 9.21. The p value is 0.09 which is not significant at 95% confidence interval indicating that null hypothesis cannot be rejected. MS (mean square error) is the SS (sum of squares) divided by degrees of freedom (df). Ratio of the two mean square errors is the value of F.

The histograms and the box plots obtained for the three sample data sets are shown in the following Figures 9.22 and 9.23, respectively. SPSS has been used for obtaining the results.

FIGURE 9.20 | *Data Snapshot (3 Samples)*

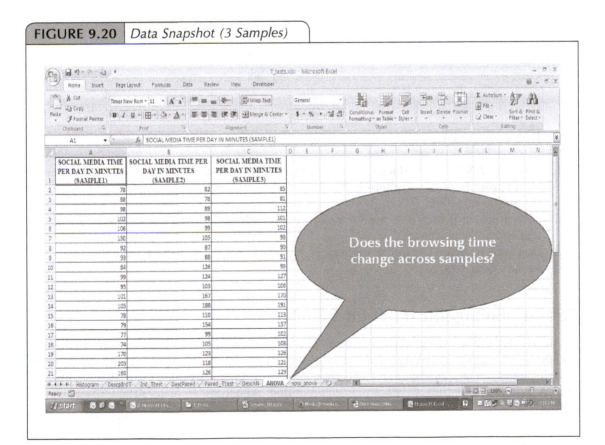

| FIGURE 9.21 | *Result Obtained from t Test in Excel (3 Samples)* |

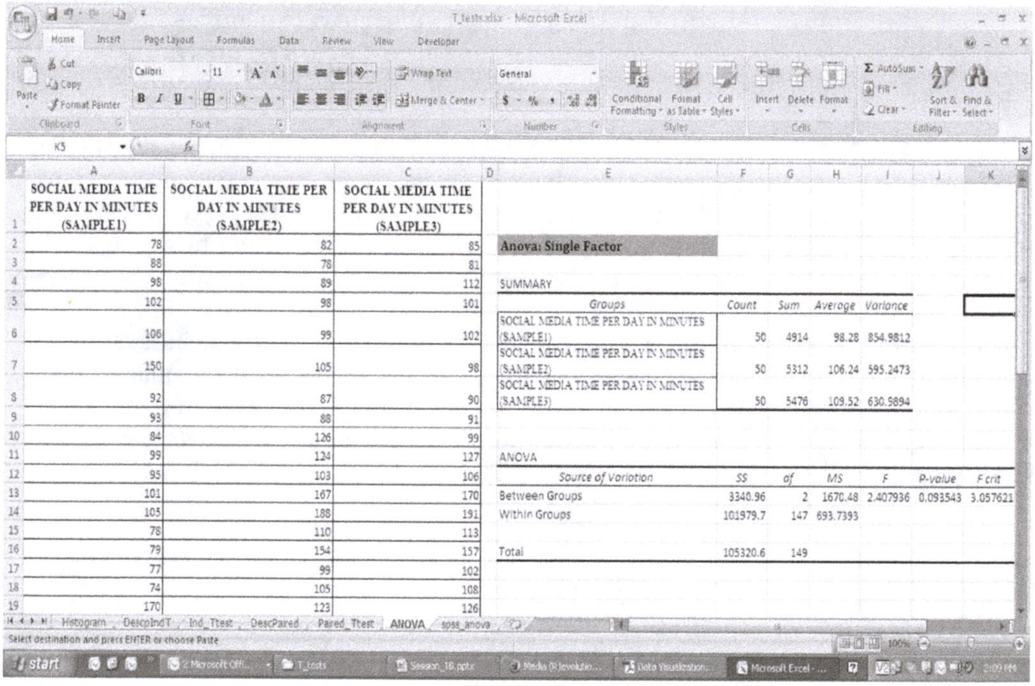

The inference for this example would be as follows:

1. One-way ANOVA test does not have a significant p value at 95% confidence interval. Hence, null hypothesis, there is no difference between the means of the three groups, cannot be rejected.
2. Histogram indicates the grand mean along with descriptive statistics showing the respective group means.
3. Box plot indicates extreme outliers in Sample Data Set 1 higher than the other two sample data sets.

Case of the Significant Third Variable

A bubble chart is a 'variation of a scatter chart' in which the data points are replaced with bubbles, and an additional dimension of the data is represented in the size of the bubbles. Bubble charts are simple visualization methods for showing data by bubbles in two-dimensional graphs. It looks at historical data and from identified indicators, compares them over a period of time.

FIGURE 9.22 *Histogram in SPSS (3 Samples)*

Anova: Single Factor						
Summary						
Groups	**Count**		**Average**	**Variance**		
Social media time per day in minutes (Sample 1)	50		98.28	854.9812		
Social media time per day in minutes (Sample 2)	50		106.24	595.2473		
Social media time per day in minutes (Sample 3)	50		109.52	630.9894		
Source of variation	**SS**	**df**	**MS**	**F**	**P value**	**F crit**
Between groups	3340.96	2	1670.48	2.407936	0.093543	3.057621
Within groups	101979.7	147	693.7393			
Total	105320.6	149				

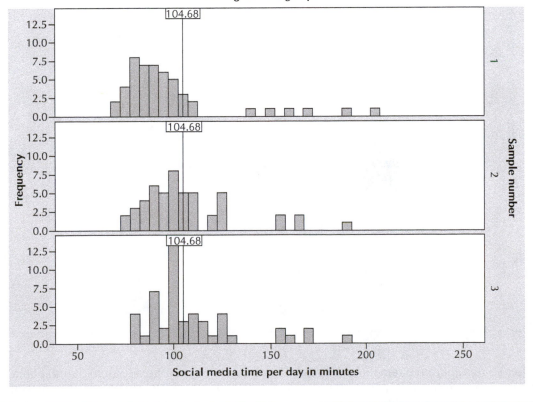

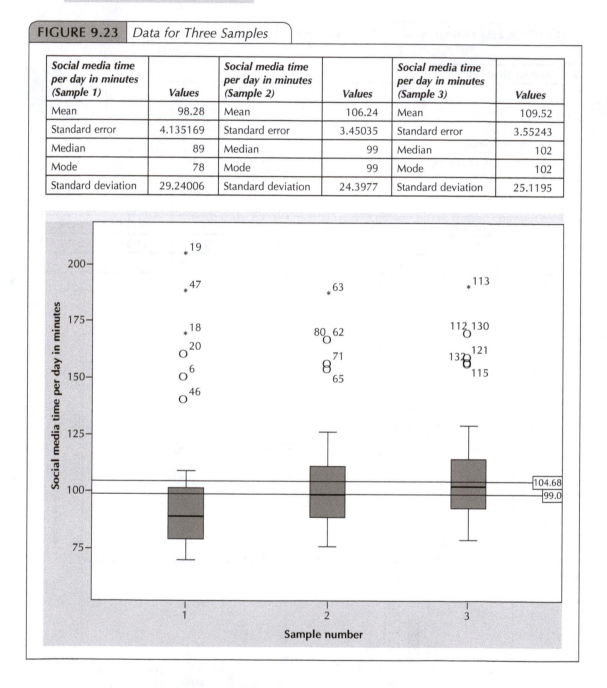

FIGURE 9.23   *Data for Three Samples*

Social media time per day in minutes (Sample 1)	Values	Social media time per day in minutes (Sample 2)	Values	Social media time per day in minutes (Sample 3)	Values
Mean	98.28	Mean	106.24	Mean	109.52
Standard error	4.135169	Standard error	3.45035	Standard error	3.55243
Median	89	Median	99	Median	102
Mode	78	Mode	99	Mode	102
Standard deviation	29.24006	Standard deviation	24.3977	Standard deviation	25.1195

Let us consider an example to understand this better. PP Brother, a leading retail chain has presence in several cities in India. It also has an online presence. The merchandise is distributed across all the locations of the store based on sales data. It uses bubble charts for monitoring region-wise sales.

FIGURE 9.24 | *Data Snapshot (8 Zones)*

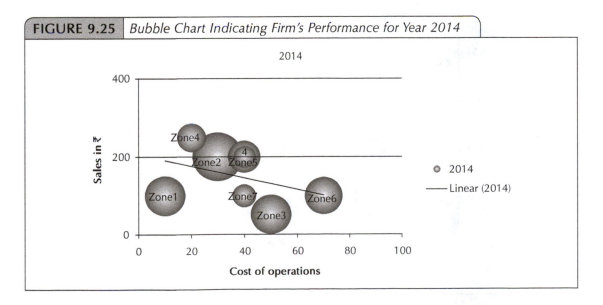

YEAR	STORE	COST IN THOUSANDS	SALES IN THOUSANDS	FOOTFALLS IN HUNDREDS
2014	ZONE1	10	100	6
2014	ZONE2	30	200	9
2014	ZONE3	50	50	6
2014	ZONE4	20	250	3
2014	ZONE5	40	200	4
2014	ZONE6	70	100	5
2014	ZONE7	40	100	2
2014	ZONE8	40	200	2
2015	ZONE1	20	100	5
2015	ZONE2	40	234	4
2015	ZONE3	70	567	6
2015	ZONE4	40	333	7
2015	ZONE5	40	456	3
2015	ZONE6	50	675	8

Data has been collected for three years across eight zones of a city. A snapshot of the data is represented in Figure 9.24. Data have been collected for the years 2014, 2015 and 2016 across all the eight zones. The remaining three columns in the data set represent the cost in INR, sales in INR and number of footfalls per zone per year.

The performance of the firm for 2014 has been shown in Figure 9.25 using a bubble chart in Microsoft Excel.

FIGURE 9.25 | *Bubble Chart Indicating Firm's Performance for Year 2014*

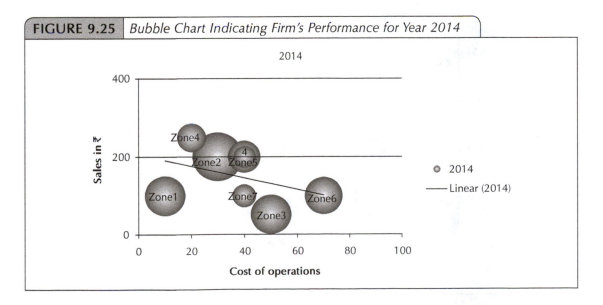

The x-axis indicates the cost of operations in thousands for each zone in INR, and the y-axis indicates the sales in thousands for each zone in INR. It is evident from the graph that in the Year 2014, Zone 4 has the lowest cost of operations and the highest sales. It is also evident that Zone 2 has the highest footfall. Zones 6 and 3 are low performing with higher cost of operations and low sales. Additionally, it is interesting to note that the high footfalls in both these zones have not converted to sales as in Zones 2 and 4.

Figure 9.26 shows the comparative performance of two years: 2014 and 2015. It is evident from the graph that the performance across all the zones was higher in the year 2015. Zone 7 had recorded a larger number of footfalls compared to the previous year and had been able to convert them to sales keeping operations cost low. Improvement was also seen in Zones 6 and 3.

Figure 9.27 shows the comparative performance of all three zones. All the stores underwent renovation in the year 2016. The stores were converted to air-conditioned stores. Other renovations were done to improve ambience and overall look and feel of the stores.

Inference of the above findings:

1. Year 2015 has been good. Low cost of operations, higher sales and more footfalls have converted to sales
2. In 2016, the cost of operations has increased. This could have probably resulted as a consequence of the renovation done to the stores and installation of air conditioners.
3. It was also observed that in 2014, in Zone 2, there were a lot of footfalls in the new store that did not convert to sales.

Let us now dig a little deeper and see the results of the Year 2015. It is observed that Zone 7 did quite well; however, Zones 1 and 3 performed badly. This is evident from Figure 9.28.

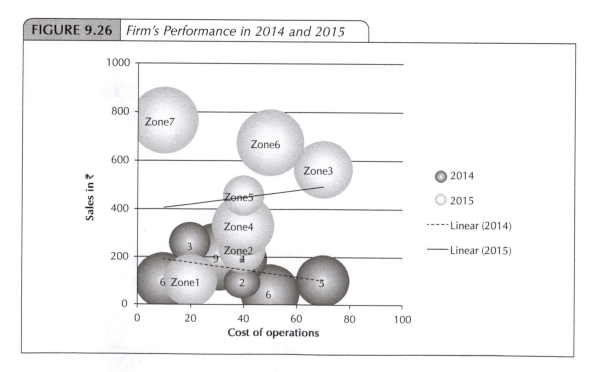

FIGURE 9.26 | *Firm's Performance in 2014 and 2015*

FIGURE 9.27 | *Firm's Performance for Three Years*

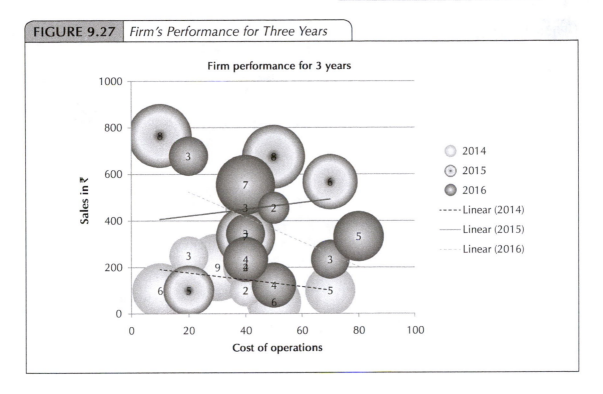

FIGURE 9.28 | *Bubble Chart Indicating Firm's Performance for Year 2015*

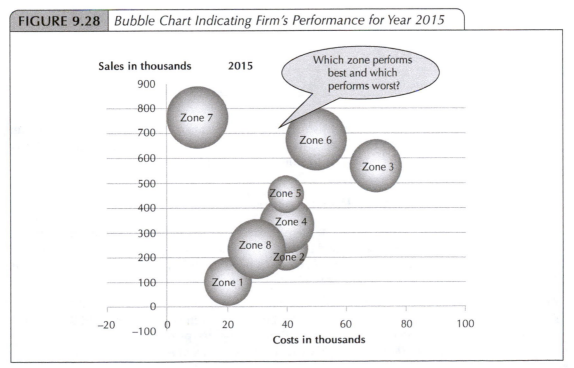

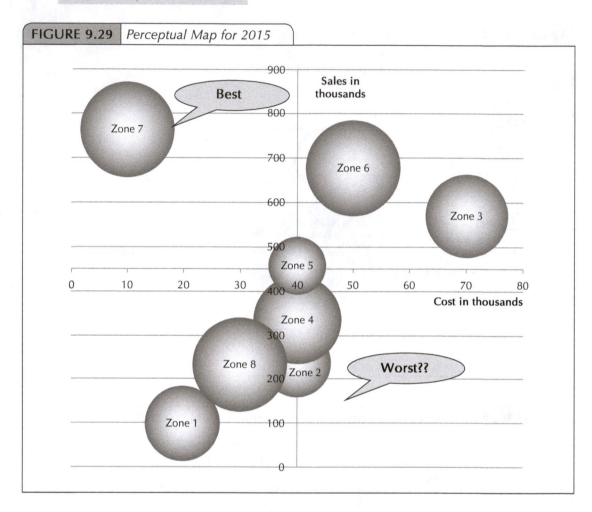

FIGURE 9.29 *Perceptual Map for 2015*

To better diagnose the results, we make use of a perceptual map as in Figure 9.29. We can infer with clarity that although the cost of operations in Zone 3 is higher, Zone 4 has performed very poorly with high footfalls not converting to sales and moderately high cost of operations.

Summarizing Data Using Pivot Tables

You have seen the use of pivot tables in Microsoft Excel while tabulating and summarizing data. Use Excel to summarize data by Zone and then by Year. Show it using bubble chart. A snapshot has been shown in Figures 9.30 and 9.31. Zone 7 has been the best performing Zone across the three years. Year 2015 has been the best performing year.

You are required to do the following class exercise using Microsoft Excel.
The data represents sales in INR of a particular businessman in seven cities. Additionally, the population of the cities and the ratio of population to sales are provided.

   Draw a bubble chart to represent the data and draw conclusions.

FIGURE 9.30   *Performance by Zone*

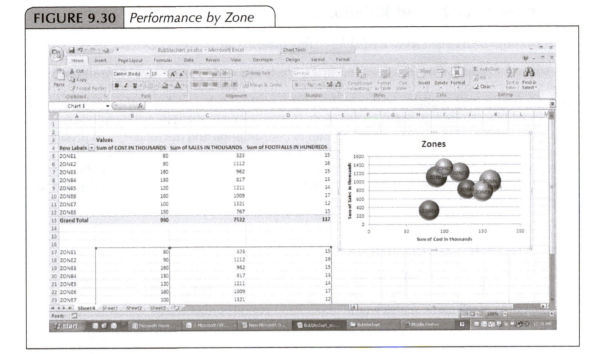

FIGURE 9.31   *Performance by Year*

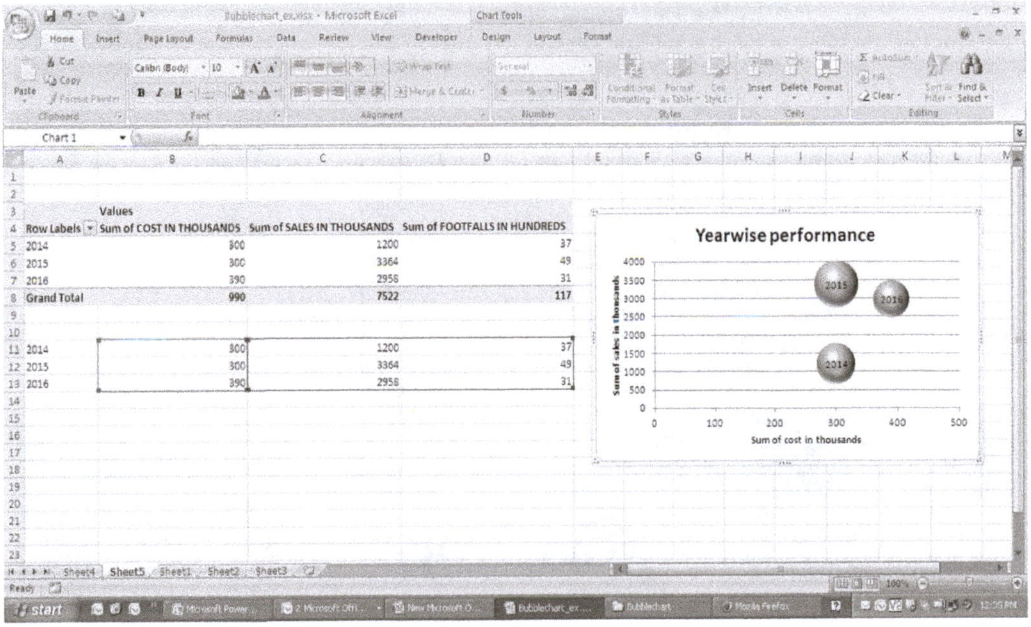

Grouping of Data and Relationships

Relationship between Two Variables: Line Graphs and Trend Lines

The snapshot of the data set provided in Figure 9.32 provides the annual production and consumption of crude oil (tonnes per year) by country from the year 2001 to 2010. Data has been taken from Gapminder.

Pivot table in Microsoft Excel has been used to summarize the data for eight countries as seen in Figure 9.33. It represents the total sum of consumption and the total sum of production by country for the 10 years. A separate pivot table represents in Figure 9.34 the total sum of consumption and the total sum of production by year for the 10 countries. The line graphs provide a visual comparison of crude oil consumption versus production by country and also across 10 years.

Heat Map for Correlation

A heat map is a two-dimensional representation of data in which values are represented by colours. A simple heat map provides an immediate visual summary of information. More elaborate heat maps allow the viewer to understand complex data sets.

FIGURE 9.32	Annual Crude Oil Production and Consumption

Country	Year	Production	Consumption
Argentina	2001	41537000	19109000
Argentina	2002	40901517.24	17107000
Argentina	2003	40243000	17558000
Argentina	2004	37788862.07	18401000
Argentina	2005	36242271.93	19676875
Argentina	2006	35767237.6	20555955
Argentina	2007	34943078.31	23192795
Argentina	2008	34123831.95	24219411
Argentina	2009	33776045.03	23700000
Argentina	2010	32549586.72	25700000
Australia	2001	34526994.3	38106000
Australia	2002	34307550.04	37970000
Australia	2003	29707666.72	38275000
Australia	2004	25920027.91	38791278

Source: https://www.gapminder.org/data/

FIGURE 9.33   *Data Summarization by Country*

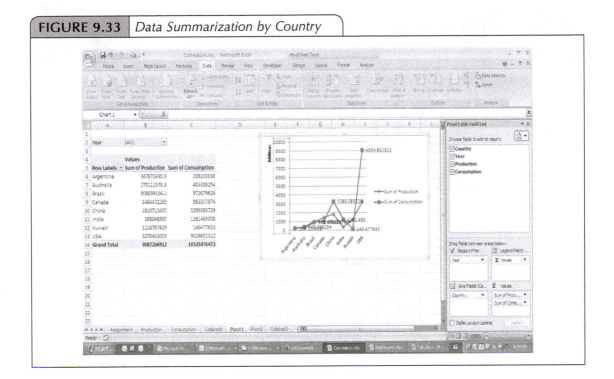

FIGURE 9.34   *Data Summarization by Year*

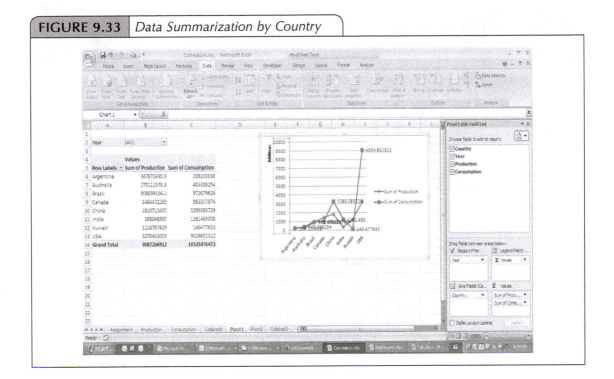

FIGURE 9.35 *Correlation*

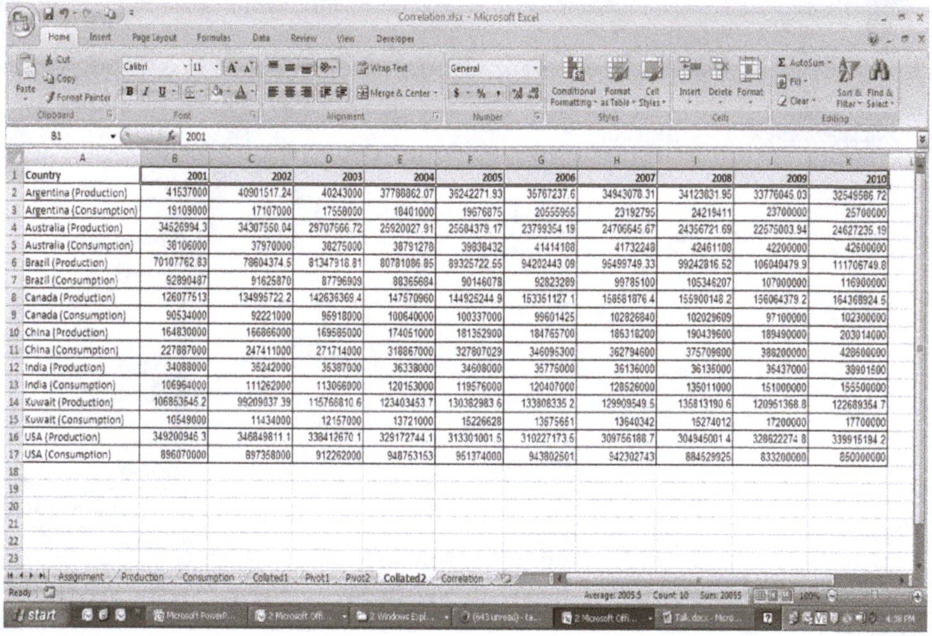

Country	2001	2002	2003	2004	2005	2006	2007	2008	2009	2010
Argentina (Production)	41537000	40901517.24	40243000	37788862.07	36242271.93	35767237.6	34943078.31	34123831.95	33776045.03	32549586.72
Argentina (Consumption)	19109000	17107000	17558000	18401000	19676875	20555965	23192795	24219411	23700000	25700000
Australia (Production)	34526994.3	34307550.04	29707566.72	25920027.91	25584379.17	23799354.19	24706645.67	24356721.69	22575003.94	24627235.19
Australia (Consumption)	38106000	37970000	38275000	38791278	39838432	41414188	41732248	42461108	42200000	42600000
Brazil (Production)	70107762.83	78604374.5	81347918.81	80781086.85	89325722.55	94202443.09	95499749.33	99242816.52	106040479.9	111706749.8
Brazil (Consumption)	92890487	91625870	87796909	88365684	90146078	92823289	99785100	105346207	107000000	116900000
Canada (Production)	126077513	134995722.2	142636369.4	147570960	144925244.9	153351127.1	158581876.4	155900148.2	156064379.2	164368924.5
Canada (Consumption)	90534000	92221000	95918000	100640000	100337000	99601425	102826840	102029609	97100000	102300000
China (Production)	164830000	166866000	169585000	174051000	181352900	184765700	186318200	190439600	189490000	203014000
China (Consumption)	227887000	247411000	271714000	318867000	327807029	346095300	362794600	375709800	388200000	428600000
India (Production)	34088000	35242000	35387000	36338000	34608000	35776000	36136000	36135000	36437000	38901500
India (Consumption)	106964000	111262000	113066000	120153000	119576000	120407000	128526000	135011000	151000000	155500000
Kuwait (Production)	106853545.2	99209037.39	115766810.6	123403453.7	130382983.6	133808335.2	129909549.5	136813190.6	120961368.8	122689354.7
Kuwait (Consumption)	10549000	11434000	12157000	13721000	15226628	13675651	13640342	15274012	17200000	17700000
USA (Production)	349200946.3	346849811.1	338412670.1	329172744.1	313301001.5	310227173.5	309756188.7	304945001.4	328622274.8	339915194.2
USA (Consumption)	896070000	897358000	912262000	948753153	951374000	943802501	942302743	884529925	833200000	850000000

FIGURE 9.36 *Correlation Output*

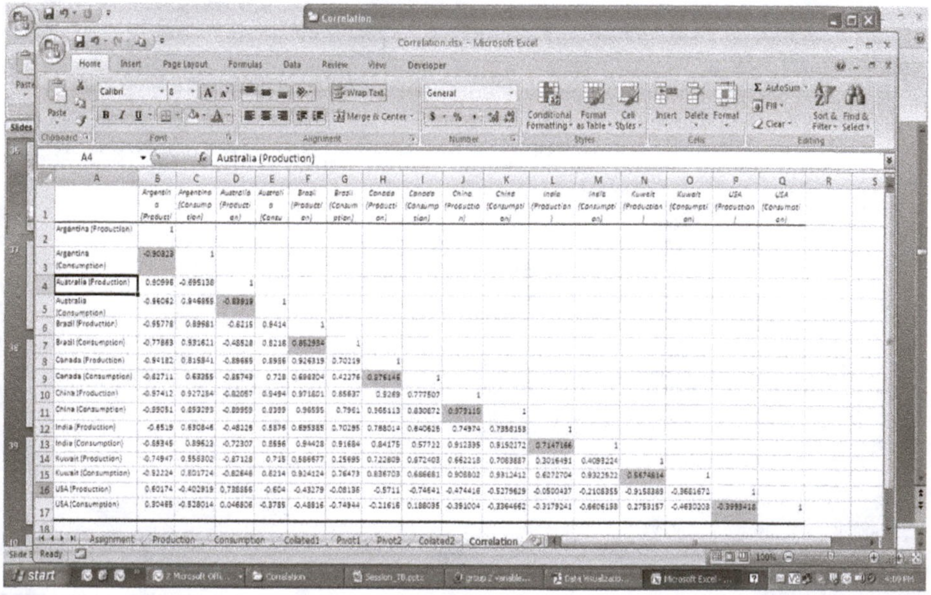

FIGURE 9.37 | *Heatmap*

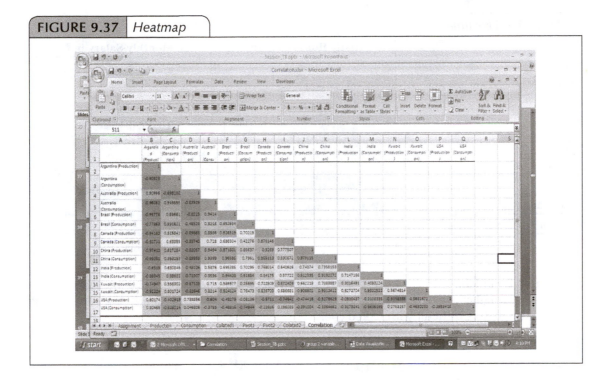

In Microsoft Excel, it can be represented using conditional formatting in the Home tab. Figure 9.37 represents the same correlation output (Figures 9.35 and 9.36) using heat map. It is visually much easier to identify significantly low and significantly high values for further interpretation. In Table 9.1, we have details on employee name, hours worked per day and monthly salary in INR. The heat map in Table 9.2 generated in MS Excel shows higher and lower values in different shades. Rumki has the least number of hours of work, whereas Shobha has the highest.

TABLE 9.1 | *Employee Table*

Employee	Daily Hours of Work	Monthly Salary in ₹
Shobha	12	800,000
Kartik	11	700,000
Nilay	7	1,000,000
Jhanvi	8	400,000
Pritesh	8	400,000
Savant	5	150,000
Rumki	4	100,000
Chandana	5	100,000
Bhavin	8	400,000
Rudra	9	1,000,000

TABLE 9.2	*Heatmap*	
Employee	**Daily Hours of Work**	**Monthly Salary in ₹**
Shobha	12	800,000
Kartik	11	700,000
Nilay	7	1,000,000
Jhanvi	8	400,000
Pritesh	8	400,000
Savant	5	150,000
Rumki	4	100,000
Chandana	5	100,000
Bhavin	8	400,000
Rudra	9	1,000,000

Rumki and Chandana have the lowest salaries, whereas Nilay and Rudra have the highest. Heat maps are particularly useful when there is large amount of data and identifying certain peak values of interest is difficult with naked eye.

Visualizing Categorical and Unstructured Data

In text documents, it is difficult to identify frequently occurring words and/or words of significance. We have seen in Chapter 8 that text mining is a methodology of interpreting unstructured data. Word clouds can be generated by analysing the textual content. A word cloud is a pictorial representation of words present in a textual document where the size of the word indicates its frequency of occurrence or its value to the context under study (Figure 9.38).

Let us do a hands-on exercise to see how this is done.

Example: An analyst and his team set out to gather relevant information which could provide insights about future talent demand in the BA roles in organizations in India. As a first step, he and his team studied and compared research reports of seven companies that provided a summary of research findings about the significance of building a skilled Analytics resource pool in India. Further, the analyst and

FIGURE 9.38	*Wordcloud*

Source: https://www.gapminder.org/data/

his team compared the reports using text mining techniques in R software thus establishing similarity documented in the research reports. These reports describe the Analytics resource requirement by companies in India in the next four–five years. The reports of seven companies from which excerpts have been taken relevant to the topic of discussion are as follows:

1. PWC, *Indian Workplace of 2022: Are Organizations Ready for the Future?* (PWC, 2014). https://www.pwc.in/assets/pdfs/publications/2014/indian-workplace-of-2022.pdf (accessed on 15 July 2019).
2. Mckinsey Global Institute, *The Age of Analytics: Competing in a Data-Driven World December 2016* (London: Nicolaus Henke, 2016).
3. Imarticus Learning, *Analytics Employment Landscape in India 2017 Study* (Imarticus Learning, 2017). https://imarticus.org/wp-content/uploads/2017/04/Industry-Report-Analytics-2017.pdf (accessed on 15 July 2019).
4. EY, *Becoming an Analytics-Driven Organization to Create Value* (EY, 2015). https://www.ey.com/Publication/vwLUAssets/EY-global-becoming-an-analytics-driven-organization/%24FILE/ey-global-becoming-an-analytics-driven-organization.pdf (accessed on 15 July 2019).
5. Deolitte, *Rewriting the Rules for the Digital Age: 2017 Deloitte Global Human Capital Trends* (Deloitte University Press, 2017). https://www2.deloitte.com/content/dam/Deloitte/global/Documents/HumanCapital/hc-2017-global-human-capital-trends-gx.pdf (accessed on 15 July 2019).
6. Oxford Economics, *How the New Geography of Talent Will Transform Human Resource Strategies* (Oxford Economics, 2012). https://www.oxfordeconomics.com/Media/Default/Thought%20Leadership/global-talent-2021.pdf (accessed on 15 July 2019).
7. Jigsaw Academy, *An Inside Look on What Influences the Indian Analytics Industry* (Jigsaw Academy, 2017). https://www.jigsawacademy.com/wp-content/uploads/2017/05/Jigsaw-Academy-Analytics-Industry-Report-2017.pdf (accessed on 15 July 2019).

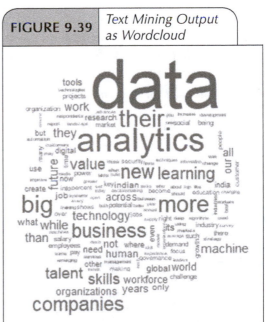

FIGURE 9.39 *Text Mining Output as Wordcloud*

The word cloud (Figure 9.39) and histogram (Figure 9.40) generated by text mining the contents of the reports using R software indicate the frequency of appearance of certain words in large numbers such as 'data', 'analytics', 'their', 'more', 'big', 'talent', 'companies', 'business', 'skills', 'future', 'work', 'new', 'value' and 'learning'. Certain words appear in greater numbers compared to others. The histogram represents the same information in the form of a chart.

Researcher needs to go back to the text to see the reason for the sentiment either positive or negative in the context of the text and topic and then workout a conclusion for the results.

Disclaimer: The above image is for representation purpose only.

| **FIGURE 9.40** | *Text Mining Output as Histogram* |

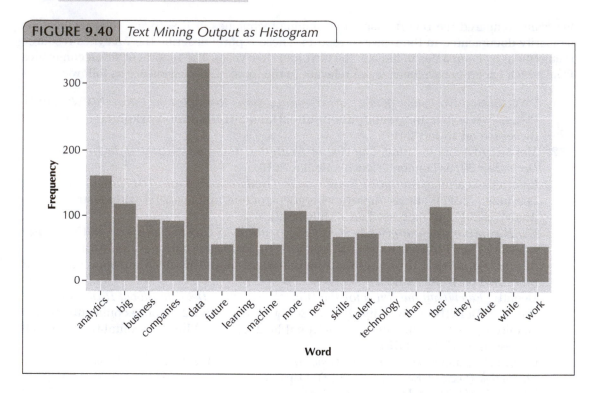

The tacit capability of the analyst in converting 'evidence' into 'implication' remains as important today in the world of Analytics as it was earlier. However, what has changed is the computational tools and implements used by the analysts today to extract evidences, and decision-makers must carefully evaluate this transition for their organizations to invest wisely in appropriate capabilities.

The R code used for generating the word cloud is as follows:

```
#First of all, create the text documents in a folder on C drive. Then
install all the packages.

library(tm)

library(SnowballC)

library(ggplot2)

library(wordcloud)

library(NLP)

library(plyr)

cname<- file.path("C:","IGITxtdocs")#Access the file

cname

dir(cname)#Will list the number of files and details
```

```
docs <- Corpus(DirSource(cname))#Loading texts into R
summary(docs)
inspect(docs)
docs<-tm_map(docs,removePunctuation)
docs<-tm_map(docs, removeNumbers)
docs<-tm_map(docs,tolower)
#docs <- tm_map(docs, PlainTextDocument)
#docs<- (docs, removeWords, stopwords("english"))

library(SnowballC)
#docs<-tm_map(docs,stemDocument)
docs<-tm_map(docs,stripWhitespace)
#docs<-tm_map(docs, PlainTextDocument)
docs<-tm_map(docs, removeWords, c("and", "are", "the", "how", "which",
"will", "this", "for", "most", "also"))
docs<-tm_map(docs, removeWords, c("have", "has", "with", "from", "can",
"these", "that"))
dtm<-DocumentTermMatrix(docs)
dtm
#tdm<-TermDocumentMatrix(docs)
#tdm
#Frequency of occurance of each word in corpus
inspect(docs)
freq<-colSums(as.matrix(dtm))
length(freq)
dtms<- removeSparseTerms(dtm, 0.1)
#Matrix is organized according to frequency of words
ord<-order(freq)
library(wordcloud)freq[head(ord)] #Least frequency
freq[tail(ord)] #Most frequency
freq<-sort(colSums(as.matrix(dtm)), decreasing=TRUE)
head(freq,10)
wf<-data.frame(word=names(freq), freq=freq)
```

```
head(wf)

library(RColorBrewer)

set.seed(142)

wordcloud(names(freq), freq, min.freq=15, scale=c(5, .1), colors=brewer.
pal(4, "Dark2"))

#Association of "analytics" with other words

findAssocs(dtms, "talent", corlimit=0.3)

findAssocs(dtms, "across", corlimit=0.1)

#Plot the word that occurs more than 50 times

#aes describes aesthetics, freq is frequency of word

p<-ggplot(subset(wf, freq>50), aes(word,freq))

#stat= "identity" option in geom_bar() ensures that the height of each
bar is proportional to the data value

p<-p+geom_bar(stat="identity")

# x axis label should be at a 45 degree angle and should be
horizontally justified

p<-p +theme(axis.text.x=element_text(angle=45, hjust=1))

p

# Hierarchical clustering

#removesparceTerms() function removes infrequent words

#this makes 15% empty space (maximum)

dtmss<- removeSparseTerms(dtm, 0.15)

library(cluster)

#Hierarchical clustering is performed in which distance between words
and then cluster them according to the similarity

d <- dist(t(dtmss), method="euclidian")

fit <- hclust(d=d, method="ward")

#The "ward" method has been remamed to "ward.D"; note new "ward.D2"

fit

plot(fit, hang=-1)

#k defines the number of clusters

groups <- cutree(fit, k=5)

#plot dendograms with red borders
```

```
rect.hclust(fit, k=5, border="red")
#k means clustering
library(fpc)
d <- dist(t(dtmss), method="euclidian")
kfit<- kmeans(d, 2)
clusplot(as.matrix(d), kfit$cluster, color=T, shade=T, labels=2, lines=0)
```

Capability Mix for BA

The conditions for analysis to flourish in organizations require different kinds of skills to be blended together. The skill set required to leverage its advantages is a concoction of data management skills, statistical/data processing prowess and business acumen. The Analytics resource with the 'right' mix (refer Figure 9.41) is in high demand and not surprisingly is available in short supply. Most organizations, in reality, have evolved their analytic processes around a mix of resources that have varying strengths in more than one of the three key strengths.

1. **Data inventory management:** Scientific enquiry requires regulated data formats that provide easy evaluation of (in) consistency in the patterns among the data, a requirement for good-quality Analytics. The new-age analysts need to be conversant with the format of the organizational data inventory and be able to 'pull' the right data bytes from the storage to be able to offer the 'right' information. Increasingly, the familiarity with unstructured data is also known to be important.
2. **Processing capabilities:** This is something that was always an integral part of business analysis. However, with the advent of large-scale databases, knowledge of sophisticated data processing engines (software and model building capabilities) is rapidly becoming a necessity—in order to mine insights from big pools of data. This is one capability that organizations find easiest to acquire given the large number of institutions that impart training. The market today has been a proliferation of this skill. It is also easy for the analysts to make themselves marketable, since this is a 'visible' and useful (though not sufficient) capability for Analytics to fructify.
3. **Business acumen:** No one can ignore the importance of converting data to meaningful insights and implications. This capability, generically termed as business acumen, is actually a mix of business conceptual knowledge along with contextual familiarity. Without this skill set, data analytics capability is at best a processing department within the organization that churns 'insipid' reports.

Business leaders trying to reap benefits of data insights need to encourage executives with high business acumen to excel in developing data-driven insight development skills. The latter need to be comfortable reading data insights and developing the knack of connecting them with their business relevance.

These are not the easiest capabilities to be developed. Usually, resources having specialized processing skills and having the urge and capability to participate actively into business

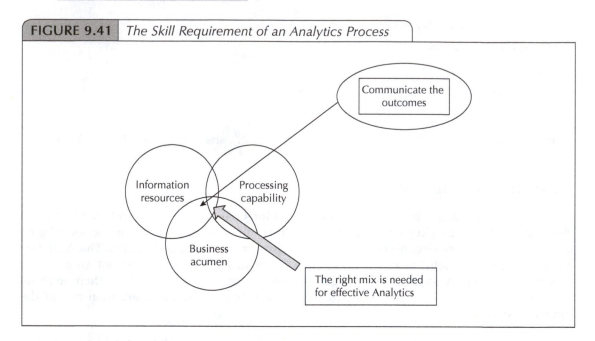

FIGURE 9.41   *The Skill Requirement of an Analytics Process*

decision-making have the right mix of skills to drive this activity. However, unlike processing skills which can be imparted through training programmes, today's Analytics skill is a strange mixture of data literacy and creative business acumen that develops with exposure to various BP contexts.

Many organizations, especially in developed markets, which are in an evolved state of adoption of Analytics, have embedded skills where policy development groups have additional expertise in data processing and management. Usually, the career graph of employees in such analytically savvy organizations requires them to transition from data processing responsibilities to policymaking with opportunities to move back and forth as required. Such organizations usually have blended skills in their employees over time and do not usually depend on specialists to manage analytical tasks. However, as mentioned earlier, this kind of evolution takes time and a proper organizational culture has to set in to make it happen successfully.

REVIEW QUESTIONS

1. The data provided in the student download section represents oil consumption (tonnes per year) of different countries across the globe. Data is available from 1965 to 2010. Draw a time series graph. Insert trend line and analyse.
2. What is the significance of bubble chart in data visualization? How can perceptual maps support better analysis?
3. Explain the capability mix for a good BA resource person.
4. Look for short stories by your favourite author. Using text mining draw a word cloud in R software.

CASE 9.1
The Dream Employee (Case Complexity: Easy)

A group of students studying MBA (second year) at a management institute in India went for a study tour to five other partnering MBA institutes. This was part of a learning intervention model that was launched by 20 MBA schools in India. Healthy academic discussions and exchange of knowledge was the primary focus areas of this activity. Clad in business suits, students were looking as industry professionals. Discussions revolved around coursework, syllabus, structure of programme, industry interventions, guest lectures, facilities at the institute (library, canteen, hostel, classrooms and so on) and placements. During one of the evening tea session discussions, one of the students, Sushma, said that Data Science is an upcoming area for recruitment by many organizations. Business analysts are getting a heavy pay package. Several heads turned towards her. Akshay said he had heard that too. Roshan said that he has his bachelor's degree in IT engineering; Data Science is just an extension of the concepts taught to him in his BTech programme. Paulomi who is a computer engineer disagreed. She said they are related concepts but in a business school one needs to see it from the lens of a manager. Devika, a science graduate is confused. She says that if Data Science is such an important area for recruitment, why are we discussing it now in second year? This should have been taught in the first year. How is it related to the four core disciplines—marketing, finance, operations and HR?[2]

Jaideep, Kartik and Vandana are majoring in BA. They said, 'Wait a minute friends; let us explain' and they narrated in detail about the relationship that exists between Data Science and the associated fields of study which includes BA. They further explained that their management institute had done a deep study in looking at the needs of organizations of constantly processing business data in large quantities for supporting managerial decision-making. Additionally, there has been a leap in quality job opportunities arising due to digital age. To build a resource pool in this area, their institute had recently launched a special major in this BA. The discussion continued till late in the evening on its merits and courses. Some who understood it participated, whereas there were others who shelved it away as too technical and not their cup of tea.

The next day there was a speaker series organized for them where senior employees from online retail giants addressed them. The marketing heads discussed among many things the relevance of analysing digital information for effective decision-making, so did the finance, HR and the operations managers in their respective domains. They reiterated in many different ways that a dream employee is one who has the domain expertise which comes with time and experience, is able to look at varied sources of data to suggest means for filtering out relevant content, is able to suggest the analytical techniques to process the data and finally read and communicate the outcomes for its appropriate use in decision-making. A resource having all of these qualities together is hard to find. However, the paperless future will value such resources and hence capabilities need to be built around them.

Exercise

1. Research and suggest the kind of capabilities that need to be built for an MBA student to be hired in HR Analytics department of an organization.

---

[2] Reference link is https://analyticstraining.com/whats-the-difference-between-data-analysts-and-business-analysts/

2. Research and suggest the kind of capabilities that need to be built for an MBA student to be hired in marketing Analytics department of an organization.
3. Research and suggest the kind of capabilities that need to be built for an MBA student to be hired in financial Analytics department of an organization.
4. Research and suggest the kind of capabilities that need to be built for an MBA student to be hired in an operations Analytics department of an organization.

CASE 9.2
Bouncing the Word Cloud (Case Complexity: Medium)

Rakila Group of Industries has been a successful effort of three brothers. Nandraj and Sohanraj Rakila are siblings of whom Nandraj is elder. Kanakraj is their paternal cousin. A humble beginning, they started their first enterprise in manufacturing bicycles. The outhouse unit had 10 employees who together worked from sourcing and assembling spare parts to build the entire bicycle. They slowly diversified into the two- and three-wheeler market.

Employee training was one of the key objectives of the organization to create and maintain an agile workforce. Timely accomplishment of processes can be achieved only when the employees are provided skill-based training in their respective fields of work. This would automatically drive the required agility and efficiency for effective supply-chain management. The entire supply chain consists of several stakeholders from supplier of suppliers to end users. Automation has revolutionized the entire supply-chain management in manufacturing companies. Employees need modern-day skill-based training to manage the technology-enabled architectures, process automation, optimum resource utilization, and hence reduce costs. It is necessary to conduct a thorough study to understand what skills already exist among the employees. Then based on what is needed, identify the gap that exists in training.

Creating agility within different processes of a supply chain is an ongoing change. Hence, focus and investment on maintaining a well-trained workforce leads to readily embrace the changes. The three brothers have themselves participated in many of these training sessions. They believe that to drive a culture of agile taskforce, it has to come from top management.

Drastic changes in processes made too often can at times be demotivating for employees. There is a learning curve associated with skill-based training that comes with returning to the job floor and applying the learnings from a training programme. If successive changes come in short durations, there is a possibility of the employees getting overwhelmed leading to their exit. Rakila Group brothers realize that it is a major loss on the balance sheet. A skilled and trained employee with experience within the organization is much more valuable than any lateral intake completely new to organizational processes. Appropriate reward programmes have been developed to encourage employees who have contributed significantly towards this mission of driving an agile supply-chain management within Rakila Industries.

Exercise

Use the R software to generate a word cloud from Case 9.2. Assist the HR manager of Rakila Industries to analyse the word cloud for integrating it into his training and development plans.

CASE 9.3
Speedometer Gauge Measures Business Performance
(Case Complexity: High)

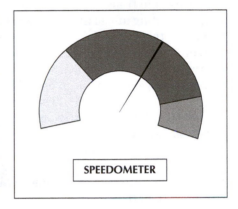

SPEEDOMETER

'Auntiji Namkeen' is now a household name in India. It started seven years ago as an entrepreneurial start-up by a group of ladies belonging to the same household. In the city of Dahod, Gujarat, Rasilaben was the eldest of the wives of four brothers. She and the other three wives of the respective three brothers had managed their household chores putting in a lot of effort in educating and raising their children. Rasilaben's husband had five other cousin brothers living within the same locality. After finishing household chores, during winter, the ladies used to sit on a cot basking in the afternoon sun. One such afternoon, during a casual conversation, Rasilaben enthusiastically told the ladies 'we have successfully completed our duty of raising our children. They are all independent now. Why don't we do something collectively that is fun and also uses our years of domestic experience?' The ladies found it to be a very interesting proposition. Rasilaben's mother-in-law, the eldest surviving member of the family, was a lady of progressive thoughts and had been supportive of the women of the household. It is this support that had led her granddaughters to pursue higher education. This time too she was the one who raised her hand in favour of Rasilaben.

The following day, the ladies came up with various propositions. One of the cousin brother's wife, Smitaben came up with a very interesting idea. She belonged to Surat, a city in south Gujarat. She said, 'I have grown up in a neighbourhood where women of the house go to work 5–6 days a week. There were often times when they seek out home-cooked food which can be delivered to their doorstep. Additionally, they seek out healthy snack time options. My mother had a passion for cooking. She used to prepare and supply food to such households on an order-to-order basis. They would relish it leading to re-orders. We can do something along those lines'.

There was instant agreement from many present. What they do every day in their kitchen can very well be extended beyond it to start a business. Skilled hands of nine women of the household soon came together to build Auntiji Namkeen. A major role in the establishment was from four of their children, Ranjana, Ketki, Soham and Kushal, who had attained their higher education from Ahmedabad. While Ranjana and Soham were commerce graduates, Ketki and Soham had completed their MBA degree. The four together decided to help their mothers and aunts to set up the family business.

Auntiji Namkeen carries two broad categories of products: 'fresh' snacks and 'dry' snacks. Fresh snacks have lower shelf life compared to dry snacks. Within the cluster of dry snacks, they carry popular snack items such as 'khakra', 'drypuri', 'sevmamra', 'chiki', dry fruits, healthy snack item ('diet') and branded items. They have tie-ups with suppliers who supply products twice a week. The fresh snack items such as 'thepla', 'handwa', 'khaman', 'dhokla' and 'patra' are prepared and distributed at 4 PM every evening. The maximum shelf life for these products is 24 hours. The 4 PM–7 PM time remains the busiest as lot of commuters stop by to pick up fresh snack on their way home from work.

Today there are 150 large stores across Gujarat, one to two stores in most major cities in India and some overseas. Each AC store has a cash counter for bill payment. Every sale transaction is captured in their store database; the items purchased, the amount purchased, bill per item and total amount of sale. Every evening at 6 PM, the total sales by category is updated from the store computer into the central server database. Ranjana and Soham feel that capturing sale transactions by category across all the stores was not very useful because the data was sitting idle in their server room with not much being experimented with. They thought that since their aunts were energetic and putting in significant effort in growing the business, it may be worthwhile to capture the information on business parameters and present it in a way for them to understand easily. That would allow them to track and monitor the health of the business as well as think of growth opportunities. They went to their MBA cousins with this suggestion. Soham and Ketki suggested building a dashboard for the company. Among many parameters that they four would be tracking via the dashboard, for their aunts, they would create speedometer gauges. As a first step, Soham and Ketki built a BA dashboard for measuring and monitoring store performance across 10 stores in Ahmedabad. An item that immediately allows the hard-working ladies to see and understand is the monthly sales volume on the speedometer gauge. The different colours and the pointer indicator help them measure the store health in the click of a second. A speedometer gauge has been included in the dashboard for each of the four items to monitor monthly store-level sales volume, store-level raw material costs, average employee hours and net profit at store level. As an experiment, the team has chosen 10 stores in Ahmedabad. Data for the month of July 2018 is given as follows:

Store	Sales Volume (Thousands)	Raw Material Cost (Thousands)	Average Employee Hours	Net Profit (Thousands)
Store 1	38	8	8	30
Store 2	115	24	7	80
Store 3	56	15	10	50
Store 4	22	9	8	10
Store 5	96	40	6	40
Store 6	100	28	8	82
Store 7	226	115	9	60
Store 8	17	2	9	5
Store 9	67	38	10	38
Store 10	238	78	7	190

Exercise

You are required to design four speedometer gauges in Microsoft Excel and/or Tableau as it would appear on the dashboard. There would be three broad indicators. First level is bad performance, second is medium and third is good. You can decide the numbers for each level as you feel fit for the business. Insert the above values given for a month.

10

Documenting the Processes

Learning Objectives

After completing this chapter, students should be able to understand about the following:

- Need for building a systematic documentation
- Documenting the processes
- Steps followed for analysis
- Capturing relevant information sources: print and digital
- Documenting client conversations
- Emphasizing relevant outcomes

Opening Example

Father Entered the Kitchen to Cook

Remember the days when your father decided to cook in the kitchen. For every ingredient, he would come to check with your mom. The salt was the most challenging of all. It did not have a measuring spoon. Rather mom, based on her years of experience, had developed a recipe engine 'model' where she knew how much to add without a measuring spoon. The recipe engine was trained to perform without pre-specified input ingredients for expected output (good food). She realized, if she wanted your dad to cook independently in the kitchen, she should write down the complete recipe for certain dishes he loved to make. This would make him independent, consume less time back and forth and make food more predictable and tasty.

NEED FOR BUILDING A SYSTEMATIC DOCUMENTATION

The above example is to draw an analogy for the readers who have begun reading the not-so-exciting part of BA—the documentation process. Many fathers are by themselves good cooks!

After the interesting, often referred to as sexy, part of BA described in Chapters 1–9, we have now reached the important chapter on the significance of documentation in BA. Documentation is primarily to bring standardization in the Analytics processes. If Employee A has performed a task which can be replicated by Employee B for a similar task, it is desirable to save the time and money by walking the steps that A has taken and taking the pain to plan and design the task. Thus, avoid building processes from scratch. A set of interrelated tasks done repeatedly can be automated. Systematic documentation is the methodology to capture, process and record significant information in required detail for appropriate use in future.

DOCUMENTING THE PROCESSES

The creator (analyst) in a BA team is usually a critical member right from the beginning of an Analytics project to the end. He/she is embedded in various responsibilities from data gathering to outcome, as the project may demand. The discussion of an Analytics project in an organization begins by the discussion of a business need or opportunity that may be important to decipher in the interest of the organization's profitability. It can be an issue relating to significant contribution of teams in companies such as sales team not able to reach potential customers, operations team not able to monitor and correct process problems in machinery due to delay in communication of malfunctioning parameters, retails stores not being able to forecast sales and inventory going out of stock often.

In such cases, often help is sought from BA teams. The first discussion with the stakeholders (clients) begins with meetings/communications that are information in semi-structured form. This information needs to be transformed into systematic notes that eventually leads to defining the 'BP/Opportunity' for the Analytics project being discussed.

Why is this important to do? Often, the initial conversations are scattered, intermixed with views and opinions from stakeholders present during the meetings. As an experienced analyst, one needs to be able to filter the important aspects of this conversation, sequence them in the way described by the client organization who has invested in the Analytics project and document it. Then in consultation with the client-side stakeholders, define and document the 'BP/Opportunity' statement. Doing so is extremely important to ensure that both sides of the team members, the client and the Analytics team, are in agreement on what needs to be done going forward.

For example, a water purifying company named Janani Enterprise manufactures drinking water purifiers. Their product range consists of five different types of water purifiers based on the purification technology used to cater to varied customer needs. It does home and office installations of water purifiers across India. For each city they have a CRM manager. About four–five zonal managers, who manage customers in different zones of the city, report to him. Domestic customers have three major service requirements: new installation, fault in the machine and mandatory service as per the warranty. The water purifier company wishes to invest in an Analytics project that will allow them to understand the service performance of their managers at every level and hence identify gaps in domestic customer service levels. The 'BP' statement here would be in the following two parts:

1. Monitor service performance of managers
2. Identify gaps in domestic customers' service level

STEPS FOLLOWED FOR ANALYSIS

After the BP has been defined and consent of all parties has been sought, the second part would be to define the 'BA Problem' statement. This would follow the following steps:

1. Break the BP into tangible deliverables that are expected by the client, here Janani Enterprise management team. For the first BP, identify if managers have been able to meet or excel their performance benchmark. For the second BP, measure customer satisfaction on service levels.
2. State the BA project objectives.
3. State the BA research questions.
4. Plan the BA project road map by creating the Analytics research matrix as discussed in Chapter 4.

These steps have to be given the necessary time for building each step to match the BP and documenting every step after approval from the client.

The next step followed for analysis would be to look at each component of the Analytics research matrix—the customer-related aspects, the employee-related (here managers) aspects, the operational model proposed, the finance involved and the competitor analysis. There could be other aspects (constructs) that need to be considered that vary from project to project. These aspects will generate the variables that need to be studied. At every stage throughout the process, detailed documentation is recommended to maintain continuity and flow of the progress in designing the Analytics research matrix.

CAPTURING RELEVANT INFORMATION SOURCES: PRINT AND DIGITAL

After the variables of interest have been identified, the next stage is to gather information on the variables for further processing. Details on each variable such as type, size, relevance, relation to which construct of study in the Analytics research matrix and method of collecting information about it need to be identified and documented. Secondary and exploratory researches are conducted at the beginning of an Analytics research project where it is needed to define the BP better. This is done in situations where enough information is not available for applied/basic research to formulate the BP. All relevant sources of secondary and exploratory data sources need to be documented.

After the Analytics research matrix has been designed and variables appropriately identified, the data source for obtaining data on each variable needs to be mapped. Many a time, analysts assume that data sources shall be accessible and available as planned. However, difficulty in accessing the data sources during data collection causes delay in executing the project. Hence, it is recommended to document the planned data sources, print or digital, and ensure appropriate access to them during the data collection process.

DOCUMENTING CLIENT CONVERSATIONS

The Analytics team begins collecting data, followed by processing information by building an Analytics model (engine) such that the outcome addresses the 'BA Problem' statement. At each stage, detailed documentation needs to be the practice of the teams. Often in the excitement of working through the repetitive process of building the EXACT model, minute details at every iteration process get missed out, leading to gaps in documentation for the future. The model at every significant stage can be tried and tested by client teams in various departments as pilot (experimental) test models. This can be done using data relevant to their domain. Incrementally building it with the client team builds trust and reduces the chance of rejection. Client inputs and feedback must be documented at every stage of testing the model. Once the model runs independently, it can be called a process—ready to use in circumstances that define similar decision-making situations. A new user will not have to spend the extra time to build from scratch.

The model in its final stage needs to be checked for quality performance by the Analytics team. Each unit of the model needs to be checked for performance and consistency. This is called Unit testing. It is then handed over to the client by completing the user acceptance test. Both sides need to be satisfied with the performance of the model with desired outcomes. Both unit and user acceptance tests must be documented for the completion of the project.

EMPHASIZING RELEVANT OUTCOMES

Nature of the corporate data is quite interesting; it can broadly be categorized into simple and complex data. Data that is easily accessible, accurately categorized and comfortably sized for the domain users to read, access and process can be termed as simple. Complexity increases with size, the sources from where the data is gathered, the type of the data that is gathered and so on. Simple and complex could be the types of analysis as well. Simple analysis could be a count or an average and then representing it in the form of charts, bar graphs and pie charts. How many employees were present for 90% of the working days? To make it complicated, certain dimensions to your query can be added. For instance, how many part-time employees were present for 90% of the working days or employees by department who were present 90% of the working days? Now, suppose I am interested in knowing senior management employees who would be given a promotion based on multiple factors of which presence of 90% of the working days is necessary, then the analysis becomes complex because it now deals with multiple variables, data from varied sources, data over a time period, comparison to historical data of similar decisions and consideration of organization's HR policies. Knowing what data analysis method to use to get the desired response can be challenging. To add to it, there are numerous tools and techniques available in the market.

While delivering an Analytics project to the client, it is thus extremely important to emphasize on the significant outcomes. What to see and how to infer. Dashboards and storytelling are discussed in Chapter 11 that deals with communicating outcomes in the language the client is able to understand.

CONCLUSION

Most BA projects begin with a concrete set of targets to be achieved by both the client and Analytics team in a given agreed upon time within a planned budget. The effort by the Analytics team is to create the model for the client team, for them to independently use and infer results. This supported by detailed documentation allows complete transfer of knowledge, thereby reducing the need for continuous hand-holding after completing service.

REVIEW QUESTIONS

1. Explain the need for building a robust documentation for BA projects.
2. What is the need for documenting client conversations?
3. For Janani Enterprise, what relevant outcomes should the analyst stress upon? Think and make a list of analyses that would be useful for them.

11 Building the Storyboard of Outcomes

Learning Objectives

After completing this chapter, students should be able to understand about the following:

- Analysing to convincing storytelling: Are they different?
- Building appropriate dashboards
- Telling relevant stories from analysis: What does it take?
- Communicating to the client

Opening Example

In an article 'Brain Movies: When Readers Can Picture It, They Understand It', the authors Donna Wilson and Marcus Conyers have explained how understanding and retention are augmented by the use of images.[1]

The authors have discussed how teachers can teach their students with the help of brain movies—image that forms in the mind as one reads something. This method helps the reader create mental images of characters and situations leading to more engaging interactions and retention. They have suggested that by creating mental images of what one sees or reads, one taps into both a verbal system for the language and a non-verbal visual spatial representational system for images. This makes the abstract system more concrete and meaningful to remember for a longer time.

The art of storytelling to clients in BA uses a similar concept. The outcomes from a BA process need to be communicated to the end user/decision-maker in a language that the audience is easily able to understand. The choices suggested by an Analytics engine or an algorithm need to be presented in a visually appealing and easily understandable form. An organization dashboard is one such means of communicating BA outcomes. It is designed keeping in mind the needs of the end user. It provides a handle to the end user to view disparate sets of processed complex information in a pleasing visual form. It focuses on sections of outcome in order of the most significant to the least. Thus, it represents information in organized partitioned layers and easily digestible bits.

---

[1] https://www.edutopia.org/blog/brain-movies-visualize-reading-comprehension-donna-wilson

ANALYSING TO CONVINCING STORYTELLING: ARE THEY DIFFERENT?

We have reached the last and crucial stage (Stage 3) of the Analytics process (see Figure 2.1). It is crucial because the true impact created by an organization's analytic capability is usually dependent on how 'well' the output is packaged and presented to the decision-maker (user group). The measure of 'goodness' of the communication is based on the user group's subjective assessment of their comprehension of the findings and their relevance to their decision-making process.

Unfortunately, this is the point where many Analytics providers are in a tough spot and yet many are not totally equipped to address the concerns of business. Also, it is our belief that in recent times, the Analytics domain has not really paid enough importance to this very critical element. Instead, the focus has been largely in improving methodology/technology. Seasoned practitioners have however realized that lack of attention on communication can be very damaging to the overall productivity of the research/Analytics process. The conversion of numeric output into narratives (storytelling), and sometimes illustrations, is important and less talked about. It is traditionally not considered to be the strength of core Analytics professionals (statisticians, computer scientists and information technologists). In fact, one of the possible reasons why Analytics, in spite of all its potential, does not still reckon well in the imagination of the many users/decision-makers is perhaps just that—it still largely uses 'machine language' to communicate results rather than higher order languages (English, for instance) which are more amenable to the user's comprehension.

There is a unique skill involved in this activity. It may require a strange concoction of scientific and creative acumen together. We admit that it is hard for one individual to excel in both; however, there lies the need to have resources in the organization who act as very good workflow managers and translators across 'machine languages' and higher order 'human intelligent' languages.

This chapter will provide some guidelines about how analysts may want to reorient their data processing output into a format that is more appetizing to the end user of Analytics. It also provides some pointers on how to structure their final output (logically) to make better impact among their user group.

BUILDING APPROPRIATE DASHBOARDS

Dashboards provide one stop location (dynamic view) of several critical key performance indicators in organizations. Every department or project group functions within its own set processes towards achieving set objectives. Measuring parameters that define the success and failure of achieving key performance indicators is important at the team level and also for collaborating across teams. The meetings that discuss performance for teams across organizations or monitor them on a continuous basis may not require every detail that the team members and managers obtain/track on a day-to-day basis. However, they require a bird's-eye view of key performance indicators with possibility of drilling down to more details, if necessary. Dashboards are built to address this need in organizations. Be it a small team preparing the key points to discuss in the forthcoming meeting with their manager, be it a department-wise meeting of medical professionals discussing new methods in medicine or a

FIGURE 11.1   *Grocery Purchase Data in MS Excel*

ID	TDS	Trips	HS	HI	FHRD1	FHRD2	FHRD3	FHRD4	ORD1	DOGS	CATS	FHA	PCD1	PCD2	PCD3	PCD4	PCD5	PCD6	PCD7
2302297.00	767.10	45.00	1.00	7.00	1.00	0.00	0.00	0.00	0.00	1.00	1.00	6.00	0.00	0.00	0.00	0.00	0.00	0.00	0.00
3302107.00	1434.32	53.00	3.00	9.00	1.00	0.00	0.00	0.00	0.00	1.00	0.00	3.00	1.00	0.00	0.00	0.00	0.00	0.00	0.00
3302292.00	940.83	21.00	2.00	5.00	1.00	0.00	0.00	0.00	1.00	0.00	2.00	3.00	0.00	0.00	1.00	0.00	0.00	0.00	0.00
5302106.00	4660.61	85.00	4.00	11.00	1.00	0.00	0.00	0.00	1.00	2.00	0.00	3.00	0.00	0.00	0.00	0.00	0.00	0.00	0.00
5302115.00	985.18	39.00	2.00	6.00	1.00	0.00	0.00	0.00	0.00	0.00	0.00	6.00	0.00	0.00	0.00	0.00	0.00	0.00	0.00
5302250.00	1223.87	18.00	2.00	5.00	0.00	0.00	1.00	0.00	0.00	1.00	1.00	1.00	0.00	0.00	0.00	0.00	0.00	0.00	0.00
6302286.00	1348.50	26.00	4.00	9.00	1.00	0.00	0.00	0.00	0.00	1.00	0.00	2.00	1.00	0.00	0.00	0.00	0.00	0.00	0.00
6302295.00	4235.26	53.00	1.00	8.00	1.00	0.00	0.00	0.00	0.00	3.00	0.00	4.00	0.00	0.00	0.00	0.00	0.00	0.00	0.00
7302281.00	1181.38	33.00	3.00	6.00	1.00	0.00	0.00	0.00	0.00	0.00	1.00	1.00	1.00	0.00	0.00	0.00	0.00	0.00	0.00
7302290.00	1059.04	21.00	2.00	7.00	1.00	0.00	0.00	0.00	0.00	3.00	0.00	3.00	0.00	0.00	0.00	0.00	0.00	0.00	0.00
9302294.00	1716.38	58.00	2.00	7.00	1.00	0.00	0.00	0.00	0.00	3.00	0.00	6.00	0.00	0.00	0.00	0.00	0.00	0.00	0.00
10302225.00	965.70	13.00	6.00	9.00	1.00	0.00	0.00	0.00	0.00	0.00	1.00	3.00	0.00	0.00	0.00	0.00	0.00	1.00	0.00
11302157.00	1131.23	16.00	4.00	10.00	0.00	1.00	0.00	0.00	0.00	0.00	0.00	3.00	0.00	0.00	1.00	0.00	0.00	0.00	0.00
11302453.00	1797.65	52.00	2.00	6.00	1.00	0.00	0.00	0.00	1.00	0.00	0.00	5.00	0.00	0.00	0.00	0.00	0.00	0.00	0.00
12302229.00	2587.64	49.00	1.00	8.00	1.00	0.00	0.00	0.00	0.00	1.00	0.00	5.00	0.00	0.00	0.00	0.00	0.00	0.00	0.00
13302210.00	1073.15	32.00	2.00	7.00	1.00	0.00	0.00	0.00	0.00	1.00	0.00	6.00	0.00	0.00	0.00	0.00	0.00	0.00	0.00
13302224.00	1561.51	38.00	1.00	5.00	1.00	0.00	0.00	0.00	1.00	0.00	0.00	0.00	0.00	0.00	0.00	0.00	0.00	0.00	0.00
13302458.00	1393.51	48.00	2.00	7.00	1.00	0.00	0.00	0.00	0.00	0.00	0.00	6.00	0.00	0.00	0.00	0.00	0.00	0.00	0.00
14302273.00	1696.17	35.00	3.00	8.00	1.00	0.00	0.00	0.00	1.00	2.00	5.00	2.00	0.00	1.00	0.00	0.00	0.00	0.00	0.00
15302200.00	1719.61	54.00	1.00	8.00	1.00	0.00	0.00	0.00	0.00	1.00	0.00	5.00	0.00	0.00	0.00	0.00	0.00	0.00	0.00
15302214.00	1251.81	30.00	2.00	7.00	1.00	0.00	0.00	0.00	0.00	1.00	0.00	2.00	0.00	0.00	0.00	0.00	0.00	0.00	0.00
15302727.00	2228.81	80.00	3.00	1.00	1.00	0.00	0.00	0.00	0.00	2.00	0.00	4.00	0.00	0.00	0.00	0.00	0.00	0.00	0.00
17302141.00	761.18	23.00	5.00	6.00	1.00	0.00	0.00	0.00	0.00	1.00	1.00	2.00	0.00	0.00	0.00	0.00	0.00	0.00	0.00
17302222.00	1200.99	15.00	3.00	3.00	0.00	0.00	1.00	0.00	0.00	0.00	0.00	0.00	0.00	0.00	1.00	0.00	0.00	0.00	0.00
17302276.00	1704.08	98.00	7.00	7.00	1.00	0.00	0.00	0.00	1.00	0.00	1.00	4.00	0.00	0.00	0.00	0.00	0.00	0.00	0.00
18302217.00	83.88	11.00	1.00	6.00	1.00	0.00	0.00	0.00	0.00	2.00	0.00	5.00	0.00	0.00	0.00	0.00	0.00	0.00	0.00
18302271.00	2158.13	104.00	1.00	9.00	0.00	0.00	0.00	0.00	1.00	0.00	4.00	0.00	0.00	0.00	0.00	0.00	0.00	0.00	0.00
19302104.00	1999.96	31.00	3.00	10.00	1.00	0.00	0.00	0.00	0.00	2.00	1.00	1.00	1.00	0.00	0.00	0.00	0.00	0.00	0.00

marketing head trying to justify the advertising and promotion budget for next five years or the company CEO of an airline industry monitoring performance across regions. These and similar other situations can represent complex capsules of information in a consolidated fashion using dashboard and storytelling methods.

Let us take an example. Figure 11.1 shows a snapshot of an Excel data sheet with grocery purchase data. There are 1,000 records. Household size variable is shown as categorical data of one–eight members. Total dollar spent (TDS) variable is continuous variable of the total amount spent per household in a six-month duration time. Household income variable has been categorized in 12 groups depending on monthly income. Trips variable is the number of trips made by a household in the six-month time that captures the data. Variable Own/Rent the house has two values: 2 for own and 1 for rent.

The data has been opened in Tableau as shown in Figure 11.2.

Figure 11.3 shows the relationship between the count of the household size category by whether they own or rent the house. It can be concluded that more number of households own a house (2) compared to rent (1). Additionally, those with two members in the house are more in number in both categories.

Figure 11.4 represents the relationship between averages of the TDS by household size in the six-month period. It can be concluded that sum of TDS spent is maximum by six-member households. From Figure 11.3, we see that the total number of six-member households in the sample data set is 26 (five families rent a house and 21 families own a house). Yet compared to two-member households, the TDS is higher for six-member households. Further, research by the company can be carried out to identify the cause for this outcome. However, before investing in research, this outcome needs to be validated using other sample data sets from the population under study.

FIGURE 11.2   *Grocery Purchase Data in Tableau*

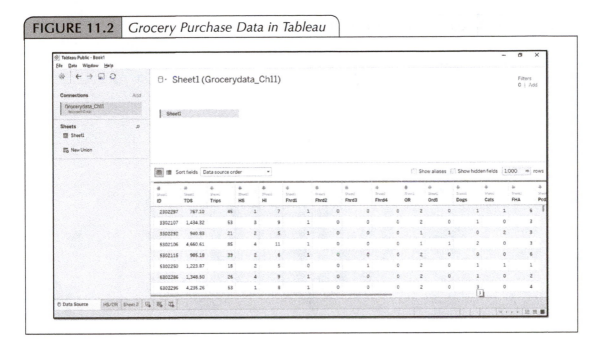

FIGURE 11.3   *Own versus Rent*

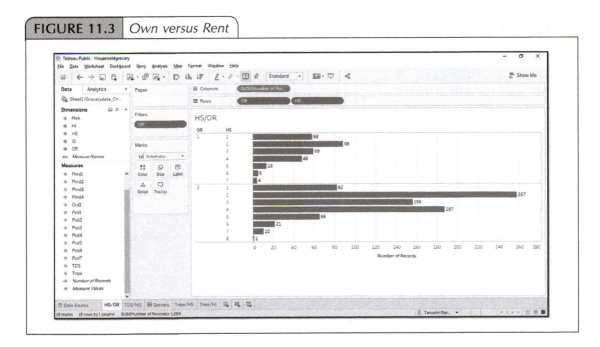

Figure 11.5 shows the average number of trips made in six months by household size. It is interesting to note that maximum trips have been made by six-member households, closely followed by two-member households.

FIGURE 11.4 | *Total Dollars Spent by Household Size*

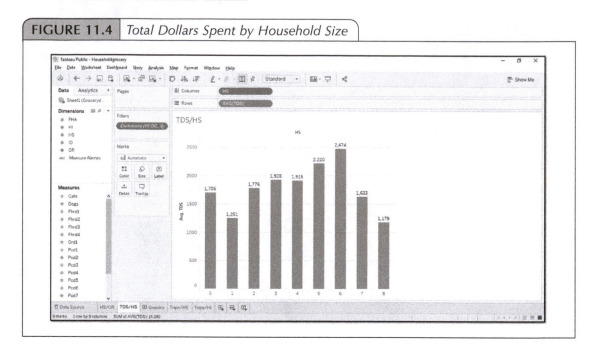

FIGURE 11.5 | *Number of Trips by Household Size*

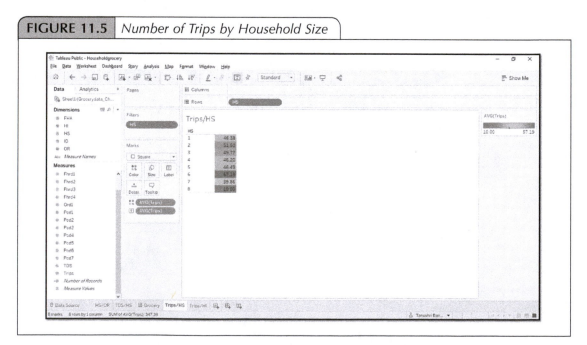

Figure 11.6 shows the average number of trips made by household income. Category 3 of household income has made the largest contribution and Category 9 the lowest.

The dashboard (Figure 11.7) created in Tableau summarizes this information for household grocery data. Here for illustration purpose, only a few variables of the data set have been

FIGURE 11.6 | Number of Trips by Household Income

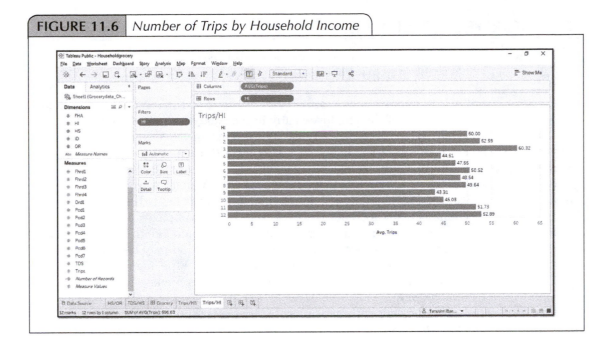

FIGURE 11.7 | Dashboard for Household

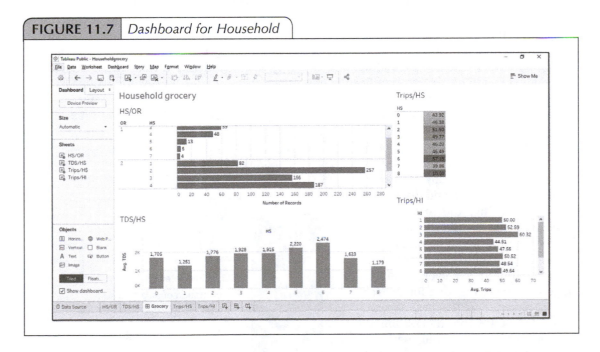

considered. You can download this data from student download section to try and add more features to the dashboard. There are three small tabs at the bottom of the Tableau interface: first to add a new worksheet, second to add a dashboard and third to create a story. The third tab will assist you in sequencing your slides to write small inference to create a story of the outcomes.

TELLING RELEVANT STORIES FROM ANALYSIS: WHAT DOES IT TAKE?

'If your words or images are not on point, making them dance in color won't make them relevant.'
—Edward Tufte, Professor Emeritus, Yale University

Making strong and logical arguments to substantiate a numeric/analysis output can go a long way in establishing credibility of the employee early in the Analytics professional curve. It is therefore important to not only have sufficient fluency in the language of business communication (English is widely used in corporate India), but also have the expertise in structuring the communication in a way that sounds logically convincing. This is not to dilute the technical competency of data processing which is indeed the core requirement. A translator's job is to translate between two languages—her proficiency of both languages has to be of superior level.

Many business communication documents appear to be a series of pages that describe what the analysts have done. That is not usually what the user group would like to hear or see in the presentation (exceptions apart). For example, a typical presentation may have (a) too much description of the process followed to do the project, (b) very little understanding of the business context in which the project has been done, (c) too much analysis of the data and description of the methodology, (d) but little or no answers to business questions raised by the end user and (e) obviously, no main message or gist of the presentation that succinctly explains the contribution made by the project.

Hence, under these circumstances, communication tends to be 'purposeless', excruciatingly boring for the listener and hard to decipher. For someone who has not been through the tedious process of culling insights from data, relating to the details of the data processing stages can be hard, unless there is some prior agenda or interest in delving into the details. Therefore, after having spent many hours working on analysing the data, a relatively misdirected presentation-cum-communication plan can significantly upset the impact of such hard work, simply because the reader (audience) of the communication does not have the patience to decipher the core message presented in a laboriously constructed treatise (see Figure 11.1). The format (Figure 11.8) exemplifies the same.

By the time the presentation reaches the 'outcome and benefit' stage, which is something of primary importance to most end users, the audience is either too tired or confused with the details of the earlier stages to pay much attention. For most impactful presentation of Analytics output to users, the last stage should set the tone for the rest of the presentation. It acts as a provocation (or builds the interest among the listeners) to continue with the rest of the discussion on the details of the Analytics/research work, if required. It may ignite thoughts as varied as—'Hmm, how did (s)he get

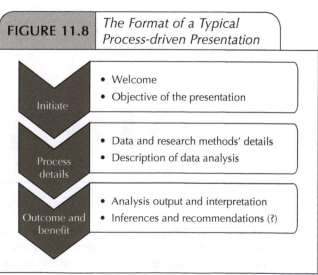

FIGURE 11.8   *The Format of a Typical Process-driven Presentation*

Initiate
- Welcome
- Objective of the presentation

Process details
- Data and research methods' details
- Description of data analysis

Outcome and benefit
- Analysis output and interpretation
- Inferences and recommendations (?)

there?' or 'Oh, I understand and completely agree with her recommendations'. Both these reactions are critical to determine the success of a very engaging business conversation.

For many aspiring Analytics professionals, it would be appropriate to adhere to some simple rules of structuring their communication documents to make them more impactful. Below are a few such guiding rules that may be considered, while packaging business presentations using numbers. Discretion may be used since not all contexts demand such presentation skills. Usually, end users and decision-makers appreciate them more, since a primary concern of theirs is answers to their questions which are somehow wrapped in the recommendations.

The three main areas that as a communicator one needs to pay attention to are[2]:

1. The synthesis of the communication.
2. Creating a compelling structure for communication.
3. Understanding the expectation of the audience.

As stated earlier, the main message is a 'synthesis' of finding (an implication or a recommendation based on the findings) rather than an exposition of facts or a summary of the same. Additionally, it should provide adequate leads into the structure of the presentation. This is an important part of the presentation. To engage the audience, the 'so what' from the analysis needs to be shared as specifically and clearly to make impact. Engagement with the presentation and subsequent conversation begins here. If the 'connect' does not happen here, the effectiveness of the subsequent conversation is lost.

Creating an Impactful Structure of Presentation

Making an impactful beginning through a well-scripted 'synthesis' can draw the audience towards the typical query—'how did (s)he get to that recommendation?'. To address such a query, the presentation must have a well-structured defence to the recommendations made.

A well thought-out structure of the defence helps in organizing the details of the presentation content effectively around the main message, so that the supporting arguments complement the veracity of the main message rather than create confusion. Business presentation experts have usually adopted two ways of creating effective logical structure (defence) of the presentation.

1. Top-down hierarchical structure
2. Sequential and logical organization

Top-Down Structure

The hierarchical organization of thoughts allows the audience to connect the recommendations (usually the main message) in the presentation to the main arguments that support the recommendations. The presentation is somewhat like opening an ensemble of arguments sequentially—from general to the specific in a hierarchical order—in the process leading the audience eventually to the core of the defence.

[2] A good reference material for this is: Barbara Minto, *The Pyramid Principle: Logic in Writing and Thinking* (London: Pitman Publishing, 1987).

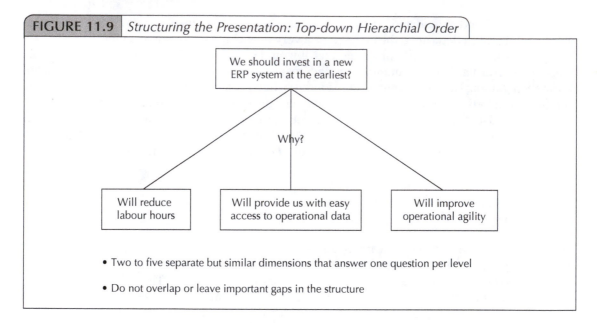

FIGURE 11.9 | *Structuring the Presentation: Top-down Hierarchial Order*

In structuring the presentation in this top-down order, the main message is supported in such a manner that the evidence appears in the consequent hierarchical (lower) level. Usually, the document layout begins with a page that answers the primary question (main message). Each subsequent layer in the pyramid is used to provide supporting evidence to the message in the layer above. Usually, up to five supporting points are used to optimally create an effective message (Figure 11.9).

This presentation format ensures a defensible argument (anticipating a query) for all assertions made in a hierarchical manner. The value of the hierarchy is that it enables the audience (reader) to sequentially move from the essence of the document to the details and allows a premature closure of the presentation without compromising on comprehensiveness, should the reader feel that (s)he does not require further factual support beyond a certain level of detail.

Sequenced and Logical Structure

This format (Figure 11.10) is useful when the argument can be posed in a logical sequence beginning with a description of the context which provides a firm background to the presented problem that may require a resolution. The main message is usually an emphatic reinforcement of the resolution. It is necessary to ensure a logical flow between the three parts of the argument, that is, situation, complication and the resolution. Specifically, the description of the context (situation) should provide logical cues for the problem definition (complication) and the latter should be so presented that arguably there can be only one resolution option, which is the one presented. In this way, the document ensures that the reader is provided with a convincing solution to the BP being addressed.

There are no firm rules of structuring a presentation. The above-mentioned points are just issues that are worth a consideration. Finally, it is about how well the 'curry is cooked' for easy

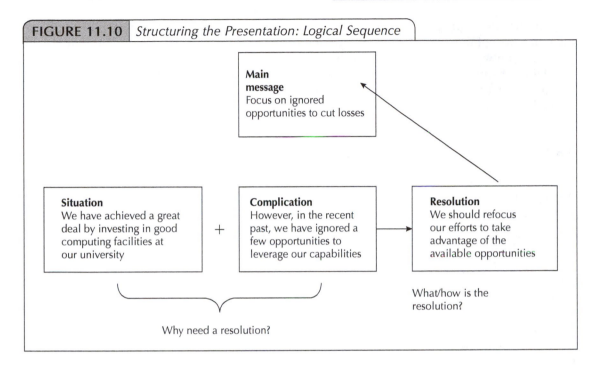

FIGURE 11.10 *Structuring the Presentation: Logical Sequence*

digestion. It should be neither too bland nor spicy, since both may have a negative response from the consumer.

COMMUNICATING TO THE CLIENT

Managing the Audience's Expectations

This should not be hard to comprehend. While we are not suggesting the presenters should 'play to the gallery', it is essential to try to get a prior notion regarding the motivations of the audience—what they might be they 'looking for' and how might one 'arrest their attention'. This endeavour may also include ascertaining as to the appropriate means of communication and the frequency at which the communication should be made. Simple but significant details regarding the communication format can go a long way in ensuring the correct impact of the same, for desired outcome.

It is necessary to remember always that the audience cares to listen to what they want to hear, not what the presenter wants to say. If it does not hear content in line what it wants to hear, it may lead to boredom and disengagement and ultimately a perceived lack of impact. On the other hand, if they hear something contradictory to its expectation, this may lead to a provocation to dispute the recommendation of the presenter, leading to an involved discussion on the research methodology. This situation serves the purpose of conducting the research and brings out useful insights and 'surprises'. Analysts must be prepared for situations where disputes arise (a sign of involvement of the audience), since they are the opportunities to prove the real worth of their analyses and research. The latter is the hard support that determines the difference between an opinion and a fact.

Whereas technology has a critical role to play in deriving subtle insights from raw data, not available otherwise, the true opportunity to create impact in the business setting is highly dependent on how these insights are creatively portrayed as an engaging story to the user group.

Telling Stories through Data

The role of the analysts (or the BP solver, in general) is therefore to 'tell useful stories, only that they need to be backed by facts'. The art of storytelling is a strange concoction of (a) understanding data insights and interpreting their impact, (b) converting them into creative language yet focused with an objective to make a point and (c) building visual imagery (where possible) to drive the impact (see Figure 11.11). In the process, the analyst ensures total engagement of the consumer of her research to the main points that she would like to drive home. That is more than a handful of skills to build for a person in this profession, not necessarily something that can be acquired overnight.

Mere reporting of facts based on a technical process is clichéd and is no longer valued as useful in the business world. Hence, creative capabilities (although incongruous with traditional analytical capabilities) have to be encouraged in organizations to ensure effective portrayal of information output.

This may be possible generally with a 'top-down' approach starting with the problem to be resolved and identifying the recommended resolution and defence for the same (as mentioned above). Sometimes, it is possible that the data and the insight do not provide concrete leads towards a plausible resolution plan. Perhaps, the problem is not what it was thought to be and now with the data, it appears to somewhat different, though unclear.

In such a situation, a 'bottom-up' approach may be helpful. This may require the following: (a) list all the points (insights) that are important, (b) try to work out a relationship between them and (c) draw a conclusion. This is sometimes known as a 'data mining' approach where there is no prior hunch to drive insight development for the data. Rather the content buried in

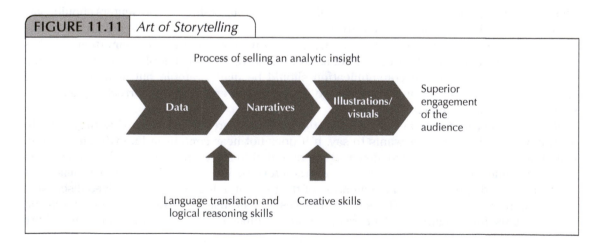

FIGURE 11.11 *Art of Storytelling*

the insights bring out the wisdom. Let us illustrate this point by using a document that needs rewriting (see Figure 11.12).

The partial report submitted by business school students is based on their secondary source research. The research has been conducted on the market comparison of available web browsers and their current usage. Assume that we know nothing about the market for web browsers other than what is presented in the report. Therefore, without passing a judgement over whether the facts are correct (or otherwise), our objective is to clearly state what the research is pointing towards a conclusion.

Is there a conclusion provided in the report or it is a collation of facts. It appears more like the latter. Of course, there is some structure, since the data is categorized into specific compartments—market share, consumer segments, usage drivers, switching patterns and competitor product analysis.

We first look for an interesting finding from the research that may arrest the user's interest. Obviously, the significant gap between the market share of 'Chrome' and other browsers

FIGURE 11.12	*Student Literature Review on Browser Comparisons*

Key Insights from Literature Review	
Market share and consumer segments	Chrome – 70.95 per cent Firefox – 10.05 per cent Edge – 4.17 per cent Internet Explorer – 5.40 per cent Segments (based on pivots): 1. Enterprises 2. Individuals – students, professionals, enthusiasts, tech savvy, loyal users
Usage drivers	How to measure usage: 1. Monthly active usage: No. of browser users in a month 2. Average time spent on the browser/amount of data (internet packets) flowing through the browser
	Strong drivers: 1. Frequency of feature addition and subsequent releases 2. Proprietary or open-source browser application development platforms
	Weak drivers: 1. Pre-installed or bundling of browser with OS 2. Aggressive promotions post launch of a new browser
Switching patterns	Enterprises-wide use – high cost involved wherein the entire firm's default apps/webpages/tools are boarded on one browser Individuals – low switching cost since co-existence of browsers is possible on a desktop Reasons for switching/churns: 1. Availability of available websites (irrespective of total compatibility with other websites) 2. Preferences of features (speed vs security for eg) 3. Delighters – (Pay integration/autofill/PDF rendering and so on)
Competitor product analysis	Major competitor products – Chrome and Firefox 1. Technical superiority using open-source platforms leading to faster advancements 2. Cross platform integration with easy portability and syncing capability 3. Better extension support and launch speed 4. Higher stability as developers tend to develop webpages compatible with the most popular browser

catches our attention. The next question is why is the gap that significant—can the data presented provide support for such a competitive position?

It appears that the 'product analysis' may be able to answer some of these queries (at least the difference between 'Edge' and 'Chrome' (and Firefox).

This is also supported somewhat by the preference for certain product features as outlined in 'usage patterns'. The research also provides opportunities for newer players to attract customer segments (enterprise/students/professionals) by providing added advantages such as 'speed', 'security' and 'pay integrations' (see 'switching patterns').

Now we have a semblance of a conclusive story to describe why 'Chrome' is ahead in the market among certain important segments and what should small players potentially do to improve their competitive position. Figure 11.13 provides this attempt at structuring the data in Figure 11.12 in a plausible business story using a 'bottom-up' approach.

BOX 11.1 | *Major Findings from Our Secondary Research*

1. Google Chrome has 71 per cent market share in the web browser market among enterprises, individuals including students, professionals and so on. Other browsers (including Microsoft Edge) have miniscule presence.
2. A major competitive advantage of the 'Chrome' over other browsers appears to be:
   a. Their technical superiority using open source platforms.
   b. Cross platform integration.
   c. Better extension support and launch speed.
   d. Higher stability.
3. These advantages are corroborated by user groups who prefer:
   a. Frequent feature additions and releases.
   b. Open-source browser application platforms.
4. However, competitors may want to bolster their market position by leveraging the following opportunity areas:
   a. Better speed and security features.
   b. Delighters such as pay integration/auto fill/PDF rendering and so on.

One other point to note is that good ideas need not be wrapped up with bad prose. Often times, analysts express their outcomes in highly dehydrated language, with technical jargons that have been liberally used to make the presentation profound. Nothing can be farther from truth, especially in environments where executives care for usefulness of the insight, rather than an expression of technical prowess. Usually, the process description is best kept in the 'appendix' and is only referred to if the veracity of the facts is questioned.

What works well sometimes is to visualize your recommendation as an image in your mind, then try to translate the same in words. Do this first, without inhibition, because it forms a very good template for you to build a creative communication. If need be, the creativity can be tempered down in the next sweep by augmenting the same with factual evidence. Where no factual defence exists, check if the assumptions that hold your recommendations are reasonable.

Example 11.1 illustrates the point being made over here.

EXAMPLE 11.1 | *How Could Raj Bhatia Have Done a Better Job of Communicating Results?*

Raj Bhatia, a data analyst employed with a large-sized FMCG company was tasked to run a regression-based model on the sales volume of the company's biggest brand. He was asked to identify the important drivers of sales and report the same to Ashok, the marketing manager.

Raj ran the regression on sales data and presented the output of the regression model to Ashok, identifying the statistically significant variables that drove sale volume of the brand.

Ashok was somewhat puzzled looking at the report. He was expecting a measure of the influence of each important marketing variable on the sales in terms of 'rupee impact', so that he could get a 'business' view of the analysis. Raj had not expected such a critique from one of his important internal clients, nor had he thought about how to convert his statistically significant result into business impact. Clearly, there was a communication gap between two important functional managers in the organization.

Raj's problem can be somewhat addressed if instead of showcasing the regression output (driver coefficients with statistical significance) which very few practitioners without statistical training appreciate, he had managed to depict the impact of the coefficients of various marketing variables in terms of the volume sales as depicted in the illustration (Figure 11.14), Ashok would perhaps have been more convinced.

The data (regression coefficients) had to be converted into an accounting metric which depicted 'sales volume attributable' to a particular marketing variable. When all such metrics are added up, they account for the total sales volume of the brand. In Figure 11.14, for instance, the incremental volume is explained by volume driven by (a) TV advertising, (b) coupons and (c) trade. In turn, the total of the 'incremental' volume (made up by these three components) and the 'base' volume made up for the volume sales of the brand. This is a practical way of accounting for volume sales and making various marketing variables 'accountable' for the same.[3]

Business storytelling is a unique 'art' that operates in the unbounded canvas of creativity but 'constrained' within the perimeter of scientific evidencing. Therefore, creative communication is not totally compatible with technical rigour (something Analytics is known for). However, 'measured' approximations to increase usefulness of the information, at the cost of precision, are something worth striving for to improve the potential for application. Admittedly, this requires the power of appropriate calibration that is achieved only with experience and a superior understanding of the underlying Analytics process.

REVIEW QUESTIONS

1. Describe the difference between hierarchical structure and sequenced logical flow.
2. When can a 'bottom-up' approach be useful in a business communication context?

---

[3] For more details on visual communication, readers may refer to Gene Zelazny, *Say It with Charts: The Executive's Guide to Visual Communication* (Irwin, IL: Irwin Professional Publication).

FIGURE 11.13	*Sales Volume Attribution to Various Marketing Mix Variables*

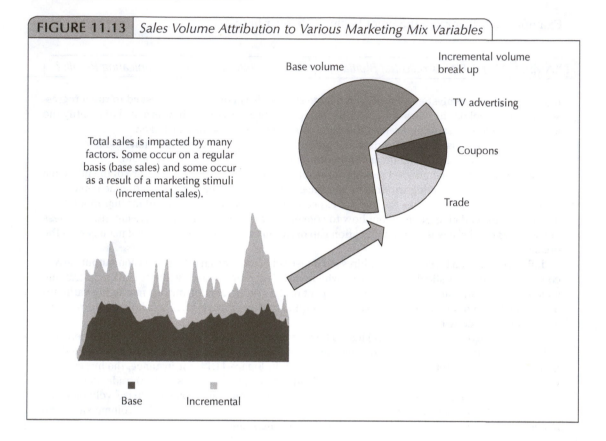

3. What is the significance of business dashboards in communicating analytical outcomes?
4. What is the difference between presenting an 'analysis' and 'telling a story' based on 'analysis'?

CASE 11.1
Creating the Two-wheeler Dashboard (Case Complexity: Low)

Sujay and his friends had a keen interest in driving two wheelers. They have always sat by the major city crossroads and admired the two wheelers on the road, often imagining themselves wearing a helmet and riding them. They, a group of four friends, had developed a passion for two wheelers over the years. The financial condition of their family was not such that they could afford a two wheeler. Their schooling and college education had been done on bicycles and the public transport city bus. All four had just completed college education and were in search of a job. The two months' time was to enjoy together as much as possible as they feared that their job will take them to different cities and away from each other.

During one such afternoon, they were remembering their courses at college. Their BI professor had very passionately taught them to design business dashboards. Sujay thought, rather than sitting idle gossiping away, why not use their interest in designing a dynamic dashboard that would capture variables that describe two wheelers in India. This would include features of the motorcycle, the purchase behaviour of customers, new trends and prices, and anything else that would be of interest to motorcycle manufacturers and dealers.

Exercise

Help Sujay with this project by suggesting the variable of interest, what kind of analysis should he and his friends do and how to represent the information on the dashboard.

CASE 11.2
'About India' Dashboard with the Data on Maps
(Case Complexity: Medium)

Tania Rao and her project group have to create a dashboard and a storyboard for her BA class presentation. You are a member of her team. She and her team members have been told to go to any of the websites where data sets can be downloaded for educational purposes. She has to represent population in India for a three-year period and its relationship to employment, health, society and education on a dashboard in the form of maps. The maps have to be colour coded with the information pertaining to each variable. You can choose the variables that you like. However, the final representation on the dashboard should be in the form of maps.

Exercise

Help Tania and your team to design the dashboard and build a story of outcomes. The map should be dynamic, which means that changing information in one location must dynamically change it in all other associated graphics.

CASE 11.3
What Should Be Naina's Dashboard Design?
(Case Complexity: High)

Naina Malhotra is preparing to present a short concise presentation to the strategic business unit (SBU) head of her company. She has to explain the following regarding their company's detergent brand 'Voor':

1. What aspects of marketing mix model impact sales of Voor?
2. What should the SBU do in the near term to support Voor?

She has taken store-level data on detergent sales from India. Total sales of detergents is impacted by many factors. As shown in Figure 11.14, some occur on a regular basis (base sales) and some occur as a result of a marketing stimuli (incremental sales).

FIGURE 11.14	*Detergent Sales Data*

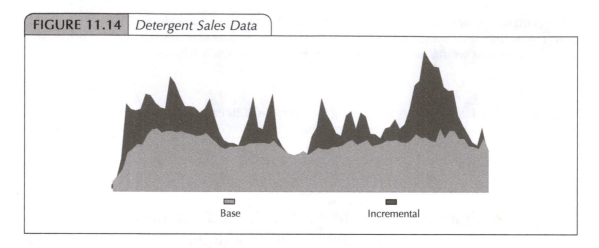

Base   Incremental

Naina has built a model to represent the customer who chooses Voor. She has tried to support it by describing what elements of marketing mix (advertisement, promotion, competition, distribution, trend, price, trade and such others) drive the choice. While competition has negative impact, all others are expected to have positive impact on sales of Voor. The model relates changes in sales to the changes in marketing support present during each week.

Naina researched that for detergent purchase by customers, there are two significant considerations: the 'pack size' of the detergent and the 'choice of the brand'. The explanatory variables for pack size are distribution, promotion and demographics. The explanatory variables for brand choice are price, distribution, pack size, promotion, satisfaction from prior purchase and demographics.

Figure 11.15 shows the three steps that were followed by Naina to complete her research for the presentation. She first tried to identify the impact each element of the marketing mix model has on the sales of Voor. Then she tried to determine the incremental volume of sales generated by investing into these efforts. Further she tried to use a logistic regression model to confirm her findings.

FIGURE 11.15	*Steps of Naina's Research*

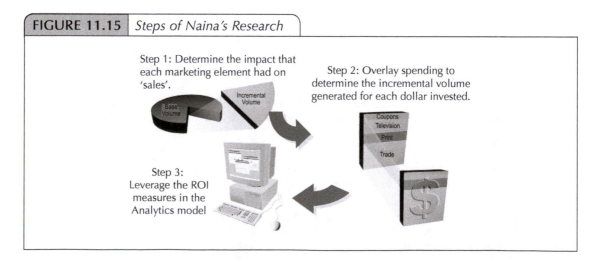

TABLE 11.1	*Outcome of Measured Variables*		
Variable	**Estimate**	**Chi-Square**	**Inference**
Distribution	0.01	9.14	Positive impact on brand choice
Total awareness	0.02	8.02	Positive impact on brand choice
Economy	0.77	6.10	Positive impact on brand choice
Performance	0.69	5.23	Positive impact on brand choice
Pack-level composite variable	−0.06	1.08	Negative impact on brand choice (insignificant)
Price	−1.39	0.31	Negative impact on brand choice (insignificant)

Table 11.1 shows the variables measured by Naina and the associated outcomes. Pack-level composite and price are insignificant, all others are significant.

Following are the broad inferences by Naina from the model:

1. Price movements do not seem to play a significant role in brand choice decisions.
2. Perceptions of 'economical wash' positively impact the choice of large-pack sizes.
3. Perceptions of 'performance' drive the choice more for smaller packs.
4. Market-level distribution measure does not impact choice; however, point of purchase (POP) and merchandising activity seemingly have an important role to play.
5. Promotion packs impact the choice of brand for large-pack sizes.

Exercise

Naina needs to design the dashboard for presenting her findings. She also has to make some suggestions for the SBU performance strategy in the near term. You are required to help her suggest the design of the dashboard with appropriate outcomes, hence create a compelling story to recommend to the SBU head on performance in the near term.

Appendix A
Case—Trasha Beverages Goes the Business Analytics Way

Customers in India have become health conscious and are seeking out food items that aid them to naturally stay fit and healthy. Among beverages, the demand for packaged fruit juices has increased over the years. Fruit juices can be either of the two types: 'fruit drinks' that have about 30% fruit content and 'fruit juices' that have 100 per cent fruit content. The fruit drinks have remained popular among consumers in India as a refreshment drink. However, as consumers are looking for including more healthy options in their diet, fruit juice consumption has increased in India. Fruit juice is available in many different package sizes. The Tetra Pak size is more popular for single consumption. Be it a mother packing lunchbox for her child or travellers stopping at a gas station for a short break, consumers have started moving to fruit juice Tetra Paks among other options. As the fruit juice market is still evolving, Trasha Beverages noticed this shift in consumer trend. They looked at the distribution data for their brand of fruit juices packed in Tetra Pak across different outlets and found that the demand for the 100 per cent natural fruit juice such as of litchi, mango, lime, apple, orange and mosambi has increased across all customer touch points, be it a grocery store, supermarket, fuel station or a student convenience store at a university.

Few years ago, the real challenge was to market the product. Trasha management was sure that their product could not be sold only in the local competitive market. Indore city and its neighbouring rural markets appeared to be attractive markets, more so because the company could employ familiar network to get willing and able distributors for their products in the moderately competitive semi-urban and rural markets. The product, fruit juice in Tetra Paks, was packaged in Bhopal and transported to Indore to be sold in the retail markets using these personal contacts. The Tetra Pak supplier was based in Bhopal.

On the face of it, this business made no sense. The cost of transportation from Bhopal to Indore was high and the distribution network had to be supported with higher margins than prevailing market rates to maintain interest among channel partners, leading to almost no operating margins for Trasha.

With such high costs, the business was soon on the brink of disaster. Trasha was left with no surplus. Nevertheless, the company continued the business for growth, with the market providing ample support through demand. Trasha's product was not perceived by consumers to be very different from the 'Tetra Paks' sold by the other competitors at that time. Given their sales volume, it did not create any negative impact on the sales of their competitors. Instead, they used to push their product with some help from the overall category 'momentum'. Trasha attributed the growth in their business to their honesty in dealing with their partners, which helped them gain their trust and loyalty.

Today, Trasha has attained a fair market share in the beverages market. The marketing and sales team commented that the fruit juice market still remains a hugely competitive but untapped market. Several questions remain unanswered:

1. Was Trasha Beverages doing enough to retain and increase their market share?
2. Was the product able to maintain the right balance between quality and affordable price for the consumer?
3. Was the Tetra Pak size of 200 ml appropriate for single consumption or would a smaller size at a lower price fetch more sales?

They approached a research agency named Quisol Insights to help them with solutions to their business problem. Trasha Beverages hoped that Quisol would be able to help them make the above decisions. Trasha provided the research firm with their company's distribution data and some other information as stated in Tables A.1–A.4. Quisol had requested this information from them in order to analyse, build models and provide BA outcomes that could be used for Trasha's business decision-making.

Table A.1 is the distribution volume data of nine years of Trasha Beverages of fruit juice in India in 200 ml Tetra Pak. There are six types of distribution channels across which the total volume in cubic metres is shown.

TABLE A.1	Distribution Volume Data for Nine Years of 200 ml Tetra Pak								
	Volume in Cubic Metres[a]								
Distribution Channels	**2010**	**2011**	**2012**	**2013**	**2014**	**2015**	**2016**	**2017**	**2018**
Grocery stores[b]	6.12	6.13	6.21	6.82	6.43	7.58	6.89	6.92	7.83
Supermarkets[c]/hypermarkets[d]	12.4	12.82	13.45	13.68	14.79	14.98	15.69	16.88	18.96
Fuel stations[e]	0.51	0.61	0.52	0.79	1.32	1.56	2.33	2.57	2.88
E-tailers[f]	0.31	0.33	0.32	0.31	0.38	0.33	0.31	0.29	0.32
Vending machines[g]	0.23	0.22	0.25	0.27	0.27	0.25	0.28	0.29	0.32
Others[h]	2.51	3.22	3.45	3.48	3.99	4.55	5.78	6.22	7.38

Notes: [a]1 cubic metre is 1,000 litres.
[b]Grocery stores: A shop that stocks large number of non-perishable food and household products. The grocer sells the products as per the requirement of the customers.
[c]Supermarkets: A store that has large variety of food and household products that are arranged in aisles. Customers can walk around and pick items of their choice.
[d]Hypermarkets: A large store similar to a supermarket that stores grocery and food items along with general merchandise.
[e]Fuel stations: Small convenient stores within fuel stations where customers can stop and purchase items of choice.
[f]E-tailers: Goods sold online.
[g]Vending machines: Stock the juice Tetra Paks.
[h]Others: University canteens, direct sales, clubs, market traders.

Data has been represented in four tables. As mentioned above, Table A.1 has information on the distribution channels used by Trasha Beverages for six types of distribution channels across which the total volume in thousand litres is shown. Distribution of fruit juice is done in six states in India: Karnataka, Madhya Pradesh, Gujarat, Punjab, Andhra Pradesh and West Bengal. Table A.2 shows the data in cubic metres volume of state- and city-wise distribution in 2018 across all the channels.

TABLE A.2	*State- and City-wise Distribution in 2018 across All Channels*		
S. No.	**State**	**City**	**Volume in 1,000 Litres in 2018**
1	Karnataka	Bangalore	5.12
2	Karnataka	Udupi	1.11
3	Karnataka	Mysore	3.12
4	Karnataka	Mangalore	4.65
5	Karnataka	Coorg	1.45
6	Madhya Pradesh	Bhopal	6.78
7	Madhya Pradesh	Indore	5.12
8	Madhya Pradesh	Sagar	1.11
9	Madhya Pradesh	Ujjain	3.12
10	Madhya Pradesh	Gwalior	4.65
11	Gujarat	Ahmedabad	1.45
12	Gujarat	Vadodara	6.45
13	Gujarat	Rajkot	4.45
14	Gujarat	Surat	4.65
15	Gujarat	Patan	5.33
16	Andhra Pradesh	Vijaywada	2.33
17	Andhra Pradesh	Visakhapatnam	5.12
18	Andhra Pradesh	Tirupati	1.11
19	Andhra Pradesh	Nellore	3.12
20	Andhra Pradesh	Guntur	4.65
21	West Bengal	Kolkata	1.45
22	West Bengal	Durgapur	4.45
23	West Bengal	Siliguri	4.65
24	West Bengal	Haldia	5.33
25	West Bengal	Bidhannagar	1.12
26	Punjab	Amritsar	5.12
27	Punjab	Ludhiana	6.45
28	Punjab	Jalandhar	4.45
29	Punjab	Patiala	4.65
30	Punjab	Pathankot	5.33

A survey has been carried out to understand customer views on their product. Table A.3 shows a sample data of 30 respondents—15 males and 15 females. To avoid complexity arising due to multiple interrelated variables, the data has been kept simple for facilitating quick understanding of concepts by students in class. In the real-life scenario, many different variables would be captured such as customer response by the channel they use to purchase the product,

TABLE A.3		Sample Data of Customer Survey for 2018					
S. No.	Gender	Monthly Consumption	Taste	Ease of Finding	Price	Overall Satisfaction	Recommend
1	1	10	5	5	5	5	1
2	1	5	5	5	5	5	1
3	1	4	4	4	4	4	1
4	1	7	4	4	4	4	1
5	1	5	4	4	4	4	0
6	1	5	2	2	2	2	0
7	1	15	5	5	5	5	0
8	1	2	4	4	4	4	0
9	1	2	4	4	4	4	0
10	1	4	4	4	4	4	0
11	1	6	2	2	2	2	1
12	1	6	2	2	2	2	1
13	1	6	2	2	2	2	1
14	1	3	5	5	5	5	1
15	1	5	5	5	5	5	0
16	2	6	5	5	5	5	0
17	2	7	5	5	5	5	0
18	2	8	5	5	5	5	0
19	2	10	5	5	5	5	1
20	2	10	3	3	3	3	1
21	2	15	4	4	4	4	1
22	2	10	3	3	3	3	1
23	2	8	4	4	4	4	1
24	2	8	5	5	5	5	1
25	2	8	5	5	5	5	1
26	2	7	5	5	5	5	1
27	2	7	4	4	4	4	0
28	2	20	2	2	2	2	0
29	2	9	2	2	2	2	0
30	2	10	3	3	3	3	0

competitor products they buy, city and state they belong to, age, family size and income. Additionally, the Tetra Paks of 200 ml carry different types of fruit juices as mentioned above. The assumption here is that their view is same for any fruit juice they buy from Trasha Beverages in 200 ml Tetra Pak. Variables in Table A.3 are gender (15 each, 1 is male and 2 are females), how many Tetra Paks they consume per month (any fruit juice in numbers), their view on taste of the product, ease of finding the product, price of the product and their overall satisfaction on the product. All of these four variables have been taken on a five-point Likert scale where 5 is high preference and 1 is low preference. The last variable is to know if the customers would recommend the product to a friend, where 1 is yes and 0 is no.

Table A.4 lists the price in 2018 in rupees of a 200 ml Tetra Pak fruit juice of Trasha Beverages and its four competitors A, B, C and D.

TABLE A.4	Price of Competing Brands in 2018	
Brand		**Price in ₹**
Trasha		15
A		18
B		20
C		12
D		14

Let us now work on some solutions to help the research firm Quisol Insights.

Question 1: State Trasha Beverage's BP and business objectives.

Solution Q1: There are three parts to the BP that Trasha Beverages has described to Quisol Insights:

1. Was Trasha Beverages doing enough to retain and increase their market share?
2. Was the product able to maintain the right balance between quality and affordable price for the consumer?
3. Was the Tetra Pak size of 200 ml appropriate for single consumption or would a smaller size at a lower price fetch more sales?

The business objective is to determine if Trasha Beverages will be the market leader in 200 ml Tetra Pak juices in the next two years.

Question 2: State Trasha Beverage's research problem.

Solution Q2: Like any other BP, Trasha Beverage's BP is abstract in nature. Quisol Insights shall convert the BP into tangible research problem that can be taken forward for analysis.

1. Is the distribution of fruit juice sufficient to meet the demand of customers?
2. Has the marketing activity (promotion, awareness, discounts, advertising) done enough to all potential customers across all regions?
3. Has price been a positive determining variable for customer satisfaction and recommendation?

(The students may want to specify research questions which are specific to each of the BPs stated above. That is left as an exercise for them.)

Question 3: State Trasha Beverage's/Quisol Insight's research dimensions (note: research problem will be defined by multiple research dimensions, which are different from business objectives).

Solution Q3:

1. Determine the distribution of fruit juice by the channels.
2. Determine the consumption by the state and the city. Then advise Trasha Beverages to compare both 1 and 2 to identify gaps.
3. Determine which variable drives customer satisfaction and what leads to recommendations (referrals) by customers.

(Students are encouraged to make research dimensions separately for each research question.)

Question 4: Identify the variable type from each row of the table and list it below.

Solution Q4: In Chapter 3, we have seen different types of variables. Here, we shall identify the variable and state it as categorical or numerical.

1. In Table A.1, there are three variables:
   a. Channel: Categorical
   b. Year: Categorical
   c. Distribution volume: Numerical
2. In Table A.2, there are three variables:
   a. State: Categorical
   b. City: Categorical
   c. Distribution volume in 2018: Numerical
3. In Table A.3, there are seven variables:
   a. Gender: Categorical
   b. Recommend: Categorical
   c. Monthly consumption: Numerical
   d. Taste: Numerical
   e. Ease of finding: Numerical
   f. Price: Numerical
   g. Overall satisfaction: Numerical
4. In Table A.4, there are two variables:
   a. Brand: Categorical
   b. Price in INR: Numerical (note that this is a continuous variable measured in INR. This is different from the price variable in Table A.3 which is measured on a five-point interval scale.)

Question 5: Determine some basic statistical outcomes described in Chapter 6 from the variables that are meaningful for Trasha Beverages.

Solution Q5: Table A.4 shows the price in 2018 of Trasha Beverages and competing brands in the market by other beverage companies. Quisol Insights observed that Trasha is somewhere in between. It wondered, what must be stopping it from increasing the price? Was that a decision

FIGURE A.1 *Distribution by Channel*

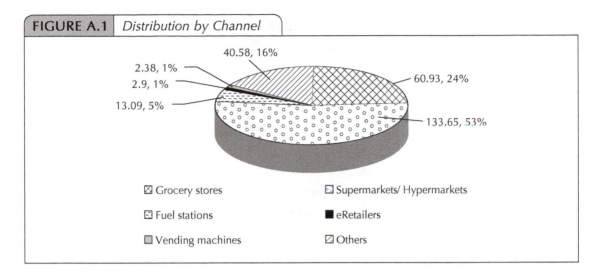

40.58, 16%

2.38, 1%

2.9, 1%

13.09, 5%

60.93, 24%

133.65, 53%

⊠ Grocery stores   ⊡ Supermarkets/ Hypermarkets

⊟ Fuel stations   ■ eRetailers

☐ Vending machines   ⊘ Others

taken by Trasha consciously after looking at possibilities or they had not done the analysis at all? Quisol's executives thought of first performing some basis analysis of the data provided to them.

As a first step, we will perform some basis analysis on the data provided in the four tables. From Table A.1, the pie chart in Figure A.1 (obtained from MS Excel) shows the total volume distribution by the six distribution channels respectively across the nine years. It also shows the percentage distribution of the total volume distributed. We can infer that the distribution was largest in supermarkets/hypermarkets and lowest in vending machines. Trasha can be recommended to check into reasons for low distribution by certain channels.

Figure A.2 (obtained from Tableau) shows similar results by indicating the average sales by channel of distribution for the nine-year period.

Quisol Insights thought it might be useful to identify if the total distribution had gone up in the nine years' time. This would tell the trend of distribution and could probably be studied in relation to the market demand. From Figure A.3 (obtained from MS Excel), we see that there has been a gradual rise in distribution from the year 2010 to the year 2018, indicating more volume of the fruit juice reaching the market. Quisol Insights will make a note of this finding and communicate to Trasha Beverages that there is a positive rise in distribution. The company needs to figure out if this was due to a pull from the market or did it lead to excess inventory. How have Trasha planned distribution vis-à-vis sales?

Let us now move to Table A.2. It will be interesting to know the consumption by city across the six states for 2018. It will help Trasha Beverages to look into their distribution strategy. They need to look into the distribution data by state and by city and then derive a comparison between distribution and consumption. Since Quisol Insights does not have the detailed distribution data by state and city, it has decided to see the consumption by state and city for 2018. From Figure A.4 (obtained from Tableau), it will report to Trasha Beverages that consumption is highest in the state of Punjab followed by Gujarat. However, if we see city wise, Bhopal has the largest consumption followed by Ludhiana and Vadodara. It is quite a scattered trend and provides enough curiosity for the firm to dig deeper and identify the reason. Possibilities are that there could be a lack in planned distribution, inventory stock-out, lost sales, low awareness of product and so on that can be corrected.

FIGURE A.2   *Average Sales by Distribution Channel*

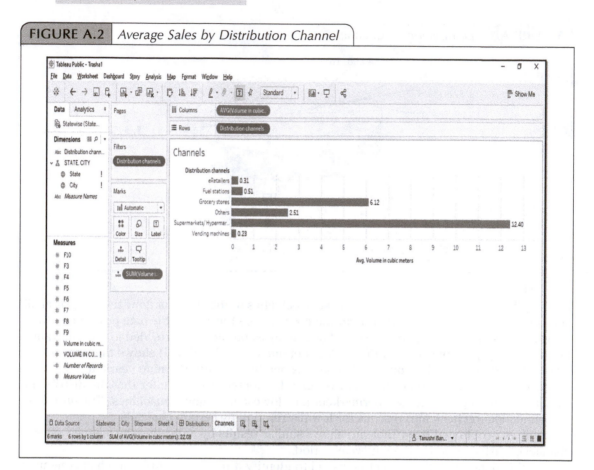

FIGURE A.3   *Volume Distribution for 9 Years*

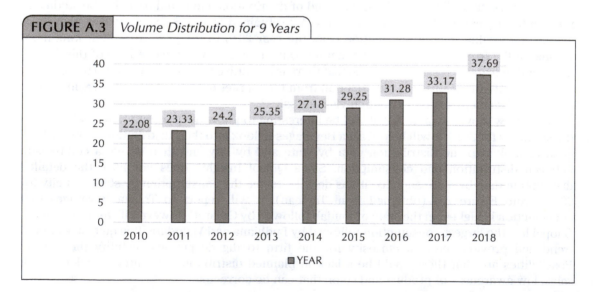

FIGURE A.4   *City-wise Consumption*

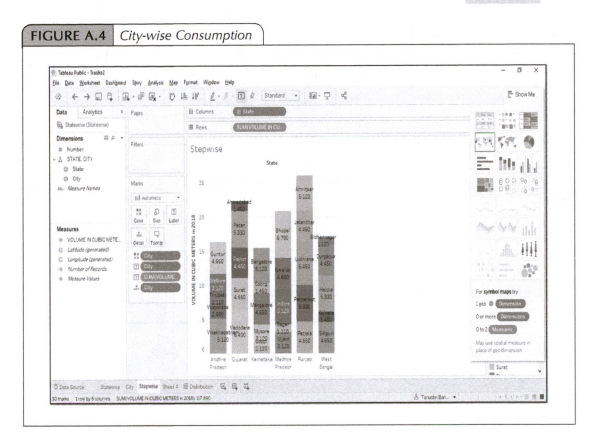

Quisol Insights executive now moved to Table A.3 which has a small sample of customer data. He wondered that the small sample will not justify the actual customer purchase behaviour as the data does not contain purchase by channel by state by city. Also, the sample size determined by the random probability sampling method was very small to represent the population. Yet, the sample had some interesting facts that the executive wanted to study. Table A.5 (obtained using SPSS) shows frequencies by gender and by recommendation. From the sample data of 30 customers obtained, 16 customers said that they would recommend the tetrapack to another friend, but 14 said that they will not recommend. The Quisol executive wondered why would they not recommend, what was wrong?

He used Tableau to determine the consumption by Tetra Pak number. Figure A.5 shows consumption of Tetra Pak (total number) by gender by recommendation. It can be inferred that females (2) consumed in general more Tetra Paks than males (1). In both cases, there was not much difference in the consumption of total number of Tetra Paks for those who recommended and those who did not. Then what led to customers not recommending even after consuming themselves? Curiosity further increased.

In the customer survey, there were three questions on the product: taste, price and ease of finding. For each of the three questions as stated below, the customer was required to rate it on a five-point Likert scale, where 5 indicated high preference/agreement and 1 indicated low preference/agreement.

| TABLE A.5 | Recommend to Another Friend | | |

Gender			
	Observed N	**Expected N**	**Residual**
Male	15	15.0	.0
Female	15	15.0	.0
Total	30		

Recommend			
	Observed N	**Expected N**	**Residual**
No	14	15.0	−1.0
Yes	16	15.0	1.0
Total	30		

| FIGURE A.5 | Gender-wise Tetrapak Consumption |

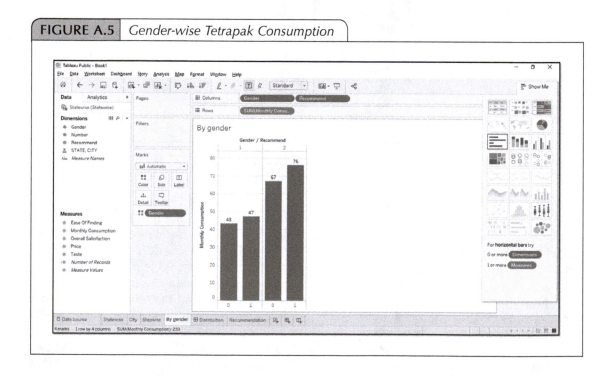

1. Do you like the taste of the fruit juice?
2. Do you feel the price fits your budget compared to other similar fruit juice brands in the market?
3. Are you able to find the product easily?

As shown in Figures A.6 and A.7 (obtained from Tableau), the Quisol Insights executive summarized the following outcome. The black blocks indicate the sum total of the responses received from males (1) and the grey blocks indicate the sum total of the responses received

FIGURE A.6   *Responses on Variables by Gender*

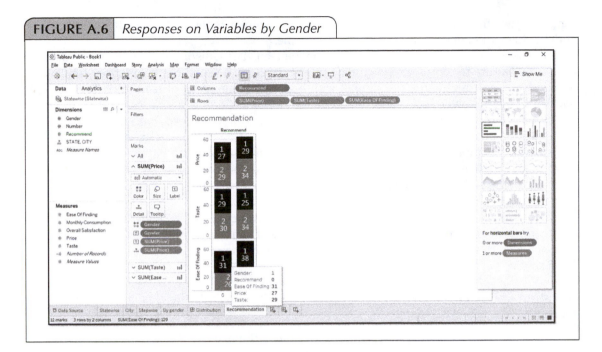

FIGURE A.7   *Consumption-based Recommendation*

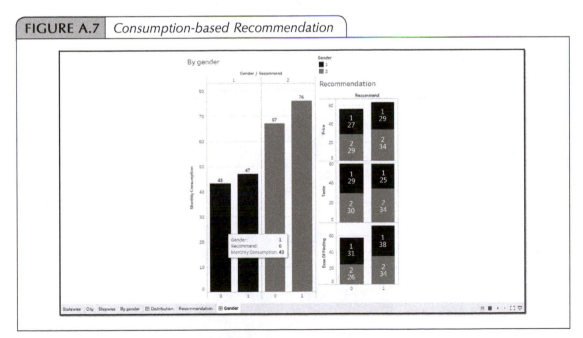

from females (2). For instance, for ease of finding, the sum of the responses of men who did not recommend was 31, whereas those who recommended was 38. Similarly, for women who did not recommend was 26 and those who recommended was 34. Thus, of those who recommended (1), both men and women rated higher indicating that it was easier to find the product. Similarly, for price, the affordability was significantly high for women, whereas for men it was lower. The variable taste did not yield any significant outcome.

There is a feature of map representation in Tableau. The Quisol Insights executive decided to use the feature to represent the consumption by state in a visual representation using maps. As can be seen from Figure A.8, Punjab with highest consumption of fruit juice Tetra Paks is darkest shade, followed by Gujarat. This is in line with our finding in Figure A.4. He now added the cities to the map and wanted to see the consumption of juice Tetra Paks by city.

The cities are represented in each of the six states in different colours by state. The cities are identified by using the latitude and longitude of the city. In case the city is not automatically identified in Tableau, you can search for the latitude and longitude of the city using the internet, feed it into the software to locate the city. Figure A.9 shows the cities by state where Trasha Beverages has distribution of the fruit juice Tetra Paks.

The Quisol Insights executive creates a pivot table using the data provided in Table A.2. This summarized the consumption of fruit juice Tetra Paks by city and by state. It provides the total sum and also the average consumption. The outcome is shown in Figure A.10 (obtained using MS Excel).

Question 6: Perform an unsupervised cluster analysis to identify the clusters in the customer responses (described in Chapter 8).

Solution Q6: The executive at Quisol Insights chose the five variables from Table A.3 which has 30 responses from the customers. The chosen variables were monthly consumption of fruit juice Tetra Paks (numbers), price, taste, ease of finding and overall satisfaction. He used RapidMiner software and obtained the result as shown in Figures A.11–A.14.

FIGURE A.8	*Graph of Consumption by State*

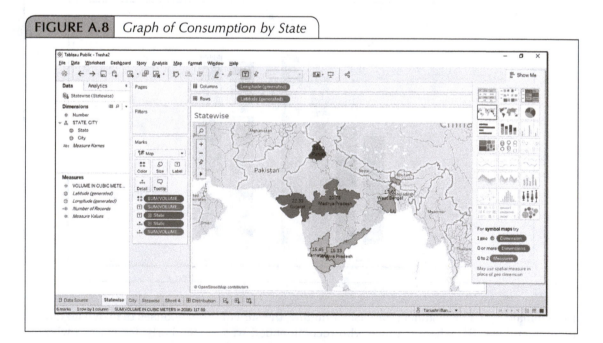

FIGURE A.9 *Graph of Distribution by City and State*

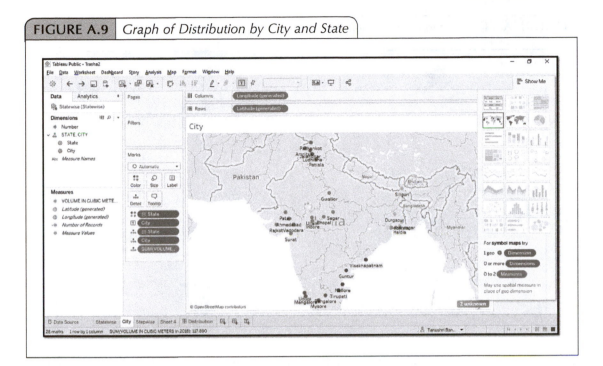

FIGURE A.10 *Total and Average Consumption by City and State*

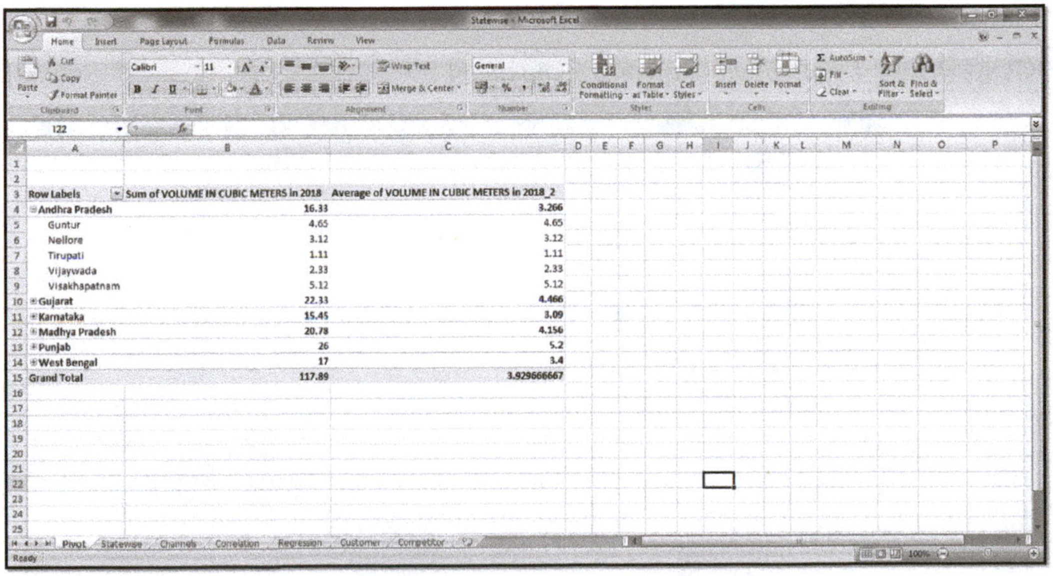

Row Labels	Sum of VOLUME IN CUBIC METERS in 2018	Average of VOLUME IN CUBIC METERS in 2018_2
Andhra Pradesh	16.33	3.266
Guntur	4.65	4.65
Nellore	3.12	3.12
Tirupati	1.11	1.11
Vijaywada	2.33	2.33
Visakhapatnam	5.12	5.12
Gujarat	22.33	4.466
Karnataka	15.45	3.09
Madhya Pradesh	20.78	4.156
Punjab	26	5.2
West Bengal	17	3.4
Grand Total	117.89	3.929666667

FIGURE A.11 *Clustering the Sample Data Set*

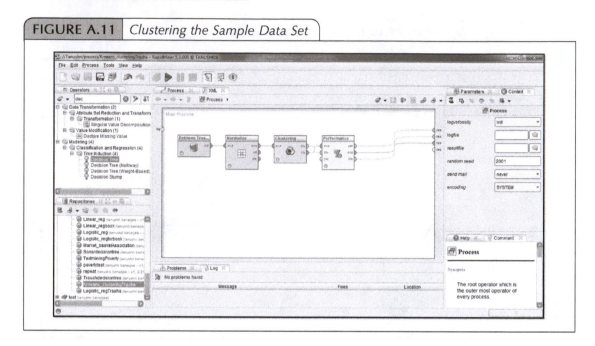

Figure A.11 shows the operators in RapidMiner to build the unsupervised cluster model. Figure A.12 shows three clusters. Of the 30 customer responses in Table A.3, Cluster 0 has six records, Cluster 1 has eight records and Cluster 2 has 16 records. Figure A.13 shows the centroid combination for the five variables. This is further represented graphically in Figure A.14.

FIGURE A.12 *Output from Clustering Technique*

FIGURE A.13   *Centroids of the Three Clusters*

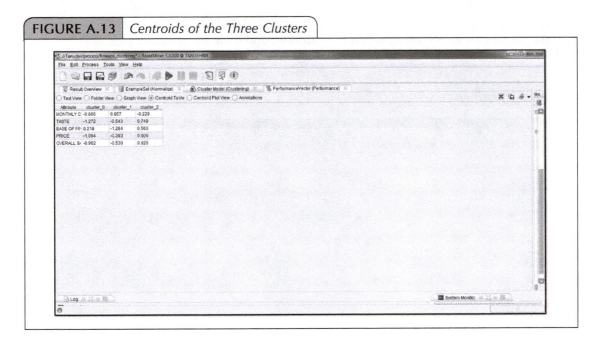

FIGURE A.14   *Graphical Representation of Centroids*

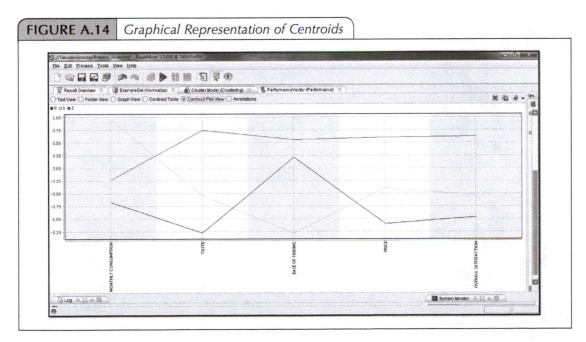

Question 7: Use a supervised classification decision tree technique on the customer response data.

Solution Q7: The executive at Quisol Insights used the same variables that he had used for the clustering technique. He has used the recommend variable as the label. As we see in Figure A.15, monthly consumption is the root node in the outcome. Until fourth level, we see that there is perfect classification of customers who recommend and do not recommend.

Figure A.16 shows the operators for creating the decision tree classification model.

FIGURE A.15 *Decision Tree of Sample Data Set*

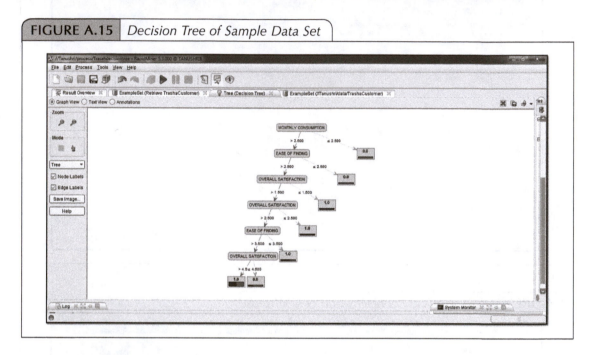

FIGURE A.16 *Decision Tree Operators*

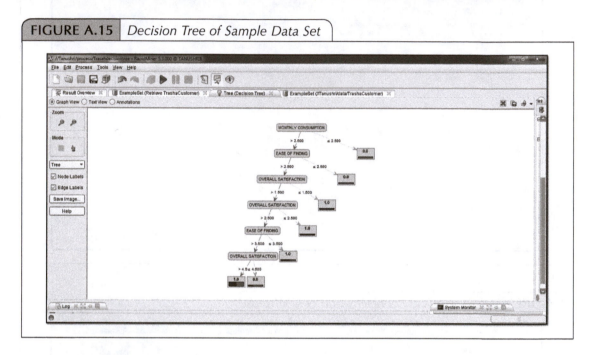

Question 8: Develop a linear regression model using the customer data. Show the correlation among the variables. Hence, determine which variables significantly impact the dependent variable.

Solution Q8: As we have seen in Chapters 7 and 8, the linear regression model allows the business decision-maker to predict the dependent variable based on the independent variables. The executive of Quisol Insights decides to build the linear regression model in two ways. Once using parametric model (Chapter 7) and the second time using the machine learning technique (Chapter 8). There are primarily two differences between these two models.

1. In parametric model we have some predetermined (known) idea about the model construction depending on the analyst's hunch about the data variables and possible relationships between the dependent and independent variables. In machine learning, the model is independently trained based on the contour of the data set, with generally no predetermined hypothesis of the relationships between independent and dependent variables.
2. There is an unexplained component of the error (with a pre-specified distribution) in a parametric model due to the predetermined relationships between the variables which are not explicitly accounted for in machine learning algorithms. In machine learning, there is only the dependent variable specified, all other variables try to explain the dependent variable by naturally learning and building the model. It depends largely on the data set used from which it learns and builds the model and can thus vary depending on the data set used. In most parametric models, there is a hunch about the independent variables impacting the dependent variable. It can thus be altered to test and see how best it replicates a real-life scenario.

Using SPSS software and the customer survey data set in Table A.3, the Quisol Insights executive performed correlation and built the linear regression model. He considered overall satisfaction as the dependent variable and monthly consumption, taste, price and ease of finding as the independent variables. Table A.6 shows the descriptive statistics: mean and standard deviation. Of the 30 response sample data sets, ease of finding variable has the highest mean and lowest standard deviation. It can thus be inferred that across both genders, customers are generally in agreement that the ease of finding the juice Tetra Paks in their desired channel of purchase is easy.

TABLE A.6 *Descriptive Statistics*

	Mean	Std. Deviation	N
Monthly consumption	7.77	3.901	30
Taste	3.93	1.258	30
Ease of finding	4.30	.915	30
Price	3.97	1.189	30
Overall satisfaction	3.97	1.351	30

TABLE A.7	Correlations					
		Monthly Consumption	**Taste**	**Ease of Finding**	**Price**	**Overall Satisfaction**
Monthly consumption	Pearson Correlation	1	−.137	−.414[a]	−.069	−.152
	Sig. (2-tailed)		.471	.023	.718	.423
	N	30	30	30	30	30
Taste	Pearson Correlation	−.137	1	−.377[a]	.691[b]	.709[b]
	Sig. (2-tailed)	.471		.040	.000	.000
	N	30	30	30	30	30
Ease of finding	Pearson Correlation	−.414[a]	.377[a]	1	.295	.343
	Sig. (2-tailed)	.023	.040		.114	.064
	N	30	30	30	30	30
Price	Pearson Correlation	−.069	.691[b]	.295	1	.643[b]
	Sig. (2-tailed)	.718	.000	.114		.000
	N	30	30	30	30	30
Overall satisfaction	Pearson Correlation	−.152	.709[b]	.343	.643[b]	1
	Sig. (2-tailed)	.423	.000	.064	.000	
	N	30	30	30	30	30

Notes: [a] Correlation is significant at the 0.05 level (2-tailed).
[b] Correlation is significant at the 0.01 level (2-tailed).

Table A.7 shows the correlation among the variables. It can be noted that overall satisfaction variable is strongly correlated at 99% confidence interval with taste (0.709) and price (0.643).

The executive then built the parametric linear regression model with the variables. As we can see from Table A.8, overall satisfaction is the dependent variable. Tables A.9 and A.10 indicate the R^2 value of 0.554 and an F value of 7.765. Thus, 55.4 per cent of the variation in the dependent variable is explained by the independent variables.

From Table A.11 we can observe that the variable which is significant at 95 per cent confidence interval is taste with a positive t value of 2.510. It can thus be inferred that taste positively impacts the overall satisfaction of consumers. Also, not that since price is not significant, Trasha Beverages can be advised to take a risk with increasing the price vis-à-vis competition. Taste can be improved with the introduction of new innovative flavours.

TABLE A.8	Variables Entered/Removed[b]		
Model	**Variables Entered**	**Variables Removed**	**Method**
1	Price, monthly consumption, ease of finding, taste	–	Enter

Notes: [a] All requested variables entered.
[b] Dependent variable: Overall Satisfaction.

TABLE A.9	Model Summary

Model	R	R^2	Adjusted R^2	Std. Error of the Estimate
1	.744[a]	.554	.483	.972

Note: [a] Predictors: (Constant), price, monthly consumption, ease of finding, taste.

TABLE A.10	ANOVA[b]

Model		Sum of Squares	df	Mean Square	F	Sig.
1	Regression	29.346	4	7.336	7.765	.000[a]
	Residual	23.621	25	.945		
	Total	52.967	29			

Notes: [a] Predictors: (Constant), price, monthly consumption, ease of finding, taste.
[b] Dependent variable: Overall satisfaction.

TABLE A.11	Coefficients[a]

Model		Unstandardized Coefficients		Standardized Coefficients		
		B	Std. Error	Beta	t	Sig.
1	(Constant)	.366	1.211		.302	.765
	Monthly consumption	−.015	.051	−.042	−.287	.777
	Taste	.515	.205	.479	2.510	.019
	Ease of finding	.086	.232	.058	.371	.714
	Price	.333	.211	.292	1.579	.127

Note: [a] Dependent variable: Overall satisfaction.

Figures A.17–A.19 show the outcome of the machine learning regression model that was built using RapidMiner software. See Chapter 8 for the operators. The executive observed from the correlation table shown in Figure A.17 that the correlation between the dependent variable overall satisfaction and the independent variables taste (0.709) and price (0.643) is significant. This is similar to the SPSS output.

Figures A.18a and A.18b shows the results of the regression model. Taste is the independent variable significantly impacting the dependent variable overall satisfaction at 95% confidence interval with a t value of 3.131. The R^2 value is 0.568. Both these values are higher than that obtained from the parametric model.

Figure A.26 shows 9 records out of the 30 records data set that have been used as the holdout sample to validate the machine learning regression model. It can be observed that the predicted value of the dependent variable overall satisfaction is close to the actual value in most cases. Only in row 2, the value is vastly different.

FIGURE A.17 *Correlation Table*

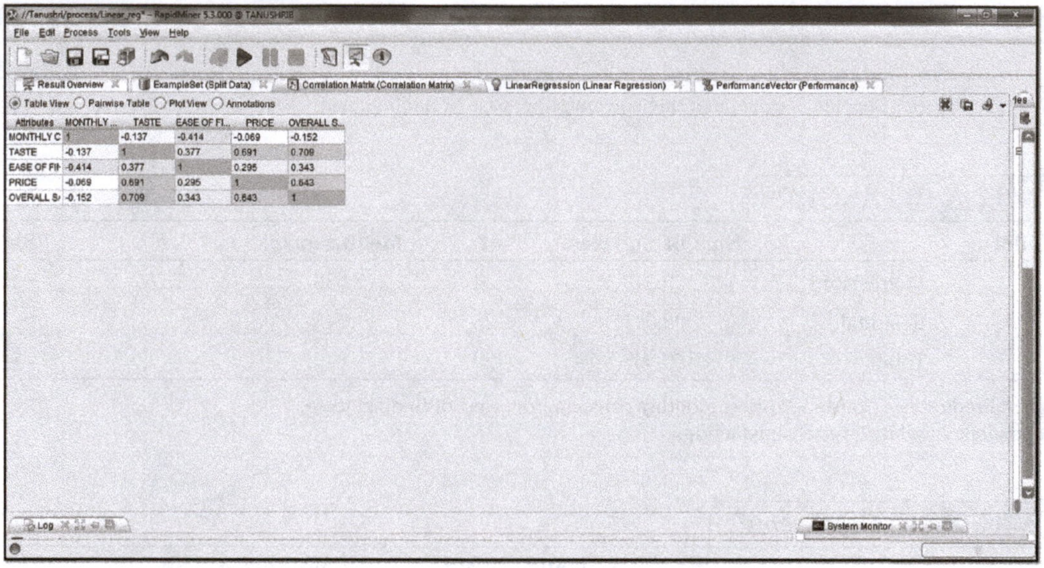

Attributes	MONTHLY ...	TASTE	EASE OF FI...	PRICE	OVERALL S...
MONTHLY C	1	-0.137	-0.414	-0.069	-0.152
TASTE	-0.137	1	0.377	0.691	0.709
EASE OF FII	-0.414	0.377	1	0.295	0.343
PRICE	-0.069	0.691	0.295	1	0.643
OVERALL S	-0.152	0.709	0.343	0.643	1

FIGURE A.18a *Regression Output*

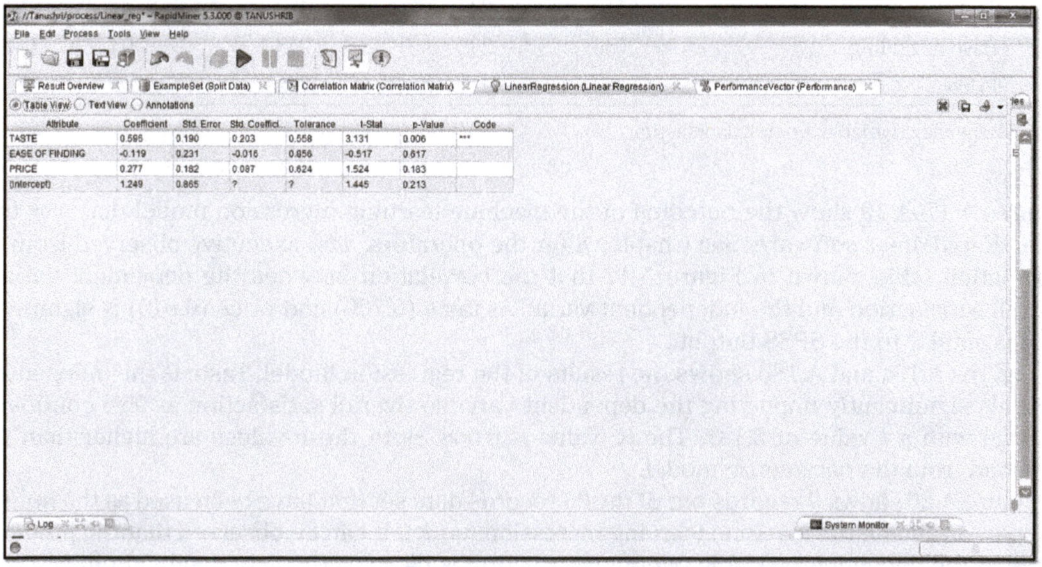

Attribute	Coefficient	Std. Error	Std. Coeffici...	Tolerance	t-Stat	p-Value	Code
TASTE	0.595	0.190	0.203	0.558	3.131	0.006	***
EASE OF FINDING	-0.119	0.231	-0.016	0.856	-0.517	0.617	
PRICE	0.277	0.182	0.087	0.624	1.524	0.183	
(Intercept)	1.249	0.865	?	?	1.445	0.213	

FIGURE A.18b *Regression Output*

FIGURE A.19 *Holdout Sample for Regression*

Row No.	OVERALL SATISFACTION	prediction(OVERALL SATISFACTION)	MONTHLY CONSUMPTION	TASTE	EASE OF FINDING	PRICE
1	3	3.509	10	3	3	3
2	1	4.262	8	4	4	4
3	5	5.015	8	5	5	5
4	5	5.015	8	5	5	5
5	5	5.015	7	5	5	5
6	4	4.657	7	5	4	4
7	2	2.756	20	2	2	2
8	5	5.373	9	5	2	5
9	3	3.509	10	3	3	3

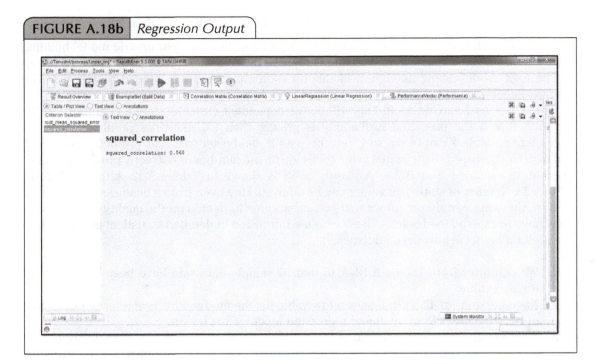

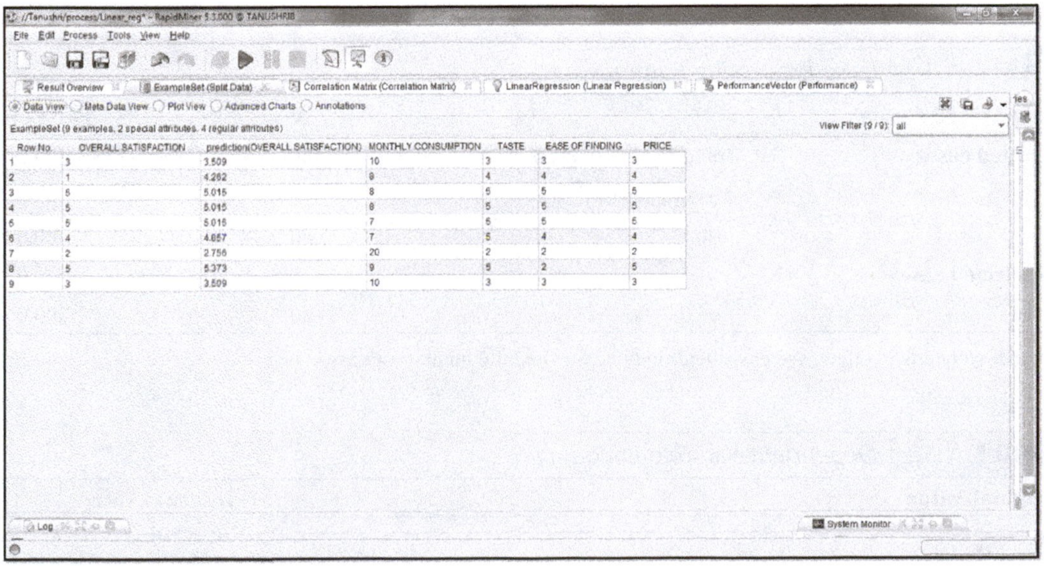

Question 9: Determine a logit classification model using the customer data.

Solution Q9: The Quisol executive performed logit using both the parametric model building method and machine learning method and compared the results.

The logit model, using maximum likelihood estimation method, is used to arrive at the results. Recommend is a categorical variable with two option 'yes' and 'no'. The table has recorded 'yes' as 1 and 'no' as 0. This will be the dependent variable. Here a condition can be set such that if the predicted probability is greater than 0.5, then the predicted value of dependent variable Y can be set to 1, or otherwise it can be set to 0. The predicted value of Y can then be compared to the actual value to decide on the number of correctly predicted values. The output obtained from Table A.3 using SPSS is shown in Tables A.12–A.16 and Figures A.20–A.23. Number of statistical values can be inferred. However, from a business analyst point of view, there are certain outcomes that you must know to decide on the quality of the model. They have been explained below. Those who are interested in detailed statistical interpretation can look up books in advanced statistics.

1. We can infer from Tables A.12–A.16 that 30 sample data sets have been used with no missing value.
2. Nagelkerke R^2 of 42.3% indicates a low value for the model. This is similar to coefficient of determination R^2 in the linear regression model (Chapter 6).
3. Wald's statistic gives a measure of the significance of each of the measured variables. It is chi-square distributed with 1 degree of freedom for numeric variables. For our example, we observe that none of the variables is significant at 95% confidence interval.
4. Table A.15 shows that 20 out of 30 cases have been correctly predicted, which results in 66.7%.

TABLE A.12 | *Case Processing Summary*

Unweighted Cases[a]		N	Per Cent
Selected cases	Included in analysis	30	100.0
	Missing cases	0	.0
	Total	30	100.0
Unselected cases		0	.0
Total		30	100.0

Note: [a] If weight is in effect, see classification table for the total number of cases.

TABLE A.13 | *Dependent Variable Encoding*

Original Value	Internal Value
No	0
Yes	1

TABLE A.14	Model Summary		
Step	**–2 Log Likelihood**	**Cox and Snell R^2**	**Nagelkerke R^2**
1	30.012[a]	.317	.423

Note: [a] Estimation terminated at iteration number 20 because maximum iteration has been reached. Final solution cannot be found.

TABLE A.15	Classification Table[a]				
				Predicted	
				Recommend	
	Observed			**No**	**Yes**	**Percentage Correct**
Step 1	Recommend	No	7	7	50.0
		Yes	3	13	81.3
	Overall percentage				66.7

Note: [a] The cut value is .500.

TABLE A.16	Variables in the Equation						
		B	**S.E.**	**Wald**	**df**	**Sig.**	**Exp(B)**
Step 1[a]	Monthly consumption	.040	.115	.121	1	.728	1.041
	Taste	–16.048	3386.918	.000	1	.996	.000
	Ease of finding	47.618	10160.753	.000	1	.996	4.791E20
	Price	.749	.806	.864	1	.353	2.116
	Overall satisfaction	–31.889	6773.836	.000	1	.996	.000
	Constant	–2.211	3.085	.514	1	.474	.110

It can be concluded that the independent variables do not decide the customers' decision on recommending the Tetra Paks for juice to their friends. Thus, Trasha needs to find out what drives recommendation by customers.

Similar result can be observed from the machine learning logit model developed using RapidMiner. Figure A.20 shows the operators used for building the model. The holdout sample shown in Figure A.22 consists of nine records of the 30 sample data sets. The training (analysis) data set consists of the remaining 21 records as shown in Figure A.23. It is seen from the confusion matrix in Figure A.21 that seven out of the nine records are wrongly predicted. Only the first two records in the holdout sample are predicted correctly. The executive at Quisol Insights needs to get additional data from Trasha Beverages to build the desired predictive model. The current model is very weak to make correct predictions.

FIGURE A.20 *Logit Model Operators*

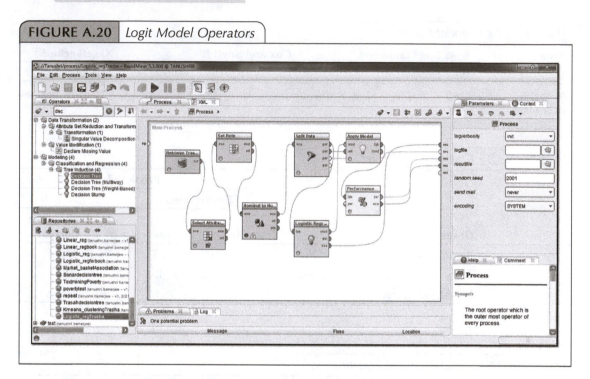

FIGURE A.21 *Confusion Matrix*

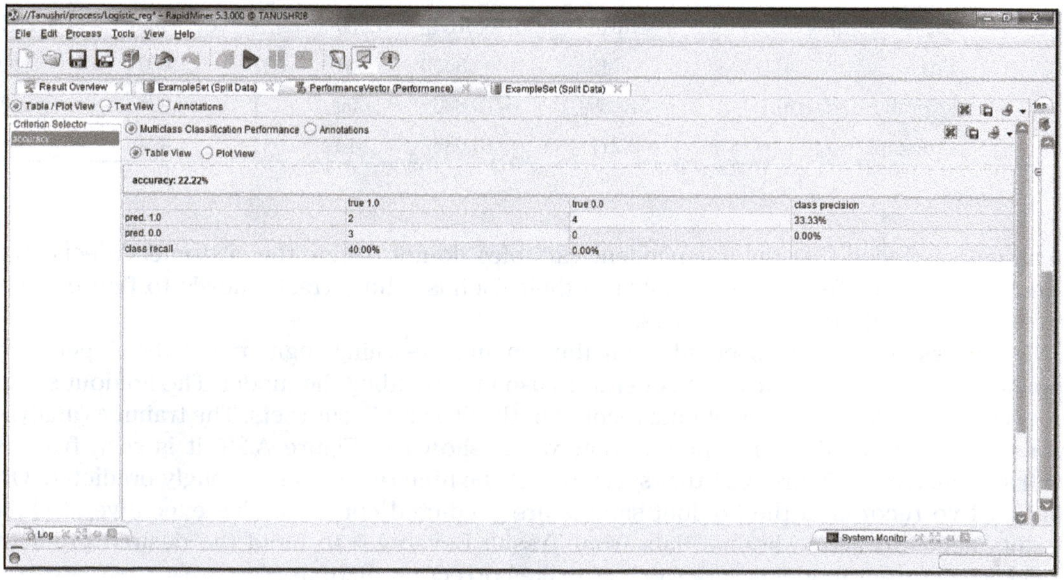

FIGURE A.22 *Holdout Sample for Logit*

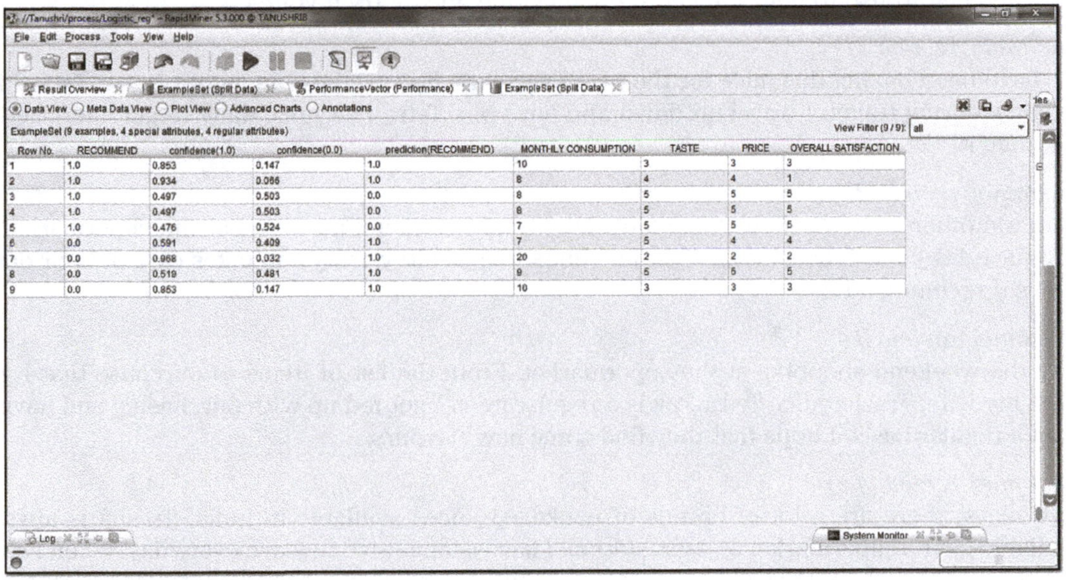

Row No.	RECOMMEND	confidence(1.0)	confidence(0.0)	prediction(RECOMMEND)	MONTHLY CONSUMPTION	TASTE	PRICE	OVERALL SATISFACTION
1	1.0	0.853	0.147	1.0	10	3	3	3
2	1.0	0.934	0.066	1.0	8	4	4	1
3	1.0	0.497	0.503	0.0	8	5	5	5
4	1.0	0.497	0.503	0.0	8	5	5	5
5	1.0	0.476	0.524	0.0	7	5	5	5
6	0.0	0.591	0.409	1.0	7	5	4	4
7	0.0	0.968	0.032	1.0	20	2	2	2
8	0.0	0.519	0.481	1.0	9	5	5	5
9	0.0	0.853	0.147	1.0	10	3	3	3

FIGURE A.23 *Training Data Set for Logit*

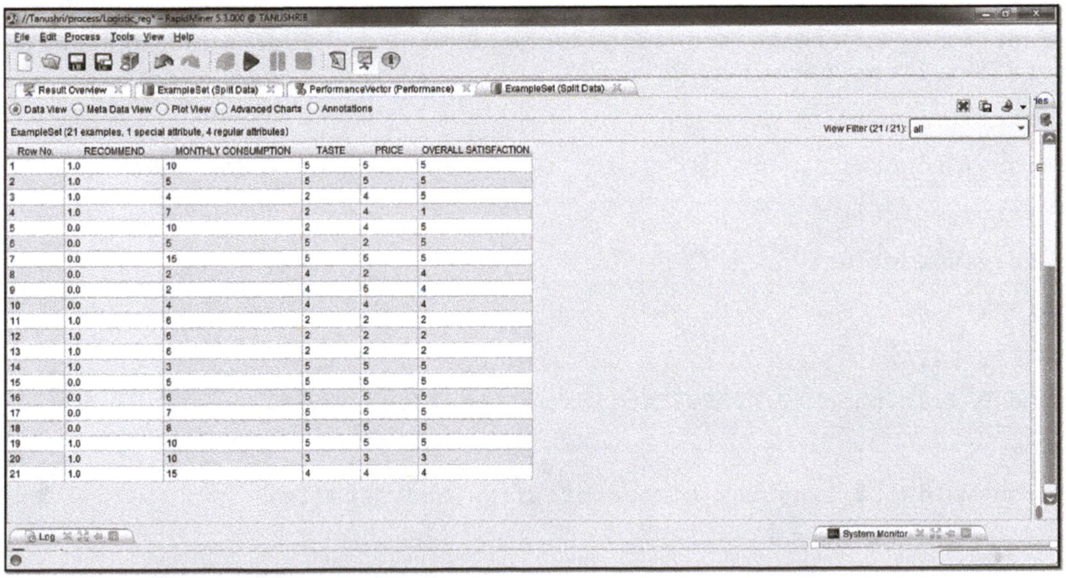

Row No.	RECOMMEND	MONTHLY CONSUMPTION	TASTE	PRICE	OVERALL SATISFACTION
1	1.0	10	5	5	5
2	1.0	5	5	5	5
3	1.0	4	2	4	5
4	1.0	7	2	4	1
5	0.0	10	2	4	5
6	0.0	5	5	2	5
7	0.0	15	5	5	5
8	0.0	2	4	2	4
9	0.0	2	4	5	4
10	0.0	4	4	4	4
11	1.0	6	2	2	2
12	1.0	6	2	2	2
13	1.0	6	2	2	2
14	1.0	3	5	5	5
15	0.0	5	5	5	5
16	0.0	6	5	5	5
17	0.0	7	5	5	5
18	0.0	8	5	5	5
19	1.0	10	5	5	5
20	1.0	10	3	3	3
21	1.0	15	4	4	4

Question 10: Perform text mining on the four customer reviews and prepare a word cloud. The process has been explained in Chapter 8 with R code for word cloud. The code has been provided below also to help you get to the outcome. Please try it yourself.

Customer review 1
We have been buying this juice for the past five years. It is available in a convenient Tetra Pak to carry during travel. I travel up down and have one Tetra Pak juice daily to get energized. I just love it.

Customer review 2
I am a mother of two school-going kids. During my weekend purchase at the supermarket, I purchase the juice Tetra Pak for their lunchbox. It is healthy, tasty and takes care of their daily needs. I recommend it.

Customer review 3
I do the weekend shopping at the supermarket. From the list of items to purchase that I get from my wife, Trasha juice Tetra Pak is a regular item. I got fed up with purchasing and having it on a regular basis. I hope that they find some new flavours.

Customer review 4
Nowadays, there are a lot of brands of packaged juices available in India. Trasha is always available be it a supermarket or a gas station. I have a long drive to work every day. When I stop by the gas station to fill petrol in my car, I go inside the small store to buy a Trasha juice. I just love the Tetra Pak. Very convenient, I just love it.

Hint on Question 10:

The R code used for generating the wordcloud is as follows:

```
#First of all, create the text documents in a folder on C drive. Then
install all the packages.

library(tm)

library(SnowballC)

library(ggplot2)

library(wordcloud)

library(NLP)

library(plyr)

cname<- file.path("C:","IGITxtdocs")#Access the file

cname

dir(cname)#Will list the number of files and details

docs <- Corpus(DirSource(cname))#Loading texts into R

summary(docs)

inspect(docs)
```

```
docs<-tm_map(docs,removePunctuation)

docs<-tm_map(docs, removeNumbers)

docs<-tm_map(docs,tolower)

#docs <- tm_map(docs, PlainTextDocument)

#docs<- (docs, removeWords, stopwords("english"))

library(SnowballC)

#docs<-tm_map(docs,stemDocument)

docs<-tm_map(docs,stripWhitespace)

#docs<-tm_map(docs, PlainTextDocument)

docs<-tm_map(docs, removeWords, c("and", "are", "the", "how", "which",
"will", "this", "for", "most", "also"))

docs<-tm_map(docs, removeWords, c("have", "has", "with", "from", "can",
"these", "that"))

dtm<-DocumentTermMatrix(docs)

dtm

#tdm<-TermDocumentMatrix(docs)

#tdm

#Frequency of occurance of each word in corpus

inspect(docs)

freq<-colSums(as.matrix(dtm))

length(freq)

dtms<- removeSparseTerms(dtm, 0.1)

#Matrix is organized according to frequency of words

ord<-order(freq)

library(wordcloud) freq[head(ord)] #Least frequency

freq[tail(ord)] #Most frequency

freq<-sort(colSums(as.matrix(dtm)), decreasing=TRUE)

head(freq,10)

wf<-data.frame(word=names(freq), freq=freq)

head(wf)

library(RColorBrewer)

set.seed(142)
```

```
wordcloud(names(freq), freq, min.freq=15, scale=c(5, .1), colors=brewer.
pal(4, "Dark2"))

#Association of "analytics" with other words

findAssocs(dtms, "talent", corlimit=0.3)

findAssocs(dtms, "across", corlimit=0.1)

#Plot the word that occurs more than 50 times

#aes describes aesthetics, freq is frequency of word

p<-ggplot(subset(wf, freq>50), aes(word,freq))

#stat= "identity" option in geom_bar() ensures that the height of each
bar is proportional to the data value

p<-p+geom_bar(stat="identity")

# x axis label should be at a 45 degree angle and should be horizontally
justified

p<-p +theme(axis.text.x=element_text(angle=45, hjust=1))

p

# Hierarchical clustering

#removesparceTerms() function removes infrequent words

#this makes 15% empty space (maximum)

dtmss<- removeSparseTerms(dtm, 0.15)

library(cluster)

#Hierarchical clustering is performed in which distance between words and
then cluster them according to the similarity

d <- dist(t(dtmss), method="euclidian")

fit <- hclust(d=d, method="ward")

#The "ward" method has been remamed to "ward.D"; note new "ward.D2"

fit

plot(fit, hang=-1)

#k defines the number of clusters

groups <- cutree(fit, k=5)

#plot dendograms with red borders

rect.hclust(fit, k=5, border="red")

#k means clustering

library(fpc)
```

```
d <- dist(t(dtmss), method="euclidian")

kfit<- kmeans(d, 2)

clusplot(as.matrix(d), kfit$cluster, color=T, shade=T, labels=2, lines=0)
```

Question 11: Prepare a dashboard in Excel by referencing all significant Excel sheets. Please try it yourself.

Hint on Question 11: An example is given in Figure A.24 of a heat map done on correlation variables. Use the slice and dice feature after preparing pivot tables. Also, try the time series feature for a variable that changes with time. Tip and process on including a speedometer gauge has been provided.

Hint: Creating a speedometer gauge/dial for BI dashboards in MS Excel (for Chapter 8, Auntiji Namkeen case). Follow the same steps using Trasha case data.

VALUE	Value (D1) 10
60 (A2)	Pointer (D2) 2
140 (A3)	End = B5click - (sum D1:D2)highlight
70 (A4)	
= B5click - (sum (A2:A4)) 360 (B5)	

FIGURE A.24   *Heatmap in Excel*

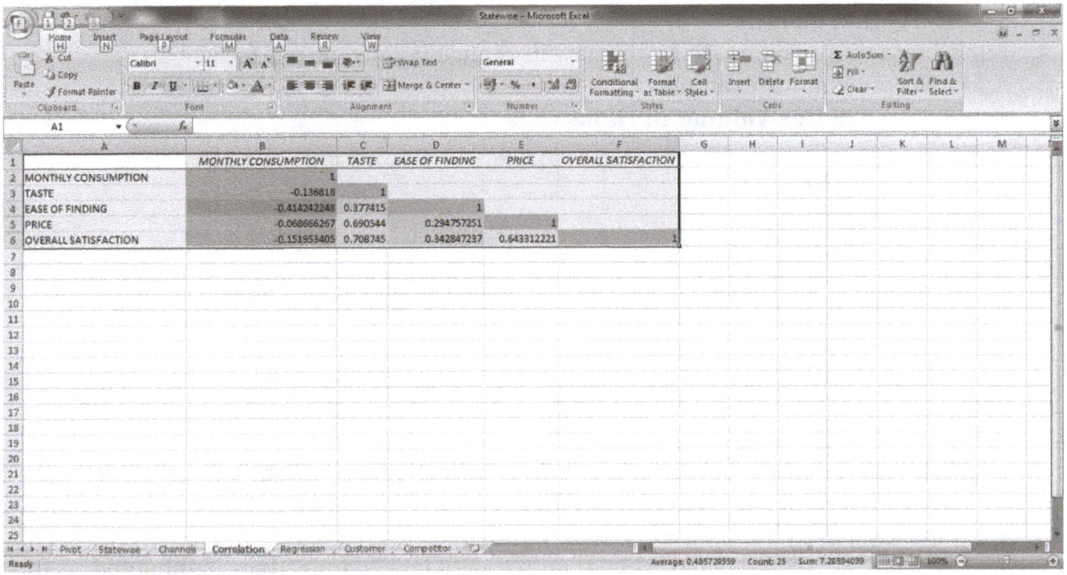

1. Decide how many segment you want. You can make as many as you want.
   a. Here we will make three segments of equal size, store level sales volume (low medium and high) and another for net profit.
   b. Last number to add up to 360.
   c. Formula to be used to add up to 360.
2. Add first donut chart
   a. Highlight first four values A2 to A5. Insert chart donut.
   b. Delete legend.
   c. Rotate the graph. Right click, format data point, no fill. Format data series and keep the angle of first slice about 228°. Remember the value.
   d. Change colour of each segment.
   e. Shape effect on top bar and choose bevel.
3. Now the pointer
   a. We want (value, pointer, end) to add up to VALUE (60, 140, 70). Hence, insert formula for End.
   b. Add another graph. Click on graph, select data: series name pointer, values highlighted (value, pointer, end).
   c. Change outer to pie chart. Right click, change chart type, pie chart secondary axis.
   d. Change the other two areas to no fill.
   e. Now change angle of the slice. Right click, change data series and rotate 228. Add black border to pointer.
   f. Test by changing 10 to 75 for pointer to show appropriate reference.
   g. Highlight pointer and change colour to black. If does not work, increase the pointer width.
   h. Draw a circle in the middle. Hold down shift to get a perfect round.
   i. Add data label to pointer by right click. Double click and select 'value' box D1 to display that number.
4. For all text that need not to be displayed, change colour of font to white
5. Add a dropdown, for example,

Store	Sales volume in thousands
Store 1	38
Store 2	115
Store 3	56
Store 4	22
Store 5	96
Store 6	100
Store 7	226
Store 8	17
Store 9	67
Store 10	238

   - Highlight the cell where you want dropdown E16. Data-data validation-settings-list-chooseStore1 to 10.
   - Add vlookup to 'values' field D1.
   - = vlookup (E16 cell click, table of stores with labels and values highlighted, 2, false).
   - Insert textbox. Put in the formula bar =D1 cell click.
6. Repeat the process to create another gauge for net profit.

Question 12: Create a dashboard and a story board for the Trasha executives.

Solution Q12: The Quisol Insights executive used Tableau software for creating the dashboard and storyboard. Figure A.25 shows the dashboard for state-wise and city-wise volume distribution of the juice Tetra Paks.

Figure A.26 shows the dashboard of juice Tetra Pak storyboard of recommendation by gender. As you have inferred from logistics regression that from the given data set, it is difficult for Trasha Beverages to identify the profile of customer who would potentially recommend the juice to a friend. However, the storyboard built by the Quisol Insights executive is to inform Trasha management of some interesting observations that could be studied further with additional data samples. As can be seen from the story in Figure A.26, females consume more Trasha juice in 200 ml Tetra Paks compared to men. Additionally, they have also recommended to a friend. Also, it is observed that males who have recommended to a friend have rated ease of finding higher compared to taste and price. Keeping these in mind, Trasha can think of means for motivating customers to recommend.

The executive thus used BA to address the BP at Trasha Beverages and provided leads on the three questions:

1. Was Trasha Beverages doing enough to retain and increase their market share?
2. Was the product able to maintain the right balance between quality and affordable price for the consumer?
3. Was the Tetra Pak size of 200 ml appropriate for single consumption or would a smaller size at a lower price fetch more sales?

FIGURE A.25 | *Dashboard*

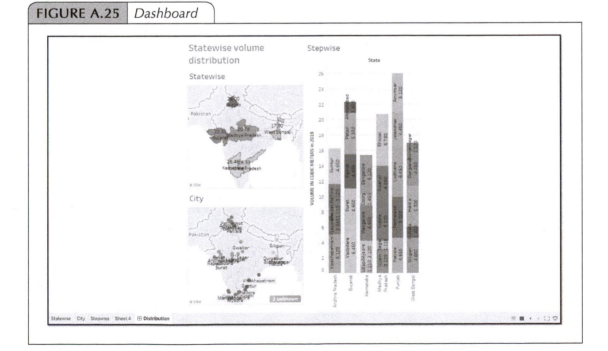

FIGURE A.26 *Storyboard*

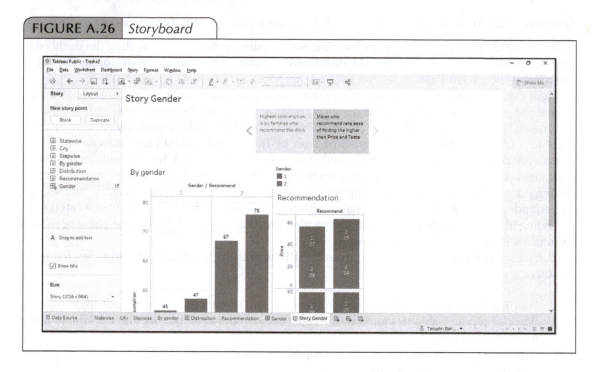

You may now use the Analytics outputs presented above to summarize the top-line responses to each of the above questions. Please be sure to provide a reference to the analysis output that supports each of your responses.

Appendix B
Business Case—Using Analytics for Business Problem-solving

Debt collection has evolved into a critical business function for the financial services industry for long-term viability, particularly in the developed Western economies. To cite an example, the credit card industry in the United States routinely accounts for over $10 billion in write-offs due to inefficient collection processes.[2] In the past four–five years, major consumer financial service-oriented companies in the United States have increasingly put emphasis on reorganizing their backend collections operations by employing intelligent use of internal information data warehouse which houses transaction history of their customers.

This case describes an attempt to use customer data such as individual characteristics, past financial transaction data to categorize customers based on their predicted responsiveness to a particular collection mechanism. The net outcome of this exercise in a banking context is to assign delinquent customers to the most-effective collection mechanism in order to optimize net debt collection (total amount of debt collected minus the operational expenditure of instituting the collection procedure). Many collection mechanisms, such as arbitration or litigation or employment of specialist collection agencies, involve a significant fixed cost per account associated with employing the procedure. For instance, for every account sent to arbitration, the credit card provider has to commit to a $130 arbitration fee irrespective of the outcome (positive or negative to the bank) of the case. Hence, careful assignment of accounts to various collection mechanisms based on their predicted responsiveness to the initiative is critical to improve the collection efficiency of the company as well as prevent excessive bad debt.

Given the increasing role of the service sector in the liberalized Indian economy and the rapid expansion of consumer financial services such as credit card, loan schemes and instalment purchases (Sanjeev, 2000), the possibility of significant bad debt creation is no

---

[1] Case describes a banking process in the period 1998–2000. Adapted from a research paper written by one of the authors. Banerjee, Arindam, 'Harnessing Customers Transaction Data for Efficient Operations: A Case of Debt Collections in the Consumer Finance Industry', *Vikalpa* 26, no. 3 (July–September, 2001): 7–18.

[2] 'SpotLight on Financial Services', American Financial Services Association, March 2000.

longer remote in the Indian environment. In this light, a significant contribution of this case study is to highlight the effective use of a marketing concept of segmentation to redesign an efficient back-office operation in the financial services industry.

THE BUSINESS OF CONSUMER CREDIT COLLECTIONS: SETTING THE CONTEXT

A significant activity in the consumer credit industry is to build and manage the credit outstanding by providing loans to responsible consumers. The revenue generation is through the interest accrual on the outstanding. The significant cost associated with managing consumer credit is due to non-payment of debts by customer leading to charge-off losses for the service provider. This loss is also proportional to the outstanding balance. Besides these major revenue and cost heads, the service provider has to incur some minor operations costs of the card business. Some minor revenue heads such as penalties and fees levied by the service provider on customers who are not diligent about on-time payment of their dues result in additional booked earnings for the service provider, although they are not critical enough to impact the viability of the business. The important issue for all credit providers is to develop a healthy customer base who will utilize the credit facility prudently, leading to healthy revenue generation, and will not default on their payments to the company[3] (see Figure B.1).

In the late 1980s, financial service providers in the United States invested in developing accurate customer acquisition models to build a portfolio of clients that would be profitable based on the above rationale. These models were primarily based on statistical modelling techniques which predicted who would be a profitable customer. However, statistical models by their nature have a built-in inaccuracy due to the parsimonious nature of their construction.

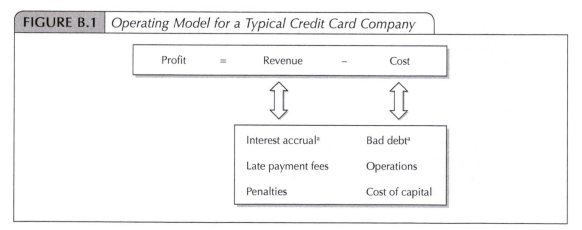

| FIGURE B.1 | *Operating Model for a Typical Credit Card Company* |

Note: [a] Function of revolving balance and customer credit handling behaviour.

[3] In the credit card industry, the term customer's propensity to pay back the debt is of notional value. Ideally, no credit card provider would like the clientele to pay back the principal amount loaned. It is only the accrued interest that is expected as a payment in the form of the 'minimum due' (min due) amount. An ideal customer is one who would dutifully pay the 'min due' amount every payment cycle and no more.

Besides, the lack of appropriate input variables may be an additional cause of inaccurate prediction of a potentially profitable client. As a result of these factors, most state-of-the-art customer acquisition models used by major financial services providers have had inherent flaws in their ability to predict who is likely to be a profitable customer (Chen and Chiou, 1999; Zhang et al., 1999).

MANAGING RISK

A major dimension of operating a credit business is to minimize the risk associated with non-payment of outstanding balances by delinquent customers. As mentioned above, inaccuracies in prediction models used for customer acquisition may also lead to the burden of servicing clients who are habitually tardy about paying back their debts. Yet, other customers may have started off with the good intention of using the credit facility extended to them by the service provider in a responsible manner, but are beset with uncontrollable financial liabilities, which upset their payment plans. Also, with increasing competition in the 1990s, service providers were forced to look for revenue-generation opportunities by soliciting relatively risky segments (sub-prime) of the consumers who were generally not sought after by many other service providers (Watkins, 2000). For these stated reasons, managing debt collections within acceptable norms is very critical to ensure that the charge-off rates do not spiral beyond control.

There are a variety of debt collection initiatives that financial service providers across the world undertake to manage their inward cash flows. The broad categories of initiatives are described as follows.

1. **Periodic letter dunning:** This method is considered to be the least expensive and also the least impactful of the various methods used by collections managers. Normally, it is used as the first attempt to notify the customer about an outstanding payment. In some instances, service providers have used a set of messages in a sequence, with a gradation in the degree of persuasion employed in the messages. Normally, the message ranges from a polite notification of a missed payment (first letter) to a firm rebuke for non-compliance, which is usually reserved for seriously delinquent customers.
2. **Telephone calls:** Usually, telephone calls are used to complement letter-dunning activity, however they are significantly more expensive than mailing letters periodically. If reliable phone numbers are available, they can serve to be more effective than sending messages by mail.
3. **Outsourcing to specialist collection agencies:** In the United States, as well as in India, collection specialists offer their services for a fee which may be a fixed fee regardless of the outcome or else they charge a commission on the collected amount. In the United States, there is a gradation of collection agencies ranging from primary collection agencies to secondary to tertiary agencies. Normally, the approach to dealing with debtors differs based on the severity of the delinquency. Early stage delinquency (30–90 days' non-payment) cases are handled in a reasonably amicable manner where customers are persuaded to adopt a periodic payment plan based on their financial condition. Serious delinquency cases normally require firmness and hard bargaining to ensure that a maximum proportion of the delinquent amount can be collected in one attempt. In some cases of genuine distress, sensitivity to the situation is required in order

to maximize the probability of collecting the debt. The methods employed are varied depending on an on-the-spot assessment of the condition of the debtor. Expertise in this activity is acquired more with experience rather than by applying any scientific management practices.

4. **Arbitration/litigation:** This is perhaps the most expensive method of collections, since it requires an up front court fee for every account that is filed for arbitration/litigation. This method is fairly coercive and can provoke the most unwilling debtors to comply if they have the ability to pay up. However, in cases of genuine customer grievance, it may turn out to be disadvantageous for the service provider to pursue arbitration/litigation since the probability of the case being overturned is high. Therefore, careful selection of delinquent customers based on their ability to pay their dues and confirmation of the fact that they do not have a history of disputes with the service provider is necessary to ensure the greater effectiveness of this collection method.

5. **Rewards programme:** Some service providers are of the opinion that rather than coercion, collection effectiveness can be improved by instituting appropriate incentive schemes for delinquent customers to motivate them to pay up to the maximum extent possible for them. Most serious delinquent customers (90 days or more) have their credit line stopped permanently by service providers. The rationale behind offering incentives such as a partial release of credit lines is to provide delinquent customers with a motivation to work towards paying up their dues to the extent possible.

THE BP TO BE ADDRESSED

While service providers have an array of options to choose from, what is not so widely known is which of these techniques is more effective on a particular type of delinquent customer. To answer the above question, running a pilot is necessary in order to assess the impact of each of these collection methods on a random sample of customers and then based on the sample result decide the best method of collection for each identifiable group (identified based on their individual characteristics and historical transaction data). An economic analysis which works out the net benefit of administering the specific collection practice on a set of customers less the cost of administration determines the net pay-off of collection. This can be used to identify customers who work out profitable for a particular collection method. For example, a rewards programme that promises a release in credit line in lieu of payment of dues may seem to be an effective measure to collect some outstanding balance from the most delinquent customers. However, it is quite likely that not all of these customers would use their open credit lines responsibly and the provider may in fact incur a loss on the new open credit line. Hence, for effective implementation of the rewards programme, it should be offered to only those customers who are expected to assume greater responsibility in handling credit in the future. The focus of the problem, therefore, is to develop the optimal routing algorithm to send each delinquent customer to the appropriate collection process in order to maximize the net inward cash flow in the future.

While it is not possible to develop a separate assignment rule for every delinquent customer, segmentation techniques have been used to identify clusters of customers based on their individual characteristics and past credit handling behaviour who may be routed to the appropriate collection department. Most routing algorithms are designed using a pilot operation that is run by randomly assigning customers to various collection mechanisms. The overall impact (net pay-off) of each collection option is gauged during the test period and the random sample for each collection mechanism is also analysed to identify any recognized segment of customers who respond to a specific collection initiative better than others. Routing algorithms are developed for each of the identified segments complying with the rationale that they are routed to the most profitable collection initiative across all available initiatives. In the absence of validated routing algorithms, many banks in the United States and elsewhere are following an assignment rule based on heuristics or 'gut feel'. While the value of experience and 'gut feel' in developing notions about collection effectiveness is significant, employing scientific validation methods like a test pilot can at the very least confirm the merits of current assignment rules if not identify opportunities to improve them.

In order to provide some more insights into this area of designing efficient customer handling facilities, the rest of this case study describes an instance of developing such a procedure at a large credit card service provider for assigning delinquent customers to an arbitration procedure. It needs to be stressed that the case of arbitration described below should be viewed as an illustration of the use of the concept of segmentation in the context of designing efficient routing algorithms. The process described below is generalizable and can be applied to develop routing algorithm for any other or even multiple collection methods at the same time. In the final section of this case, some validity of developing similar management practices in the Indian context will be provided.

The Arbitration Route to Effective Debt Collection

The general methodology used to design effective backend customer handling facilities at a large bank in the eastern United States is described here. The details and the financial implications of the project are disguised to protect the interest of the bank.

In early 1998, the operations head at this bank realized the need for streamlining its collection activities for its credit card operations. At that point in time, write-off (bad debts written off as losses) rate was close to 12%. With an annual outstanding balance close to $30 billion in its credit card business, this amounted to a significant amount of annual losses. Prudent measures were needed to arrest the trend towards huge write-offs. The head of operations decided to set up an initiative to reallocate collection activities to gain maximum impact. As a first step, it was decided to evaluate the arbitration procedure to subject only to those delinquent customers who respond positively to this procedure. One of the major considerations in selecting arbitration as the first initiative was the high fixed cost to the bank for each delinquent customer. For every customer sent to arbitration, the bank had to pay up an arbitration fee of $130, irrespective of outcome. Hence, it was essential to send only those delinquent customers against whom the bank had a reasonable case for arbitration and who would have the ability to pay up the debt amount as well as the arbitration fee at the time of a favourable ruling.

Arbitration Procedures in Consumer Debt Collections

Traditionally, credit providers have resorted to litigation procedures available under the law of the state to coax their delinquent customers to pay up their debts. Usually, when all other reasonable means of persuasion are exhausted, creditors resort to this extreme measure.

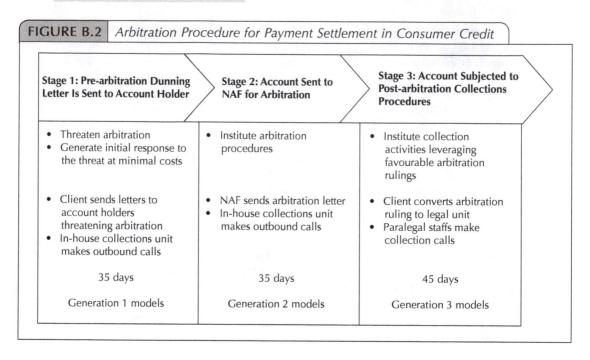

FIGURE B.2   *Arbitration Procedure for Payment Settlement in Consumer Credit*

Certain countries, like the United States, provide customers of financial products an additional protection against a litigation suit by making it mandatory for the dispute to be handled by an arbitration forum (acts as a semi-formal dispute handling body) prior to its decisions being ratified by the court of law. The ruling of the arbitration forum is binding in most respects and usually it can be converted into a judgement based on a routine filing at the court of law.

In the United States, two major recognized arbitration forums operate in the domain of consumer credit disputes, the National Arbitration Forum (NAF) and the American Arbitration Forum (AAF).

The procedure of arbitration for payment settlement in consumer credit (see Figure B.2) is normally initiated by sending a letter of intent by the service provider to the delinquent customer about its decision to resort to arbitration procedures to recover the due amount from the customer. Normally a one-month period is given for the customer to respond favourably to the notification and if he decides to accede to the credit provider's demand for payment of the debt, the arbitration application is dropped.

If the response from the communication is not favourable or there is no response, the service provider has to follow up its intention by filing for arbitration against the delinquent customers and paying up the arbitration fees to the statutory body that oversees the process.[4]

The procedure normally takes about four months for completion from the time the application is filed. Usually, the arbitration forum refers the case to one of its arbitrators on roll, who would send a communication to the delinquent customer regarding the procedure and invite a response. If there is a dispute on the amount or there is a grievance that the customer voices, a formal hearing is fixed for the two parties (service provider and the delinquent

[4] National Arbitration Forum (in the United States).

customer) to state their cases in front of the arbitrator. Based on the respective statements, the arbitrator provides a ruling, which then becomes binding on the warring parties. If the ruling is in favour of the customer, the service provider will have to drop the case for getting the delinquent amount. Otherwise, the customer is obliged to pay up the delinquent amount as well as the arbitration fees. If the customer does not have the ability to pay the entire amount, the service provider may get the settlement ratified in the court of law and have the customer's fixed assets attached to the delinquent amount. In some cases, as required, the customer's wages are garnished to repay the delinquent amount.

There are some general implications that can be drawn from the description of the arbitration procedure. One, it is expensive for the bank to institute this procedure for all its delinquent customers (the fee is $130 per filing) and two, it is a fairly prolonged process and there is no guarantee that the debt will be returned immediately after a favourable ruling is received by the service provider. Hence, judicious choice of customers who may be assigned to this collection procedure is very necessary to be able to make this a profitable venture.

DESIGNING THE TEST PILOT OPERATION

Designing the appropriate pilot operation involves the following:

1. Setting up the arbitration process at an appropriate level for the pilot.
2. Selecting a random sample of delinquent customers to be sent through the process.
3. Tracking the response or lack of response from each customer on an ongoing basis.
4. Identifying all sources of historic information available on the customers who were used in the pilot.

Setting Up the Arbitration Process

Since this procedure was adopted for the first time, careful planning was required to set up the arbitration procedure. A separate routing channel was created in operations to allow selected arbitration cases to an arbitration collections cell. The cell handled the generation of the letter serving as a notice to delinquent customers about the bank's intention to seek arbitration, it handled the telephone calls from the customers that were served notice and also transferred the relevant papers to the arbitration forum at the end of the notice period. The cell also tracked if the customers made the payment of their debt anytime during the process. Since this was a pilot study of a limited scale, at least in the initial stages, the size of the arbitration cell was modest. The plan was to scale up the operations, when a decision was made on a full roll-out.

Selection of Customers for Arbitration

A random sample of customers was chosen for assignment to the arbitration process. The randomization was undertaken after rejecting from the available population of delinquent customers all non-operational cases such as accounts with no proper addresses, multiple names and cases with disputes. The logic was that it would serve no purpose to send such cases deemed unfit for arbitration. The universe of cases sans the cases mentioned above were subjected to a random sort and a small sample of 1,500 cases were selected over a period of about a month to be sent through the arbitration process. Simultaneously, another set of approximately 2,200 cases was flagged as control cases. The cases in the latter set were sent to the various collection cells as they normally are, and hence were appropriately termed as the 'business as usual' cases. The control group served as a benchmark for evaluating the performance (response) of the arbitration group. This is a standard methodology adopted to run natural experiments to test out the effect of a new initiative. Theoretically, the difference in the response between the group subjected to the initiative and the control group is attributed to the new initiative.

The sample of customers was chosen from a universe of customers who had become delinquent in the recent past. The logic applied was that delinquent customers who were identified and administered the appropriate collection procedure early enough (one–two months delinquent) would have a higher chance of paying up than cases that were sufficiently old (six–seven months delinquent).

Tracking Responses from Delinquent Customers

From the initiation of the experiment (pilot), all customers' accounts, in both arbitration and the control groups, were monitored continuously for any response or payment from customers. This was not a problem since the bank had established processes to track and update accounts based on any new payment or response behaviour. A reporting system was created to track the number of customers paying up or responding positively (e.g., calling up the bank to promise to pay) on a monthly basis. The first month-end report from the time accounts were assigned to the experiment coincided with the end of the notice period following the letter communicating the bank's intention of instituting arbitration procedures against the customer. This response rate served as the surrogate for effectiveness of the letter threatening arbitration procedures.

Customer Database for Profiling Customers

The challenging part of the pilot operation was the identification of sources of data on the individual accounts that were tracked through the testing phase. Any information byte available on the customers which described his/her demographics, psychographics, past transaction and payment behaviour and any syndicated source of information on the customer's dealings with other financial service providers was identified. Data were accumulated from various sources housed in the bank's data warehouse.

1. **Bank's customer application database:** All credit card companies, at the time of a new application for credit, elicit information about the potential customer in a standardized format. This includes details regarding the customer's address, income, age, education levels and other routine demographic characteristics that are kept on record. The application database contains the electronic version of these data and is often the primary source of information regarding individual characteristics of a respondent that can be used as predictor variables for segmentation.
2. **Files from credit bureaus:** Syndicated agencies, also referred as credit bureaus, collate credit handling history of all customers from all service providers and develop

standardized models that predict a customer's credit behaviour in the future based on her history of handling credit. These models are robust since they are built using transaction history of a particular customer from multiple service providers (provided the customer uses multiple credit options). Also, the models are able to represent a larger cross section of the market since they are built by pooling data from a larger database unlike the ones available with a single credit provider. The disadvantage of these models is that they are standardized and hence not always appropriate for custom applications for a particular card company. Nevertheless, credit bureaus are an excellent source for syndicated transaction data of customers from multiple sources. Also, the standardized outputs from prediction models run by these agencies are used as input into the custom models built by individual card companies (these outputs are better known as credit scores).

3. **Bank's internal customer transaction database:** The bank's internal databases on the history of transaction between the bank and a particular customer provide a rich source of information regarding the behaviour of the customer. Information such as annual charges to the card and interest accrual and delinquency history (number of times the customer has been delinquent in the recent past and severity of his delinquency) may be candidate predictor variables about her payment behaviour in the future, and therefore may help determine the 'right' collection method to be used.

4. **Bank's internal customer-wise collections history database:** To complement the data available from the bank's internal transaction database, individual customer's history of interaction with the collections department was accessed. This database contained information on any previous records of delinquency and the collection department's interaction with the customer while recovering the delinquent amount. More specifically, it recorded instances of the number of promises made to pay by the customer in a previous delinquency, if she kept her promise and how much of what she promised was actually honoured. This data was kept on an annual basis and the bank could track for at least three years in history about the exact payment behaviour of a delinquent customer.

5. **Demographic data on customers provided by third party providers:** Many times the individual characteristics data available in the applications database is augmented with available data from third-party sources (Donnelley Marketing Services, Claritas and Metro Mail are the major providers of demographic data in the United States). Apart from individual-level information, these sources provide information at the neighbourhood level (based on the address of the customer). Important neighbourhood-level information such as racial mix, economic parameters, income distribution and real estate value are available from this database.

For the success of the project, it was crucial to have access to historical information, which was (a) available for a majority of the customers, (b) reliable and (c) relevant for developing a model that identified the right customer to be sent through the arbitration process. In order to do so, a plausible outcome of this project was to build a prediction model using the customer data on demographics and past behaviour, which would be able to select the right customers to be sent to arbitration. Hence, identifying information sources on individual customers that could potentially be used as predictor variables was very important. At the same time, it must be pointed out that the model building exercise was exploratory in nature. Unlike conventional statistical model development, we undertook this model building exercise with little prior notion about what variables or characteristics of customers would determine their responsiveness to an arbitration threat. Hence, it was necessary to access as many variables associated with delinquent customers as we could possibly locate to develop a robust model. In this respect, the model development process had the resemblance to a typical data mining exercise. In this search across the bank, about 150 unique variables were tracked that described an individual's characteristics and past behaviour, which were found suitable to be used as potential predictor variables.

PLANNED ANALYSIS OF THE OUTPUT OF THE PILOT

The first attempt to analyse the results based on the pilot was made when a significant number of arbitration cases had been in the arbitration cell for at least a month. Across all the cases that had been sent to arbitration the average positive response rate at the end of month 1 was about 24%. Correspondingly, the response rate in the control sample was about 13%. Hence, it was concluded that the initial letter sent out to the customers served as a sufficient threat to increase the response rate significantly over the control group. However, the average response rate was not good enough to assign all customers to arbitration (given the cost involved). The conclusion was that not all customers from the defined universe (used for the experiment) could be sent through the arbitration process. Perhaps, there were certain types of customers who responded to the intervention better than others. The next step was to see if such customer profiles could be identified using their profiling variables by building a prediction model.

Hence, a statistical procedure to identify segments of customers (based on the customer-related variables identified) was conducted. The objective was to uncover groups of customers who responded significantly more than the average response of the sample.

A decision tree analysis (data mining method) was conducted on the data set consisting of the responses of the customers in the arbitration sample and their corresponding characteristics (demographics and past transaction data). This type of analysis is popularly known as classification and regression trees (CART) as well. The technique was employed on a sample of 1,500 cases. The technique employs a hierarchical rote search process by which it examines the separation between cases that respond and do not respond. The hierarchical combination of variables that splits the sample into groups that provide the maximum separation among the two response groups is chosen as the predictor model (see Box B.1). A set of about 150 candidate predictor variables (as described earlier) was considered to evaluate the appropriate combination of customer variables that best separated the responders from the non-responders. The model estimated is presented in Figure B.3.

Box B.1	*Comparison of Methodologies Used*

CART is conceptually similar to the Automatic Interaction Detection (AID) techniques. It is a tree-based model that uses a criterion variable, either categorical or interval scaled and attempts to split the sample into homogeneous and heterogeneous clusters with respect to the criterion variable. The methodology used to achieve this is by sequentially splitting the sample into smaller clusters based on the predictor variable that leads to the maximum separation in the value of the criterion variable across the clusters. The search algorithm identifies the predictor variable and the splitting rule (the value of the predictor variable across which the maximal separation is achieved).

A comparison between CART and a traditional regression model reveals similarity in methodology since both explain causality.

$$\text{Response} = f \text{ (individual characteristics, past credit handling behaviour)}$$

$$f = \text{non-parametric function.}$$

However, unlike regression models, which validate a mathematical relationship among predictor variables that predicts the value of the dependent (criterion) variable, the family of tree-based models identifies splitting rules that regroup the sample of responses into sub groups that are maximally heterogeneous in their responses. More details on this technique are available from the authors of this technique (see Brieman et al., 1984). A similar technique in vogue in marketing research industry in India is chi-square automatic interaction detector (CHAID). Whereas, CART invokes a binary splitting rule (at every step in the sequence the sample is split into two sub samples), CHAID adopts a multiple cluster splitting algorithm at each step.

FIGURE B.3 | *CART Model for Arbitration Sample*

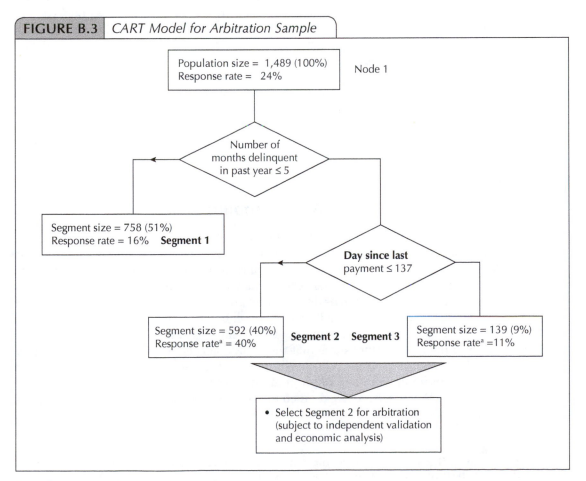

Note: [a]Response is defined as paid currently.

INTERPRETATION OF THE MODEL RESULT

The model in Figure B.3 shows that the original sample of respondents had a response rate of 24 per cent (see Node 1), meaning 24% of the sample responded favourably to the letter sent out by the bank indicating its intention to initiate arbitration proceedings. The respondents either called back and promised to pay up or sent in their payment for the amount due.

The CART methodology split the sample based on the variable called 'number of months delinquent in the past year'. All cases which had exhibited less than five months of delinquency in the past year had a lower than average response rate of 16% (Segment 1). The cases that did not satisfy the above condition were further split by the variable 'days since last payment'. Cases that had not made any payment in the past 137 days were grouped as 'Segment 3' and had a very low response rate of 11%.

The model identified 'Segment 2' to be the most favourable in terms of response (40%). They are delinquent customers who have in the last one year been in the delinquency pool for at least five months, but have also shown some inclination not to be considered a 'serious' case of delinquency by paying up some amount, though not necessarily the entire delinquent amount periodically. This is indicated by their having made some payment to the bank in the past three–four months (137 days, as the model predicts).

The implications are that if one were to calibrate the assignment rule for sending a debtor to arbitration, using his past delinquency history and payment patterns, this may yield a better 'hit rate'. It is all the more significant for the bank to select this segment since a high response to a letter stating intention to initiate arbitration is a less risky proposition for the bank since it is yet to pay up the fixed fee associated with filing a case with the arbitration forum.

What Is Profile of Customers Who Respond?

It may be prudent at this point to delve into the characteristics of the debtors who have responded favourably. As the model identifies them, they are customers who are more prone to remain delinquent as per the past year's financial transactions. However, they appear to be relatively less serious cases of delinquency since they have made some form of payment in the recent past. They can be described as debtors who are not serious about meeting payment schedules and remain recycling in the delinquency pool. It is possible to conjecture that they may be customers who are able to pay up but are unwilling (careless) to pay on time since there were no credible censure measures that the bank could adopt against them until now. These are simply conjectures based on past financial transaction behaviour and in the absence of actual attitudinal data and appropriate demographic data,[5] validating the above hypothesis is difficult. A validation based on contextual data would be helpful in confirming these hunches.

---

[5] In spite of a comprehensive survey of information resources, no reliable source of demographic data was available that could be used extensively in the modelling exercise.

IS THE EXPERIMENT SUCCESSFUL? RESPONSE RATES IN THE CONTROL GROUP

It is important to cross-check whether the segment identified as responding to arbitration notice shows similar response in the control group. This is important because we need to be sure that it was the letter that was creating the positive impact. However, if the segment exhibited a strong positive response regardless of the collection mechanism, it would be pointless to assign it to arbitration since it would unnecessarily expose the bank to an additional fixed expense of the filing fee (for the proportion of customers in this segment who do not respond anyway).

Similar CART output of the control group revealed a tree structure as shown in Figure B.4. From an overall response rate of 13%, the model identified a small segment (size: 5% of original sample), which had a high response rate of 43%. Going by the description of the segment

FIGURE B.4   *CART Segments within Control Sample*

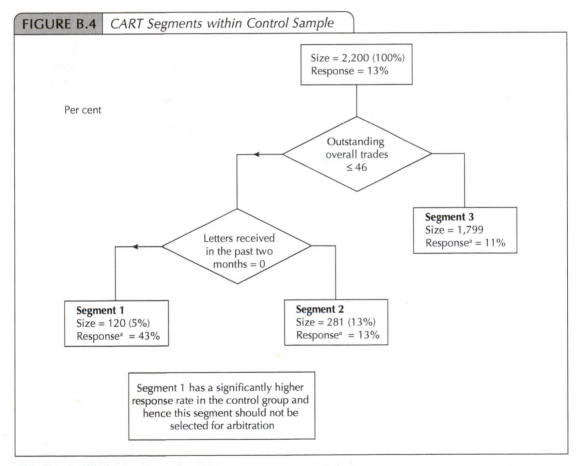

Note: [a]Response defined as paid currently.

(debtors who had an outstanding balance of less than 46% across all their credit instruments and had not corresponded with the bank in the past two months), it may seem that they exhibit a frivolous attitude towards managing their debt. This description seems somewhat similar to the description of the segment that responded well to arbitration. An attempt to find the accounts that satisfied the description of the segments that responded significantly in both the groups (arbitration and control) resulted in very few matches. Hence, we concluded that they were different sets of customers. A separate identification of the particular segment that responded in arbitration, in the control group revealed a corresponding response rate of 16%. Hence, the pilot revealed an incremental response rate of 24% due to the initial letter-dunning activity. This preliminary result was used to forecast the financial implication of arbitration, especially its role in reducing the final write-off percentage.

FINANCIAL IMPLICATIONS OF THE ANALYSIS

The net positive response of arbitration letter-dunning activity was extrapolated in terms of its effect in reducing the write-off rate and therefore its consequent impact on reducing the losses to the bank (see Figure B.5). A conservative estimate on reduction in charge-off and its impact on the additional savings led to an estimate of $217 per account.[6] Since 40% of the accounts in the cardholder database (excluding the preliminary rejects) qualify to be assigned to arbitration, this amounted to a savings of $40 million annually for the bank. The savings calculated took into account the number of new accounts that flowed into the delinquency pool each month. This served as the true measure of the worth of the initiative and played an important part in taking decisions regarding a national ramp up.

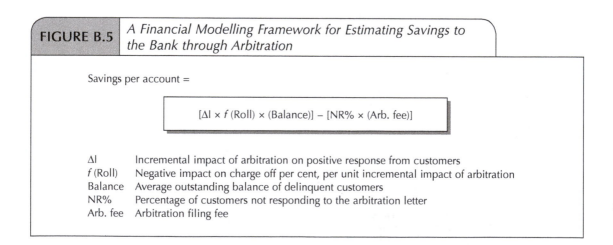

| **FIGURE B.5** | *A Financial Modelling Framework for Estimating Savings to the Bank through Arbitration* |

Savings per account =

$$[\Delta I \times f\,(Roll) \times (Balance)] - [NR\% \times (Arb.\ fee)]$$

ΔI Incremental impact of arbitration on positive response from customers
$f\,(Roll)$ Negative impact on charge off per cent, per unit incremental impact of arbitration
Balance   Average outstanding balance of delinquent customers
NR%   Percentage of customers not responding to the arbitration letter
Arb. fee   Arbitration filing fee

---

[6] The details of the financial model used to calculate the impact are proprietary to the bank. However, this logic for building the model is based on the reduction in flow of accounts towards charge-off due to a positive response to the arbitration letter dunning.

FOLLOW-UP AND VALIDATION

Based on these promising estimates, the bank decided to increase the flow rate (number of accounts sent to arbitration each month) using the assignment rules identified. The initial samples sent using the new assignment rule served as validation for the estimated responses. The validation exercise lent credibility to the original estimates since the variance in the response rates was of the order of ±8 per cent. With the passage of time, the original sample sent through arbitration revealed insignificant responses beyond the letter-dunning stage. Most arbitration cases were approved in favour of the bank without a hearing, however, the immediate cash flow from them was negligible and the due amount had to be attached to the customer's assets. Hence, it was realized that the true potential of the arbitration process in securing immediate collections was mainly through the letter-dunning process and that the prediction model needed to be refined to get a homogenous segment with a higher response rate.

An area of concern in running these pilots is the management of transition from the pilot phase to the actual roll-out, especially when the results are very optimistic. The scale of operations used to man the process during the pilot phase does not match the enormous investments required to manage a full-scale roll-out. While this may not sound very prosaic, experience in this project had proven to the contrary. Immediately after the scale up, the arbitration handling process had a temporary process failure. Lack of personnel manning the arbitration call handling centre and paucity of staff handling paper work for the filing of arbitration led to large-scale pile up of cases in the pipeline which significantly affected efficiency of the collection process for significant interval of time. The implications are that organizations pursuing the option of redesigning their internal processes need to focus on the analysis and development as well as the seamless implementation of the process to reap maximum benefits in a reasonable amount of time.

IMPLICATIONS ON THE INDIAN FINANCIAL SERVICES INDUSTRY

The fledgling financial services industry in India is on a growth phase. According to a survey conducted by the *Financial Times*, the total market size in India is close to $50 billion.[7] Borrowing which was hitherto considered a taboo in the Indian society has been replaced by a healthy dose of openness to credit facilities.

One problem that creditors will face in this high-growth market is ensuring acceptable credit quality. Newer markets will tend to be constituted by less sophisticated borrowers and ensuring good management of bad loans will be a major challenge. One manager in a leading consumer finance company stated that managing bad loans was currently not a problem since the company followed strict measures to ensure that the clientele was of the premium segment. Such measures may well be appropriate for a nascent market as it stands today. However, with increasing competition many service providers may find it profitable to develop new products for the sub-prime markets, which will also entail astute management of credit risk through

---

[7] Survey on 'Indian Banking and Finance/Future Trends—Consumer Credit: The Middle Class Mantra', *Financial Times*, 5 May 2000.

effective collection measures. Increased competition in the premium segments may put pressure on interest rates such that increased focus on the unsophisticated borrower may be imperative for long-term profitability.[8]

Therefore, credit service providers may face the repercussions of catering to riskier segments of the market in terms of a greater responsibility in managing their collections operations. This will require creative designs of various collection procedures in the Indian context, within the purview of the Indian Consumer Laws. Subsequently, banks would have to develop some efficient assignment rules based on the segmentation concept described in this case study to optimally manage their backend collections activity.

Some consumer credit service managers in the Indian environment are likely to voice scepticism about the availability of customer data to develop prediction models as described in this case. While this scepticism is valid to some extent, it needs to be pointed out that a bulk of the data related to past transaction data and customer descriptors are available with all credit card companies electronically since the operating procedures of the business require maintenance and updating of transaction data of the bank's customers on an ongoing basis. Also, most banks maintain the records of the application data that are obtained from customers when they apply for a new credit card.

In the context of a potentially high growth market as it exists in India, this case is meant to highlight the need for adopting internationally acceptable best practices in the industry. For survival in the long run in an industry, which can rapidly exhaust all opportunities for differentiation, implementation of efficient backend operations is essential. In this regard, this case highlights an example of prudent use of statistical modelling along with appropriate financial analysis to design an optimal debt collection procedure. While the specific collection mechanism may vary across environments, the premise of using an economic trade-off analysis to design the process has universal appeal. Also, to be able to incorporate these best practices, some degree of information sharing in the industry is necessary through syndication of internal data across financial service providers.

END NOTE

Readers may note that the case presented above is a typical example of an application of Analytics for resolving a BP. To summarize, it has a detailed description of the context and the problem that needs to be resolved. It then details out the research methodology to be used and visualizes the end result to be obtained that may spell the success/failure of the project. There is a plan developed for the analyses of the data with a logical sequence of looking at top-line results and the need for more granular analysis (customer segmentation using CART). The validation of the results and the financial implications of the analytical results are also presented to prove the worthiness of the findings.

There is an important point that is being made in this case. Good analysis is about diagnosing a problem well so that it assists in designing an appropriate resolution plan. The latter may include a selection of appropriate methods to collect data (experimentation in this case). In other instances, it may be to look for appropriate sources of existing data that can help in providing the right insights.

[8] 'Kotak Exits Consumer Goods Funding', *Economic Times*, 26 March 2001.

It also includes a plan of data analyses which logically sequences out the nature of analysis to be done (and reasons thereof), where the earlier analyses feed results (and implications) into the latter ones to build on the final results. In this case, the results of the experiment provided a direct measure of performance between the results of the test and control groups. When the results were not found to be very promising, a segmentation approach was employed to find more granular results. In the process, the selection of methods to analyse the data were identified. The emphasis here is on the need to sense the resolution path, which determines the appropriate methods (analytic techniques) to be used. Specifically, the choices here were (a) a test of significance of means between groups and (b) a decision tree analysis to conduct segmentation. While other tools exist, they were not required in this context.

The point to be made through this case is quite clear. The profession of Analytics is less about the application of data processing tools, and it is more to do with sensing the problem to be resolved and choosing the 'right' tool to be used, given the format of the available data. Knowledge of operating data analytic tools is therefore just a basic condition in being an effective Analytics professional in the business domain.

REFERENCES

Breiman, Leo, Jerome Friedman, Richard Olsen, and Charles Stone. 1984. *Classification and Regression Trees.* Wadsworth, OH: Pacific Grove.

Chen, Liang-Hsuan, and Tai-Wei Chiou. 1999. 'A fuzzy Credit-Rating Approach for Commercial Loans: A Taiwan Case'. *Omega: The International Journal of Management Science* 27: 407–419.

Sanjeev, Gunjan. 2000. 'Debt Burden: No Longer a Problem'. *Indian Management* January 39(1): 58–61.

Watkins, John P. December, 2000. 'Corporate Power and the Evolution of Consumer Credit'. *Journal of Economic Issues* XXXIV (4): 909–932.

Zhang, Guoqiang, Michael Y. Hu, B. Eddy Patuwo, and Daniel C. Indro. 1999. 'Artificial Neural Networks in Bankruptcy Prediction: General Framework and Cross-Validation Analysis'. *European Journal of Operations Research* 116: 16–32.

Appendix C
Online Grocery Case

The paper 'Web Content Analysis of Online Grocery Shopping Websites in India'[1] by the authors provides more insights into the practical application of data mining concepts:

INTRODUCTION

Shopping for grocery and everyday household products is an integral part of life. In India, buying from a nearby *kirana* store (small retail store in the neighbourhood in India), ordering products via phone call from the *kirana* store, picking up groceries from the supermarket are some of the methods adopted by consumers. With changing time, consumers have started becoming technology savvy, resulting in widespread use of Internet and mobile phones. E-tailers have identified an opportunity to reach consumers via the online platform, thus beginning the era of online shopping. The online grocery portal provides features such as comparative pricing, deals and coupons, home delivery options and such others. According to a Nielsen survey [10], the urban and affluent consumers in India have opted for the e-commerce as an alternate means of shopping. This platform has provided the Indian customer the product, service, conversations, query resolutions, content all under the same umbrella of digital shopping.

Grocery market growth in the online space presents a challenge for supermarket chains competing for share, where their investments in online and offline need to be balanced [9]. Earlier research related to internet grocery shopping has concentrated on comparing online and offline purchase behaviour in various ways like the importance of brand names [6], brand loyalty [5], shopping pattern [1] and consumers' perceptions of the advantages and disadvantages of online grocery shopping [7]. Study has also been conducted on consumer traits of the internet shoppers, either in terms of their general shopping orientation [4], their web-usage-related lifestyle [3] or psychographic characteristics [2]. Additionally [8], based upon motivations for shopping online attempts at developing a typology of the internet grocery shoppers.

Another Nielsen survey [11] evaluated the parameters that drive increased consumer interest in online grocery shopping. *Convenience, selection* and *savings* have been stated as primary reasons for choosing online grocery over store shopping. *Shipping costs, inability to inspect perishables* and having *to wait for deliveries to arrive* have been mentioned as disadvantages of online grocery shopping. There is a significant number of people who continue to shop from stores in person and have not yet experienced online shopping. Reasons stated have been the habit and preference of the individual or insufficient means to use it due to lack of awareness/availability of online grocery options.

There is opportunity for growth of online grocery due to the following reasons:

1. **Convenience:** Online grocery shopping from home avoids the trips that have to be made to the grocery stores. It frees up the time for other activities and maintain better work-life balance.
2. **Generation Y:** Generation Y has a large number of online users. Hence, habit and preference of in-store shopping that exists with earlier generations is less with Generation Y. Usage of the internet and mobile applications are leading to increase in online shopping.
3. **Broadband and media:** Growth and penetration of Internet has increased at a rapid pace. Technology savvy customers have ventured into the online shopping space looking for information. Advertisements on media have promoted the advantages of online shopping.
4. **Customization:** Online grocery shopping tracks customer purchase behaviour and hence is able to provide customized recommendations to the customer during following visits to the website based on previous shopping habits (e.g., product recommendations or promotions for combinations of offerings/kits).

With growing number of e-tailers providing online platform for grocery shopping, competition has entered the online grocery shopping market in India. Research and academic discussion forums debate competitive strategies for their growth and survival. Some of the common attributes of measuring online presence in a competitive market include the bouquet of product categories offered, the ability to service PAN India, competitive pricing, on-time delivery of products and services, discounts offered through deals and coupons, maintaining quality, managing suppliers and handling consumer complaints effectively. While the content displayed on the website is important along with the look and feel, easy loading of pages, quick navigation between web page links, appearing in searches, referrals from other websites and a desirable revenue model, equally important is to maintain the optimum products in the inventory, on-time delivery, cashback options, deals and discounts, payment options and handling customer queries and complaints. All of these activities generate a huge amount of data that are structured as well as unstructured in nature. Some of the data are consciously captured by the organizations which are used by their Analytics teams to do descriptive and predictive analyses and devise competitive strategies and metrics for measurement of their success online.

A huge amount of data exists in unstructured form like the textual data of the website content, customer buying habits, queries and complaints and so on. Analysts have developed ways of mining this rich source of data for developing insights that can be useful for business growth and profitability. Statistical methods like web and text mining for evaluating web and textual content on the websites have become important in analysing unstructured data.

Text mining, also known as text data mining or knowledge discovery in textual databases, is the semi-automated process of extracting patterns (useful information and knowledge) from large amount of unstructured data sources. Text mining is the same as data mining in that it has the same purpose and uses the same processes, but with text mining, the input to the process is a collection of unstructured (or less structured) data files such as Word documents, PDF files, text excerpts XML files and so on. In essence, text mining can be thought of as a process (with two main steps) that starts with imposing structure to the text-based data sources followed by extracting relevant information and knowledge from this structured text-based data using data mining techniques and tools.

The World Wide Web is perhaps the world's largest data and text repository, and the amount of information on the Web is growing rapidly every day. A lot of interesting information can be found online: whose homepage is linked to which other pages, how many people have links to a specific Web page and how a particular site is organized. In addition, each visitor to a website, each search on a search engine, each click on a link and each transaction on an e-commerce site creates additional data. Although unstructured textual data in the form of Web pages coded in HTML or XML are the dominant content of the Web, the Web infrastructure also contains hyperlink information (connections to other Web pages) and usage information (logs of visitors' interactions with Web sites), all of which provide rich data for knowledge discovery. Analysis of this information can help us make better use of Web sites and also aid us in enhancing relationships and value to the visitors of our own Web sites. Web mining (or Web data mining) is the process of discovering intrinsic relationships (i.e. interesting and useful information) from Web data, which are expressed in the form of textual, linkage or usage information [12].

This paper evaluates 10 online grocery shopping sites in India comparing the content on their homepages, customer reviews and also analysing their business performance as summarized on public websites that use search optimization tools and analytical processes. This paper aims to study attributes from structured and unstructured data that lead to success of online grocery business in India.

The public websites that have been considered for this study are as follows:

Bigbasket.com (Bangalore, Mumbai, Delhi, Mysore, Chennai, Hyderabad, Pune, Madurai, Coimbatore, Vijayawada, Ahmedabad, Nashik, Lucknow and Vadodara): bigbasket.com has over 18,000 products and over 1,000 brands in their catalogue that include fresh fruits and vegetables, rice and dals, spices and seasonings to packaged products, beverages, personal care products and meats [51].

AaramShop.com (97 cities): AaramShop is a hybrid retail platform that is completely focused on ensuring that customers can shop for daily essentials and grocery brands from the comfort of their homes or offices [52].

RelianceFreshDirect.com (Mumbai): RelianceFreshDirect.com provides the convenience of ordering groceries online or on phone. Customers can buy various brands and pack sizes of fruits and vegetables, dairy and bakery, staples, packaged food and household and personal care products [53].

Askmegrocery.com (PAN India): Askmegrocery.com aims at fulfilling customers' daily grocery requirements and brings a gamut of products ranging from staples, dairy products, personal care products to other household utilities and thousands of brands [54].

ZopNow.com (Bangalore, Hyderabad, Mumbai, Navi Mumbai, Thane, Pune and Gurgaon): As a starting point for their vision, they plan to achieve the first mission of delivering 'daily needs' items at customers' doorstep in less than three hours. They currently carry items ranging from home needs, personal needs, staples, beverages, spices, edible oil, cleaning utilities, baby products and many more [55].

FabGrocery.com (Kolkata): FabGrocery.com is a virtual departmental store, serving across Kolkata. FabGrocery.com is created to fit into the lifestyle of every Kolkatan. They want to ease the grocery shopping experience for every household with wide range of products, on-time delivery, competitive prices and much more [58].

BazaarCart.com (Delhi, Noida, Ghaziabad): At BazaarCart.com one can expect the best prices in Delhi/NCR on favourite grocery items because when they sell online, they can sell stuff cheaper [59].

GrocerMax.com (Gurgaon): They promptly deliver what you really want, from an assortment of 10,000+ quality merchandise, at customers' doorsteps, always at a price less than the MRP [56].

Naturesbasket.com (Mumbai, Delhi, Bangalore, Hyderabad, Pune): Godrej Nature's Basket is the retail venture of Godrej Group started in 2005 as a single fresh food store. They have today morphed into a 36-store chain of premium gourmet stores strategically located at high street locations in Mumbai, Delhi/NCR, Pune, Hyderabad and Bangalore and have created online presence via this portal [60].

SaltnSoap.com (Kolkata): SaltnSoap, a BlueBeaks initiative, intends to provide its consumers a convenient, social, enjoyable and rewarding experience of shopping their daily grocery needs online from the comfort of their homes and offices [57].

Definition of Terms Used in This Research Study

Cosine similarity index: Cosine similarity is a measure of similarity between two vectors of an inner product space that measures the cosine of the angle between them. The cosine of 0° is 1, and it is less than 1 for any other angle. It is thus a judgement of orientation and not magnitude: two vectors with the same orientation have a cosine similarity of 1, two vectors at 90° have a similarity of 0 and two vectors diametrically opposite have a similarity of –1, independent of their magnitude. Cosine similarity is particularly used in positive space, where the outcome is neatly bounded in [0,1]. In information retrieval and text mining, each term is notionally assigned a different dimension and a document is characterized by a vector where the value of each dimension corresponds to the number of times that term appears in the document. Cosine similarity then gives a useful measure of how similar two documents are likely to be in terms of their subject matter [61].

Images on site: Search engines send out automated programmes called 'spiders' that crawl websites and search for what type of content it contains. Although spiders are not able to 'see' images, they are able to read the text which is associated with those images [63].

Alexa traffic ranking: Alexa traffic rank is traffic rank of a site. The traffic rank is based on 3 months of historical traffic data collected from the users of Alexa Toolbar. It is combined with different traffic data source and page views. Alexa counts the number of visitors and number of page views of all the sites for Alexa traffic rank [67].

Page load time: Page speed can be described in either 'page load time' (the time it takes to fully display the content on a specific page) or 'time to first byte' (how long it takes for your browser to receive the first byte of information from the web server). No matter how you measure it, a faster page speed is better [62].

Revenue per day: Revenue of the website on a daily basis.

Website's worth: There are several factors that determine the website valuation price. These include age of the website, domain authority, SEO analysis, page rank, traffic rank, social media interaction, website content and many other factors. These factors are all considered to calculate the estimate of how much the website is worth [66].

Number of unique visitors: A visit is one individual visitor who arrives at your website and proceeds to browse. A visit counts all visitors, no matter how many times the same visitor may have been to your site. A unique visit will tell you which visitors are visiting your site for the first time. The website can track this as unique by the IP address of the computer. The number of unique visits will be far less than visits because a unique visit is only tracked if cookies are enabled on the visitors computer [65].

Number of page views: Once a visitor arrives at a website, they will search around on a few more pages. On an average, a visitor will look at about 2.5 pages. Each individual page a visitor views is tracked as a page view [65].

Traffic source via organic search: This indicates the percentage of visitors who visit the site via a search engine. There are primarily four different types of traffic sources (the way visitors find the website) [65].

Direct navigation: Type URL in traffic, bookmarks, email links w/o tracking codes and so on.

Referral traffic: From links across the web, social media, in trackable email, promotion and branding campaign links.

Organic search: Queries that sent traffic from any major or minor web search engines.

Pay per click (PPC): Click through from PPC-sponsored ads, triggered by targeted key phrases.

Methodology

The authors have conducted this study in 3 parts, all based on secondary data collected from public websites.

Part A

In Part A, the authors have captured unstructured data (textual) from homepage of 10 grocery shopping websites using the RapidMiner tool's web mining operators. Hence, established a cosine similarity index amongst them. The obtained result allows the authors to understand the similarity in terms of the homepage content and keywords among the websites.

The authors have observed that websites that are designed as retail interface for online grocery shopping have certain design aspects in common. A quick look at the websites indicates that certain content like product categories, product names, login corner, payment link, mobile app link and so on appear in all the pages. However, in the competitive space the content and design remains different in their own unique ways. In this research work, in part A, the authors have attempted to identify the similarity amongst the homepage textual content of the websites, thus indicating the difference that exists between them in terms of the online interface content. Using RapidMiner operators, the authors have used the web crawler to connect to the specified websites and read the content from the homepage. A comparative statistical analysis of the textual content obtained using web mining establishes the similarity index as shown in Table C.1.

Output of the Analysis for Part A

From the result obtained from RapidMiner (Table C.1), it can be concluded that the websites are significantly different in terms of content on the homepage. The highest similarity is seen between the 2nd (askmegrocery.com) and 5th (fabgrocery.com) websites of 8.1%. The least similarity is seen between the 1st (bigbasket.com) and the second (aaramshop.com) and the 3rd (naturesbasket.com) and the 5th (FabGrocery.com) websites of 0.28%.

In addition to homepage content, the keywords specified for organic search for the respective websites have been documented in Table C.2. Organic search is used by majority of online users for seeking information by typing search words in search engines. In India, due to the recent

TABLE C.1 *Similarity Index in %*		
First website	**Second website**	**Similarity in %**
1. Bigbasket.com	2. Askmegrocery.com	0.28
1. Bigbasket.com	3. Naturesbasket.co.in	1.03
1. Bigbasket.com	4. Bazaarcart.com	0.5
1. Bigbasket.com	5. Fabgrocery.com	0.72
1. Bigbasket.com	6. Saltnsoap.com	1.91
2. Askmegrocery.com	3. Naturesbasket.co.in	1.63
2. Askmegrocery.com	4. Bazaarcart.com	3.27
2. Askmegrocery.com	5. Fabgrocery.com	8.13
2. Askmegrocery.com	6. Saltnsoap.com	1.89
3. Naturesbasket.co.in	4. Bazaarcart.com	3.93
3. Naturesbasket.co.in	5. Fabgrocery.com	0.28
3. Naturesbasket.co.in	6. Saltnsoap.com	1.25
4. Bazaarcart.com	5. Fabgrocery.com	0.77
4. Bazaarcart.com	6. Saltnsoap.com	0.94
5. Fabgrocery.com	6. Saltnsoap.com	1.68

TABLE C.2 *List of Keywords*		
S. No.	**Website**	**Keywords**
1	Bigbasket.com	Online supermarket, online grocery store, buy groceries online, grocery online, buy food online, grocery, online grocery shopping, online grocery, food shopping online, online grocery shopping India [29]
2	AaramShop.com	CPG, FMCG, free home delivery, online grocery shopping, aaramshop, India, lizol, neighbourhood retailers, hybrid commerce, All Out mosquito repellent [30]
3	Reliancefreshdirect.com	Reliance fresh, buy grocery online, online grocery shopping, online grocery, reliance one card [31]

(Table C.2 Continued)

(Table C.2 Continued)

S. No.	Website	Keywords
4	Askmegrocery.com	Grocery shopping online, online grocery store, online grocery shopping, online grocery store in India, online vegetable shopping, online fruits shopping, askme grocery, askmegrocery, ask me grocery, askme grocery offers [32]
5	Zopnow.com	Buy online, supermarket, grocery delivery, ZOP, hypermarket, grocery, online grocery shopping, online grocery, Tata Tea Gold, zopnow [28]
7	Fabgrocery.com	Online grocery Kolkata, best online grocery store in Kolkata, online grocery shopping in Kolkata, online grocery store Kolkata, grocery store in Kolkata, grocery shopping in Kolkata, online grocery products in Kolkata, fabgrocery, grocery product Kolkata, grocery home delivery in Kolkata [33]
8	Grocermax.com	Vegetables, frozen, grocery online, non veg, grocery, online grocery shopping, online grocery, online grocery Gurgaon [35]
9	Saltnsoap.com	Online supermarket, online grocery store, buy grocery online, grocery, online grocery shopping, grocery store India, home delivery, best online grocery store, online grocery Kolkata, grocery store Kolkata [34]
10	Naturebasket.co.in	Online grocery shopping, grocery shopping online, online grocery, online supermarket, food online, gourmet food India [27]

interest and growth of online shopping, search keywords become an important dimension of website design. Keyword optimization (the act of researching, analysing and selecting the best keywords to target to drive qualified traffic from search engines to your website) [68] is an important consideration in the overall website design for reaching maximum number of prospective customers. It is observed that the most common keywords appearing across all the sites are 'online grocery shopping', 'home delivery' and 'supermarket'.

Part B

In Part B, the authors have analysed customer reviews from the online grocery websites. Fourteen customer reviews have been considered for the study. The authors have used Rapid-Miner's text mining operators and association rules operators to analyse them and establish association rule from the textual content. Association rule mining finds interesting associations and correlation relationships among large sets of data items. Association rules show attribute value conditions that occur frequently together in a given data set. They provide information in the form of if–then statements and are probabilistic in nature. In addition to the **antecedent** (if) and the **consequent** (then), an association rule has two numbers that express the degree of uncertainty about the rule. In association analysis, the antecedent and consequent are sets of items (called item sets) that are disjoint (do not have any items in common). The first number is called the 'support' for the rule. 'Support' is the number of transactions that include all items in the antecedent and consequent parts of the rule. The other number is known as the 'confidence' of the rule. Confidence is the ratio of the number of transactions that include all items in the consequent as well as the antecedent (the support) to the number of transactions that include all items in the antecedent. 'Lift' is a value that gives us information about the increase in probability of the then (consequent) given the if (antecedent) part [69]. The authors have evaluated the customer reviews using these parameters and text mining operators of RapidMiner.

The shopping experience of a customer who shops online is considered satisfactory only when the customer is happy with the overall shopping experience. The authors have addressed this hypothesis from the textual content documenting the customer reviews. Using 'happy' as the indicator, the authors have identified the words that are associated with happiness. The strength of the 'support' of those words existing together across the reviews indicates the areas of focus for the e-tailer to provide an overall satisfactory experience to their customers. The authors have further evaluated the 'confidence' and 'lift' for the associated words that have high 'support' value.

Output of the Analysis from Part B

Analysing the 'support', 'confidence' and 'lift' values from association rule for conclusion word 'happy' identifies the words to which happiness of a customer is associated. As seen from Figure C.1, the 'support' value is 35.7%, meaning 35.7% times of the customer reviews, the word 'happy' exists together with the words 'delivery' and 'products'. This indicates that the mention of happiness due to delivery of products has been made only in 35.7% of the total number of reviews. The authors have further noted that there is an 83.3% chance of 'happy' existing in customer reviews that mention delivery of products indicating a 'confidence' value of 83.3%. This indicates that if the customer mentions about delivery of products, there is 83.3% chance of them mentioning happiness. Additionally, the value of 'lift' is 1.667, indicating that occurrence

| FIGURE C.1 | Association Rule Output from RapidMiner |

of words 'delivery' and 'products' has a positive effect on the occurrence of 'happy' or that they are positively correlated. We also note that words 'delivery' and 'groceries' along with 'time' and 'happy' has a 'lift' value of 3.5, indicating that customers who receive delivery of groceries view it as time saving and are happy with the experience.

Part C

In Part C, the authors have captured the parameters (attributes) used by search engine optimization (SEO) sites for analysing the online grocery websites. Then we have tried to identify the correlation amongst these attributes. Several online sites like stattools.com, statvoo.com, informer.com, similarityweb.com and so on have used website usage metrics information and have analysed it using SEO tools and statistical methods. Information used for our study include the following parameters for the 10 websites: daily visitors, daily page views, Alexa rank, page speed score, images on the site in % compared to other content on the site, traffic source on the website of which organic search traffic in %, website worth in dollars, income per day in dollars. The parameters have been defined in the Methodology section. Using a correlation matrix, the authors have tried to understand the relationship between income per day in dollars made by the websites to the other parameters, thus identifying the ones that are strongly (> 0.9) correlated. The parameters that have strong correlation to income per day in dollars are the ones that have higher impact on the revenue.

Output of the Analysis from Part C

The correlation matrix in Table C.3 indicates a strong correlation between 'daily page views' –0.97, 'daily visitors' –0.98, 'website's estimated worth in dollars' –0.99 to 'income per day in dollars'. The Alexa ranking is negatively correlated as less the Alexa ranking more visited is the website. However, from the findings, the Alexa ranking does not seem to be affecting the income per day. Similarly, the amount of images on the website, the time taken by the pages to load and the traffic source via search engines do not have a significant impact.

TABLE C.3 *Correlation Matrix*

	Income per Day ($)	Daily Visitors	Daily Page Views	Alexa Rank	Page Speed Score (%)	Estimated Worth ($)	Images (%)	Search Traffic (%)
Income per day ($)	1							
Daily visitors	0.978	1						
Daily page views	0.970	0.998	1					
Alexa rank	–0.392	–0.366	–0.338	1				
Page speed score (%)	0.225	0.161	0.167	–0.103	1			
Estimated worth ($)	0.988	0.969	0.968	–0.313	0.277	1		
Images (%)	–0.459	–0.436	–0.452	0.278	–0.318	–0.523	1	
Search traffic (%)	–0.077	–0.152	–0.155	0.022	0.768	–0.051	–0.270	1

Overall Findings

In Part A, we find the following:

Maximum similarity between the homepage content of online grocery shopping websites (10 considered for this study) is 8.1% and minimum similarity is 0.28%.

The most common keywords appearing across all the 10 websites are 'online grocery shopping', 'home delivery' and 'supermarket'.

In part B, we find the following:

Happiness with the experience of using the online grocery website is positively correlated to delivery of groceries.

The correlation is stronger when the delivery of the grocery is done timely.

In part C, we find the following:

The income per day in dollars made by the e-tailers of grocery online is strongly correlated to number of visitors on the website, number of page views and websites' worth in dollars.

It is not affected by Alexa ranking, images on the website, the time taken by the pages to load and the traffic source via organic search engines.

PRACTICAL IMPLICATIONS

Results of the study will help identify the keywords that e-tailers of online grocery anticipate the Indian consumers to use while using a search engine to get to online grocery websites. Common keywords used in search engines would fetch all the websites containing the keywords. Thus the results will encourage e-tailers to uniquely differentiate from competitor websites by keyword optimization. It will also identify consumer preferences from the customer review analysis. With the statistically obtained result, the e-tailer is reassured that timely delivery of groceries makes an Indian customer happy. It may be important to identify what else is associated with happiness which did not show significantly due to the limited number of samples used for the study. The result obtained from the correlation matrix will help identify the parameters that drive per day revenue for the online retailer. Due to the limited sample size further statistical analysis could not be carried out to establish the strength of the impact of the independent variable on per day revenue, however, the strength of the correlation identifies the impacting variables. Further studies can help devise creative strategies for optimizing website metrics for increasing revenue.

ORIGINALITY/VALUE

While study on individual online grocery shopping sites in India has been conducted, the authors have not come across a comparative study of the sites both from the point of content analysis as well as usage information. Results obtained from the study will be useful for online retailers in designing their websites for generating more revenue and increase number of happy customers. The similarity index will identify the similarity in terms of textual content that exists between their and competitor websites. The keywords similarity and difference highlight what competing sites use to show up in organic searches. The academic researchers who work in online retailing space can use the results of the study to carry out similar research with larger data sets.

REFERENCES

Andrews, R.L. and Currim, I.S. (2004), "Behavioural differences between consumers attracted to shopping online versus traditional supermarkets: implications for enterprise design and marketing strategy", International Journal of Internet Marketing and Advertising, Vol. 1 No. 1, pp. 38-61.

Barnes, S.J., Bauer, H.H., Neumann, M.M. and Huber, F. (2007), "Segmenting cyberspace: a customer typology of the internet", European Journal of Marketing, Vol. 41 No. 1/2, pp. 71-93

Brengman, M., Heuens, M., Weijters, B., Smith, S.M. and Swinyard, W.R. (2005), "Segmenting internet shoppers based on their web-usage related lifestyle: a cross cultural validation", Journal of Business Research, Vol. 58 No. 1, pp. 79-88.

Brown, M., Pope, N. and Voges, K. (2003), "Buying or browsing? An exploration of shopping orientations and online purchase intention", European Journal of Marketing, Vol. 37 No. 11/12, pp. 1666-84.

Danaher, P.J., Wilson, I.W. and Davis, R.A. (2004), "A comparison of online and offline consumer brand loyalty", Marketing Science, Vol. 22 No. 4, pp. 461-76.

Degeratu, A., Rangaswamy, A. and Wu, J. (2000), "Consumer choice behavior in online and traditional supermarkets: the effects of brand name, price and other search attributes", International Journal of Research in Marketing, Vol. 17 No. 1, pp. 55-78.

Francesca, R. and Rettie, R. (2009), "Online Grocery Shopping: The Influence of situational factors", European Journal of Marketing, Vol 43, No. 9/10, pp. 1205-1219.

Ramus, K. and Nielsen, N.A. (2005), "Online grocery retailing: what do consumers think?", Internet Research, Vol. 15 No. 3, pp. 335-52.

Rohm, A.J. and Swaminathan, V. (2004), "A typology of online shoppers based on shopping motivations", Journal of Business Research, Vol. 57 No. 7, pp. 748-57.

Francesca, R. and Rettie, R. (2009), "Online Grocery Shopping: The Influence of situational factors", European Journal of Marketing, Vol 43, No. 9/10, pp. 1205-1219.

Terron Adrian, The Nielsen Company, 2012, Nielsen Featured Insights: The Advent of 'Me'-tailing and how India's shoppers are now buying online, retrieved from http://www.nielsen.com/content/dam/corporate/india/reports/2012/Me-tailing-and-how-India-shoppers-are-now-buying-online.pdf

Swedowsky Maya, The Nielsen Company. September 2009 "Analyst Report: Online Grocery Shopping: Ripe time for Resurgence", retrieved from http://www.nielsen.com/content/dam/corporate/us/en/newswire/uploads/2009/10/Nielsen-OnlineGroceryReport_909.pdf

Turban, E., Sharda, R., Delen, D., and King, D. (2011), Business Intelligence: A Managerial Approach, Second Edition, Pearson, ISBN: 978-93-325-1814-8

Appendix D
Tips on Using Software Used in This Book

MICROSOFT EXCEL

All of you are familiar with the spreadsheet software Microsoft Excel. Your laptops or desktops have MS Excel installed as part of the Microsoft Office suite. This is a handy software that you have used to create tables for recording survey results and information on entities of interest. Each column represents an attribute for the entity (table) and each row represents an instance of the table.

In order to work with the data in the table, the Formulas tab shown in Figure D.1 provides several functions to process and analyse the data.

Use of filters is also a very useful method of interpreting data. It is on the Home tab as shown in Figure D.2. It additionally provides an option of sorting the data either in the ascending or descending order before or after applying the filter. The AutoSum function also on the Home tab is a quick way of data summation.

The Conditional Formatting feature on the Home tab is useful in creating heat maps. You can play around to build creative heat maps for visually appealing representations of data that aids better interpretation. It has been discussed in Chapter 8.

Another commonly used function for summarizing data in the pivot table has been discussed in Chapter 6. As shown in Figure D.3, after clicking the Insert tab, you will be required to insert a pivot table for the data you wish to summarize.

Different types of charts are available on the Insert tab for visually representing information. The bubble chart discussed in Chapter 9 is also discussed here.

The Slicer and Timeline features, shown in Figure D.4, on the Insert tab are useful for dashboard creation as discussed in Chapter 11.

The statistical analysis of data present in tables can be performed using the methods available on the Data Analysis ToolPak. The 'Analysis ToolPak' is an add-in available for download in MS Excel. If you have not already done so, follow the steps below to add the add-in.

1. Go to File in MS Excel and click on Options.
2. Click on Add-ins.

FIGURE D.1 *Formula Tab in Excel*

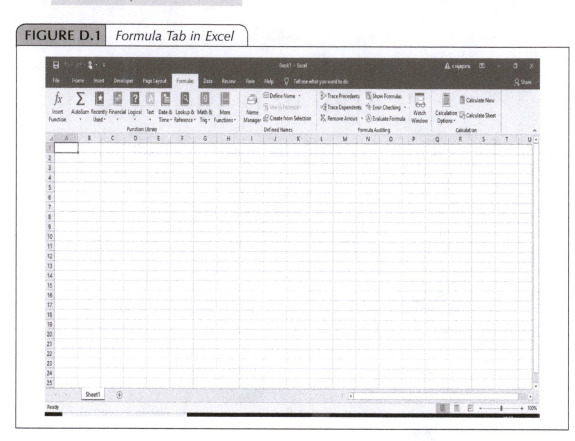

FIGURE D.2 *Sort and Filter in Excel*

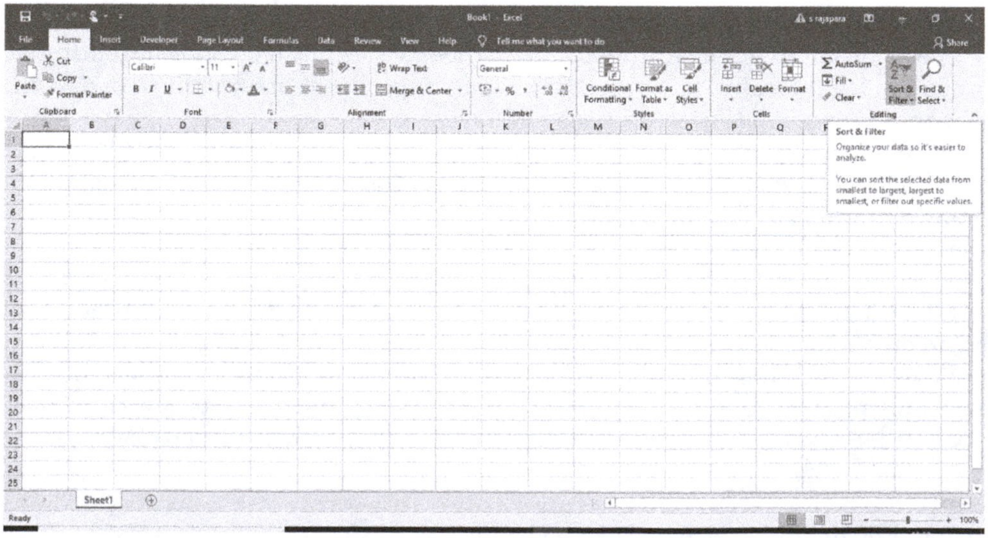

FIGURE D.3   *Inserting Pivot Table in Excel*

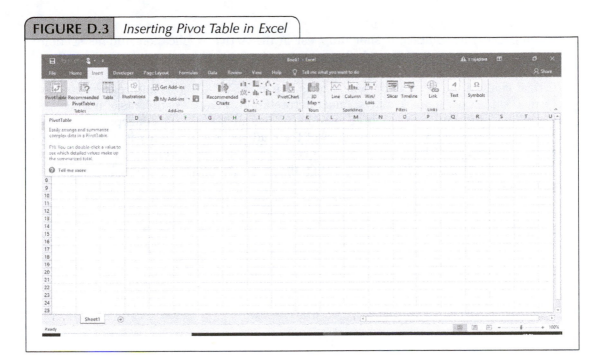

FIGURE D.4   *Slicer and Timeline in Excel*

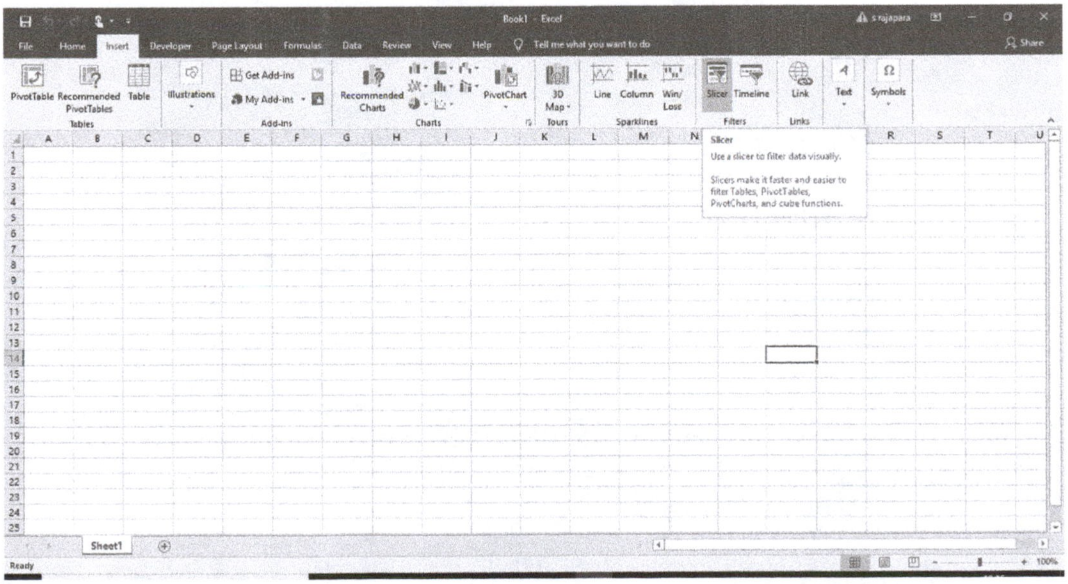

3. Add the 'Analysis ToolPak' add-in.
4. On successful addition, it should appear in the Active Application Add-ins section as shown in Figure D.5. It should also appear on the Data tab as shown in Figure D.6.

Statistical analysis such as histograms, t tests, z test, ANOVA, F test and regression can be performed with ease for quick analysis and interpretation of data. As students of management, you shall be spending two to three months in learning business concepts during your internship experience. In most cases, part of the students' responsibility is of working with data and analysing it. The authors recommend that right from your introduction to data-related activity in your coursework, using the Data Analysis ToolPak should be your companion for data analysis.

| FIGURE D.5 | Adding Analysis ToolPak in Excel |

FIGURE D.6	*Analysis ToolPak in Data Tab*

R SOFTWARE

R software provides an environment for statistical computing with data and its associated graphics. It is available free of cost. It is 'open source' meaning it allows collaborative contributions from its users. It can be downloaded from http://cran.r-project.org which is the Comprehensive R Archive Network (CRAN).

Following is the method of downloading R for Windows operating environment. The CRAN website provides options for downloading R for either Windows, Linux or Mac operating systems. The following are the instructions for downloading it for Windows:

1. Click on 'Download R for Windows'.
2. On the displayed screen, click 'base' for next steps.
3. Click on R (latest version) to install the executable file and the R program as shown in Figure D.7.

There is a graphical user interface (GUI) that needs to be installed after the installation of R. This is called RStudio interface. It can be downloaded from the site http://www.rstudio.org/. Follow the below steps for installation:

1. Click on 'Download RStudio'.
2. Click on 'RStudio Desktop' as shown in Figure D.8.
3. After the installation of RStudio is complete, it will display an icon on the desktop.

FIGURE D.7 | *Installation of R Program*

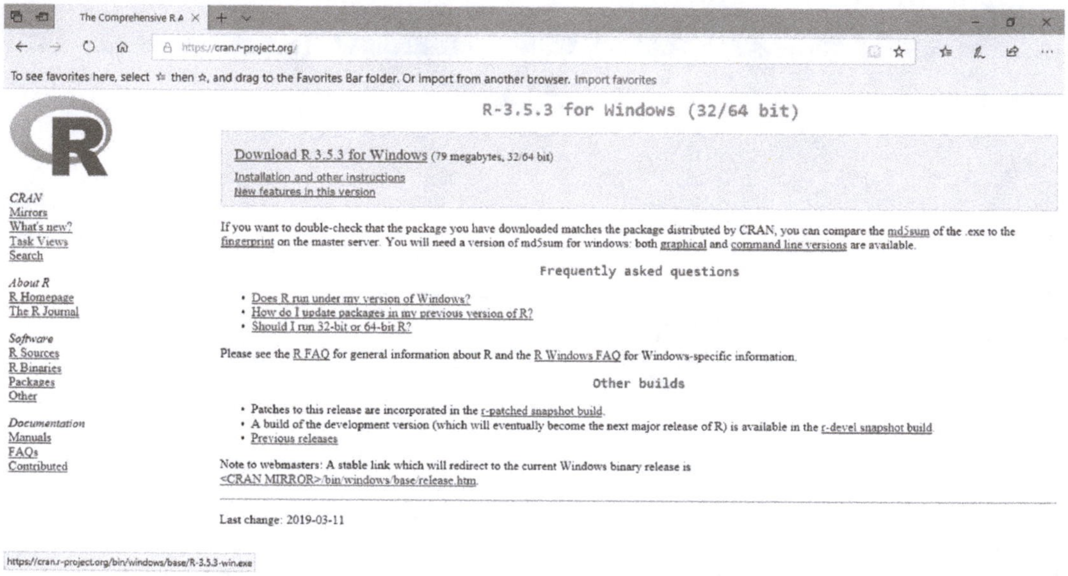

RStudio provides a user-friendly interface for R to the user for integrated development environment. It provides a console, a workspace for codes in R, a window for script and graphs respectively. It provides easy access to files along with a list of packages for R that can be downloaded by the user. It facilitates user activity by providing a dedicated workspace and a graphical display of the work done. It also retains and shows the history of the activities of the user.

Loading packages in R

There are two ways of loading the packages in R software environment:

1. Click on 'Packages' in the top menu bar. Then click on 'Load Packages'. Selecting a particular package allows use and access of commands and operations contained in that package.
2. If you know the name of the package to be installed, then open an R session and type the following command: install.packages ("<package name>").

R Commander is the GUI of R that does not require code to be written in R. It provides all the basic statistical analysis with the click of buttons. For beginners, it is a good way to begin and eventually move into R programming.

For installing R Commander, as shown in Figure D.9, go to 'Packages' and click on 'Install Packages'. Type 'Rcmdr', you shall see it in the list. Download it. You are now all set to use RStudio and R Commander.

Chapters 7 and 9 have examples that discussed using R.

FIGURE D.8 Installation of RStudio Desktop

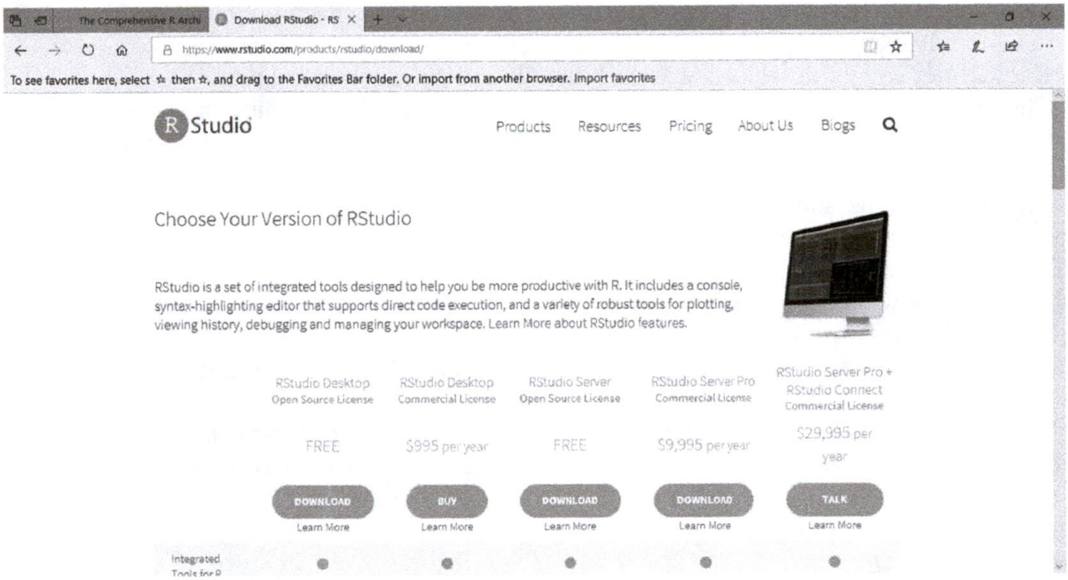

FIGURE D.9 Installation of R Commander

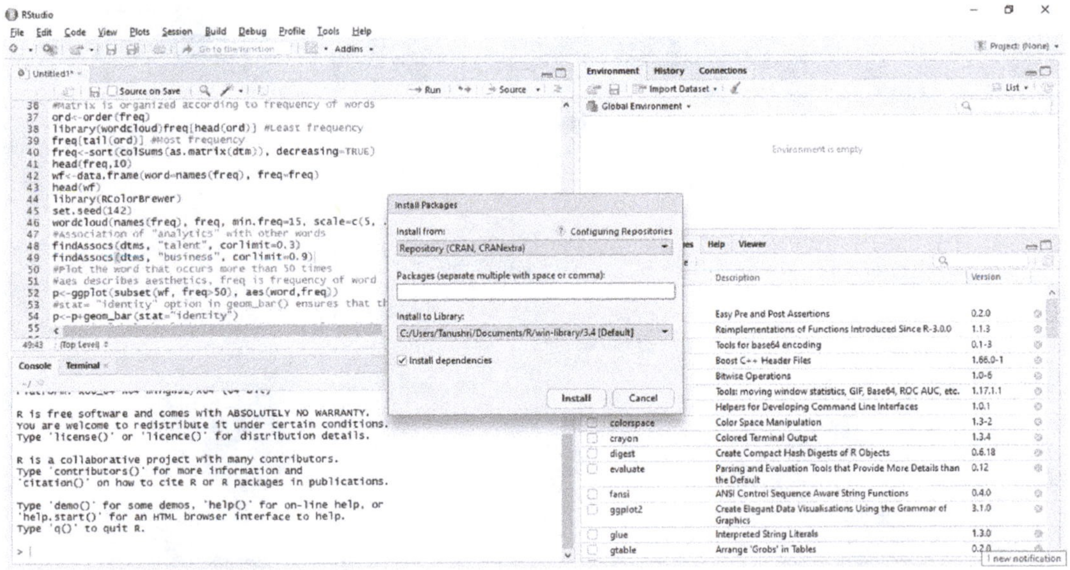

RAPIDMINER SOFTWARE

RapidMiner is an open source platform for data science and machine learning. Chapter 8 on data mining has examples that have used RapidMiner as a software tool.

RapidMiner can be downloaded from https://RapidMiner.com/products/.

The new versions of RapidMiner Studio and RapidMiner Server editions provide use of the software as open source trail versions. Older versions of RapidMiner are available as open source for free download.

The interface, as shown in Figure D.11 is user friendly with option of drag and drop for operators required for data mining and machine learning algorithms. It does not require you to write code, hence easy to learn and use during your course of study for data analytics. The interface has a workspace for the user where one can link and proceed by adding subsequent operators. Unsupervised and supervised methods have been discussed in detail in Chapter 8. Help on each operator used is provided on the interface for guidance and support. In Figure D.11, it is on the lower right corner of the interface.

RapidMiner software can read data files of several types as shown in Figure D.12. It is recommended to begin by creating your own working directory on your laptop and store all your RapidMiner files in that directory. There are two folders by default in the directory. As shown in Figure D.13, one is the 'data' folder, where you shall be required to store all your data for processing. The second is the 'processes' folder, where you can store all the data mining models that you build over time. The operators are shown on the upper left corner of the interface in Figure 13. To search for a particular operator, you can type it in the space provided. The operators need to be pulled to the workspace and linked to each other using appropriate

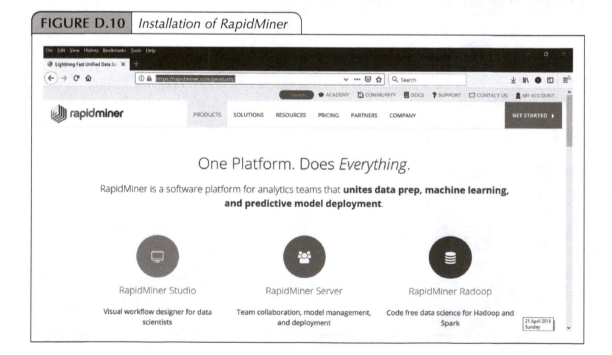

| **FIGURE D.10** | *Installation of RapidMiner* |

FIGURE D.11   *The RapidMiner Interface*

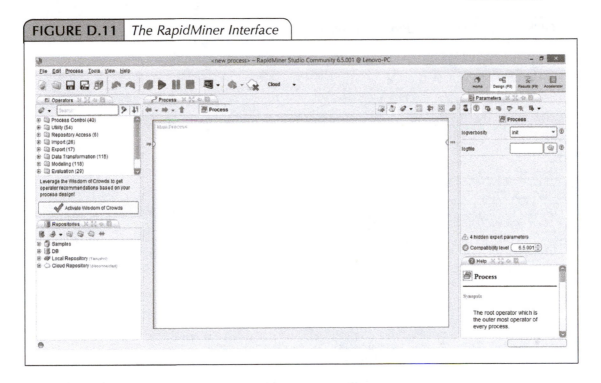

FIGURE D.12   *Data File Types That Can Be Imported*

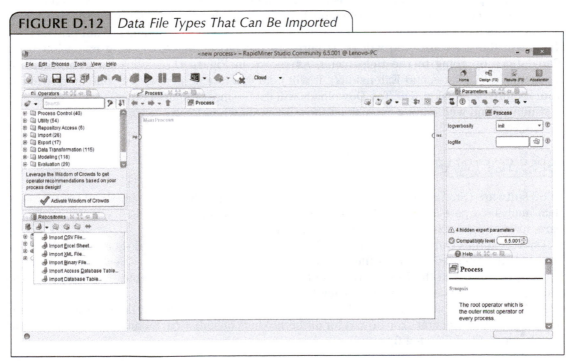

FIGURE D.13 | *Data and Processes Folder*

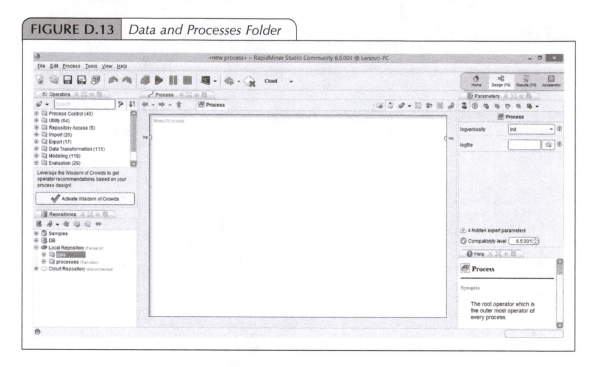

input/output ports. Each time you finish building a process using the operators, you can run it to see the outcome of the model. The models in Chapter 8 have been built using the operators.

Operators for certain functionalities which include text and web mining are not provided by default in the software. You will be required to download the text mining extension from RapidMiner by going to the Help menu. As shown in Figure D.14, click on Help, then on Marketplace (Updates and Extensions). It will take you to a screen where you can download your required extension. The Top Downloads will list the most frequent downloads. Usually, the text mining and web mining extensions show up as shown in Figure D.15. Install them.

SPSS SOFTWARE

SPSS software (Statistical Package for Social Science) is a widely used statistical software for data analysis. Apart from social science, it is used in management studies, education, health care, market research and survey data in various fields.

Data from files can be opened in SPSS by using File—Open in the Menu section as shown in Figure D.16. Alternatively, data files can be created in SPSS using File—New. The Data view shows the records in the form of rows and columns in the form of a table. The Variable view provides the interface for defining each attribute of the table.

Different statistical methods can be used on the data to be analysed. The Analyze tab on the Menu section has several drop downs for different kinds of statistical techniques of which some are shown in the following figures:

1. Descriptive statistics and compare means discussed in Chapter 6—Figure D.17.
2. Correlation and regression analysis discussed in Chapter 7—Figure D.18.

FIGURE D.14 *Marketplace*

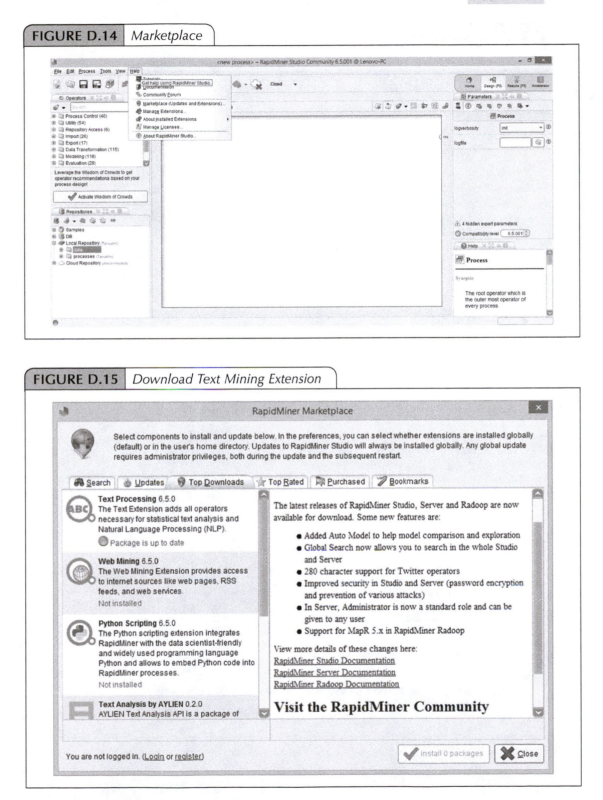

FIGURE D.15 *Download Text Mining Extension*

FIGURE D.16   *Data Files in SPSS*

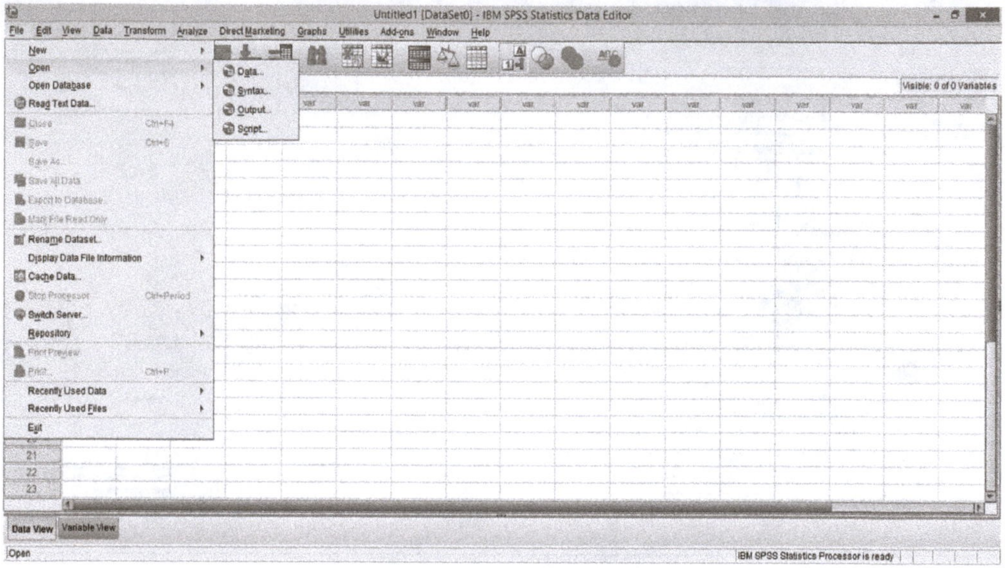

FIGURE D.17   *Comparing Means in SPSS*

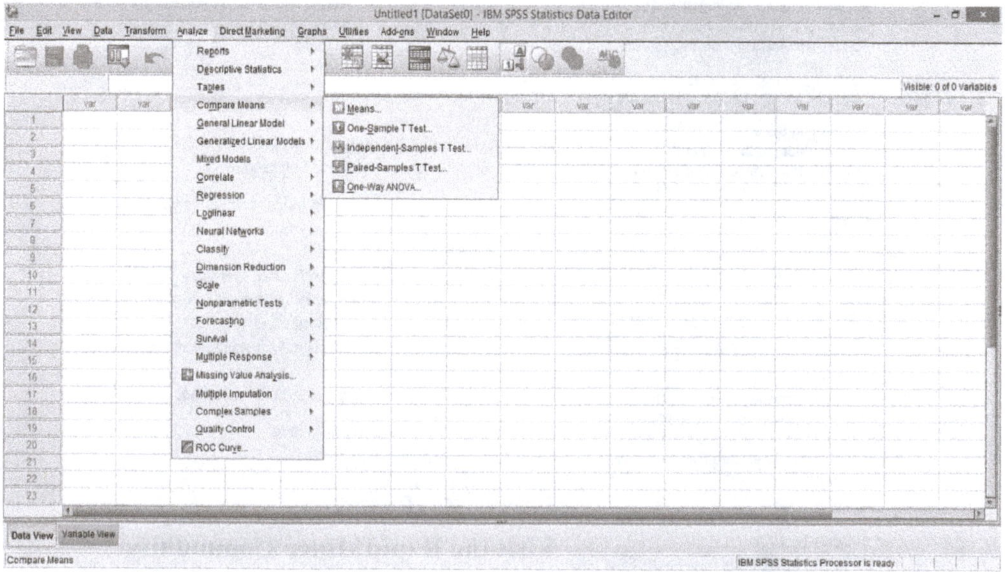

FIGURE D.18 *Regression in SPSS*

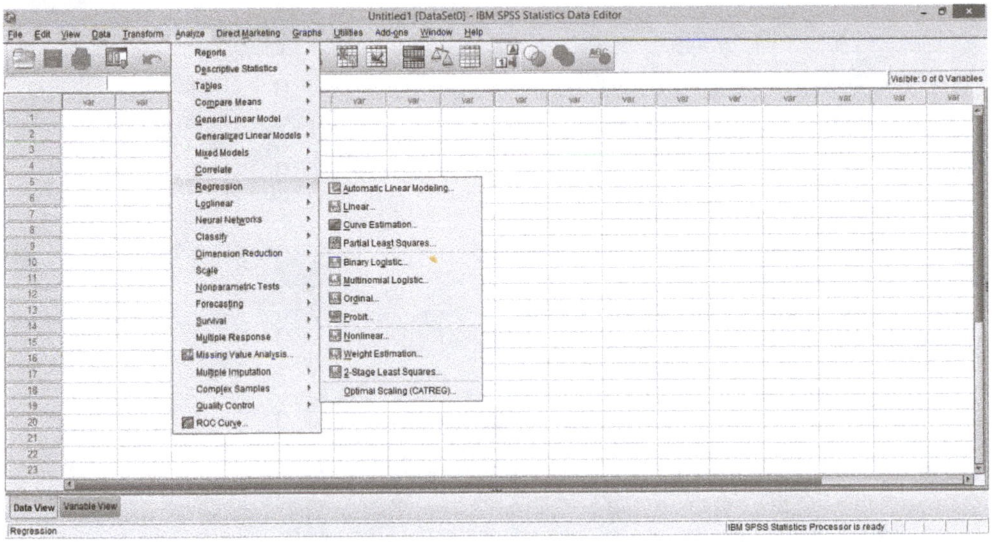

3. Classification techniques discussed in Chapters 7 and 8—Figure D.19.
4. Non-parametric tests and graphical representations discussed in Chapter 9—Figures D.20 and D.21.

After completing your work, save both the data and the output obtained in your local folder.

FIGURE D.19 *Classification in SPSS*

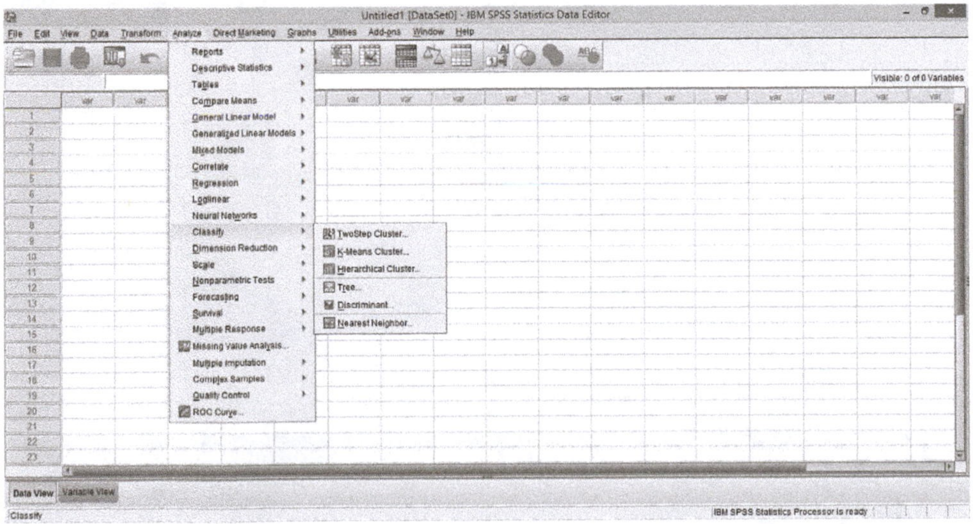

FIGURE D.20 | *Non-parametric Tests in SPSS*

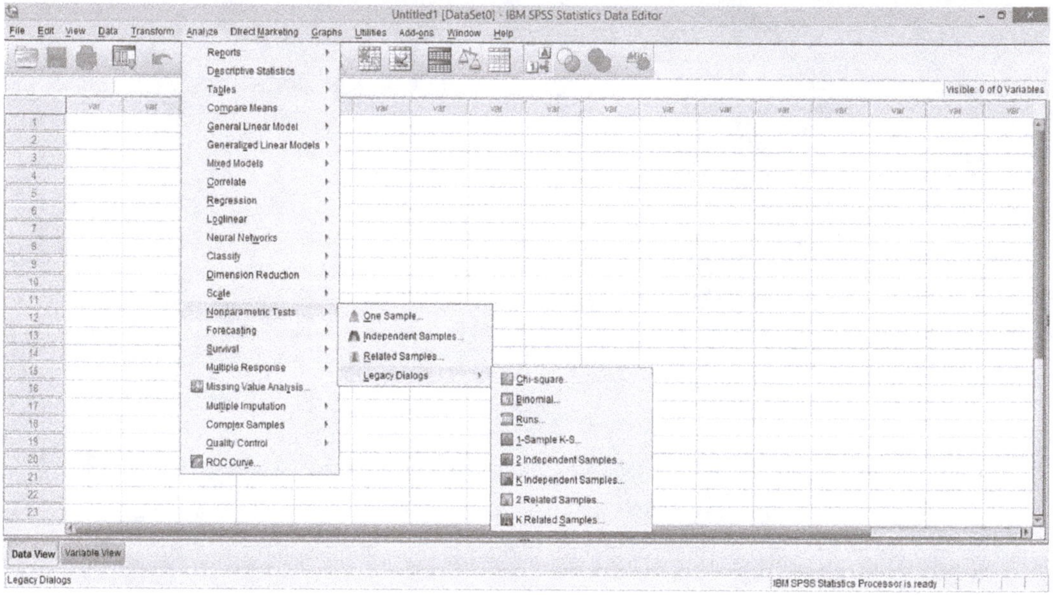

FIGURE D.21 | *Graphs in SPSS*

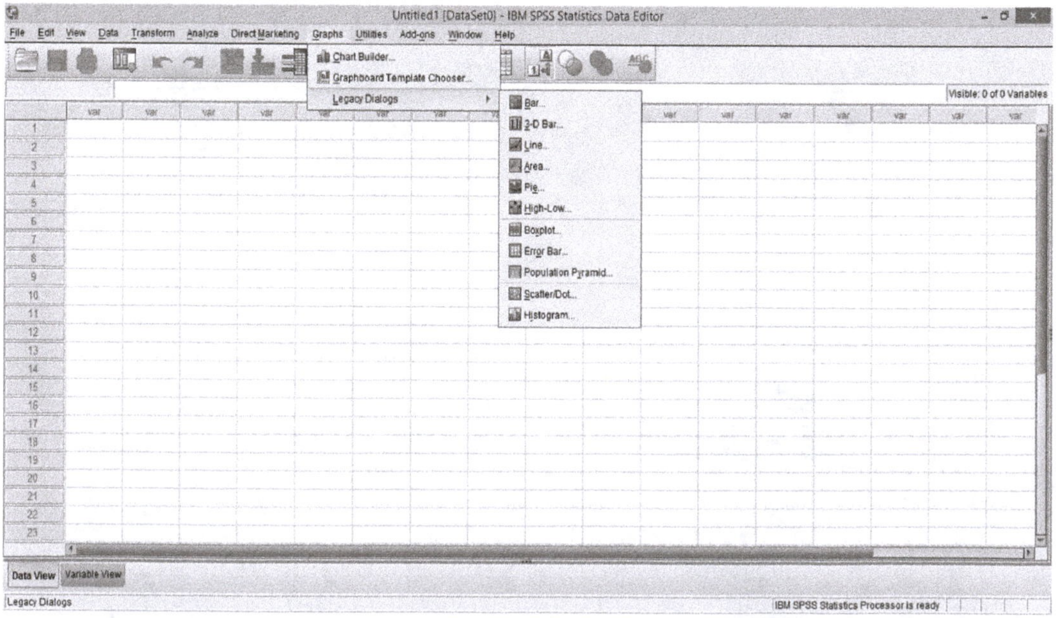

TABLEAU SOFTWARE

Tableau is a BI tool that provides a visual method of interpreting statistical outcomes. In real-life scenarios, when organizations work with complex data, the number of variables and the relationships between them can be equally more complex. For an analyst or data science expert to comprehend and then communicate the outcomes to the client effectively is often a challenge. Tableau allows better visualization for quick interpretation of this data during tabulation and summarization that can be represented effectively using dashboards and storytelling during meetings. We have discussed the creation of dashboard and storytelling in Chapter 11.

Tableau Public is free for download. Click here to install https://public.tableau.com/s.

Before downloading, create your profile by signing in. This will allow you to save your work. As you open Tableau, you will see that it has three different sections. Middle section is where you can open local hard disk files and also see the progress of your work. The Connect section on the left allows you to connect to different data sources. The Right section is the discover section to learn more about Tableau. Lower right section contains sample data sets.

First, connect to worksheet to import data on which you would want to work upon. Then open the worksheet in Tableau workspace. As shown in Figure D.22, here you shall see two sections—Dimensions (categories) and Measures (numeric)—for the data types. Drag and drop various operators as is required for the analysis.

Summary tables can be created similar to pivot tables in MS Excel. After creating summary table, go to show me and choose chart. You can sort horizontal bar graph and add other design features available on the interface. You can change the data type if necessary. Geographic locations can be represented as maps, an example is shown in the case on Trasha Beverages. After completing your work, save your work by clicking the File menu to Tableau public.

| FIGURE D.22 | Tableau Interface |

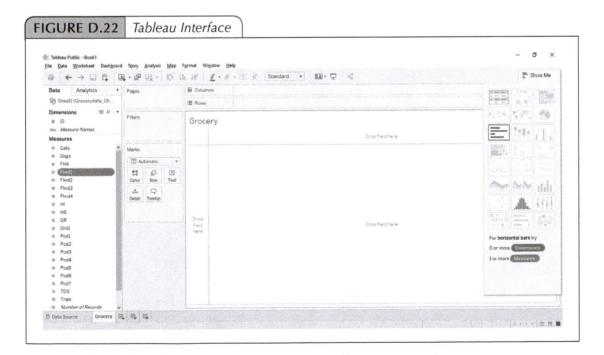

Index